Global Political Economy
UNDERSTANDING THE
INTERNATIONAL
ECONOMIC ORDER

Robert Gilpin

WITH THE ASSISTANCE

OF Jean M. Gilpin

PRINCETON UNIVERSITY PRESS

PRINCETON AND OXFORD

Copyright © 2001 by Princeton University Press
Published by Princeton University Press, 41 William Street,
Princeton, New Jersey 08540
In the United Kingdom: Princeton University Press, 3 Market Place, Woodstock,
Oxfordshire OX20 1SY

Library of Congress Cataloging-in-Publication Data
Gilpin, Robert.
    Global political economy : understanding the international economic order /
Robert Gilpin with the assistance of Jean M. Gilpin.
        p. cm.
    Includes bibliographical references and index.
    ISBN 0-691-08676-1 (alk. paper) — ISBN 0-691-08677-X (pbk.)
    1. International economic relations.   2. Free trade.   3. International finance.
    4. Technological innovations—Economic aspects.   5. Economic development.
    I. Gilpin, Jean M.   II. Title.
    HF1359 .G5516 2001
    337—dc21   00-051684

This book has been composed in Sabon.

The paper used in this publication meets the minimum requirements of ANSI/NISO
Z39.48-1992 (R 1997) (Permanence of Paper)

www.pup.princeton.edu

Printed in the United States of America by Princeton University Press,
Princeton & Oxford

10 9 8 7 6 5 4 3 2

10 9 8 7 6 5 4
(Pbk.)

Global Political Economy

Contents

Abbreviations and Acronyms

ADC	advanced developed (or industrialized) countries
AFL-CIO	American Federation of Labor and Congress of Industrial Organization
APEC	Asia-Pacific Economic Cooperation
BWS	Bretton Woods System
CAP	Common Agricultural Policy
ECLA	Economic Commission for Latin America
EEC	European Economic Community (Common Market)
EMS	European Monetary System
EMU	Economic and Monetary Union
ERM	Exchange Rate Mechanism
EU	European Union
FDI	foreign direct investment
GATT	General Agreement on Tariffs and Trade
GDP	gross domestic product
G-7	group of seven major developed economies
Group of 77	coalition of less developed countries
HST	hegemonic stability theory
ILO	International Labor Organization
IMF	International Monetary Fund
IO	international organization
IPE	international political economy
ITO	International Trade Organization
LDC	less developed country
MITI	Ministry of International Trade and Investment (Japan)
MNC	multinational corporation
MOF	Ministry of Finance (Japan)
NAFTA	North American Free Trade Agreement
NATO	North Atlantic Treaty Organization
NBER	National Bureau of Economic Research
NEG	new economic geography

NICs	newly industrializing countries
NIEs	newly industrializing economies
NGO	nongovernmental organization
NIEO	New International Economic Order
OCA	optimum currency area
OECD	Organization of Economic Cooperation and Development
OPEC	Organization of Petroleum Exporting Countires
R & D	research and development
RTA	Regional Trade Agreement
SDR	Special Drawing Right
SII	Structural Impediments Initiative
STT	strategic trade theory
UN	United Nations
UNCTAD	United Nations Commission for Trade and Development
VER	voluntary export restraint
WB	World Bank
WTO	World Trade Organization

Preface

SINCE PUBLICATION of my book, *The Political Economy of International Relations*, in 1987, the international economy has experienced a number of fundamental changes.[1] These changes include the end of the Cold War and the victory of democratic capitalism over authoritarian communism, the rise of the information or Internet economy, and the triumph of neoliberal market-oriented economic ideology (deregulation, privatization, and a decreased role for the state in the economy). Important technological advances in telecommunications, transportation, and information technology have significantly increased the interdependence of national economies. These several developments have transformed the international economy and ushered in a new era of economic globalization.

In addition to these important steps toward the creation of a truly global economy, since the mid-1980s the world has also witnessed the extraordinary growth of economic regionalism as a countermovement to economic globalization.[2] Western Europe has been the leading player in what Jagdish Bhagwati has called the "Second Regionalism."[3] The North American Free Trade Agreement (NAFTA) and less formal arrangements in Pacific Asia have, along with the European Union, moved the world toward regional economic arrangements. Regional and other important developments in the real world of economic and political affairs have been accompanied by innovations in economic theory that are highly relevant for an understanding of international political economy (IPE). Theoretical innovations include the "new growth theory," the "new economic geography," and the "new trade theory."[4] Taken together, these novel theories constitute

[1] Robert Gilpin, *The Political Economy of International Relations* (Princeton: Princeton University Press, 1987).

[2] The historic tension between the forces of unification and of fragmentation is the subject of Ian Clark, *Globalization and Fragmentation: International Relations in the Twentieth Century* (New York: Oxford University Press, 1997).

[3] Jagdish Bhagwati and Arvind Panagariya, eds., *The Economics of Preferential Trade Agreements* (Washington, D.C.: AEI Press, 1996), 2

[4] Although I discussed the new trade theory or theory of strategic trade in my 1987 book (see footnote 1 above), I did not consider it in detail; nor did I consider it in conjunction with the new growth and economic geography theories.

a significant contribution to our understanding of the political economy of international relations. Thus, both real world and theoretical developments have set the stage for this book's interpretation of global political economy.

At one point in my work on this book, I intended it to be a second edition of my 1987 book. However, I eventually realized that the political, economic, and theoretical changes mentioned above, as well as changes in my own thinking about international political economy, warranted a wholly new book on the subject. This book should be considered a complement to my recent book, *The Challenge of Global Capitalism: The World Economy in the 21st Century* (2000).[5] Whereas the latter book is primarily an analysis and discussion of the post–Cold War international economy, the present work is more theoretical and focuses more directly on IPE. The overlap of the two books is modest and is confined mainly to a few chapters dealing with policy areas such as trade and money.

In preparing this book, I have benefited greatly from the support and assistance of many institutions and individuals. My most important debt is to the Woodrow Wilson School and the Center of International Studies of Princeton University for their financial and other support. The Abe Fellowship Program, funded principally by the Japan Foundation Center for Global Partnership, also generously supported my research. I also wish to thank the John Sloan Dickey Center for International Understanding at Dartmouth College and its director, Michael Mastanduno, for providing me with an intellectual home during the winter term 1998. Special thanks are due to Joanne Gowa, Robert Keohane, and Atul Kohli, who gave me excellent comments on an early version of the manuscript. Seminars sponsored by the Dickey Center, the Department of Political Science of MIT, the Department of Political Science at the University of Vermont, the Central European University (Budapest), and the Department of Political Science at Boston College enabled me to receive outstanding criticisms of my ideas. Special thanks are due to Charles Myers of Princeton University Press, especially for his patience with missed deadlines and other trying experiences with the author as he shepherded this book through the Press and also to Joan Hunter for her expert and conscientious copyediting of this book. Last, but not least, special thanks are due to my wife, Jean. In search of errors, duplications, and improved clarity, she and I have read aloud the text more times than I care to remember. Such a practice is a strain on a marriage, but hopefully it improves the quality of the book.

[5] *The Challenge of Global Capitalism: The World Economy in the 21st Century* (Princeton: Princeton University Press, 2000).

xii

Global Political Economy

CHAPTER ONE

The New Global Economic Order

T HIS BOOK analyzes the globalization of the world economy and
its real as well as its alleged implications for the international
political economy. Since the end of the Cold War, globalization has
been the most outstanding characteristic of international economic
affairs and, to a considerable extent, of political affairs as well. Yet,
as I shall argue throughout this book, although globalization had
become the defining feature of the international economy at the beginning of the twenty-first century, the extent and significance of economic globalization have been greatly exaggerated and misunderstood in both public and professional discussions; globalization in
fact is not nearly as extensive nor as sweeping in its consequences
(negative or positive) as many contemporary observers believe. This
is still a world where national policies and domestic economies are
the principal determinants of economic affairs. Globalization and increasing economic interdependence among national economies are indeed very important; yet, as Vincent Cable of the Royal Institute of
International Affairs has pointed out, the major economic achievement
of the post–World War II era has been to restore the level of international economic integration that existed prior to World War I.[1]

My 1987 book lacked an adequate domestic dimension. It analyzed
the international economy as if domestic economic developments
were of only minor importance. In part, this neglect was due to my
desire to help advance an autonomous, self-contained *international*
political economy. The present book attempts to overcome this unfortunate weakness through a focus on what I call "national systems
of political economy" and their significance for both domestic and
international economic affairs. As national economies have become
more and more integrated, the significance of the fundamental differences among national economies has greatly increased. The 1987
book had several other serious limitations, including its treatment of
the multinational corporation, economic development, and economic
regionalism; although I discussed all three of these important subjects

---

[1] Vincent Cable, "The Diminished Nation-State: A Study in the Loss of Economic
Power," in *What Future for the State?*, *Daedalus* 124, no. 2 (spring 1995): 24.

at that time, much more needs to be said, especially in light of subsequent developments.

In the mid-1980s, a revolution in international economic affairs occurred as multinational firms (MNCs) and foreign direct investment (FDI) began to have a profound impact on almost every aspect of the world economy. In the 1960s and 1970s, increased international trade transformed international economic affairs. Subsequently, in the 1980s, the overseas expansion of multinational firms integrated national economies more and more completely. Moreover, whereas the term "multinational" had been synonymous with the expansion of American firms, in the 1980s firms of other nationalities joined the ranks of multinationals. Most importantly, MNCs led the way in internationalization of both services and manufacturing.

My discussion of economic development in the 1987 book has become totally outdated; scholarship at that time gave serious attention to quasi-Marxist dependency theory and the deep division between the less developed and the developed world. Today, the debate over economic development centers on the appropriate role for state and market in the development process. In the conclusion to the 1987 book, I referred to economic regionalism as the wave of the future. Today, economic regionalism has reached flood tide and is having a significant impact on the international economy. Financial developments since the mid-1980s have greatly increased the integration of the world economy and, therefore, deserve attention. This book also addresses the question of whether or not the increased importance of the market in the organization and functioning of the global economy means the end of the nation-state and of international political economy as that term is defined in this book. Those familiar with my past work will not be surprised to learn that I think not.

The principal purpose of this book is to draw upon these real-world and recent theoretical developments in order to formulate a more comprehensive understanding of international political economy than in my earlier publications. The eclectic 1987 book presented what I considered to be the three major perspectives on international political economy (IPE)—liberalism, Marxism, and nationalism; this book takes a consciously realist or state-centric approach to analysis of the international economy. Differing from many contemporary writings on the global economy, I believe that the nation-state remains the dominant actor in both domestic and international economic affairs. Believing that both economic and political analyses are necessary for an understanding of the workings of the international economy, this book integrates these distinct modes of scholarly inquiry.

CHANGES IN THE WORLD ECONOMY

This book has been motivated largely by the huge changes in the international economy that have occurred since 1987. The most important change, of course, has been the end of the Cold War and of the Soviet threat to the United States and its European and Japanese allies. Throughout most of the last half of the twentieth century, the Cold War and its alliance structures provided the framework within which the world economy functioned. The United States and its major allies generally subordinated potential economic conflicts to the need to maintain political and security cooperation. Emphasis on security interests and alliance cohesion provided the political glue that held the world economy together and facilitated compromises of important national differences over economic issues. With the end of the Cold War, American leadership and the close economic cooperation among the capitalist powers waned. Simultaneously, the market-oriented world grew much larger as formerly communist and Third World countries became more willing to participate in the market system; this has been exemplified by the much more active role taken by the less developed countries (LDCs) in the World Trade Organization (WTO). While this development is to be welcomed, it has made the task of managing the global economic system more daunting.

Economic globalization has entailed a few key developments in trade, finance, and foreign direct investment by multinational corporations.[2] International trade has grown more rapidly than the global economic output. In addition to the great expansion of merchandise trade (goods), trade in services (banking, information, etc.) has also significantly increased. With the decreasing cost of transportation, more and more goods are becoming "tradeables." With the immense expansion of world trade, international competition has greatly increased. Although consumers and export sectors within individual nations benefit from increased openness, many businesses find themselves competing against foreign firms that have improved their efficiency. During the 1980s and 1990s, trade competition became even more intense as a growing number of industrializing economies in East Asia and elsewhere shifted from an import substitution to an

[2] For a strong attack on globalization and its alleged evils, see Richard Falk, *Predatory Globalization* (Oxford: Polity Press, 1999).

export-led growth strategy. Nevertheless, the major competitors for almost all American firms remain other American firms.

Underlying the expansion of global trade have been a number of developments. Since World War II, trade barriers have declined significantly due to successive rounds of trade negotiations. During the last half of the twentieth century average tariff levels of the United States and other industrialized countries dropped from about 40 percent to only 6 percent, and barriers to trade in services have also been lowered.[3] In addition, from the late 1970s onward, deregulation and privatization further opened national economies to imports. Technological advances in communications and transportation reduced costs and thus significantly encouraged trade expansion. Taking advantage of these economic and technological changes, more and more businesses have participated in international markets. Nevertheless, despite these developments, most trade takes place among the three advanced industrialized economies—the United States, Western Europe, and Japan, plus a few emerging markets in East Asia, Latin America, and elsewhere. Most of the less developed world is excluded, except as exporters of food and raw materials. It is estimated, for example, that Africa south of the Sahara accounted for only about 1 percent of total world trade in the 1990s.

Since the mid-1970s, financial deregulation and the creation of new financial instruments, such as derivatives, and technological advances in communications have contributed to a much more highly integrated international financial system. The volume of foreign exchange trading (buying and selling national currencies) in the late 1990s reached approximately $1.5 trillion per day, an eightfold increase since 1986; by contrast, the global volume of exports (goods and services) for all of 1997 was $6.6 trillion, or $25 billion per day! In addition, the amount of investment capital seeking higher returns has grown enormously; by the mid-1990s, mutual funds, pension funds and the like totaled $20 trillion, ten times the 1980 figure. Moreover, the significance of these huge investments is greatly magnified by the fact that a large portion of foreign investments is leveraged; that is, they are investments made with borrowed funds. Finally, derivatives or repackaged securities and other financial assets play an important role in international finance. Valued at $360 trillion (larger than the value of the entire global economy), they have contributed to the

---

[3] Gary Burtless, Robert Z. Lawrence, Robert E. Litan, and Robert J. Shapiro, *Globaphobia: Confronting Fears about Open Trade* (Washington, D.C.: Brookings Institution, 1998), 5–6.

complexity and the instability of international finance. It is obvious that international finance has a profound impact on the global economy.

This financial revolution has linked national economies much more closely to one another and increased the capital available for developing countries. As many of these financial flows are short-term, highly volatile, and speculative, international finance has become the most unstable aspect of the global capitalist economy. The immense scale, velocity, and speculative nature of financial movements across national borders have made governments more vulnerable to sudden shifts in these movements. Governments can therefore easily fall prey to currency speculators, as happened in the 1992 European financial crisis, which caused Great Britain to withdraw from the European Exchange Rate Mechanism, and in the 1994–95 punishing collapse of the Mexican peso, as well as in the devastating East Asian financial crisis in the late 1990s. Whereas, for some, financial globalization exemplifies the healthy and beneficial triumph of global capitalism, for others the international financial system is "out of control" and must be better regulated. Either way, international finance is the one area to which the term "globalization" is most appropriately applied.

The term "globalization" came into popular usage in the second half of the 1980s in connection with the huge surge of foreign direct investment (FDI) by multinational corporations. MNCs and FDI have been around for several centuries in the form of the East India Company and other "merchant adventurers." In the early postwar decades, most FDI was made by American firms, and the United States was host to only a small amount of FDI from non-American firms. Then, in the 1980s, FDI expanded significantly and much more rapidly than world trade and global economic output. In the early postwar decades, Japanese, West European, and other nationalities became major investors and the United States became both the world's largest home and host economy. As a consequence of these developments, FDI outflows from the major industrialized countries to the industrializing countries rose to approximately 15 percent annually. The largest fraction of FDI, however, goes to the industrialized countries, especially the United States and those in Western Europe. The cumulative value of FDI amounts to hundreds of billions of dollars. The greatest portion of this investment has been in services and especially in high-tech industries such as automobiles and information technology. Information, in fact, has itself become a "tradeable," and this raises such new issues in international commerce as the protection of intellectual property rights and market access for service industries. In combination with increased trade and financial flows, the increasing importance of MNCs has significantly transformed the international economy.

Although the end of the Cold War provided the necessary political condition for the creation of a truly global economy, it is economic, political, and technological developments that have been the driving force behind economic globalization. Novel technologies in transportation have caused the costs of transportation, especially transoceanic travel, to fall greatly, thus opening the possibility of a global trading system. In addition, the computer and advances in telecommunications have greatly increased global financial flows; these developments have been extremely important in enabling multinational firms to pursue global economic strategies and operations. The compression of time and space resulting from these technological changes has significantly reduced the costs of international commerce. Globalization has also been produced by international economic cooperation and new economic policies. Under American leadership, both the industrialized and industrializing economies have taken a number of initiatives to lower trade and investment barriers. Eight rounds of multilateral trade negotiations under the General Agreement on Tariffs and Trade (GATT), the principal forum for trade liberalization, have significantly decreased trade barriers. In addition, more and more nations have been pursuing neoliberal economic policies such as deregulation and privatization. These developments have resulted in an increasingly market-oriented global economy.

Many observers believe that a profound shift is taking place from a state-dominated to a market-dominated international economy. Humanity, many argue, is moving rapidly toward a politically borderless world.[4] The collapse of the Soviet command economy, the failure of the Third World's import-substitution strategy, and the outstanding economic success of the American economy in the 1990s have encouraged acceptance of unrestricted markets as *the* solution to the economic ills of modern society. As deregulation and other reforms have reduced the role of the state in the economy, many believe that markets have become the most important mechanism determining both domestic and international economic and even political affairs. In a highly integrated global economy, the nation-state, according to this interpretation, has become an anachronism and is in retreat. Many also believe that the decline of the state is leading to

[4] The evolution and increasing importance of the market is the subject of John Hicks, *A Theory of Economic History* (London: Oxford University Press, 1969).

an open and truly global capitalist economy characterized by unrestricted trade, financial flows, and the international activities of multinational firms.

Although most economists and many others welcome this development, critics emphasize the "high costs" of economic globalization, including growing income inequality both among and within nations, high chronic levels of unemployment in Western Europe and elsewhere, and, most of all, environmental degradation, widespread exploitation, and the devastating consequences for national economies wrought by unregulated international financial flows. These critics charge that national societies are being integrated into a global economic system and are buffeted by economic and technological forces over which they have little or no control. They view global economic problems as proof that the costs of globalization are much greater than its benefits. Foreseeing a world characterized by intense economic conflict at both the domestic and international levels, and believing that an open world economy will inevitably produce more losers than winners, critics argue that unleashing market and other economic forces has caused an intense struggle among individual nations, economic classes, and powerful groups. Many assert that what former German chancellor Helmut Schmidt called "the struggle for the world product" could result in competing regional blocs dominated by one or another of the major economic powers.

The idea that globalization is responsible for most of the world's economic, political, and other problems is either patently false or greatly exaggerated. In fact, other factors such as technological developments and imprudent national policies are much more important than globalization as causes of many, if not most, of the problems for which globalization is held responsible. Unfortunately, misunderstandings regarding globalization and its effects have contributed to growing disillusionment with borders open to trade and investment and have led to the belief that globalization has had a very negative impact on workers, the environment, and less developed countries. According to an American poll taken in April 1999, 52 percent of the respondents had negative views regarding globalization.[5] Yet, even though globalization is an important feature of the international economy that has changed many aspects of the subject of international political economy, the fact is that globalization is not as perva-

---

[5] Andrew Kohut, "Globalization and the Wage Gap," *New York Times*, 3 December 1999, sec. 1, reporting on a Pew Research Center's national survey in April 1999, which found that 52 percent of all respondents were negative toward globalization. Low-income families were much more negative than wealthier ones.

sive, extensive, or significant as many would have us believe. Most national economies are still mainly self-contained rather than globalized; globalization is also restricted to a limited, albeit rapidly increasing, number of economic sectors. Moreover, globalization is largely restricted to the triad of industrialized countries—the United States, Western Europe, and, to a much lesser extent, Japan—and to the emerging markets of East Asia. Most importantly, many of the attacks on globalization by its critics are misplaced; many, if not most, of its "evils" are really due to changes that have little or nothing to do with globalization.

The end of the Cold War and the growth of economic globalization coincided with a new industrial revolution based on the computer and the rise of the information or Internet economy. Technological developments are transforming almost every aspect of economic, political, and social affairs as computing power provides an impetus to the world economy that may prove as significant as those previously produced by steam power, electric power, and oil power. The economics profession, however, has been deeply divided about whether or not computing power represents a technological revolution on the same scale as these earlier advances. Although the computer appears to have accelerated the rate of economic and productivity growth, it is still too early to know whether or not its ultimate impact will affect the overall economy on a scale at all equivalent to that produced by the dynamo. A growing number of economists, however, believe that computers have an important impact not only on productivity but also on economic affairs in general. For example, some economists believe that the organization of and the ways in which national economies function are experiencing major changes in response to the computer and the Internet. Although it is still much too early to gauge the full impact of the computer on the economy, it is certain that the computer and the information economy are significantly changing many aspects of economic affairs. Most importantly, in the industrialized countries, they have accelerated the shift from manufacturing to services (financial, software, retailing, etc.). This pervasive economic restructuring of the industrialized economies is economically costly and politically difficult.

During the last decades of the twentieth century, there was a significant shift in the distribution of world industry away from the older industrial economies—the United States, Western Europe, and Japan—toward Pacific Asia, Latin America, and other rapidly industrializing economies. Although the United States and the other industrialized economies still possess a preponderant share of global wealth and industry, they have declined in relative (not absolute) terms, while the industrializing economies, especially China, have gained economic importance. Before the 1997 financial crisis, which began in Thailand and eventually plunged East Asia into political and economic turmoil, Pacific Asia's economic success had been extremely impressive; many of these economies achieved average annual growth rates of 6 to 8 percent. And despite the financial crisis, such economic "fundamentals" as high savings rates and excellent workforces support the belief that these emerging markets will continue to be important actors in the global economy.

Economic regionalism has spread in response to these political, economic, and technological developments. Compared to the earlier regional movement of the 1950s and 1960s (the European Economic Community is the only surviving example of that movement), the new regionalism has much greater significance for the global economy. The movement at the beginning of the twenty-first century is nearly universal; the major economies, with a few exceptions that include China, Japan, and Russia, are members of a formal regional arrangement. Regionalism at the turn of the twenty-first century entails increased regionalization of foreign investment, production, and other economic activities. Although there is no single explanation for this development, every regional arrangement represents cooperative efforts of individual states to promote both their national and their collective economic and political objectives. Economic regionalism is an important response by nation-states to shared political problems and to a highly interdependent, competitive global economy. As the international economy has become more closely integrated, regional groupings of states have increased their cooperation in order to strengthen their autonomy, improve their bargaining positions, and promote other political/economic objectives. Regionalization is not an alternative to the nation-state, as some believe, but rather embodies the efforts of individual states to collectively promote their vital national interests and ambitions.

These developments have made the governance of the global economy a pressing issue. Effective and legitimate governance requires agreement on the purpose of the international economy. During the Cold War, the purpose of the world economy was primarily to strengthen the economies of the anti-Soviet alliance and solidify the political unity of the United States and its allies; this goal frequently necessitated acceptance of trade discrimination and other illiberal policies. Today, many Americans and others assert that the purpose of governance should be to promote unrestricted free and open mar-

11

kets. The global economy and the rules governing it, they believe, should be guided by the policy prescriptions of neoclassical economics and be based on market principles. Free trade, freedom of capital movements, and unrestricted access by multinational firms to markets around the globe should be the goals of international governance. With the triumph of the market, economic logic and the relative efficiencies of national economies should determine the distribution of economic activities and wealth (and, of course, of power) around the world. Critics of globalization, on the other hand, challenge this emphasis on the importance of free trade and open markets.

Despite the growing importance of the market, historical experience indicates that the purpose of economic activities is ultimately determined not only by markets and the prescriptions of technical economics, but also (either explicitly or implicitly) by the norms, values, and interests of the social and political systems in which economic activities are embedded. Although economic factors will play an important role in determining the character of the global economy, political factors will be of equal, and perhaps greater, importance. The nature of the global economy will be strongly affected by the security and political interests of, and the relations among, the dominant economic powers, including the United States, Western Europe, Japan, China, and Russia. It is highly unlikely that these powers will leave the distribution of the global economic product and the impact of economic forces on their national interests entirely up to the market. Both economic efficiency and national ambitions are driving forces in the global economy of the twenty-first century.

In this book, I have taken a "political economy" approach that integrates economic and political analysis with other modes of scholarly analysis. Formal economic theories provide indispensable tools, facilitating comprehension of economic developments; the conventional theory of international trade, newly gained insights from the theory of industrial organization, and other theoretical developments in economic science provide important additional ideas. However, economic theories alone are not sufficient for an understanding of developments and their significance for economic and political affairs. One must also draw upon ideas and insights from history, political science, and the other social sciences. In brief, a true "political economy" is prerequisite to an improved comprehension of the implications of new developments for international (and, where relevant, domestic) economic affairs.

The intensity and importance of the debate over the nature of the changing world economy makes one aware of a troubling paradox. At the same time that economic issues have moved to the center of national concerns, the discipline of economics itself has become increasingly remote from the realities of public affairs. Over decades the increasing emphasis of the economics profession on abstract models and mathematical theories made economics less and less relevant to public discourse and inaccessible not only to the larger public but also to academic colleagues. This is especially unfortunate because economics, despite its frequently esoteric nature, is or at least should be at the heart of public discourse. The problem is particularly troubling because the intellectual vacuum left by economists is too frequently filled by individuals who misunderstand economics or deliberately misuse the findings of economics in their promotion of one panacea or another to solve the problems of both domestic and international economies.

INTELLECTUAL PERSPECTIVES

In 1987, I identified three ideologies or perspectives regarding the nature and functioning of the international economy: liberalism, Marxism, and nationalism. Since the mid-1980s, the relevance of these perspectives has changed dramatically. With the end of both communism and the "import-substitution" strategies of many less developed countries (LDCs), the relevance of Marxism greatly declined, and liberalism, at least for the moment, has experienced a considerable growth in influence. Around the world, more and more countries are accepting liberal principles as they open their economies to imports and foreign investment, scale down the role of the state in the economy, and shift to export-led growth strategies. Marxism as a doctrine of how to manage an economy has been thoroughly discredited, so that only a few impoverished countries such as Fidel Castro's Cuba and Kim Jong Il's North Korea cling to this once strong faith. Yet, Marxism survives as an analytic tool and a critique of capitalism, and it will continue to survive as long as those flaws of the capitalist system emphasized by Marx and his followers remain: the "boom and bust" cycle of capitalist evolution, widespread poverty side by side with great wealth, and the intense rivalries of capitalist economies over market share. Whether under the guise of Marxism itself or some other label, concerns over these problems will surface in discussions of the world economy.[6]

[6] An example is William Greider, *One World, Ready or Not: The Manic Logic of Global Capitalism* (New York: Simon and Schuster, 1997). Although Greider is not a Marxist, his book raises the specter of what Marxists call the "underconsumption" or "glut" theory of capitalist crisis; that is, the contradiction between the capacity of capitalism to produce goods and the inability of workers to purchase these goods.

13

One criticism of my 1987 book was that I did not adequately state my own intellectual position: Was I a liberal, a Marxist, or a nationalist? The short answer is "none of the above." However, before giving my longer answer, I must comment on the three perspectives and on a weakness in my 1987 book. I failed to make clear that each of these perspectives is composed of both analytic and normative elements. Economic liberalism, for example, is not only an analytic tool based on the theories and assumptions of neoclassical economics, but it is also a normative commitment to a market or capitalist economy. As I mentioned, Karl Marx himself accepted the basic analytical ideas of the liberal economics of his time, but he despised capitalism—a term he coined—and asked questions that he considered more fundamental than those asked by earlier nineteenth-century classical economists: questions about the origins of the capitalist system, the laws governing its evolution, and its ultimate destiny. As Joseph Schumpeter has emphasized, whereas economists are interested in the day-to-day functioning of the capitalist system, Marx and Schumpeter himself were interested in the long-term dynamics of the capitalist system.

Nationalism or, more specifically, economic nationalism, is also composed of both analytic and normative elements. Its analytic core recognizes the anarchic nature of international affairs, the primacy of the state and its interests in international affairs, and the importance of power in interstate relations. However, nationalism is also a normative commitment to the nation-state, state-building, and the moral superiority of one's own state over all other states. Although I accept "economic nationalism," or what I below call a "state-centric" approach, as an analytic perspective, I do not subscribe to the normative commitment and policy prescriptions associated with economic nationalism. My own normative commitment is to economic liberalism; that is, to free trade and minimal barriers to the flow of goods, services, and capital across national boundaries, although, under certain restricted circumstances, nationalist policies such as trade protection and industrial policy may be justified.

In retrospect, I should have distinguished clearly between economic nationalism as a normative position and political realism as an analytic perspective. Or, to put the matter another way, while all nationalists are realists in their emphasis on the crucial role of the state, security interests, and power in international affairs, not all realists are nationalists in their normative views regarding international affairs. Therefore, in this book I employ the broader term "realism" or, more specifically, "state-centric realism" to characterize my approach to analysis of the international political economy. But even the very term "realism" requires further elaboration.

My Perspective: State-centric Realism

Realism is a philosophical position and an analytic perspective; it is not necessarily a moral commitment to the nation-state. Many realists, in fact, lament a world in which the nation-state is not adequately restrained by international rules and moral considerations. Nor is realism a scientific theory. As a philosophic or intellectual perspective, realism is not subject to the Popperian criterion of falsifiability and, like other philosophic positions such as liberalism and Marxism, realism can neither be proved nor disproved by empirical research.[7] However, international relations scholarship in the realist tradition has led to a number of theories or hypotheses such as the theories of the balance of power and hegemonic stability that can be and have been subjected to empirical testing to determine their validity.

Several years ago, I was asked if there was a difference between realism and nationalism. The question startled me, as I had always thought that any reader of Hans Morgenthau, Hedley Bull, and other prominent realist writers would be fully aware that while these scholars were realists in their analysis of international affairs and their sober expectations regarding human possibilities, they were by no means nationalists. The realist diagnosing the illnesses of the human condition is not endorsing what he or she sees any more than a physician endorses the cancer found in a patient. Morgenthau's writings, in fact, attacked unbridled nationalism and, in *Politics Among Nations* (1972), he set forth rules for diplomatic behavior that could assist nations to live in peace with one another at the same time that they safeguarded their national interests. As critics charge, Morgenthau may have been naive in believing that it was possible to prescribe moral and diplomatic principles based on his own realist assumptions. The point, however, for Morgenthau and other realists (myself included), is that realism and nationalism are not identical. Nationalists may be realists, but realists are not necessarily nationalists.

Although realists recognize the central role of the state, security, and power in international affairs, they do not necessarily approve of this situation. The teacher who first introduced me to realism as an

---

[7] According to the philosopher of science Karl Popper, if an idea or hypothesis, etc., cannot be refuted, at least in principle, it is not a "scientific" statement.

analytic perspective, Professor George Little of the University of Vermont, was a Quaker pacifist; yet, when I was an undergraduate, Little once chided me for my naive and unrealistic views on a particular development in international politics. Martin Wight, the author of one of the most important tracts on realism in this century, *Power Politics* (1986), was also a Christian pacifist.[8] Even Hans Morgenthau in his influential *Politics Among Nations*, having Adolf Hitler in mind, condemned "universal nationalism," that is, imperialistic behavior, as immoral. One of his basic messages was that states should try to respect the interests of other states.[9] It is possible, I believe, to analyze international economic affairs from a realist perspective and at the same time to have a normative commitment to certain ideals.

As Michael Doyle reminds us in his *Ways of War and Peace* (1997), there are many varieties of realist thought.[10] Yet all realists share a few fundamental ideas such as the anarchic nature of the international system and the primacy of the state in international affairs. However, one should distinguish between two major realist interpretations of international affairs, that is, between state-centric and system-centric realism. State-centric realism is the traditional form of realism associated with Thucydides, Machiavelli, and Morgenthau, as well as many others; it emphasizes the state (city, imperial, or nation-state) as the principal actor in international affairs and the fact that there is no authority superior to these sovereign political units; this position asserts that analysis should focus on the behavior of individual states. Systemic realism, or what is sometimes called structural realism or neorealism, is a more recent version of realist thought and is primarily associated with Kenneth Waltz's innovative and influential *Theory of International Politics* (1979).[11] In contrast to state-centric realism's emphasis on the state and state interest, Waltz's systemic version emphasizes the distribution of power among states within an international system as the principal determinant of state behavior.

The state-centric realist interpretation of international affairs makes several basic assumptions regarding the nature of international

---

[8] Wight's essay can be found in the collection of his writings edited by Hedley Bull and Carsten Holbraad, *Power Politics* (Harmondsworth, England: Penguin Books, 1986).

[9] Hans J. Morgenthau, *Politics Among Nations* (New York: Knopf, 1972).

[10] Michael W. Doyle, *Ways of War and Peace: Realism, Liberalism, and Socialism* (New York: W. W. Norton, 1997).

[11] Kenneth N. Waltz, *Theory of International Politics* (Reading, Mass.: Addison-Wesley, 1979).

affairs. Because it assumes that the international system is anarchic, this interpretation views the state, in the absence of a higher authority, as the principal actor in international affairs. The existence of anarchy, however, does not mean that international politics is characterized by a constant and universal Hobbesian war of one against all; states obviously do cooperate with one another and do create institutions in many areas.[12] Anarchy means rather that there is no higher authority to which a state can appeal for succor in times of trouble. In addition, although the state is the primary actor in international affairs, realism should acknowledge the importance of such nonstate actors as multinational firms, international institutions, and nongovernmental organizations (NGOs) in the determination of international affairs. Realism, however, insists that the state remain the principal actor.

The central concerns of the state are its national interests as defined in terms of military security and political independence; however, state-centric realism does not reject the importance of moral and value considerations in determining behavior. While it follows that power and power relations play the major roles in international affairs, power can assume the form of military, economic, and even psychological relationships among states, as E. H. Carr has pointed out. Moreover, despite this emphasis on power, other factors such as ideas, values, and norms do play an important role in interstate affairs.[13] The criticism, for example, that all realists are unaware of the role of ideas or intellectual constructs in international affairs is patently false. As Morgenthau argued in his classic *Scientific Man vs. Power Politics* (1946), the liberal beliefs of the Western democracies made them incapable of recognizing and being able to react decisively to the threat of fascism in the 1930s. Recognizing the importance of ideas, Morgenthau warned that it was dangerously unwise to place one's faith solely in the power of ideals.[14]

In this book I define "global political economy" as the interaction of the market and such powerful actors as states, multinational firms,

[12] An important critique of the realist emphasis on anarchy is Alexander Wendt, "Anarchy Is What States Make of It: The Social Construction of Power Politics," *International Politics* 46, no. 2 (spring 1992): 391–425.

[13] On the role of ideas or "epistemic communities" in international affairs, consult Peter M. Haas, ed., "Knowledge, Power, and International Policy Coordination," *International Organization* 46, no. 1 (special issue; winter 1992). See also E. H. Carr, *The Twenty Years' Crisis, 1919–1939*, 2d ed. (London: Macmillan, 1951).

[14] Hans J. Morgenthau, *Scientific Man vs. Power Politics* (Chicago: University of Chicago Press, 1946).

and international organizations, a more comprehensive definition than in my 1987 book, *The Political Economy of International Relations,* although both take a state-centric approach to the subject.[15] While I do assume that the territorial state continues to be the primary actor in both domestic and international economic affairs, I do not contend that the state is the *only* important actor. Other significant players include the World Bank, the International Monetary Fund (IMF), and the Commission of the European Union. Despite the importance of these other actors, however, I emphasize that national governments still make the primary decisions regarding economic matters; they continue to set the rules within which other actors function, and they use their considerable power to influence economic outcomes. The major political players, namely Germany, France, and the United Kingdom, are central in even such a highly integrated international institution as the European Union. Whatever the ultimate shape of the European Union, national governments will continue to be important actors within this regional arrangement.

My interpretation of international political economy assumes that the interests and policies of states are determined by the governing political elite, the pressures of powerful groups within a national society, and the nature of the "national system of political economy." As I argued in *War and Change in World Politics* (1981), the economic/ foreign policies of a society reflect the nation's national interest as defined by the dominant elite of that society.[16] As conceptualists correctly argue, there is a subjective element in an elite's definition of the national interest. However, objective factors such as the geographic location of a society and the physical requirements of the economy are of great importance in determining the national interest. Only objective factors, for example, can explain why Great Britain's foremost national interest for approximately four hundred years was to prevent the occupation of the lowlands (Belgium and the Netherlands) by a hostile power. Clearly, British behavior and the numerous wars England fought to keep these lands out of unfriendly hands suggest that the English nation under many different rulers and political regimes possessed interests that transcended the more narrowly defined interests of the governing elite of the moment.

My state-centric position assumes that national security is and always will be the principal concern of states. In a "self-help" interna-

[15] Robert Gilpin, *The Political Economy of International Relations* (Princeton: Princeton University Press, 1987).

[16] Robert Gilpin, *War and Change in World Politics* (New York: Cambridge University Press, 1981), 18–19.

tional system, to use Kenneth Waltz's apt expression, states must constantly guard against actual or potential threats to their political and economic independence. Concern with security means that power—military, economic, and/or psychological—will be vitally important in international affairs; states must be continually attentive to changes in power relations and the consequences for their own national interests of shifts in the international balance of power. Although, as Richard Rosecrance correctly argues, the "trading state" has become a much more prominent feature of international affairs, it is important to recognize that successful development of the international economy since 1945 has been made possible by the security system provided by the alliances between the United States and its allies in Europe and Asia. Trading states like Japan and (West) Germany emerged and grew while protected by American military power; moreover, toward the end of the twentieth century they established and began to maintain an independent military option.[17] Indeed, these trading states now possess substantial defensive military forces and defense industries as an insurance policy; even Japan, with its "peace" constitution, has become one of the world's foremost military powers.

One of the most important contemporary critiques of realism is "constructivism."[18] According to this increasingly influential position, international politics is "socially constructed" rather than constituting an objective reality. As defined by Alexander Wendt, the two basic tenets of constructivism are that (1) human structures are determined mainly by shared ideas rather than material forces, and (2) the identities and interests of human beings are constructed or are the product of these shared ideas rather than being products of nature. If valid, these ideas undermine not only realism, Marxism, and liberalism but also neoclassical economics and much of political science. Although constructivism is an important corrective to some strands of realism and the individualist rational-choice methodology of neoclassical economics, the implicit assumption of constructivism that we should abandon our knowledge of international politics and start

---

[17] Richard N. Rosecrance, *The Rise of the Trading State: Commerce and Conquest in the Modern World* (New York: Basic Books, 1986); Rosecrance, *The Rise of the Virtual State: Wealth and Power in the Coming Century* (New York: Basic Books, 1999).

[18] Alexander Wendt, *Social Theory of International Politics* (New York: Columbia University Press, 1999); and Peter. J. Katzenstein, ed., *The Culture of National Security: Norms and Identity in World Politics* (New York: Columbia University Press, 1996).

19

afresh from a tabula rasa wiped clean by constructivism is not compelling.

Constructivism's principal critique of realism is that realism is purely materialistic and analyzes the political world only in terms of technological forces, physical circumstances, and other objective factors; realists are said to be overly deterministic and to portray a political world over which human beings have no control (or "agency"). Constructivism, on the other hand, is said to emphasize the role of ideas, social structures, and human volition in political affairs; people can construct a better political and more humane universe than that described by realists. Although I cannot do justice in several paragraphs to these ideas, several comments are in order. Constructivism makes too great a distinction between realism, at least as I use the term in this book, and constructivism with respect to the role of ideas, ideology, and constructs. Classical realists from Thucydides forward have emphasized the role of ideas and "identity" in political affairs. What better example than the powerful idea of nationalism and the importance of national identity that have been staples of realist thought since Machiavelli and Hobbes! While constructivists are right in stressing the importance of shared ideas and the social construction of the world, it is not clear how far they are willing to take this position. Ideas are obviously important, but the world is composed of many economic, technological, and other powerful constraints that limit the wisdom and practicality of certain ideas and social constructions. Any theory that seeks to understand the world must, as do liberalism, Marxism, and realism, seek to integrate both ideas and material forces.

One of the key ideas in constructivist analysis of international affairs is the idea of identity, or how a society defines itself; for example, whether a society is democratic or authoritarian in nature affects its behavior. According to constructivists, realists neglect the importance of identity and focus only on material interests and power considerations. In some cases, this criticism is valid. In general, realists do stress "interest" over "identity." However, many state-centric realists recognize the importance of identity in state behavior; for example, the nature of the domestic political system. As I have already mentioned, I myself emphasize the importance of the national system of political economy in determining the economic behavior of individual states. Whether a national society defines itself as a stakeholder (e.g., Germany or Japan) or a shareholder (Great Britain or the United States) economy, the type of economy has a significant impact on its economic behavior.

Political and economic identities or ideologies can have a strong influence on national behavior. Certainly, one can not explain the Cold War without reference to the ideological conflict between the democratic-capitalist identity of the United States and the totalitarian-communist identity of the Soviet Union. In fact, George Kennan, a realist to the core, based his "containment" doctrine on the authoritarian identity of the Soviet state.[19] In time, Kennan correctly predicted, the policy of containment would transform this identity and hence the behavior of the Soviet state. Morgenthau also emphasized the importance of identity. The theme of *Scientific Man versus Power Politics* was that liberal democratic societies exhibited moral failure when they did not recognize the evil nature (identity) of Nazi Germany in the 1930s.[20] The sociopolitical nature of a society, the national ideology, and the political identity all contribute to a society's definition of its interests and influence its behavior. Realists disagree, however, with the constructivist's position that identity is the most important or the only determinant of a nation's foreign policy.

The state-centric interpretation of international political economy (IPE) rejects a belief popular among many scholars, public officials, and commentators that economic and technological forces have eclipsed the nation-state and are creating a global world economy in which political boundaries and national governments are no longer important.[21] It is certainly true that economic and technological forces are profoundly reshaping international affairs and influencing the behavior of states. However, in a highly integrated global economy, states continue to use their power and to implement policies to channel economic forces in ways favorable to their own national interests and the interests of their citizenry. These national economic interests include receipt of a favorable share of the gains from international economic activities and preservation of national autonomy. Movement toward such regional arrangements as the European Union (EU) and the North American Free Trade Agreement (NAFTA) exemplifies collective national efforts to reach these goals.

Many commentators correctly point out that the nation-state in the last quarter of the twentieth century increasingly came under attack from within and from without; both transnational economic forces

[19] For Kennan's views, see John Lewis Gaddis, *Strategies of Containment: A Critical Appraisal of Postwar American National Security Policy* (New York: Oxford University Press, 1982).

[20] Morgenthau, *Scientific Man vs. Power Politics*.

[21] For an early expression of this "end of the state" thesis, see Edward Hallett Carr, *Nationalism and After* (London: Macmillan, 1945).

21

and ethnic nationalisms were tearing at the economic and political foundations of the nation-state. Yet the nation-state remains of supreme importance even though there is no certainty that it will exist forever. Like every human institution, the nation-state was created to meet specific needs. The state arose at a particular moment in order to provide economic and political security and to achieve other desired goals; in return, citizens gave the nation-state their loyalty. When the nation-state ceases to meet the needs of its citizens, the latter will withdraw their loyalty and the modern state will disappear as did the feudal kingdoms, imperial systems, and city-states that it displaced. However, there is no convincing evidence that such a transformation in human affairs has yet occurred. On the contrary, the world is witnessing a rapid increase in the number of nation-states accompanied by creation of powerful military forces.[22] Moreover, if and when the nation-state does disappear, it will be displaced by some new form of formal political authority.

Economic issues certainly have become much more important since the end of the Cold War and have displaced, for the United States and its allies, the prior overwhelming concern with military security. It is misleading, however, to draw too sharp a distinction between international economic and security affairs. While the weight placed on one or the other varies over time, the two spheres are intimately joined, always have been, and undoubtedly always will be. Although the two policy areas can be distinguished analytically, it is extremely difficult to isolate them in the real world. Their intimate connection was set forth initially by Jacob Viner in his classic "Power versus Plenty as Objectives of Foreign Policy in the Seventeenth and Eighteenth Century."[23]

As the British economist Ralph Hawtrey demonstrated in his important *Economic Aspects of Sovereignty* (1952), the relationship of economic affairs and national security, at least over the long term, is

---

[22] In 1945, there were about 50 states in the UN. At the end of the century there were nearly 200. They all seek to possess the accoutrements of nationhood: currency, airlines, and national armies. Obviously, statehood is attractive.

[23] Jacob Viner, "Power versus Plenty as Objectives of Foreign Policy in the Seventeenth and Eighteenth Centuries," in Jacob Viner, *The Long View and the Short: Studies in Economic Theory and Practice* (Glencoe, Ill.: Free Press, 1958). More recent writings on economics and security are discussed in Michael Mastanduno, "Economics and Security in Statecraft and Scholarship," *International Organization* 52, no. 4 (autumn 1998).

reciprocal.[24] The international political and security system provides the essential framework within which the international economy functions; domestic and international economies generate the wealth that is the foundation of the international political system. Then, over time, the economic base of the international political system shifts according to "the law of uneven growth";[25] the resulting transformation of the international balance of power causes states to redefine their national interests and foreign policies. Such political changes frequently undermine the stability of the international economic/political system and can even lead to international conflict.

The ways in which the world economy functions are determined by both markets and the policies of nation-states, especially those of powerful states; markets and economic forces alone cannot account for the structure and functioning of the global economy. The interactions of the political ambitions and rivalries of states, including their cooperative efforts, create the framework of political relations within which markets and economic forces operate. States, particularly large states, establish the rules that individual entrepreneurs and multinational firms must follow, and these rules generally reflect the political and economic interests of dominant states and their citizens. However, economic and technological forces also shape the policies and interests of individual states and the political relations among states, and the market is indeed a potent force in the determination of economic and political affairs. The relationship of economics and politics is interactive.

PURPOSE OF ECONOMIC ACTIVITY

Most economists, trained in the discipline of neoclassical economics, believe that the purpose of economic activity is to benefit individual consumers and maximize efficient utilization of the earth's scarce resources. While other values and goals may be important, they are not of fundamental concern to economists qua economists. The basic task of economists is to instruct society on how markets function in the

---

[24] Ralph G. Hawtrey, *Economic Aspects of Sovereignty* (London: Longmans, Green, 1952). Hawtrey's book is still one of the very best ever written on the subject of economics and national security. A more recent and excellent discussion of the relationship of power and plenty is Theodore H. Moran, "Grand Strategy: The Pursuit of Power and Plenty," *International Organization* 50, no. 1 (winter 1996): 176–205.

[25] Gilpin, *War and Change in World Politics*, 94.

production of wealth and how these markets can be made most efficient. How societies then choose to distribute that wealth among alternative ends is a moral and political matter lying outside the realm of economic science.

In the study of political economy, however, the purpose of economic activity is a fundamental issue: Is the purpose of economic activity to benefit individual consumers, to promote certain social welfare goals, or to maximize national power? The question of purpose is at the core of political economy, and the answer is a political matter that society must determine. The purpose that a particular society (domestic or international) chooses to pursue in turn determines the role of the market mechanism in the economy. Whether a society decides that the market or some other mechanism should be the principal means to determine the allocation of productive resources and the distribution of the national product is a political matter of the utmost importance. The social or political purpose of economic activities and the economic means to achieve these goals cannot be separated. In every society, the goals of economic activities and the role of markets in achieving those goals are determined by political processes and ultimately are responsibilities delegated by society to the state. Yet, the market has its own logic, and its dictates must be heeded; as economists are fond of reminding us, every benefit has a cost and in a world of scarcity, painful choices must be made. Therefore, the market and economic factors do impose limits on what states can achieve.

Conclusion

The functioning of the world economy is determined by both markets and the policies of nation-states. The political purposes, rivalries, and cooperation of states interact to create the framework of political relations within which economic forces operate. States set the rules that individual entrepreneurs and multinational firms must follow. Yet, economic and technological forces shape the policies and interests of individual states and the political relations among states. The market is indeed a potent force in determination of economic and political affairs. For this reason, both political and economic analyses are required to understand the actual functioning and evolution of the global economy. A comprehensive analysis necessitates intellectual integration of both states and markets.

The Nature of Political Economy

THE STUDY of political economy is now very much in vogue among historians, economists, and social scientists.[1] This interest reflects a growing appreciation that the worlds of politics and economics, once thought to be separate (at least as fields of academic inquiry), do in fact importantly affect one another. The polity is much more influenced by economic developments than many political scientists have appreciated, and the economy is much more dependent upon social and political developments than economists in general have admitted. Recognition of the interrelationships between the two spheres has led to increased attention from historians and social scientists. I shall explore the nature of political economy and contrast it with economics before turning to the subject of international political economy itself.

During the last two centuries several different definitions of the term "political economy" have been set forth.[2] A brief summary of the changes in those definitions provides insight into the nature of the subject.[3] For Adam Smith in *The Wealth of Nations* (1776), political economy was a "branch of the science of a statesman or legislator" and a guide to the prudent management of the national economy, or as John Stuart Mill, the last major classical economist, commented, political economy was the science that teaches a nation how to become rich. These thinkers emphasized the wealth of *nations*, and the term "political" was as significant as the term "economy."

In the late nineteenth century, this broad definition of what economists study was narrowed considerably. Alfred Marshall, the father of modern economics, turned his back on the earlier emphasis on the

[1] The references to economists discussed in this section draw from the review of the varieties of political economy in David K. Whynes, ed., *What Is Political Economy?: Eight Perspectives* (Oxford: Basil Blackwell, 1984).

[2] An analysis of various approaches to the subject can be found in James A. Caporaso and David P. Levine, *Theories of Political Economy* (New York: Cambridge University Press, 1992).

[3] This discussion of the various meanings of political economy is based on Colin Wright, "Competing Conceptions of Political Economy," in James H. Nichols Jr. and Colin Wright, eds., *From Political Economy to Economics—And Back?* (San Francisco: Institute for Contemporary Studies, 1990).

nation as a whole and on the political as important. In his highly influential *Principles of Economics* (1890), Marshall substituted the present-day term "economics" for "political economy" and greatly restricted the domain of economic science. Following Marshall's precept that economics was an empirical and value-free science, his disciple Lionel Robbins in *The Nature and Significance of Economic Science* (1932) provided the definition to which most present-day economists subscribe: "Economics is the science which studies human behavior as a relationship between ends and scarce means which have alternative uses." In more modern terminology, economics is defined by economists as a universal science of decision-making under conditions of constraint and scarcity.

At the end of the twentieth century, the term "political economy" has come back into fashion even among economists, but there are important differences from earlier usages; also there is considerable controversy over the meaning of the term. For many professional economists, especially those identified with the Chicago School, political economy means a significant broadening of the *scope* or subject-matter that economists study.[4] These economists have greatly extended the social domain to which the methods or formal models of traditional economics are applicable. The underlying assumptions regarding motivation and the analytical tools of mainstream economics, they argue, are pertinent to the study of all (or at least almost all) aspects of human behavior. For such Chicago School economists as Gary Becker, Richard Posner, and Anthony Downs, the methodology of economics—that is, methodological individualism or the rational actor model of human behavior—is applicable to all types of human behavior from individuals choosing a sexual partner to voters choosing the American President. According to this interpretation, behavior can be explained by the efforts of individuals to maximize, satisfy, or optimize their self-interest.

Many economists and other social scientists enamored with economics attempt to use the individualistic or rational-choice methodology of economics to explain social institutions, public policy, and other forms of social activities that have traditionally been regarded as noneconomic in nature. Such "economic imperialism," identified most closely with the Chicago School, covers several scholarly areas that include neoinstitutionalism, public-choice theory, and what economists themselves call "political economy." The essence of this

---

[4] Warren J. Samuels, ed., *The Chicago School of Political Economy* (University Park, Pa.: Association of Evolutionary Economists, 1976).

26

approach to social institutions and other sociopolitical matters is to assume that individuals act alone or together to create social institutions and promote other social/political objectives to advance their private interests. Two fundamental positions may be discerned within this broad range of scholarly research. On the one hand, some scholars assume that individuals seek to create social institutions and advocate public policies that will promote overall economic efficiency. On the other hand, the term "political economy" is used by neoclassical economists to refer to rent-seeking behavior by individuals and groups.[5] Trade protectionism is an example of this approach. There is, however, a powerful normative bias among economists that economic institutions or structures are created to serve market efficiency.

The long-term objective of this body of scholarship is to make *endogenous* to economic science those variables or explanations of social phenomena that have traditionally been assumed to be *exogenous* and therefore the exclusive province of one of the other social sciences such as psychology, sociology, or political science. By "endogenous," economists mean that a particular human action can be fully explained as a self-conscious effort of an individual to maximize his or her economic interests; for example, according to the "endogenous growth theory," to be discussed in the next chapter, a firm invests in scientific research in order to increase its profits. By "exogenous," economists mean that a particular action can be explained best by a noneconomic motive; for example, Albert Einstein may be said to have been motivated in his work by curiosity or by the desire for fame rather than a desire to increase his income.

Economic imperialists assume that political and other forms of social behavior can be reduced to economic motives and explained by the formal methods of economic science. Government policies, social institutions including the state itself, and even whole economic systems, these economists claim, can be explained through application of formal economic models. For example, economist Edmund S. Phelps broadly defines political economy as the *choice* of the economic system itself.[6] Underlying this sweeping definition of political economy is the conviction, expressed by Jack Hirshleifer, that economics is the one and only true social science. The universality of economics, he argues, is due to the fact that its analytic abstractions such as scarcity,

---

[5] Rent-seeking refers to the use of a resource to obtain a surplus over the normal economic return to that resource. An example is a tariff that raises the cost of domestic goods.

[6] Edmund S. Phelps, *Political Economy: An Introductory Text* (New York: W. W. Norton, 1985), xiii-xiv.

27

cost, and opportunities are themselves universally applicable and can be used effectively to explain both individual behavior and social outcomes.[7] As we shall note many times in this book, the belief that there is only one universal social science, namely economics, is a powerful dogma embraced by many, if not most, economists.

At least three different schools of economists employ an economic approach to human behavior: neoclassical institutionalism, the public-choice school, and what is sometimes called the "new political economy." Neoclassical institutionalism attempts to explain the origin, evolution, and functioning of all types of institutions (social, political, economic) as the result of the maximizing behavior of rational individuals. The public-choice school is also interested in applying the methods of formal economics to analysis of political behavior and institutions, especially to the *political* organization of free men.[8] The new political economy is interested primarily in the political determinants of economic policy. Although I shall make only occasional references to these schools of political economists, their insights have influenced the argument of this book.

The public-choice approach is most closely associated with Nobel Laureate James Buchanan and his co-author, Gordon Tullock.[9] Using the framework of conventional economics, Buchanan and Tullock in their highly influential *The Calculus of Consent* (1962) promoted the important subfield of public choice.[10] For most economists in the public-choice school, the subject matter is the same as that of political science; they believe that they are applying superior methods of economic science to political affairs.[11] What defines the public-choice school more than anything else, however, is its political coloration. With certain important exceptions, such as Nobel Laureates Kenneth Arrow and Paul Samuelson, both of whom have made important contributions to the subject of public choice, this school of political econ-

---

[7] Jack Hirshleifer, "The Expanding Domain of Economics," *American Economic Review* 75, no. 6 (December 1995): 53.

[8] Wright, "Competing Conceptions of Political Economy," 71.

[9] A useful overview of the public-choice literature is Dennis C. Mueller, *The Public Choice Approach to Politics* (London: Edward Elgar, 1993).

[10] James M. Buchanan and Gordon Tullock, *The Calculus of Consent* (Ann Arbor: University of Michigan Press, 1962). The relevance of the public-choice approach to the international economy is set forth in Thomas D. Willett, *The Public Choice Approach to International Economic Relations* (Charlottesville: University of Virginia, Center for Study of Public Choice, 1996).

[11] The term "positive political economy" is frequently applied to this position. An example is James E. Alt and Kenneth A. Shepsle, *Perspectives on Positive Political Economy* (New York: Cambridge University Press, 1990).

omists, especially Buchanan and Tullock themselves, is distinguished by its explicitly normative commitment to unfettered markets and strong opposition to government intervention in the economy. While some economists emphasize *market failures* as a reason for government intervention in the economy, the more conservative branch of public-choice economics considers *government* failure—that is, economic distortions caused by the policies of governments—to be more of a threat to economic well-being. Politicians and government officials are not the disinterested public servants they are assumed to be by many economists and advocates of government interventionism; they have interests of their own that they seek to maximize in their public activities. This position asserts that politicians, liberal reformers, and others distort the efficient functioning of the market as they use the apparatus of government to further their own private interests.

Neoclassical institutionalism is one of the most interesting developments in contemporary economics. According to neoinstitutionalist economists, economic institutions (and other institutions, including the state) and their characteristics can be explained by the methods of neoclassical economics. Nobel Laureate Douglass C. North, one of the foremost representatives of this school, maintains that economic institutions (like all forms of economic activity) are the consequence of intentional actions by rational individuals to maximize their economic interests.[12] Economic actions may be motivated by the desire to increase economic efficiency or may be simply rent-seeking. However, there is a predilection among neoinstitutionalists and other economists to assume that economic institutions have been produced by rational efforts to increase efficiency.[13] This neoinstitutionalist school is weakened by the fact that it overlooks the noneconomic factors responsible for the creation of social institutions and the rules governing societies.

Most mainstream economists frequently use the term "political economy" pejoratively to refer to the self-serving behavior of individuals and groups in the determination of public policy. According to the "new political economy," national policy is most frequently the

---

[12] Douglass C. North, *Structure and Change in Economic History* (New York: W. W. Norton, 1981); also, North, *Institutions, Institutional Change, and Economic Performance* (New York: Cambridge University Press, 1990).

[13] A notable example is Richard A. Posner, *The Economics of Justice* (Cambridge: Harvard University Press, 1981). A valuable critique of neoclassical institutionalism is Alexander James Field, "On the Explanation of Rules Using Rational Choice Models," *Journal of Economic Issues* 13, no. 1 (March 1979): 49–72.

result of private groups' efforts to employ public means to further their own private interests rather than the result of selfless efforts to advance the commonweal. Economic policy, this positon argues, is the outcome of distributional politics and competition among powerful groups for private advantage. For example, the economics literature on trade protection (endogenous trade theory) exemplifies this approach as it argues that tariffs and other obstructions to free trade can best be understood as rent-seeking behavior by particular interest groups.

A very different concept of political economy is used by those critics (especially Marxists) who believe that the discipline of economics has become too formal, mathematical, and abstract. The study of economics as the development of formal models, many charge, has become largely irrelevant to the understanding and solving of real social and economic problems. A major reason for this isolation of economics from the real world, they argue, is that economics neglects the historical, political, and social settings in which economic behavior takes place. As a consequence, some assert that economics, at least as it is taught and practiced in traditional departments of economics, has little relevance to the larger society and its needs.

Closely associated with this general criticism is what many critics regard as the pretension of economics to be a "science" modeled on physics and other natural sciences. Economics, they contend, cannot be value-free, and economists should not pretend that it is. According to Marxists and others, conventional economics reflects the values and interests of the dominant groups of a capitalist society. Rather than being value-free, economics is alleged to be infused with an implicit conservative social and political bias that emphasizes market and efficiency and neglects such social problems as inequality of income and chronic unemployment. In the opinion of Robert Heilbroner and William Milberg, contemporary economics is nothing but a handmaiden of modern Western capitalism, and its primary purpose is to make this troubled system work.[14]

By the end of the twentieth century, the term "political economy" had been given three broad and different meanings. For some scholars, especially economists, political economy referred to the application to all types of human behavior, including behaviors that would not be classified by others as economic, of the *methodology* of formal economics; that is, methodological individualism or the rational actor

---

[14] Robert L. Heilbroner and William Milberg, *The Crisis of Vision in Modern Economic Thought* (New York: Cambridge University Press, 1995).

model of human behavior. Other scholars used the term to mean employment of a specific economic *theory* or theories to explain social behavior; a good example is found in Ronald Rogowski's use of the Stopler-Samuelson theorem to explain political outcomes over time and space.[15] For those political scientists, including myself, who believe that social and political affairs cannot be reduced to a subfield of economics, political economy refers primarily to *questions* generated from the interactions of economic and political affairs. Proponents of this broad approach to the subject are eclectic in their choice of subject matter and methods (economic, historical, sociological, political, etc.).

WHAT YOU SEEK IS WHAT YOU FIND

Interpretations of economic affairs are highly dependent upon the analytic perspective of the observer and upon his or her assumptions as these determine what the observer looks for or emphasizes. Fundamental differences between economics and political economy are exemplified in their differing definitions of the economy to be studied, of the basic economic entities or actors, and of the forces responsible for economic and, more broadly, sociopolitical change. Members of each academic specialization differ in their perspectives on economic affairs, questions asked, and methods employed. The differences, illustrated in the coming paragraphs, are important because they profoundly influence the ways in which economists and political economists study economic affairs at both the domestic and international levels.

Definition of an Economy

In April 1992, the prestigious National Bureau of Economic Research (NBER) sponsored a conference to analyze whether or not Japan was deliberately creating an exclusive economic bloc in East and Southeast Asia. According to Martin Feldstein, NBER director, in his charge to conference participants, the conference was the first attempt by the Bureau to bring together a group of economists and political scientists (the latter included experts on Japanese and international politics) to address an issue of mutual concern. The results of the conference were published in *Regionalism and Rivalry: Japan and the United States in Pacific Asia* (1993), edited by Jeffrey Frankel (an

---

[15] Ronald Rogowski, *Commerce and Coalitions: How Trade Affects Domestic Political Alignments* (Princeton: Princeton University Press, 1989).

economist) and Miles Kahler (a political scientist).[16] The contributions to the book revealed that these two groups of specialists, as they attempted to answer Feldstein's questions, asked different questions, used different methods, and reached different conclusions regarding the nature of the evolving Pacific Asia economy.

The political scientists' analysis concentrated on the trade/investment behavior of Japanese firms and on official Japanese foreign aid to the region (Official Development Assistance). Evidence, they asserted, revealed that Japanese corporations, with the active support of the state, were attempting to incorporate the Pacific Asian economies into regional industrial and financial structures or networks organized, managed, and dominated by large Japanese corporations. Through their trade, investment, and other activities, these giant multinational firms working together with Japanese foreign aid agencies were consciously fashioning a regional division of labor composed of highly integrated production and distribution networks centered on the Japanese home economy. The political scientists concluded that the Japanese, as they had done in the 1930s, were again attempting to create and dominate an East Asian sphere of influence, albeit this time by peaceful economic means. The political scientists defined the Pacific Asian economy as a hierarchical structure increasingly determined and dominated by Japanese multinational corporations and the Japanese state.

The economists, on the other hand, concentrated their analysis on trade flows and other measurable economic quantities that could be formally modeled. Their analysis of the data led to the conclusion that the Japanese state and corporations were not attempting to create an exclusive economic sphere in Pacific Asia. On the contrary, they insisted that what was taking place in the region could be explained entirely in terms of market forces and the responses of individual firms to those forces. For example, the increasing Japanese investment in the region and growing trade with the region were considered responses to the substantial appreciation of the yen following the Plaza Agreement of September 1985 and to subsequent changes in Japanese comparative advantage. Moreover, analysis of gross trade statistics showed that, although intraregional trade in Pacific Asia was growing, it was growing less rapidly than trade between Pacific Asia and the rest of the world. Thus, economists found no

---

[16] Jeffrey A. Frankel and Miles Kahler, eds., *Regionalism and Rivalry: Japan and the United States in Pacific Asia* (Chicago: University of Chicago Press, 1993).

evidence either for the existence of a distinctive Pacific Asian economy or for any Japanese effort to create a regional sphere of influence.

Whereas the political scientists' analysis defined the Pacific Asian economy as composed of powerful economic and state actors, the economists defined the regional economy in terms of economic forces and quantities. The opposed conclusions of the two groups of specialists reflected the differences in their basic assumptions about the nature of economic reality, the evidence studied, and the methodology employed. I believe that the differing analytic approaches and conclusions of the economists and the political scientists are actually complementary rather than contradictory. Considered together, both intellectual approaches increase awareness of the role of both political and economic factors in shaping economic reality and thereby deepen our comprehension of developments in the world economy.

Nature of Economic Actors

In the late 1960s, a group of graduate students in public affairs at Princeton University's Woodrow Wilson School of Public and International Affairs asked a professor of economics to offer a course on the multinational corporation (MNC). During the 1960s the rapid overseas expansion and increasing importance of these giant firms (at that time mostly American) had captured public attention and become intensely controversial. Raymond Vernon and other commentators believed that these business firms would greatly facilitate efficient utilization of the world's scarce resources and speed economic development of the entire globe.[17] However, Stephen Hymer and other radical critics regarded such powerful corporations as nothing more than instruments of an expanding American capitalist imperialism that was exploiting countries throughout the world.[18] The students believed that the MNC was a novel and important phenomenon that should be the focus of at least one course in the School's substantial economics curriculum.

The students were firmly rebuffed with the professor's response that "the multinational corporation does not exist." Corporations exist, the economist granted, but there is no such thing as a distinctive *multinational* corporation that behaves differently from other corporations. Every corporation, whatever its nationality or scope of its

---

[17] Raymond Vernon, *Sovereignty at Bay* (New York: Basic Books, 1971).

[18] Stephen Hymer, *The International Operation of National Firms: A Study of Direct Foreign Investment* (New York: Cambridge University Press, 1976).

activities, behaves in the same way that all others behave. All corporate leaders make their decisions in response to market signals and in order to maximize their profits. (Or, as the economist told the students, the purpose of the postman is to deliver the mail regardless of the color of the uniform.) Economists in general believe that, whether the firm is American, European, or Japanese, it must optimize within given constraints and respond effectively to market opportunities in highly competitive markets or go out of business. The fact that a firm happens to be of a particular nationality and competes in a world market through establishment of overseas subsidiaries does not significantly change matters. In language that a Marxist or a realist would use, the ownership of the means of production and the national origins of a business firm are totally irrelevant.

This experience illustrates the view of neoclassical economics regarding the nature of economic actors. The world of the economist is populated solely by individuals (consumers and producers) pursuing their self-interest; firms, states, or other economic actors are assumed to be merely aggregates of such individual actors. Every individual (regardless of ethnicity, class, or national identity) is assumed to act rationally (employing a cost/benefit calculation) in pursuit of his or her self-interest. There are no fundamental differences among American, Japanese, or Bantu economic actors. Everyone is assumed to be seeking the same broad range of economic objectives. The only things that differ from one society to another are the external constraints on decision-making and the opportunities among which the individual must choose.

Within other intellectual perspectives, the nature of economic actors appears very different. A Marxist, for example, regards economic classes (defined by the ownership or nonownership of the basic means of production) or such representatives of class interests as politicians or interest groups as the fundamental actors in economic affairs. According to this view, all corporations (national or multinational) are representatives of the capitalist class that dominates every capitalist economy. For proponents of a state-centric approach, on the other hand, the primary economic actors are nation-states or other powerful political groups, and, therefore, the nationality of the MNC is of great importance because its behavior is strongly influenced by the policies and culture of its home society. Viewed from this perspective, a "multinational" corporation is, in its essence, a corporation of a particular nationality whose international activities are, on the whole, intended to promote the primary interests (economic, political, or even security) of its nation of origin.

34

Dynamics of the World Economy

In September 1992, an important and disturbing event occurred when, without warning, private investors suddenly transferred huge sums of money out of the British pound, the Italian lira, and other currencies into the German mark, thereby forcing an unwanted devaluation of the pound and other currencies. This devaluation significantly reshaped the economic and political landscape of Western Europe and tore apart the Exchange Rate Mechanism (ERM) of the European Monetary System (EMS), whose purpose was to maintain the values of the European Community currencies within specified narrow bands. As a consequence of this financial crisis, Great Britain withdrew from the ERM and caused the movement toward European economic and monetary integration to divide into a "two-speed" process of European unification.

Interpretations of this episode illustrate the differences between an "economic" and a "political economic" analysis of the dynamics of the world economy. Economists were certainly aware that political developments like German reunification and the Danish rejection, in June 1992, of the Maastricht Treaty had important roles in generating the financial crisis of that fall. However, such political developments were treated by economists as factors external to the formal economic modeling of the crisis. Economists were interested in the dynamics of the crisis itself and not the political dynamics that led to the crisis. Therefore, the underlying political and other causes of this crisis were not closely examined by economists. Instead, analysis of the crisis by economists focused only on its economic aspects. For example, formulation of a general model of financial crises was a central purpose in one excellent study by economists.[19]

Political economists, on the other hand, were more interested in the political genesis of the crisis, its political resolution, and the longer-term economic/political consequences. That is to say, they were most interested in the external or exogenous political factors that lead to a crisis, contribute to its resolution, and determine its long-term effects. The point of this comparison is that economists and political economists were interested in different phenomena and asked different questions. The 1992 financial crisis illuminated the relationship and

---

[19] This is the case, for example, of an excellent study of the crisis by Willem H. Buiter, Giancarlo Corsetti, and Paolo A. Pesenti, *Financial Markets and European Monetary Cooperation: The Lessons of the 1992–93 Exchange Rate Mechanism Crisis* (New York: Cambridge University Press, 1998).

interaction of the economic and political forces that provide the dynamics of the international economy.

Since the mid-1970s, the size of international financial flows has grown to hundreds of billions of dollars a day. These immense capital flows can easily overwhelm national economies, as they did the Italian and British economies in 1992 and many other economies in the late 1990s. Increasing integration of global financial markets has caused national governments to surrender a portion of their economic autonomy to global market forces. Although a government may pursue inappropriately expansionary economic policies for a time, powerful market forces will eventually overturn these policies. The huge outflow of capital from Italy and Great Britain in 1992 and subsequent devaluations of their currencies forced both nations to withdraw from the Exchange Rate Mechanism (ERM), although Italy eventually returned.

Many observers believe that the September 1992 financial crisis demonstrated the triumph of transnational economic forces and economic globalization over the nation-state. In this popular and influential interpretation, the integration of global financial markets and the resulting huge flows of capital across national boundaries have led, in the words of one enthusiastic writer, to "the end of geography."[20] Some commentators allege that national governments are rapidly losing their economic autonomy and have even become hostage to global market forces and the whims of international speculators. Some argue that if a national government fails to heed the interests of the controllers of international capital, the errant government will not be able to obtain the capital required to carry out its economic and political plans. International capital markets are alleged to have created a web of economic interdependence that has transformed the nature of international affairs and destroyed the economic and political independence of nation-states. Hence, many have concluded that markets are firmly in control of the world economy. Some believe that the 1997 East Asian financial crisis supports this conclusion.

An alternative interpretation of the earlier 1992 crisis emphasizes the role of government decisions and political developments in convincing international investors that the currency situation in Western Europe was highly unstable. The July 1990 decision to eliminate intra-European barriers to capital flows had increased the risk of currency speculation that could cause exchange rate disequilibria. This

[20] Richard O'Brien, *Global Financial Integration: The End of Geography* (London: Pinter Publishers, 1992). Published for the Royal Institute of International Affairs.

potentially risky situation was exacerbated when additional restrictions were placed on exchange rate flexibility within the ERM. These economic developments laid the groundwork for the crisis. Political developments that raised questions about the movement toward European monetary unity included the Danish rejection in June 1992 of the Maastricht Treaty. This startling action was followed in September by the narrow (51 percent) passage in France of a national referendum on the Treaty. However, the most important developments leading to the financial crisis were the several decisions of the German Central Bank (Bundesbank), from November 1990 on, to raise German interest rates substantially in order to offset the inflationary consequences of German reunification. Then the American Federal Reserve lowered interest rates in early 1992 to stimulate the stagnant American economy. Also, in order to stay within the ERM currency bands, the British government had attempted to maintain an overvalued pound and thereby caused the worst British recession in the postwar era. These political developments raised serious doubts that the British could continue to maintain the value of the pound.

The large gap between Germany's excessively high and America's excessively low interest rates, plus the economic troubles of Italy and Great Britain, created a disequilibrium in exchange rates. Hedge-fund managers like George Soros of the Quantum Fund saw an opportunity for a huge windfall and fled from the overvalued lira and pound to the mark. Others followed suit in what economists have called a "speculative overreaction." Thus, although it is correct to say, at one level of analysis, that Italy and Great Britain were overwhelmed by market forces, at a deeper level of analysis it is equally correct to say that the financial crisis was due to policy decisions taken by American, German, and British financial authorities. Government decisions and the actions of individual economic actors were responsible for that crisis. Indeed, French government officials, economic nationalists to the core, denounced the financial crisis as an "Anglo-Saxon plot" to destroy the movement toward European unity.

The 1992 financial crisis illustrates that both impersonal market forces and the deliberate actions of a few powerful states can determine the dynamics of the world economy. While Italy and Great Britain were overwhelmed by market forces, deliberate policy decisions by American and German central banks produced such economic fundamentals as the differentials in interest rates. Interactions of impersonal markets and state policies constitute the driving forces in the world economy and the subject matter of the study of international political economy. Whereas market forces are the domain of economic analysis, the explanation of economic policies is primarily the province of political economy. Because each mode of analysis is limited by its assumptions, both should be utilized to improve understanding of the dynamics of the world economy.

THE NATURE OF AN ECONOMY

Whereas economists regard an economy as a market composed of impersonal economic forces, specialists in political economy interpret it as a sociopolitical system populated by powerful actors. Such conceptual differences distinguish the study of economics from that of international political economy (IPE).

The *neoclassical economic interpretation* is that the economy is a market or a collection of markets composed of impersonal economic forces over which individual actors, including states and corporations, have little or no control. As former *New York Times* economic commentator Leonard Silk has described it, for economists the economy is nothing more than a collection of flexible wages, prices, interest rates, and similar forces that move up and down allocating resources to their profitable use as buyers and sellers rationally pursue their own interests.[21] Such an economic universe is a self-regulating and self-contained system composed solely of changing prices and quantities to which individual economic actors respond. Economic actors are assumed to be "price-takers" who seek to maximize, or at least satisfy, their private interests as they respond to changes in relative prices or to changes in economic constraints and opportunities.

The *political economy interpretation* used in this book defines the economy as a sociopolitical system composed of powerful economic actors or institutions such as giant firms, powerful labor unions, and large agribusinesses that are competing with one another to formulate government policies on taxes, tariffs, and other matters in ways that advance their own interests.[22] And the most important of these powerful actors are national governments. In this interpretation, there are many social, political, or economic actors whose behavior has a powerful impact on the nature and functioning of markets. This conception of the economy as an identifiable social and political structure composed of powerful actors is held by many citizens and by most social scientists other than professional economists.

[21] *New York Times*, 26 March 1980, D2.
[22] Ibid.

The role of institutions in determining economic behavior and outcomes is of particular interest in the political economy interpretation. Social, political, and economic institutions are significant in that they determine, or at least influence, the incentives that shape the interaction of individuals and groups as political and economic actors. In economics the two principal explanations for the creation of institutions are neoclassical institutionalism and the theory of public choice. Both of these theories assume that institutions can be explained as resulting from conscious action by economic actors to further their economic interests. These two positions differ, however, regarding the purpose of institutions. Neoclassical institutionalism is based on the belief that institutions are created primarily to solve economic problems and will result in increased economic efficiency; for example, neoinstitutionalists believe that business corporations are created to reduce transaction costs. The public-choice position, on the other hand, believes that government institutions are created by powerful groups, public officials, and politicians to promote their own self-interest and that they decrease efficiency; for example, tariffs are essentially rent-seeking devices to shift income from consumers to domestic producers. Both positions, however, explain the creation of institutions as resulting from rational intentions.

Political economists, on the other hand, believe that institutions are created for a variety of rational, irrational, and even capricious motives. Moreover, in contrast to economists' emphasis on efficiency or rent-seeking, the political economists argue that institutions are built on the idea of path dependence and that economic and other institutions are the result of accidents, random choices, and chance events that frequently cannot be explained as the result of rational economic processes. Institutions are sometimes the consequence of historical accident and self-reinforcing and cumulative processes. (One of my favorite examples is the constitutional prohibition against foreign-born Americans becoming President; its purpose was to bar the detested Alexander Hamilton from the presidency.) As a consequence, many institutions are neither efficient nor do they necessarily represent the economic interests of the individuals who brought them into existence. However, once these institutions are created, for whatever chance or irrational reason, they have a powerful advantage over new and more efficient institutions that could otherwise displace them.

Institutions are even more tenacious than neoinstitutionalism and public-choice theory suggest, and it is frequently difficult to replace an inefficient institution with a more efficient one. Neoclassical institutionalism, for example, is based on the assumption of constant returns to scale in which economic actors who desire to replace an older and less efficient institution or business firm with a newer and more efficient one can do so without any overwhelming difficulty. However, the established institution or business firm may enjoy economies of scale (and hence lower costs) merely as a consequence of having established itself in the market ahead of potential rivals. An existing institution may also have gained a legitimacy and a powerful constituency whose interests it serves. Thus, even though the potential efficiency of the new institution or business firm may be much greater than the efficiency of the existing institution or business firm, the "barriers to entry" are too great to accomplish a change. In the economic universe of political economists there are many inefficient economic institutions and oligopolistic businesses that result from random events and irrational decisions.

The study of political economy requires integration of these two fundamentally different meanings of "economy." Both the neoclassical and the political economy interpretations of economic activities are necessary and important ingredients in the effort to understand how the economy functions. Impersonal markets and powerful actors interact to produce those economic and political outcomes of interest to students of political economy. The study of political economy requires an understanding of how markets work and how market forces affect economic outcomes as well as an understanding of how powerful actors, of which the nation-state is by far the most important, attempt to manipulate market forces to advance their private interests. The science of economics, as it has been developed by generations of professional economists, possesses highly useful analytical tools and a rich body of theoretical insights (or as economists prefer, models) for understanding markets. The scope of economic science, however, is too limited and its theories much too abstract for the purposes of international political economy. The strength of political science lies in its broad emphasis on the "realities" of the universal struggle among human beings, groups, and states for power and position. Its weakness lies in the intuitive nature of its methods and its limited theoretical foundations.

The study of political economy and international political economy requires an analytic approach that takes into account economics, political science, and other social sciences. It must incorporate the many economic, political, and technological factors that determine, or at least influence, the nature and dynamics of the international economy. Yet, such an approach will undoubtedly always be limited in its explanatory, and certainly in its predictive, powers. There is simply too much that we do not know and perhaps never will know. As international economist Robert Baldwin has commented, an adequate theory of international political economy would have to be built upon a theory of how governments reach decisions, and, of course, there is no such theory.[23] Achievement of our goal of comprehending how the international political economy functions will probably always be elusive no matter how hard we work to improve the study of the international economy.

EMBEDDEDNESS OF THE ECONOMY

The central idea that markets are embedded in larger sociopolitical systems underlies my interpretation of both political economy and international political economy. The government, powerful domestic interests, and historical experiences determine the purpose of the economy and establish the parameters within which the market (price mechanism) functions. Contrary to economists' belief that economic activities are universal in character and essentially the same every-where, the specific goals of economic activities are in actuality socially determined and differ widely over the face of the earth. For example, although neoclassical economists assert that the primary purpose of economic activities is to satisfy the desires of individual consumers, this characterization applies to the United States but not to every other economy. Japan and many Asian societies, for example, place a high priority on the welfare of the community and on social cohe-sion. In fact, the idea that markets should be free to promote the private interests of individuals is a rather recent belief, and the strength of the welfare state in Western Europe indicates that even in the West this idea is not universally accepted.

In addition to determining the purpose of economic activity, the sociopolitical system and a society's values determine the role that the market or price mechanism in a particular society legitimately plays and the socially approved ways in which economic objectives may be pursued. Every society has values and beliefs that circumscribe the ways in which the market is permitted to function; societies establish rules and set boundaries that govern the range of activities in which the price mechanism is considered legitimate; what is considered to be "fair" economic behavior in one society may not be considered fair in another. For example, bribery is a serious offense in the United

[23] Robert Baldwin, in Jaime De Melo and Arvind Panagariya, eds., *New Dimensions in Regional Integration* (New York: Cambridge University Press, 1993).

States, but what Westerners would call "bribery" has long been a normal and accepted business practice in China. Many Americans complain that competition from low-wage Asian labor is unfair; many Asians retort that the American criticism is unfair because low wages constitute their only important comparative advantage. Such national differences have been a major source of misunderstandings and even of political conflict as national economies have become more closely linked to one another through trade and investment.

The international economy is also embedded in a sociopolitical system, although not as deeply as are national economies; the international economy is embedded in an international system of regimes, public and private organizations, and, most important of all, nation-states. As I shall argue in greater detail below, the dominant power/s in the international system plays/play a major role in defining the purpose of the international economy and the principal rules governing international economic activities. For example, during the Cold War, the Western international economic system, under American leadership, was intended to strengthen security ties against the Soviet Union.

Economists in general believe that an international economy easily and automatically emerges because, in the words of Adam Smith, it is natural for mankind to "truck, barter, and trade." However, it is in fact politically very difficult to create an open world economy. As Mancur Olson has pointed out, the decision of a government to open its economy to imports and other commercial activities constitutes a politically risky action because it immediately results in many resentful losers and, at least initially, produces just a few winners.[24] Necessarily then, Olson argues, the creation of an international economy is the result of costly actions taken by powerful states (hegemons) for economic, political, and especially security reasons. Private economic interests, especially those of powerful business groups, also obviously play an important role in the efforts of powerful states to create an international economy. However, the political and security interests of states themselves play the central role in its creation.[25]

The primacy of the national economic and political interests of dominant powers is illustrated in the nature of successive international economies since the mid-seventeenth century. During the mercantilist age of the seventeenth and eighteenth centuries, the major

[24] Mancur Olson provides an illuminating discussion of this subject in De Melo and Panagariya, eds., *New Dimensions in Regional Integration*.

[25] The nexus of economic and security affairs is discussed by Edward D. Mansfield in his *Power, Trade, and War* (Princeton: Princeton University Press, 1994).

powers of Western Europe fought on land and sea to create empires that would support their political rivalries. Although companies of merchant-adventurers such as the British and Dutch East India Companies benefited from these commercial conflicts, the primary concern of states was to acquire a favorable balance of trade/payments to finance their external military and political ambitions. Great Britain's victory in the Napoleonic Wars resulted in a new and differently ordered international economy. Formal imperialism and possession of colonies were deemphasized and what historians called "the imperialism of free trade" emerged. Or, in the words of Stanley Jevons, one of England's foremost economists in the late nineteenth century, "Unfettered commerce . . . has made the several quarters of the globe our willing tributaries."[26] The Pax Britannica and Britain's dominant global position were thus built on economic foundations.

Following World War II, the United States launched a concerted effort to create an open world economy. The origins of this effort can be traced to the Reciprocal Trade Act of 1934 and the Tripartite Monetary Agreement a few years later. In addition, American postwar planners working mainly with their British counterparts began to lay the foundations for an open world economy following the war; this cooperative effort culminated in the Bretton Woods Conference (1944) that created the institutional framework for the postwar international economy. However, strong assertion of American postwar economic leadership occurred *only* after the emergence of a clear Soviet threat. With the outbreak of the Cold War, the United States undertook a number of important initiatives to strengthen the wartorn economies of its allies, to forge a powerful anti-Soviet alliance, and subsequently, to fasten these allied economies firmly to the United States. The most important American action was, of course, the Marshall Plan that transferred billions of dollars to Western Europe; this extraordinary transfer of wealth would not have taken place if not for the Cold War. In effect, the United States used its political, economic, and other resources to create an open world economy embracing its political allies and much of the Third World.

This analysis suggests that the creation and maintenance of an open and unified world economy requires a powerful leader or "hegemon" that possesses both the political interest and the resources to pay the high costs associated with such a task. It is highly unlikely that an open and unified world market economy could be created and maintained unless there were a dominant power able and willing to use its

[26] Stanley Jevons, *The Coal Question* (London: Macmillan, 1906), 411.

political, economic, and other resources to encourage other states to lower trade and other economic barriers, to prevent free-riding, and to apply sanctions to states that failed to obey the rules or regimes governing the liberal world economy. If there were no such strong leader, international cooperation among egocentric states would be exceedingly difficult, and there is a likelihood that the open, unified world economy would fragment into national protectionism and regional blocs.

The emphasis in this book on the role of political actors using their power to influence market outcomes has some similarities to the position of the public-choice school that argues that all political behavior, including that of public officials, can be explained as the pursuit of private interests by self-centered individuals and groups. However, my position differs from this perspective in important respects. The public-choice school implies that politics and markets can, at least in theory, be separated; it argues that if there were no state intervention in the economy, the price system by itself would determine all outcomes. I believe, on the other hand, that the market is inherently political. For example, the distributive effects of markets are determined primarily by the nature and distribution of property rights, and property rights themselves and their distribution are inevitably affected by political developments. Further, whereas the public-choice position believes that public officials are motivated primarily by economic interests, I myself believe that national security and prestige play an equal and frequently an even greater role in motivating the behavior of national governments.

Another difference between the public-choice position and my own is based on different concepts of the nature of the state and the national interest. The public-choice position believes that the state is simply a collection of those individuals who comprise the government at a particular moment; the national interest is the combined interests of the individual members of the society or of those members who dominate the government. On the other hand, I believe that the state is more than the sum of its component parts, that it has some autonomy from society, and that the national interest is distinct from the combined interests of its parts. The state and the national interest cannot be reduced, as the public-choice position asserts, to the individuals who happen to be in power at any particular moment.[27] Most

----

[27] Willett, I believe, concedes this point when he acknowledges that foreign policy cannot be reduced to interest group politics. Willett, *The Public Choice Approach to International Economic Relations,* 14.

adherents of the public-choice position believe in free trade, as do I. However, the commitment to free trade must be based on a concept of a national interest and the belief that free trade will benefit that national interest and not just the interests of those in power at the time.

A state or national government must fulfill several social, economic, and political functions to retain the loyalty of its citizens. Provision of security for its citizens both at home and abroad is the primary function of the state; no other institution can relieve it of this responsibility. Another function is to promote the social and economic welfare of its citizens and to guarantee minimal standards of individual justice; although the social welfare function has long existed, as James Mayall has emphasized in discussing what he calls "the new economic nationalism," economic welfare has become intimately joined to national citizenship in the modern world.[28] Without a state of their own, individuals have no access to welfare programs. The state also provides an identity for its citizens; it appears to be inherent in human nature that individuals need to be part of some larger social grouping. In many societies there is growing concern that globalization is leading to loss of a separate identity for individual citizens and individual states. This situation reinforces my belief that political economy's concept of an economy as markets embedded in a sociopolitical system is not only accurate but that it also provides a very useful tool of analysis.

Conclusion

This book defines political economy as the interaction of the market and powerful actors. Both components are necessary, and one cannot comprehend how either domestic or international economies function unless he or she understands both how markets work and how states and other actors attempt to manipulate markets to their own advantage. As I stated above, markets have an inherent logic of their own as they respond to changes in relative prices, constraints, and opportunities. Therefore, to analyze the functioning of an economy, one must begin with at least a rudimentary knowledge of how the discipline of economics understands the economy as a market or price mechanism, and this is the focus of the next chapter.

---

[28] James Mayall, *Nationalism and International Society* (New York: Cambridge University Press, 1990), chap. 6.

CHAPTER THREE

The Neoclassical Conception of the Economy

D URING THE past two centuries, professional economists have studied the economy as a market system; economists from David Ricardo (1772–1823) to the present have formulated theories to explain economic affairs. These theories have had a significant influence on the trade, monetary, and other policies of national governments. Because the foundation provided by the discipline of economics is essential to comprehension of the economy as a "market," this chapter will discuss the science of economics, its strengths, and its limitations.

THE DISCIPLINE OF NEOCLASSICAL ECONOMICS

In the 1955 edition of his influential textbook, *Economics*, Nobel Laureate Paul Samuelson coined the term "neoclassical synthesis" to characterize the theoretical consensus of professional economists. Samuelson was referring to the consensus that economists had achieved through integration of microeconomics (associated with Alfred Marshall and other leading economists of the late nineteenth century) with the new macroeconomics set forth by John Maynard Keynes in his *General Theory of Employment, Interest, and Money* (1936).[1] Even though this consensus later broke down in the 1970s when the economics profession fragmented into a number of competing schools of macroeconomic thought, the term neoclassical economics is still used to refer to mainstream, orthodox, or conventional economics. It is applied to the economics of the Keynesian, monetarist, or other divergent schools of contemporary economic thought because they all are based on similar assumptions regarding the nature of the market. Perhaps one could say simply that neoclassical economics can be defined as the body of methods and theories accepted and utilized by most members of the economics profession. In this book, I use the term "neoclassical economics" (or simply "economics") in this general sense.

[1] John Maynard Keynes, *The General Theory of Employment, Interest, and Money* (New York: Harcourt, Brace, 1936).

46

Neoclassical economics constitutes a systematic examination of economic affairs as they are defined by professional economists. Economics is a discipline or profession into which its practitioners have been thoroughly socialized. It is the most systematic and rigorous of the social sciences and the necessary starting point for understanding not only the economy but also many other aspects of society. However, economics is only that—a starting point; it is the beginning and not the end of analysis. The systematic approach taken by neoclassical economics provides many advantages but also embodies certain limitations. Social reality, despite the efforts of economic imperialists and many rational-choice analysts to persuade us to the contrary, cannot be reduced solely to the prices and quantities of economic science.

Modern economics, like physics and the other hard sciences and unlike the other social sciences (with the possible exception of demography and certain fields in psychology), had a founder or lawgiver who, in effect, defined the purposes, parameters, and methodology of the discipline. The role of the lawgiver in an academic discipline has been well characterized by Charles Gillispie in his portrayal of Galileo Galilei who founded physics, the first science worthy of the name. As Gillispie described his genius, Galileo earned recognition as the first true physicist and founder of modern physics because he asked the right questions, proposed answers (hypotheses or theories), and created an appropriate methodology (experimental techniques) with which to test possible answers.[2] In such other physical sciences as chemistry and biology, there are other creative geniuses who laid the foundations of their disciplines.

The foundations of a scientific discipline, or any academic discipline for that matter, must contain several elements. Each discipline requires a commonly accepted definition of the subject and general agreement on the questions that the members of the discipline must attempt to answer. Another component is a generally preferred means or methodology; the principal method of economics is methodological individualism (the rational-actor method), which assumes that rational, self-centered individuals are the basic economic actors. Possible answers, hypotheses, and eventually theories (perhaps laws) satisfy, at least for a time, the questions of interest to the discipline. The questions, methods, and answers evolve, accumulate, and are discarded over time, through open competition among ideas. The win-

---

[2] Charles Coulston Gillispie, *The Edge of Objectivity: An Essay in the History of Scientific Ideas* (Princeton: Princeton University Press, 1960), 7.

ning ideas in this intellectual struggle become part of the ever-evolving consensus of the profession.

The foundations of modern economics were laid by David Ricardo in the early decades of the nineteenth century.[3] Ricardo and his fellow classical economists shared a number of basic assumptions, including the idea that everything of value was created by labor (the labor theory of value) and a belief that the three basic factors of production (land, labor, and capital) could not move across national boundaries. Ricardo and other classical economists were particularly interested in learning (1) what laws govern the distribution of income among the factors of production and (2) the determinants of international trading patterns; that is, the composition of the imports and exports of different countries. Seeking answers to these questions, Ricardo utilized basic mathematical techniques and formal models that continue to be the accepted methodology of professional economics. Ricardo also formulated the law of diminishing returns (or rent) to account for the distribution of national income and the principle or theory of comparative advantage to explain trade patterns. With that principle, he explained why Great Britain exported textiles and imported port from Portugal. While the questions, methods, and theories of the economics profession have changed over the past century and a half, Ricardo's basic approach to the subject has continued to guide his economist successors.

Economics as the Science of Rational Choice

Most contemporary economists would join Paul Samuelson in defining economics as the study of choice under conditions of scarcity.[4] According to this definition, the study of economics originates in the fundamental fact that, in a world where everything is scarce, choices must be made. Economics is the science that guides individuals to make an efficient allocation of scarce resources to alternative and frequently equally desirable goals. In other words, modern economics is basically a science of rational choice or decision-making under conditions of scarcity or constraints. Economics, according to many if not most economists, can provide a comprehensive explanation of human behavior based on market principles.[5]

Every decision, whatever benefits it may bring, involves a cost or

---

[3] David Ricardo, *The Principles of Political Economy and Taxation* (New York: E. P. Dutton, 1911; first published in 1817).

[4] Paul A. Samuelson, *Economics: An Introductory Analysis* (New York: McGraw-Hill, 1967), 5.

[5] Gary S. Becker, *The Economic Approach to Human Behavior* (Chicago: University of Chicago Press, 1976), 5.

what economists call an "opportunity cost." In choosing to do one thing, one must necessarily forgo the opportunity of doing something else that might be of equal or even greater value. As economists frequently quip, "There is no such thing as a free lunch" (TSTFL). Even a free lunch involves an investment of time and, therefore, surrender of an opportunity to do something else. In more stark terms, everything incurs a cost as well as a benefit. The economist's constant awareness that every decision involves a necessary trade-off between costs and benefits casts a conservative mantle over the social and political outlook of the profession and may explain why Thomas Carlyle characterized economics as "the dismal science."

Although some economic theorists such as Adam Smith, Karl Marx, and Joseph Schumpeter have attempted to comprehend the economy as a complete, dynamic, and ever-changing system of human interaction, economics in the early twenty-first century is essentially a toolbox of formal models and analytic techniques. In Keynes's words, "The Theory of Economics does not furnish a body of settled conclusions immediately applicable to policy. It is a method rather than a doctrine, an apparatus of the mind, a technique of thinking, which helps its possessor to draw correct conclusions."[6] While its methodology provides economics with its analytic rigor, it encourages economic theorists to oversimplify economic reality and frequently has no social relevance. In the inevitable trade-off between rigor and relevance, economists will choose the former over the latter almost every time. One of the highest compliments that one economist can give another is to describe his or her work as "robust," regardless of its utility in furthering understanding of the actual working of the economic system.

A formal economic model is an intellectual device used to explain a particular event or variable; such a model is an abstraction based on an economic theory. Although a model may take a literary form, the economics profession, ever since publication of Samuelson's *Foundations*, has preferred that models be expressed in formal, mathematical, and abstract terms. Stated simply, a formal model contains a number of *endogenous* variables whose values (prices or quantities) are determined logically within the model.[7] Explanation of an event

---

[6] Quoted in G. R. Hawke, *Economics for Historians* (New York: Cambridge University Press, 1980), 7–8.

[7] Economists frequently state that a particular action is "endogenous," meaning that the action can be explained by an individual's self-conscious effort to promote his or her economic interests. For example, if a scientific discovery were motivated by a desire for profits rather than being due to intellectual curiosity, one would say that the cause of the discovery was endogenous.

also requires *exogenous* or external variables and one or more behavioral assumptions that connect the exogenous and endogenous variables. The central behavioral assumption is that individual actors are rational and are always seeking to satisfy their own economic interests. The exogenous variable or variables are the "givens," or initial conditions, that determine or influence the value of the endogenous variables. These explanatory or independent variables are external to the model; they could include a change in consumer tastes, innovation of a new technology, and/or other factors.

Economics, then, is essentially a collection of formal models applied to analysis of specific problems and to an explanation of economic phenomena. The fundamental purpose of economic research is to create new models or to extend existing ones.[8] The professional training of the economist centers on the task of learning analytic tools and knowing which model is applicable to a particular circumstance. To paraphrase Paul Krugman, to say that models define the subject of economics means that, if there is no model available to explain a particular phenomenon, that phenomenon is of little interest to the economics profession regardless of its importance for the real world. Krugman has suggested that this explains why little attention has been given to the determinants of economic development, an area for which economists have not yet developed an adequate model.[9]

The utility of a model is situation-specific, and as situations are seldom identical, it can be difficult to know which model is in fact applicable and whether the model can actually predict or explain the outcome of a particular situation. Indeed, economists disagree on the validity of various models and on which model is applicable to a particular situation. As Charles Kindleberger has commented, the answer to every important question in economics is "it depends!" Or, in more formal terms, every economic model is qualified by the caveat of *ceteris paribus* (or, providing that all other things are equal!). Because all economic theories are partial theories and even such basic laws as supply and demand are contingent on specific circumstances,

---

[8] Models play a crucial selective role in determining what economists choose to study. If a theory, for example, cannot be expressed in a formal model that, at least in principle, is subject to testing, then it is very likely not to be of interest to the economics profession. What this means in practice is that many ideas and theories that might, and I emphasize might, explain economic affairs are ignored by economists in favor of ideas that can be tested. This tendency leads to the frequently deserved charge that economics lacks relevance. Economists would no doubt respond that they would prefer to be irrelevant than to be wrong.

[9] Paul R. Krugman, *Development, Geography, and Economic Theory* (Cambridge: MIT Press, 1995).

50

the utility of models is strictly limited. Economists must deal with a large number of variables and must employ simplifying assumptions.

Economics as the Universal Social Science

For many economists, economics is better defined by its methodological approach than by its precise subject matter. As Krugman has noted, the tools define the subject for the economist, and the domain of economics is determined by the range and applicability of its methods. Gary Becker, an influential proponent of this view, sets forth in his book, *The Economic Approach to Human Behavior* (1976), the basic assumptions underlying economics methodology and, thus, the economic approach to the study of social, political, and all other forms of behavior. The assumptions he discusses are:

(1) Economics assumes rational end/means calculations, or "maximizing behavior more extensively and explicitly" than do other social sciences.

(2) Rational or maximizing behavior guides efforts to obtain or maintain "stable preferences." These preferences are not for specific items such as oranges versus apples, but for such basic aspects of life as food, honor, prestige, health, benevolence, and especially wealth. Economics assumes that people everywhere, regardless of their social condition, differ little on these basics. Economics is therefore considered to be a universal science of human behavior, and its methods and assumptions are believed applicable to all times and to all places, whether fifth-century Greece or contemporary industrial Japan.

(3) Markets develop naturally in order to coordinate, with varying degrees of efficiency, the actions of different participants.[10]

The methodology based on these assumptions is known as *methodological individualism* or the *rational-choice model* of human behavior. Economic analysis assumes that individuals (individual consumers, producers, and households) are the only social reality. These individuals are further assumed to be rational optimizers; that is to say, they are individuals who make conscious choices to maximize (or at least satisfy) their interests at the lowest possible cost to themselves.[11] According to this doctrine of "constrained optimization,"

---

[10] Becker, *The Economic Approach to Human Behavior*, 3–14.

[11] In the economic universe composed of supply and demand factors and prices and quantities, individual economic actors are treated as the bearers of these abstract variables or of processes explained by a formal model. For example, a worker is the bearer of a wage demand.

since every individual exists in a world of scarcity and constraints, an economic actor wishes to make the most efficient use of the limited resources available to him or her. This rational-choice model applies only to endeavor and not to outcome. An individual's failure to achieve an end or objective due to ignorance or some other cause does not, at least in the rational-choice model of human behavior, invalidate the premise that individuals act on the basis of a cost/benefit or means/ends calculus.

In the abstract world of the economist, all individual consumers are assumed to be alike; that is, homogeneous. All individual producers are assumed to be alike also. For example, every corporation, regardless of its nationality or ownership, is believed to make its decisions on the basis of prices, market considerations, and other objective factors, and their primary objective is assumed to be increased profits. Even though different cultures and historical settings provide differing constraints and opportunities, individuals everywhere are still believed to be essentially the same. While Americans, Japanese, and Brazilians find themselves in very different circumstances, their basic wants do not differentiate one from the other. The environment determines the constraints and opportunities that shape the means available to individuals to reach their goals. The belief that individuals everywhere are rational optimizers provides the foundation for the neoclassical economist's certainty that economics is a universal science based on the objective laws of the market and is applicable to every economy regardless of its level of development or its culture.

The behavior of individual consumers and producers in the rational pursuit of their objectives is governed by the principle of marginal utility, or marginality. On the demand side of the economy, according to marginal-utility analysis, as consumers consume more and more of a good they experience diminishing utility; that is, while the first ice cream sundae consumed may be devoured with great pleasure, each additional sundae provides less pleasure (decreasing utility) and the demand of the individual for more sundaes decreases. On the supply side of the ledger, in situations when there are no economies of scale, as producers expand production of a given good they begin to encounter diminishing returns and rising costs per unit. These diminishing returns and rising costs mean that, at some point, the producer no longer has an incentive to produce more of the commodity. In effect, a small change in one economic variable results in a small change in another economic variable. A competitive equilibrium in which the actor has no further incentive to consume or to produce is eventually attained through such a process of incremental change. The one possible exception to the principle of marginal utility, at least for most individuals, is the desire for wealth itself, a desire that appears insatiable.

The model of competitive equilibrium is intellectually and morally attractive. A free-market competitive equilibrium becomes efficient when demand equals supply in every market and all the resources of an economy are fully utilized. Such an equilibrium has been reached when no individual or firm can achieve greater welfare by altering the allocation of resources in any way whatsoever without decreasing at least one other person's welfare; this is the concept of the Pareto optimum discussed below in this chapter. In other words, the distribution of income and wealth that emerges in such an equilibrium cannot be altered by economic policies without hurting at least one other person. In effect, economic policy necessarily must either have no effect or must hurt some group of citizens. Therefore, most economists believe that the role of government should be minimal.

An important and far-reaching implication of these fundamental ideas is that economics and its emphasis on individual choice is applicable to all aspects of human behavior. As a universal science of choice, economics has no clear and separate domain of its own but can be used to analyze and understand almost every facet of human behavior. Moreover, the theories of economic science (like those of physics and chemistry) are considered objective, universal, and applicable across all societies and historical periods. The fundamental principles of economic science and its methodology are not limited by boundaries of any kind.

This proposition, that economics is the "one and universal" social science, has been defended by Lionel Robbins in the following words:

It has sometimes been asserted that the generalizations of Economics [the upper-case letter is his] are essentially historico-relative in character, that their validity is limited to certain historical conditions, and that outside these they have no relevance. . . . This view is a dangerous misapprehension. . . . No one will really question the universal applications of such assumptions as the existence of scales of relative valuation, or of different factors of production, or of different degrees of certainty regarding the future. . . . It is only failure to realize this, and a too exclusive preoccupation with the subsidiary assumptions, which can lend any countenance to the view that the laws of Economics are limited to certain conditions of time and space.[12]

[12] Lionel Robbins, quoted in Lloyd G. Reynolds, *The Three Worlds of Economics* (New Haven: Yale University Press, 1971), 19–20.

Despite claims of the universality of economic laws, economists have extreme difficulty identifying such laws, and agreement on the validity of any specific law may be impossible to achieve.[13] For this reason, John Stuart Mill referred to economics as an inexact science and characterized its laws as *tendency* laws; that is, as generalizations regarding what will happen if no disturbing event should intervene.[14] Obviously, differing national policies and social systems can become intervening variables.

NATURE OF A MARKET

The concept of the market as a self-regulating and self-correcting "smoothly functioning machine" governed by objective laws and universal principles is at the heart of economics. Moreover, this concept leads to the conclusion that the free-market system, under certain circumstances and assumptions such as complete information and non-oligopolistic competition, leads to an optimal allocation of given resources. Economists work to define the laws governing markets of all kinds, and their principles and generalizations are the best available guide to explain how markets work and, to a lesser extent, why they sometimes do not work. Although all of us have observed and participated in markets where goods, services, and money are exchanged, "the market" conceived by economists is an abstraction or intellectual construct. While some markets may have a physical location like a stock market or an auction, many markets do not have a physical existence that one can experience directly. Indeed, the market economy as conceived by economic theory consists only of interdependent equations that are solved continuously and simultaneously.

Economists believe that a market arises spontaneously to satisfy needs. Human beings are by nature economic animals who, according to Adam Smith, have an inherent propensity to "truck, barter and exchange." To facilitate exchange and improve their well-being, people create markets, money, and economic institutions. However, once a market exists, it is believed to function in accordance with its own internal logic and without central direction. Coordination among the

---

[13] Obvious candidates are the laws of supply and demand and the law of diminishing returns. However, even if they do qualify as laws, the claim that they are laws of economics rather than physics or psychology is in dispute.

[14] This discussion is based on Roger E. Backhouse, *Economists and the Economy: The Evolution of Economic Ideas.* 2d ed. (New Brunswick, N.J.: Transaction Publishers, 1994), 225.

activities of individuals participating in a market is spontaneous and is guided by the "invisible hand" of self-interest.

The rational and homogeneous individuals of economic science live in an economic universe composed solely of prices (p) and quantities (q) that possess no ethnic, national, or other identity. Changes in prices and quantities constitute the signals to which individuals respond in their efforts to maximize their goals or, as economists prefer, their utilities. Individual consumers and producers make decisions based on changes in relative prices, market opportunities, and external constraints. Prices, at least over the long term, are determined by such objective economic laws as the law of diminishing returns and the law of supply and demand. The law of demand is the most important of the laws that drive or govern the economy. This "law" holds that people will buy more of a good if the relative price falls and less if the relative price rises; people will also tend to buy more of a good as their relative income rises and less as it falls. Any development that changes the relative price of a good or the relative income of an actor will create an incentive or disincentive for an individual to acquire (or produce) more or less of the good. This simple yet powerful law of demand is fundamental to the functioning of the market system.

One of the most important concepts employed by economists to understand market functioning is static equilibrium (or simply equilibrium). An equilibrium exists when there is no tendency for the balance between such interrelated variables as prices and quantities to change.[15] In less technical language, an equilibrium means that no economic actor has an incentive to change his or her behavior and the costs and benefits of the existing situation are judged to have achieved the best balance that an individual could reasonably expect. Therefore, the potential gains from changing the situation are not worth the potential costs, so no change takes place.

The concept of equilibrium is central to explanations of both economic stability and economic change. Neoclassical economics assumes that markets, at least over the long term, tend toward an equilibrium in which supply matches demand. When a disequilibrium exists, powerful forces will bring the system back into equilibrium. Economists use the term "disequilibrium" to mean any change in demand, opportunities, or relative prices that gives an economic actor an incentive to change his or her behavior in order to increase his or her gains or decrease his or her costs. For example, an increase in the

---

[15] Fritz Machlup, quoted in Yanis Varoufakis and David Young, eds., *Conflict in Economics* (New York: Harvester Wheatsheaf Press, 1990), 14.

supply, and hence a decline in the price of a good, will give some actors an incentive to increase their consumption of the good (subject, of course, to the principle of diminishing returns). Over time, the imbalance between the increased supply and the increased demand for the good will be overcome, and the market will be restored to an equilibrium condition in which no actor has an incentive to change her or his behavior. Thus, a market equilibrium is defined by economists as a system of prices and quantities in which there is a balance between opposing forces.

The concept of equilibrium is a powerful analytic tool. Yet, this concept can also be quite misleading. Economists generally use the term as if they really could determine at any particular moment whether or not an equilibrium actually exists in a particular market. However, as Fritz Machlup emphasized, the concept of equilibrium is an abstract concept and cannot tell us whether in reality equilibrium actually exists.[16] Moreover, rather than being a neutral term, the concept may be loaded with policy and political biases. The equilibrium concept is central to economists' study of the market, but there are problems in using equilibrium as an explanatory or predictive tool.

Markets are highly dynamic and are continually revolutionizing societies. Certain characteristics of a market economy explain its dynamic nature: (1) changes in relative prices in the exchange of goods and services, (2) competition as a determinant of individual and institutional behavior, and (3) the effect of efficiency in determining the survivability of economic actors. The market's profound consequences for economic, social, and political life flow from these characteristics. The pressures of market competition and the imperative to achieve ever greater efficiency lead to the continuous innovation of new technologies, organizational forms, and productive techniques, and to discarding of the old in what Joseph Schumpeter called a "process of creative destruction." At both the domestic and international levels, a market system creates a hierarchical division of labor and distribution of wealth among producers, a division based principally on specialization and the law of comparative advantage. Market forces lead to the reordering of society (domestic or international) into a dynamic core and a dependent periphery. The core is characterized principally by its more advanced levels of technology and economic development; the periphery is, at least initially, dependent on the core as a market for its exports and as a source of productive

---

[16] Fritz Machlup, *Economic Semantics*, 2d ed. (New Brunswick, N.J.: Transaction Publishers, 1991), 43–72.

techniques. In the short term, as the core of a market economy grows, it incorporates into its orbit a larger and larger periphery; in the long term, however, due to the growth process and diffusion of productive technology, new cores tend to form in the periphery and then to become growth centers in their own right. Examples of these tendencies for the core to expand and to stimulate the rise of new competitive cores and the profound consequences for economic and political affairs produced by such developments will appear throughout this book.

Method of Comparative Statics

The concept of equilibrium constitutes the foundation of the method of comparative statics, one of the most important analytic techniques in the economist's toolbox.[17] It is a method of analyzing the impact of a change in a model by comparing the equilibrium resulting from the change with the original equilibrium. In their analysis of economic change, economists rely on this presumed tendency of a market to return to an equilibrium. The method of comparative statics is as old as economics itself and was used by David Hume (1711–1776) in his theory of the price-specie flow mechanism—his analysis of the domestic and international effects of a change in a nation's balance of payments. The method, however, was not formalized until the 1930s and the 1940s in the work of John Hicks (1939) and in Paul Samuelson's classic *Foundations of Economic Analysis* (1947).[18] Consideration of this method of comparative statics enables one to appreciate both the strengths and the limitations of the economic analysis of economic change.

In an equilibrium condition, as already noted, no participants in a market have an incentive to change their behavior. This situation is assumed to continue until an exogenous factor is introduced. A change in relative price, a technological innovation, or a shift in consumer tastes provides an incentive for economic actors to alter their behavior; an exogenous change may also involve imposition of new constraints on economic actors or appearance of new economic opportunities. In response, say, to a change in relative prices, a rational economic actor will have an incentive to maximize gains or minimize losses. Or, a new technology that reduces the cost of producing a

---

[17] For a technical discussion of the method, consult Paul A. Samuelson, *Foundations of Economic Analysis* (Cambridge: Harvard University Press, 1983), 7–8.

[18] Ibid.

particular good might be adopted by an entrepreneur to cut costs, expand market share, and/or increase income. Then, competitors would either have to adjust to this development or else be forced out of business; in either case, the exogenous change has powerful ramifications throughout the economy as actors adjust to its consequences. When equilibrium is restored, there is no longer any incentive for actors to change their behavior until another exogenous change enters the market.

Exogenous developments that cause disequilibrium and give individuals an incentive to change their behavior are frequently quite minor and may require little more than a small adjustment by the economic actors. This means that the evolution of an economy is a generally continuous and relatively smooth process consisting of an equilibrium, a destabilizing disequilibrium, and eventual creation of a new equilibrium. Economists agree with Gottfried Leibnitz (1646–1716) that nature does not take jumps and that change tends to be incremental.[19] However, upon occasion, exogenous developments can be revolutionary and can cause a profound shock to the economy; then the resultant adjustment or transition to a new equilibrium can have significant implications for both economic and political affairs. The sudden large increase in petroleum prices in 1973 exemplified dramatically how a change in relative prices could have a disproportionately huge impact on international economic and political affairs when the increase in world energy prices plunged the world economy into a decade of economic "stagflation." Throughout the 1970s and beyond, the economies of the world struggled to adjust to this dramatic increase in energy prices.

According to neoclassical economics, the outcome of a disequilibrium is totally dependent upon the interplay of economic forces and the interaction of many individual decisions responding to changes or anticipated changes in relative prices. The focus of analysis is on the disequilibrium itself and on the economic forces it generates. The history of the events leading up to the disequilibrium or initial conditions is not relevant for the outcome or to restoration of an equilibrium. As Paul Samuelson has argued, whatever initial conditions may be, eventually prices and quantities converge to a new equilibrium

---

[19] For example, an economist wrote that the stock market crash of October 1987 could not have been caused by such a small event as the American-German clash over interest rates. Causes and effects, he argued, must equal one another. Chaos theory, on the other hand, teaches us that small events can have disproportionately large consequences.

without regard to initial conditions.[20] In other words, history is generally irrelevant to an *economic* explanation of an event. All one needs to know is the vectors and the strength of the forces at work. The attitude of economists toward dynamics is not unlike that of physicists; a physicist does not need to know the history of a baseball game nor have a detailed knowledge of the batter to calculate the trajectory of a batted ball. Nevertheless, introduction of the idea of path dependence into economic analysis has helped moderate antihistorical thinking in economics.

Although the method of comparative statics is a powerful tool of analysis, its usefulness as a means of understanding economic change in the real world is severely limited. The method cannot provide an analysis of the historical forces responsible for the original equilibrium position nor of the transitional process involved in the move from one equilibrium position to another. In effect, economics cannot account for the causes of the disequilibrium because the exogenous variables that produced the equilibrium lie outside the realm of economic analysis. Moreover, economics cannot predict, nor is it concerned with, the course of historical events that lead to the new equilibrium; yet, as the path dependence concept informs us, the many important developments on the way to the new equilibrium will have a determining effect on the nature of the new equilibrium and hence on the overall condition of the economic system. Finally, even though an economic system eventually finds a new equilibrium, the system never returns to the old equilibrium. In brief, the world has been transformed, but economics is of no more than limited utility in explaining the outcome and how it was achieved.

At the time of the 1973 oil crisis, some economists argued that the price rise was caused solely by market forces. The high inflation of the late 1960s and early 1970s, they asserted, had caused a wide gap, or disequilibrium, between the nominal price and the real price of petroleum. According to this interpretation, the oil price change was merely a rapid movement toward the new equilibrium between the price and the supply of petroleum. While this comparative statics analysis does indeed tell part of the story, it omits the crucial role played by the Yom Kippur War between Israel and its Arab neighbors and the impact of the oil price rise on world affairs. It is actually highly doubtful that the huge rise in the price of oil would have taken

---

[20] Paul Samuelson, quoted in Rod Cross, ed., *Unemployment, Hysteresis and the Natural Rate Hypothesis* (Oxford: Basil Blackwell, 1988), 3.

place, at least at that time, if the Arab-Israeli war had not occurred. In addition, the ways in which different countries adjusted to the oil shock and returned to equilibrium had profound consequences for the world economy. Whereas the United States responded to the deflationary effects of the oil price rise with efforts to stimulate its economy, West Europeans were more concerned about the inflationary effects and restrained their economies. Important policy conflicts resulted from these differing responses, and the conflicting paths chosen by the United States and other major economies contributed to instabilities in the world economy throughout the 1970s.

Economic analysis is a necessary ingredient in any effort to understand the dynamics of the world economy; indeed, the comparative statics analysis of the oil price rise is very useful. However, economics provides only a partial explanation of the event and leaves out such essential parts of the story as the war that triggered it, the different paths taken toward new equilibria, and the overall consequences for the international economic and political system. While it would be too much to expect the method of comparative statics to take account of these matters, the point is that economic analysis alone does not substitute for historical, political, and sociological analysis.

INTELLECTUAL LIMITATIONS

As many economists themselves acknowledge, economics has a number of intellectual limitations that weaken both its claims to be an exact science and its usefulness as an analytic tool. Perhaps most important of all, certain assumptions underlying economics are unrealistic. For example, the central assumption of individual rationality has frequently been demonstrated to be inaccurate.[21] Nor is the assumption that an economic actor has *complete* information always correct. And markets are frequently not the perfect competitive markets they are assumed to be by conventional economic analysis. Even though they have given considerable attention to these issues and have dealt with them in various ways, economists still assume that such problems are exceptions rather than inherent limitations. Economists have given increased attention to the problem of uncertainty; yet there has been a tendency to ignore the problem of uncertainty and/or to wish

---

[21] An attack on the assumption of rationality is found in the research of Daniel Kahneman. Consult his "New Challenges to the Rationality Assumption," *Journal of Institutional and Theoretical Economics* 150, no. 1 (1994): 18–35.

it away. Economists do, however, utilize various techniques to sidestep difficulties raised for economic analysis by the unrealistic assumptions of their discipline.

Economists' treatment of uncertainty and technological change provides a valuable illustration of unrealistic assumptions. Although the profession recognizes technological advance as the most important determinant of long-term economic growth and hence the most important factor propelling economic change in the modern world, it also acknowledges that technological innovation is uncertain and unpredictable by its very nature. Nevertheless, Gene M. Grossman and Elhanan Helpman in their pioneering *Innovation and Growth in the Global Economy* (1991) explicitly base their analysis of technological advance and its consequences on the unrealistic assumption of *certain* and *complete* information about the nature and consequences of technological innovation.[22] The very nature of technological developments, on the other hand, is that they and their effects are highly unpredictable.

From my perspective, one of the most important intellectual limitations of economics is its neglect of the role of the state in economic affairs and especially in international economic developments. The discipline focuses on the behavior and interactions of autonomous individuals and enterprises responding to impersonal market signals. It is obvious, of course, that economists are well aware that national policies and activities can be relevant for economic outcomes. However, political considerations tend to be either ignored or conveniently forgotten.[23] Economists formulate laws of economic behavior on the assumption that markets count and states do not.

Although many economists acknowledge the unrealistic assumptions underlying economic science and do their best to transcend them, many and perhaps even most would agree with Milton Friedman's methodological prescription that it is of no significance whether or not the assumptions underlying economics are realistic.[24] What is important, according to Friedman, is whether those assumptions lead to fruitful propositions that can be tested empirically and thereby shown to be valid or invalid. In other words, do the assump-

[22] Gene M. Grossman and Elhanan Helpman, *Innovation and Growth in the Global Economy* (Cambridge: MIT Press,1991).

[23] Benjamin J. Cohen, *Organizing the World's Money: The Political Economy of International Monetary Relations* (New York: Basic Books, 1977), 41.

[24] Milton Friedman, "The Methodology of Positive Economics," in his *The Methodology of Positive Economics* (Chicago: University of Chicago Press, 1953), 3–43.

tions of rational individuals, perfect markets, and complete information enable economists to make accurate predictions about economic behavior?

In principle, of course, Friedman is quite correct that what is important is the empirical testing of a theory. However, his attack on those who call for realistic assumptions would be more convincing if economists' predictions and forecasts were indeed as accurate as he apparently assumes. Also, if economists really did choose among theories solely on the basis of empirical evidence, Friedman's argument would be strengthened. However, as Donald McCloskey has noted, few theories are tested empirically and economists choose theories for a number of ideological, philosophical, and, in his language, "rhetorical" reasons. More devastating is the fact that few theories or hypotheses meet the Popperian test of falsifiability. In other words, they cannot be tested empirically to determine their validity. Moreover, economics, like the other social sciences, is frequently hampered by absence of a counterfactual against which a theory may be tested.[25]

In addition, economists frequently redefine the terms of a theory to make it consistent with empirical evidence. A notable example relevant to this book was the discovery by Wassily Leontief that the United States had a comparative advantage in agriculture, which, at the time of his research, was considered to be a labor-intensive activity.[26] Prior to Leontief's research, conventional trade theory had predicted that the United States should have a comparative advantage in capital-intensive goods. To resolve what became known as the "Leontief Paradox," economists introduced the concept of "human capital." According to this reformulation of the meaning of capital, the comparative advantage of the United States in agriculture was explained by the fact that it had invested heavily in agricultural skills, knowledge, and equipment. Broadening the concept of capital to include human capital greatly weakened the predictive power of conventional trade theory based on the idea of factor endowments.

This modification of the definition of capital and, by implication, of conventional trade theory, raises the important epistemological

[25] Donald N. McCloskey, *The Rhetoric of Economics* (Madison: University of Wisconsin, 1985). On the failure to meet the test of verifiability, consult Mark Blaug, "Disturbing Currents in Modern Economics," *Challenge* 41, no. 3 (May/June 1998): 11–34; interview with Mark Blaug, "The Problem with Formalism," *Challenge* 41, no. 3 (May/June 1998): 35–45.

[26] W.W. Leontief, "Domestic Production and Foreign Trade: The American Capital Position Re-examined", *Proceedings of the American Philosophical Society* 97 (September 1953), 332–49. Reprinted in *Readings in International Trade*, ed. H. G. Johnson and R. E. Caves (Homewood, Ill.: R. D. Irwin, 1968).

question of whether or not the idea of human capital is a logical extension of the conventional theory of international trade based on factor endowments or whether it actually is an ad hoc hypothesis intended to rescue a theory that is crumbling in the face of contrary evidence. As Thomas Kuhn demonstrated in *The Structure of Scientific Revolutions* (1962), scholars and scientists are frequently strongly tempted to resort to ad hoc hypotheses to defend a long-accepted "truth" that has become subject to serious attack.[27] In fact, use of ad hoc hypotheses and of ex post facto redefinitions of important terms in a theory makes it difficult to prove a theory or hypothesis wrong. Proponents of a theory whose validity is threatened by contrary evidence sometimes merely change the terms of the theory to make it conform to the empirical evidence. Modification of the meaning of capital in the above example suggests that economists do change their assumptions in order to make their predictions work. At the least, the inclusion of human capital significantly enlarged and modified the content of conventional trade theory.

The predictions of economists are in fact notoriously poor. As some quip, "Economists have successfully predicted seven of the last five recessions." Moreover, a significant portion of the accepted body of economic theory has never been adequately tested. For students of political economy, the ceteris paribus (other things being equal) caveat offered by economists is exceptionally significant because political factors and social institutions do affect the outcome of economic activities and are rarely equal in their consequences. For this reason alone, the problem of the validity of the assumptions on which economics is based cannot be as easily dismissed as Friedman and other economists would like.

Economists' efforts to employ econometrics, the principal mathematical technique/s to test theories against facts, have produced only moderate success in resolving theoretical controversies. While econometrics has had many successes, it has failed to transform economics into the formal and mathematical science foreseen by Samuelson. Successful application of econometrics has been limited by the lack of good data and the sheer complexity of the economy. In the harsh judgment of *The Economist*, econometric studies have not settled a single major theoretical dispute.[28] Moreover, many if not most economic theories are never submitted to empirical testing. In the ab-

---

[27] Thomas S. Kuhn, *The Structure of Scientific Revolutions* (Chicago: University of Chicago Press, 1962).

[28] *The Economist*, 9 May 1987, 68–69.

sence of empirical testing of their theories, strong differences flourish. Rather than a theoretical consensus on macroeconomics, one encounters Keynesians, New Keynesians, Post-Keynesians, Classicists, New Classicists, monetarists, proponents of rational expectations, and other fractious schools of economists, all using formal mathematical techniques and coming to quite different conclusions, largely because they start with differing assumptions.

Another problem limiting the usefulness of economics as an analytic tool is found in large and important subfields of economics that have never been tested or are in fact nonempirical and therefore not really testable. One such subject is the field of industrial organization. The theory of industrial organization has made major theoretical strides, especially through application of the model of noncooperative games from game theory, a development that has made industrial organization one of the most theoretically developed subfields of economics. Even so, the field of industrial organization is confronted by the serious methodological problem that, although many alternative models of corporate behavior applicable to specific industries have been developed, there is still no general model or overarching theory of industrial organization. In fact, as Joseph Stiglitz has observed, economists do not even agree on the fundamental model for analyzing or describing the economy.[29] As Daniel Bell and Irving Kristol have pointed out, most economic controversies involve differences over the nature of economic reality.[30] And prospects for a science of economics are indeed limited without agreement on the nature of the economy itself; that is, which economic model/s should be applied to describe the market. This leads to a situation where political and ideological biases play a larger role in the acceptance of theories than economists generally admit.[31]

Economists' assumption that economics is a universal science applicable to all times and places can lead to analytic distortions and faulty policy prescriptions. Their inability or unwillingness to recognize the significance of differences among states and societies and/or the influence of cultural and historical settings limits the usefulness of economics. The imposed policy prescriptions of the International Monetary Fund (IMF) following the East Asian financial crisis provide an

[29] Joseph E. Stiglitz, "Another Century of Economic Science," *Economic Journal* 101, no. 404 (January 1991): 134–39.

[30] Daniel Bell and Irving Kristol, eds., *The Crisis in Economic Theory* (New York: Basic Books, 1981), viii.

[31] John Tiemstra, "Why Economists Disagree," *Challenge* 41, no. 3 (May/June 1998): 46–62.

unfortunate example of economists' failures to comprehend local social and political conditions. An understanding of the international political economy must be based on appreciation of state policies, social norms and institutions, and historical legacies, and also of the ways in which economic outcomes are shaped by such external factors.

Although neoclassical economists claim that economics is an objective science like physics, economics is actually built upon a number of normative assumptions or value judgments accepted by most economists. These normative assumptions influence the choice of subjects that economists study and the answers they will accept. Economics offers many conflicting explanations of the causes of trade flows and the determinants of exchange rates; indeed, value preferences frequently play a significant role in determining which model a particular economist accepts or rejects. In this way, normative assumptions sometimes influence economists' policy prescriptions. Although one may share some of their assumptions, as I do, including the desirability of free trade and of open economies, these assumptions can have a distorting effect on analysis and resulting policy recommendations.

Modern economics, based on the philosophy of political liberalism, assumes that the individual rather than groups or classes is the basic unit of society,[32] and that there is a harmony of interests among individuals, at least over the long term, with this harmony accounting for social and political stability. The underlying harmony in a market system is the result of what Adam Smith called "the invisible hand," which means that the actions of each individual, as he or she pursues selfish interests, lead automatically to betterment of the human race. Belief in the harmony of interests among individuals also constitutes the basis of the liberal belief in moral and social progress. Liberals argue that, despite frequent setbacks, history is moving toward achievement of the greatest good for the greatest number.

Liberalism incorporates a normative commitment to individual rights, the free market, and political democracy. Or, to put the point differently, liberal thought tends to believe that all good things go together. As Charles E. Lindblom has pointed out, political democracy and economic liberalism have tended generally to accompany one another in the modern world.[33] Tension does exist, however, between liberalism's commitment to equality (equity) and its commit-

---

[32] The idea that society is composed of conflict groups, of which the state is the principal example, was set forth by Ralf Dahrendorf, *Class and Class Conflict in Industrial Society* (Stanford: Stanford University Press, 1959).

[33] Charles E. Lindblom, *Politics and Markets: The World's Political Economic Systems* (New York: Basic Books, 1977).

ment to freedom (liberty). The split between those liberals who give priority to one or the other of these fundamental values underlies dissension in modern democracies over the role of the state in the economy. Americans apply the term "liberals" to those partisans who give precedence to equality and therefore urge government intervention in the economy to promote equality. Conservatives, on the other hand, give precedence to liberty and, at least in principle, oppose government intervention in the economy. From this perspective, both Franklin D. Roosevelt, with his New Deal policies of state intervention in the economy to promote economic equality, and Ronald Reagan, whose economic policies (Reaganomics) began to roll back the New Deal in the interest of economic freedom, were "liberals." They simply placed a differing degree of emphasis on equality versus liberty.

An important normative assumption held by mainstream economists is that the purpose of economic activity is to increase the welfare of the individual consumer and to maximize global wealth. The harmony-of-interest doctrine assumes that if the market is left alone and "prices are right," resources will be employed efficiently, and over the long term everyone's welfare will improve. Such beliefs lead to the conclusion that the state should not intervene in the economy. Politicians, economists believe, invariably get prices wrong and thereby distort the efficient functioning of the market.

Defining economics as a science of efficient resource allocation, economists tend to have a strong bias in favor of efficiency over equity. That is, economists generally prefer the efficient allocation of economic resources to maximize production of wealth rather than distribution of wealth according to some subjective standard of what is fair. This emphasis on the driving force of efficiency encourages economists to believe that, despite frequent setbacks caused by such developments as war, trade conflicts, and other disruptions, the world is moving inexorably in the direction of free trade and a global market economy. The movement toward integration of national economies and increasing global economic interdependence has developed because markets are more efficient than other forms of economic organization.[34] The collapse of the Soviet-type command economy strongly reinforced this conviction.

Most neoclassical economists accept implicitly the existing distribution of wealth and property rights. Yet economists have, of course,

---

[34] This argument is set forth in John R. Hicks, *A Theory of Economic History* (London: Oxford University Press, 1969).

addressed the equity-efficiency trade-off and have also carried out research on the most efficient distribution of wealth and property rights to achieve the social conditions most conducive to rapid economic growth. Many economists have strong personal concerns about wealth inequities; even an economic conservative like Milton Friedman has proposed a negative income tax as a solution to growing inequalities in American society. Nevertheless, concern over the distribution of income lies outside the primary focus of the discipline. Instead, economists generally accept and seldom challenge the legitimacy of the status quo distribution of wealth and property rights in society, an attitude that sometimes leads to indifference to social issues. An admittedly unscientific survey of Princeton University economists regarding the economic priorities of the first Clinton Administration revealed such a conservative social bias. All but one of the half-dozen economists interviewed proclaimed that the newly elected President's first priority should be to leave the economy—then in a recession—alone. The one exception was the economist-president of Princeton, Harold Shapiro, who stressed the importance of maintaining healthy social welfare programs![35]

At the international level, economists generally assume what Charles Kindleberger calls a "cosmopolitan" rather than a nationalist stance.[36] With few exceptions, economists believe in free trade and oppose protectionist practices; they strongly believe that open and unrestricted markets are the best way to increase consumer choice and maximize efficient use of the planet's scarce resources. At the same time, however, economists qua economists place a low priority on the distribution of wealth within and among national economies. They eschew the controversial issue of "distributive justice" because it involves a value judgment and thus lies outside the realm of economic science. Many critics regard mainstream economics as politically conservative and therefore tolerant of the evils of the domestic and international status quo. Indeed, the beliefs that resources are scarce and must be used efficiently, and that hard choices must be made among alternative uses, reinforce the conservative bias pervading the discipline.

Economists in general believe that trade and economic intercourse promote peaceful relations among nations because the mutual benefits of trade and expanding interdependence foster cooperative rela-

---

[35] *Princeton Alumni Weekly,* 10 March 1993, 56.
[36] Charles P. Kindleberger, *Power and Money: The Economics of International Politics and the Politics of International Economics* (New York: Basic Books, 1970).

tions. Whereas politics tends to divide, economics is believed to unite peoples. A liberal world economy based on openness and free trade should have a moderating influence on international politics because it creates bonds of mutual interest and a commitment to the status quo. However, it is important to emphasize again that although everyone will, or at least could, benefit in absolute terms under a system of free exchange, individual relative gains will differ depending on the marginal contribution to the social product made by those individuals. This issue of relative gains and the uneven distribution of the wealth generated by the market system has given rise to Marxist and nationalist criticisms of economic liberalism.

Neoclassical economists believe that markets should be left alone by politicians. Except in rare cases of market failure, the government should neither intervene in the economy nor try to influence market outcomes. Economists use the term "market failure" to describe a situation in which markets fail to produce either economically optimal or socially desirable outcomes, and they define four principal types of market failure. One type occurs when there are externalities or "spillovers" of economic activities so that one actor's economic activities harm those of another (as in environmental pollution). Increasing returns and declining marginal costs that lead to a monopoly constitute another type of market failure. Still another is found in such market imperfections as market rigidities and consumer lack of information. And a more controversial type is distributional inequalities. While most economists acknowledge market failures, they are far from agreement on ways to resolve such failures. There is a particularly clear difference of opinion about income inequalities.

Although there is intense controversy within the economics profession concerning market failure and what, if anything, should be done about it, most economists would agree that the problem of government failure—policies that distort the market and cause gross inefficiencies—constitutes a more serious problem. This laissez-faire attitude holds that if the market were left alone, it would get prices (of wages, profits, and rents) right, incentives and disincentives would encourage individuals to make their maximum contribution to the economy, and the economy would produce optimum outcomes for society. On the other hand, economists believe that government intervention in the economy invariably gets prices wrong, distorts incentives, and produces economic outcomes that are suboptimal for the society as a whole.

Finally, commitment to Pareto optimality provides a guiding normative principle for economics.[37] As a moral principle for individuals, this idea cannot be faulted. However, its relevance for the real world of political affairs is not only dubious, but the principle is highly questionable in political terms because it assumes that absolute gains are important but related losses are insignificant.[38] State-centric analysts, on the other hand, stress the importance of relative gains or losses as much or more than absolute gains.

This difference in emphasis can be crucial to evaluation of a particular development. For example, viewed by the criterion of Pareto optimality, an absolute gain to one state is justifiable. However, a state-centric assessment could be very different. A case in point would be an absolute gain in the wealth and hence in the power of an aggressive state such as Nazi Germany in the 1930s. Such a development would have been morally justifiable according to the Pareto criterion. However, in political terms, a wealthier Nazi Germany could shift the international distribution of power in favor of that potentially aggressive state and thus the likelihood of war could increase. Economists' emphasis on absolute gains and state-centric analysts' emphasis on relative gains in a world of competitive states arise from their very different assumptions.

ECONOMISTS AND PUBLIC POLICY

The prominent role of professional economists in American public life has been an important feature of American society since the end of World War II. In 1946 the Full Employment Act assigned the important task of ensuring full employment to the federal government; the Council of Economic Advisors, whose members have included some of America's most distinguished economists, was created by that Act to assist the President and the federal government to carry out this responsibility. Gradual acceptance within the economics profession of the Keynesian doctrine of demand management provided the Council with the rationale and tools for macromanagement of the American economy.

Celebrating the elevated status of the economist in American public affairs, Walter Heller, chairman at that time of President Lyndon

[37] This term is named after Vilfredo Pareto (1848–1923), an Italian economist and sociologist.
[38] A Pareto-optimum equilibrium is one in which at least one individual's welfare would be improved and no other individual's welfare would be lessened.

Johnson's Council of Economic Advisors, proclaimed in his 1965 Godkin Lectures at Harvard University the arrival of "the age of the economist."[39] The theoretical triumph of Keynesian economics, Heller told his audience, meant that economists now knew how to "fine tune" the economy in order to avoid the twin perils of recession and inflation; at long last, the destructive business cycle had been conquered. Moreover, he added, the American political elite had accepted Keynesian macroeconomics. (Even President Richard Nixon agreed a few years later that "we are all Keynesians now!"). Heller pointed out that, as a consequence, economists now sat at the right hand of the President and advised the President on how to guide the economy to ever-increasing prosperity. A few years later, Harry Johnson, an economist of a much more conservative inclination, proclaimed that the ability of economists to quantify and predict constituted their claim to superiority over most intelligent individuals with an interest in economic problems.[40]

These statements by Heller and Johnson reflected economists' confidence in the efficacy of their methods and theories in the early decades after World War II. Unfortunately, economists frequently have been overly confident in their methods; believing that if something cannot be measured, quantified, or tested by the methods of economics, it either does not exist or at least is irrelevant, economists have often excluded other analytic approaches. The economics profession often ignores crucial aspects of social reality that cannot be modeled or made consistent with neoclassical assumptions. Kenneth Arrow, one of the truly great minds of modern economics, has suggested a plausible explanation for this excessive self-confidence. Economists, Arrow points out, see themselves as privileged purveyors of rationality; certainly the intellectual confusion and imprecise thinking encountered in public debate on economic issues lends credence to such a self-perception. Yet, as Arrow continues, "Unfortunately, there is a close connection between rationality and intolerance: If you know a thing *a priori*, the way you know a column of figures is right when it is correctly calculated, there is no room for argument and anyone who disagrees must be either stupid or dishonest."[41]

---

[39] Walter W. Heller, *New Dimensions of Political Economy* (Cambridge: Harvard University Press, 1966).

[40] Harry G. Johnson, *On Economics and Society* (Chicago: University of Chicago Press, 1975).

[41] Kenneth Arrow, quoted in E. L. Jones, "Economics in the History Mirror," Economic Discussion Papers No. 6/88, School of Business, La Trobe University, Bundoora, Victoria, Australia, 7–8.

The predilection among economists to ignore those social and political aspects of public affairs that cannot be modeled means that economists generally analyze public problems or make policy pronouncements as if the fundamental issues at stake were solely, or at least primarily, economic. Of course, experts in many other fields have similar predilections. The knowledge (expertise) of experts is frequently more limited than they are willing to admit to themselves or to anyone else. In this way economists and other experts exhibit a "trained-incapacity."[42] Robert Keohane, in his incisive critique of the McCracken Report, has demonstrated superbly the tendency of economists to disregard the opinions of experts in other fields, to be totally unaware of the political/ideological biases inherent in their own policy recommendations, and to go beyond their competence when advising governments.[43]

During the early decades following World War II, the world economy experienced rapid economic growth and relatively low rates of inflation. In the early 1970s, this happy situation suddenly turned sour. During the previous decade, particularly after escalation of the Vietnam War, the rate of inflation had accelerated, and this began to dampen the rate of growth. Other developments, including a slowdown in the rate of growth in productivity in the United States and in Europe, had contributed to growing problems in the world economy. In 1973 the crisis caused by a sudden large increase in the price of oil changed matters dramatically and plunged the world economy into stagflation (an unprecedented combination of low economic growth, rising unemployment, and severe inflation). Much to their embarrassment, economists had to admit that at this time they knew neither how to "fine-tune" the economy nor how to avoid the scourge of the business cycle. Trying to find out what had gone wrong, the Organization of Economic Cooperation and Development (OECD) in Paris appointed a commission of eight eminent economists from advanced capitalist economies, led by chairman Paul McCracken, to study the situation. The commission was asked to prepare a report on the "main policy issues involved in the pursuit by member countries, of non-inflationary economic growth and high employment levels in the light of the structural changes which have taken place in the recent past." After eighteen months of work, the OECD Secretariat

---

[42] This thesis is elaborated in my book, *American Scientists and Nuclear Weapons Policy* (Princeton: Princeton University Press, 1962).

[43] Robert O. Keohane, "Economics, Inflation, and the Role of the State: Political Implications of the McCracken Report," *World Politics* 31, no. 1 (October 1978): 108–28.

published the commission's report, entitled *Towards Full Employment and Price Stability* (1977).

The thesis of the report was that the economic troubles of the 1970s had been caused primarily by certain policy errors of OECD member governments, errors that included overexpansionary economic policies and failure to respond properly to the inflationary consequences of the breakdown of the system of fixed exchange rates. Although presented as economic truth, the report's analysis was actually based on a politically conservative, market-oriented ideology. As Keohane writes, "Pervading the report is the view that contemporary democratic governments are unwilling to exercise sufficient domestic discipline, particularly monetary discipline."[44] Governments, the report suggests, had been too lax and had given in to the temptation of easy monetary policies in order to win favor with their electorates. The solution offered by the report was reimposition of economic discipline and limitation of the public's economic aspirations. The report's idea that a "disciplinary" (rather than a welfare) state was needed to make capitalism work was adopted by economic conservatives and put into practice by President Ronald Reagan and Prime Minister Margaret Thatcher in the 1980s.

Although the McCracken Report concluded that the causes of the economic disarray of the 1970s were located in the realms of social and political affairs, none of the economists on the committee were experts in those areas. As Keohane pointed out, the fundamental issue confronting the McCracken committee was the conflict, or at least the apparent conflict, between the necessary conditions for modern economic growth and the nature of both modern democracy and the welfare state. Yet the economist-authors of the report, Keohane suggests, appear to have been totally unaware that they were dealing with a classic conflict between capitalism and democracy. Nor did they make any attempt to judge the political feasibility of their recommendations for resolving this fundamental clash. In Keohane's words, "A more profound understanding of macroeconomic events will only be achieved by combining the economic argument with the analysis of conflicts of interests, and the exercise of power, as they take place within different national societies and the international political economy."[45]

Economists' neglect of the social and political dimensions of public affairs and public policy originates in their tendency to treat economic

[44] Ibid., 111–12.
[45] Ibid., 116.

issues as if they were solely or at least primarily technical problems. Because economists believe that reality consists of only those matters that they can model and quantify, even when they are aware of the role of social factors or political forces that shape economic and public affairs, they deem such matters to be outside the scope of economics and therefore irrelevant because they cannot be measured or modeled. Therefore, economists deliberately ignore or downgrade such factors in their analyses and policy recommendations. Whereas economists believe that economics is scientific, they frequently regard social and political affairs as matters of personal taste and private opinion.

Nonetheless, as Paul Krugman's popular writings have indicated, economists' confidence in their ability to guide the economy and to advance the commonweal had significantly weakened after Heller's 1965 Godkin Lectures, mentioned earlier. The discovery of the "natural rate of unemployment" and development of the theory of rational expectations revealed the limitations of economists' macroeconomic policy tools.[46] Moreover, Krugman bemoaned the fact that "policy entrepreneurs" frequently displaced economists in providing economic advice to society. Referring to supply-side economics and other questionable economic doctrines, Krugman, using less than elegant words, suggested that a major task for economists must be "to flush such economic cockroaches down the toilet."[47]

As I discuss both the strengths and limitations of economics, I note that the strengths generally outweigh the weaknesses. With the rigor of their methods and the insights of their theories, economists have made major contributions to public affairs and have tried, not always with success, to safeguard the public against such a dubious idea as trade protectionism and against the excesses of economic regionalism. The economics profession itself, however, is deeply divided on such issues as trade, monetary affairs, and economic development even though the problems of the global economy and possible solutions are often treated by economists as if they were solely technical matters amenable to the methods of economic science. Although the contributions of economics have been crucial to our understanding of the world economy, one must also appreciate the role of political and

[46] In nontechnical terms, the natural rate of unemployment is the lowest rate that an economy can sustain without experiencing inflation. The doctrine of rational expectations posits that the market will always anticipate government policy and will neutralize its intended effects.

[47] Paul R. Krugman, *Peddling Prosperity: Economic Sense and Nonsense in the Age of Diminished Expectations* (New York: W. W. Norton, 1994), 291–92.

other factors in determining the nature and dynamics of the world economy.

COMPARISON OF ECONOMICS AND POLITICAL ECONOMY

Economics is clearly a more rigorous and theoretically advanced field of study than are political economy and the other social sciences. However, economics is based on highly restrictive methodological assumptions and, despite flourishing "economic imperialism," the domain of formal economic analysis is quite limited. Moreover, efforts to apply the rational choice techniques of economic analysis to the messy world of politics and social affairs more generally have not achieved consistent success. Although economic theories and methods are important and provide an essential foundation for the study of political economy, they are not in themselves sufficient to explain the nature and dynamics of the "real" world economy. This writer believes that combining the insights and theories of economics with the more intuitive and less rigorous techniques of history and the other social sciences leads to a more profound and useful comprehension of economic affairs than does adherence to any one field alone.

The most fundamental difference between neoclassical economics and the study of political economy is in the nature of the questions asked and of the answers given. Neither is superior to the other, nor is there any necessary conflict between the answers given by neoclassical economists to the questions that interest them and the answers given by political economists to their different questions. The two subjects complement one another, and political economists of almost every persuasion do, in fact, accept most, or at least much, of the corpus of conventional neoclassical economics. Even though political economists frequently consider the theories of neoclassical economics to be too limited, too abstract, and in many cases not directly relevant to the particular questions of interest to them, insofar as they are technically competent to do so, they draw upon the accepted theories of economics as they study many specific issues.

Economics and political economy differ significantly in their view of the role of the market in economic affairs and of the relationship of the market to other aspects of society. Whereas neoclassical economists believe that the market is autonomous, self-regulating, and governed by its own laws, almost all political economists assume that markets are embedded in larger sociopolitical structures that determine to a considerable extent the role and functioning of markets in social and political affairs and that the social, political, and cultural environment significantly influences the purpose of economic activities and determines the boundaries within which markets necessarily must function.[48]

Neoclassical economists and scholars of political economy also disagree with one another regarding the limitations of economics as an analytic tool useful for understanding the dynamics of social, political, and even economic affairs. While economic science provides a useful framework for static analysis, it seldom can explain changes in fundamental economic variables; for example, despite the central role of technological developments in economic affairs, economists do not have an explanation for technological change. In fact, the crucial determinants of economic change lie outside the framework of economic analysis. Reviewing the economics literature on the subject of economic change, Joseph Stiglitz comes to the astonishing conclusion that economists have not learned much about the dynamics of the economy.[49]

Despite the attempts of economic imperialists and rational-choice theorists to explain all forms of human behavior through application of the techniques of microeconomics, these techniques have limited utility for analyzing and explaining human behavior. Most political economists, I believe, would agree with the distinguished economist Joseph Schumpeter that economic analysis progresses until it inevitably encounters social, political, and psychological factors that economics cannot explain.[50] Although the research strategy of economic science is to "endogenize" exogenous variables, economic analysis and explanation are unlikely ever to exceed a certain limit.[51] There will always be exogenous variables such as culture, technology, and institutions that affect economic outcomes but cannot themselves be

[48] The concept of "embeddedness" is taken from the literature on economic sociology. An excellent discussion of this field of scholarship is Neil J. Smelser and Richard Swedberg, eds., *The Handbook of Economic Sociology* (Princeton: Princeton University Press, 1994). While this field of scholarship has produced classic works by Max Weber, Talcott Parsons, and others, economic sociology, with the major exception of radical sociology, has not devoted much attention to the international economy.

[49] Joseph E. Stiglitz, "Another Century of Economic Science," *Economic Journal* 101 (January 1991): 139.

[50] Joseph A. Schumpeter, *The Theory of Economic Development: An Inquiry into Profits, Capital, Credit, Interest, and the Business Cycle* (Cambridge: Harvard University Press, 1934), 4–5. I am indebted to Robert Keohane for bringing Schumpeter's comments to my attention.

[51] To endogenize an exogenous variable, such as the behavior of a politician, means that the exogenous variable can be explained by the logic of economics: individuals rationally seek to increase their own interests. This assumption is of course the basis of the public-choice school.

explained endogenously by the methods of economics; that is, in terms of rational individuals attempting to maximize their economic self-interest.

As Schumpeter states in another context, conventional economics can tell us how to manipulate the existing economic apparatus in order to increase its efficiency, but economics cannot explain how that economic apparatus came into existence in the first place.[52] Yet, identifying the determinants of an economic system is one of the most important problems that should be solved by economists and political economists alike. Indeed, how can economic development be understood without an answer to this question?

CONCLUSION

The analytic techniques, rich empirical data, and theoretical insights of neoclassical economics are essential ingredients in the study of political economy in general and international political economy in particular. Nevertheless, it is important to keep in mind the fact that economic activities occur within differing sociopolitical structures and that these structures greatly influence their outcomes. Understanding of the international economy must therefore be based on the contributions of international political economics as well as on economics itself.

[52] Joseph A. Schumpeter, *Capitalism, Socialism, and Democracy* (New York: Harper and Brothers, 1947).

The Study of International Political Economy

T HE STUDY of international political economy (IPE) is of necessity highly dependent on the theories and insights of neoclassical economics. However, IPE and neoclassical economics ask different questions as they apply their own mode of analysis.[1] Whereas economics is primarily concerned with efficiency and the mutual benefits of economic exchange, international political economy is interested not only in those subjects but also in a broader range of issues. IPE is particularly interested in the distribution of gains from market activities; neoclassical economics is not. Although, at least over the long term, every society gains absolutely from the efficient functioning of international markets, the gains are seldom distributed equally among all economic actors, and states generally are very much concerned over their own relative gains. Whereas economists regard markets as self-regulating mechanisms isolated from political affairs, specialists in IPE are interested in the fact that the world economy has a considerable impact on the power, values, and political autonomy of national societies. States have a strong incentive to take actions that safeguard their own values and interests, especially their power and freedom of action, and they also attempt to manipulate market forces to increase their power and influence over rival states or to favor friendly states.[2]

Whereas economists and economic analysts are generally indifferent to the role of institutions in economic affairs (due to their focus on the market), the nature of the international institutions and those international regimes that govern international markets and economic activities constitute a central concern of international political economists. As regimes may significantly affect the distribution of gains from economic activities and the economic/political autonomy of in-

[1] An excellent history of IPE, albeit too focused on American contributions, is Peter Katzenstein, Robert O. Keohane, and Stephen D. Krasner, "International Organization and the Study of World Politics," in Peter Katzenstein, Robert O. Keohane, and Stephen D. Krasner, *International Organization at Fifty: Exploration and Contestation in the Study of World Politics, International Organization* 52, no. 4 (autumn 1998).

[2] Joanne Gowa, *Allies, Adversaries, and International Trade* (Princeton: Princeton University Press, 1994).

dividual states, states—especially powerful states—attempt to influence the design and functioning of institutions in order to advance their own political, economic, and other interests. Thus, the study of international political economy presumes that states, multinational corporations, and other powerful actors attempt to use their power to influence the nature of international regimes.[3]

DISTRIBUTION OF WEALTH AND ECONOMIC ACTIVITIES

Whereas the science of economics emphasizes the efficient allocation of scarce resources and the absolute gains enjoyed by everyone from economic activities, state-centric scholars of international political economy emphasize the distributive consequences of economic activities. According to economics, exchange takes place because of mutual gain; were it otherwise, the exchange would not occur. IPE's state-centric interpretation, on the other hand, argues that economic actors are attentive not only to absolute but also to relative gains from economic intercourse; that is, not merely to the absolute gain for themselves, but also to the size of their own gain relative to gains of other actors. Governments are concerned about the terms of trade, the distribution of economic returns from foreign investment, and, in particular, the relative rates of economic growth among national economies. Indeed, the issue of relative gains is seldom far from the minds of political leaders.

The significance of relative gains for economic behavior and in the calculations of nation-states was recognized at least as early as the economic writings of the eighteenth-century political philosopher David Hume (1711–1776). Hume's mercantilist contemporaries argued that a nation should seek a trade and payments surplus, basing their arguments on the assumption that it was only *relative* gains that really mattered. In today's language of game theory, international commerce during the mercantilist era was considered to be a zero-sum game in which the gain to one party necessarily meant a loss to another. Hume himself demonstrated the folly and self-defeating nature of this mercantilist argument by introducing the "price-specie flow mechanism" into economic thought.[4] Subsequently, formulation by

[3] Stephen D. Krasner, ed., *International Regimes* (Ithaca: Cornell University Press, 1983).

[4] In oversimplified terms, the "price-specie flow mechanism" states that the flow of specie (gold or silver) into an economy as a consequence of a trade/payments surplus increases the domestic money supply and raises prices of a country's exports. This price rise in turn decreases the country's trade/payments surplus. In short, any attempt to have a permanent trade/payments surplus is self-defeating. See David Hume, in Eugene Rotwein, ed., *Writings on Economics* (London: Nelson, 1955).

David Ricardo (1772–1823) of the law or principle of comparative advantage revealed that every nation could gain in absolute terms from free trade and from an international division of labor based on territorial specialization. Subsequent modifications of Ricardo's theory suggested that states were also interested in the relative gains from trade. Ricardo's demonstration that international economic exchange was not a zero-sum game but rather a positive-sum game from which everyone could gain led Paul Samuelson to call the law of comparative advantage "the most beautiful idea" in economic science. However, both absolute gains and the distribution of those gains are important in international economic affairs.

A number of political economists have addressed the issue of absolute versus relative gains in international affairs, and the ensuing debate has largely centered on Joseph Grieco's argument that states are more concerned about relative than absolute gains and that this creates difficulties in attaining international cooperation.[5] Although I know of no political economist who dismisses altogether the role of relative gains in international economic affairs, scholars of IPE do differ on the weight each gives to relative versus absolute gains. Whereas many scholars stress the importance of relative gains, liberals emphasize the importance of absolute gains and believe that Grieco has overstated the significance of relative gains. Absolute gains, they argue, are more important than Grieco's analysis suggests, and therefore international cooperation should be easier to attain than he postulates. While Grieco's emphasis on the importance of relative gains is, I believe, basically important, and states do, in general, prize relative gains, sometimes even at the expense of absolute gains, this argument cannot be elevated into a general law of state behavior.[6] One can say about this generalization in political economy no more than Kindleberger has said of most generalizations in economics: "It depends!"

The importance of absolute versus relative gains in state calculations is actually highly dependent upon the circumstances in which a specific trade-off occurs. While it may be true that states can never be

---

[5] Joseph M. Grieco, *Cooperation Among Nations: Europe, America, and Non-Tariff Barriers to Trade* (Ithaca: Cornell University Press, 1990). An excellent volume on the debate over the importance of relative versus absolute gains is David A. Baldwin, ed., *Neorealism and Neoliberalsim: The Contemporary Debate* (New York: Columbia University Press, 1993).

[6] This point is also made in Robert Powell, *The Shadow of Power: States and Strategies in International Politics* (Princeton: Princeton University Press, 1999): 80. Also, Michael Mastanduno, "Do Relative Gains Matter? America's Response to Japanese Industrial Policy," *International Security* 16, no. 1 (summer 1991): 73–113.

totally unconcerned about the distributive consequences of economic activities for their relative wealth and power, they frequently do, largely for security reasons, ignore this concern in their dealings with others. During the height of the Cold War, for example, the United States fostered the economic unification of Western Europe for political reasons despite the costs to its own economic interests. Kenneth Waltz has noted that the conscious decision of the United States in the late 1940s to build the power of its European allies at a sacrifice to itself was a historically unprecedented action.[7]

States are particularly interested in the distribution of those gains affecting domestic welfare, national wealth, and military power. When a state weighs absolute versus relative gains, military power is by far the most important consideration; states are extraordinarily reluctant, for example, to trade military security for economic gains. Modern nation-states (like eighteenth-century mercantilists) are extremely concerned about the consequences of international economic activities for the distribution of economic gains. Over time, the unequal distribution of these gains will inevitably change the international balance of economic and military power, and will thus affect national security. For this reason, states have always been very sensitive to the effects of the international economy on relative rates of economic growth. At the beginning of the twenty-first century, concern is focused on the distribution of industrial power, especially in those high-tech industries vitally important to the relative power position of individual states. The territorial distribution of industry and of technological capabilities is a matter of great concern for every state and a major issue in international political economy.

NATIONAL AUTONOMY

One of the dominant themes in the study of international political economy (IPE) is the persistent clash between the increasing interdependence of the international economy and the desire of individual states to maintain their economic independence and political autonomy. At the same time that states want the benefits of free trade, foreign investment, and the like, they also desire to protect their political autonomy, cultural values, and social structures. However, the logic of the market system is to expand geographically and to incorporate more and more aspects of a society within the price mechanism, thus making domestic matters subject to forces external to the

[7] Kenneth Waltz, *Theory of International Politics* (Reading, Mass.: Addison-Wesley, 1979).

society. In time, if unchecked, the integration of an economy into the world economy, the intensifying pressures of foreign competition, and the necessity to be efficient in order to survive economically could undermine the independence of a society and force it to adopt new values and forms of social organization. Fear that economic globalization and the integration of national markets are destroying or could destroy the political, economic, and cultural autonomy of national societies has become widespread.

The clash between the evolving economic and technical interdependence of national societies and the continuing compartmentalization of the world political system into sovereign independent states is one of the dominant motifs of contemporary writings on IPE. Whereas powerful market forces (trade, finance, and investment) jump political boundaries and integrate societies, governments frequently restrict and channel their economic activities to serve the interests of their own societies and of powerful groups within those societies. Whereas the logic of the market is to locate economic activities wherever they will be most efficient and profitable, the logic of the state is to capture and control the process of economic growth and capital accumulation in order to increase the power and economic welfare of the nation. The inevitable clash between the logic of the market and the logic of the state is central to the study of international political economy.

Most economists and many political economists believe that the international economy has a positive impact on international political affairs. The international economy, many argue, creates webs of mutual interdependence and common interests that moderate the self-centered behavior of states. Underlying this benign interpretation is a particular definition of economic interdependence as dependence. However, as Albert Hirschman pointed out in *National Power and the Structure of Foreign Trade (1969)*, while economic interdependence may be characterized by mutual dependence, dependence is frequently not symmetrical.[8] Trade, investment, and markets establish dependencies among national societies that can be and are exploited. Integration of national markets creates power relations among states where, as Hirschman notes, economic power arises from the capacity to interrupt economic relations.[9] Economic ties among states almost always involve power relations.

Robert Keohane and Joseph Nye (1977) extended this analysis of economic power and the political aspects of economic interdepen-

[8] Albert O. Hirschman, *National Power and the Structure of Foreign Trade* (Berkeley: University of California Press, 1969).
[9] Ibid., 16.

dence by distinguishing "sensitivity" interdependence from "vulnerability" interdependence. Most economists really are referring to sensitivity interdependence exemplified by responsiveness among economic variables, such as changes in interest rates in one country that influence interest rates in another. Vulnerability interdependence, on the other hand, is what Hirschman and political economists frequently have in mind when they speak of economic interdependence; this latter term refers to the possibilities of political exploitation of market interdependencies.[10] Individual states have a powerful incentive either to decrease their own dependence on other states through such policies as trade protection and industrial policies or to increase the dependence of other states upon them through such policies as foreign aid and trade concessions. International economic relations are never purely economic; they always have profound implications for the economic autonomy and political independence of national societies.

THE POLITICS OF INTERNATIONAL REGIMES

All economists and political economists acknowledge the need for some minimal rules or institutions to govern and regulate economic activities; even the most ardent public-choice economist would agree that laws are needed to enforce contracts and protect property rights. A liberal international economy—that is, an international economy characterized (at least in ideal terms) by such factors as open markets, freedom of capital movement, and nondiscrimination—certainly needs agreed-upon rules. A liberal economy can succeed only if it provides public goods like a stable monetary system, eliminates market failures, and prevents cheating and free-riding.[11] Although the primary purpose of rules or regimes is to resolve economic problems, many are actually enacted for political rather than for strictly economic reasons. For example, although economists may be correct that an economy benefits from opening itself to free trade whether or not other countries open their own markets to it, a liberal international economy could not politically tolerate too many free-riders who benefit from the opening of other economies but refuse to open their own markets.

[10] Robert O. Keohane and Joseph S. Nye Jr., *Power and Interdependence: World Politics in Transition* (Boston: Little, Brown, 1977).

[11] In nontechnical language, a public or collective good is one that everyone can enjoy without having to pay for the use of the good. A frequently used example is a lighthouse. Because of this free use, no one usually has an incentive to provide them, and therefore public goods tend to be "underprovided." The literature on this subject and on proposed solutions to the underprovision problem is extensive.

In the past, the rules governing the international economy were quite simple and informal. Insofar as the implicit rules were enforced at all, they were enforced by the major powers whose interests were favored by those rules. For example, in the nineteenth century under the Pax Britannica, overseas property rights were frequently upheld by British "gunboat diplomacy,"[12] and the international gold standard, based on a few generally accepted rules, was managed by the Bank of England. Now, formal international institutions have been created to manage today's extraordinarily complex international economy. The most important institutions are the Bretton Woods institutions such as the World Bank, the International Monetary Fund, and the World Trade Organization. The world economy would have difficulty functioning without these institutions. Therefore, understanding their functioning has become an extremely important concern of political economists.[13]

The concept of international regimes, defined as "sets of implicit or explicit principles, norms, rules, and decision-making procedures around which actors' expectations converge in a given area of international relations," has been at the core of the research on international institutions.[14] Although a distinction can be made between an international regime as rules and understandings and an international institution as a formal organization, the word "regimes" and the word "institutions" are frequently used interchangeably in writings on international political economy. Moreover, what is really important for the functioning of the world economy are the rules themselves rather than the formal institutions in which they are usually embodied. To simplify the following discussion, I shall use "international regime" to encompass both rules and such formal international organizations as the International Monetary Fund or the General Agreement on Tariffs and Trade.

---

[12] Charles Lipson, *Standing Guard: Protecting Foreign Capital in the Nineteenth and Twentieth Centuries* (Berkeley: University of California Press, 1985).

[13] Many realists would disagree with my belief that international organizations are important, at least in the area of economic affairs and insofar as they do not infringe on the security interests of powerful states.

[14] Stephen Krasner, "Structural Causes and Regime Consequences: Regimes as Intervening Variables," *International Organization* 36, no. 2, (spring 1982): 186. As Krasner himself points out, there are several variants of regime theory. For this reason, I shall focus on what I consider to be the common denominators in these theories. Richard N. Cooper coined the term "international regime" in his "Prolegomena to the Choice of an International Monetary System," *International Organization* 29, no. 1 (winter 1975): 64. The term "regime" was introduced into the IPE literature by John Ruggie, "International Responses to Technology: Concepts and Trends," *International Organization* 29, no. 3 (summer 1975): 570.

Robert Keohane has been the most influential scholar in the development of regime theory. In his book, *After Hegemony* (1984), Keohane set forth the definitive exposition and classic defense of regime theory.[15] He argues that international regimes are a necessary feature of the world economy and are required to facilitate efficient operation of the international economy. Among the tasks performed by regimes are reduction of uncertainty, minimization of transaction costs, and prevention of market failures. International regimes are created by self-centered states in order to further both individual and collective interests. Even though a particular regime might be created because of the pressures of a dominant power (or hegemon), Keohane argues that an effective international regime takes on a life of its own over time. Moreover, when states experience the success of an international regime, they "learn" to change their own behavior and even to redefine their national interests. Thus, according to Keohane's analysis, international regimes are necessary to preserve and stabilize the international economy.

From its beginning, regime theory has been surrounded by intense controversy. One major reason for the intensity of this debate is that regime theory arose as a response to what Keohane labeled "the theory of hegemonic stability."[16] Proponents of the latter theory had argued that the postwar liberal international economy was based on the economic and political leadership of the United States. Some theorists had argued that the hegemonic stability theory also suggested that the relative decline of American power due to the rise of new economic powers and the slowing of American productivity growth in the early 1970s placed the continued existence of a liberal world economy in jeopardy. As Steven Weber has pointed out, regime theory was largely a response to the perceived decline of American power, the 1973 energy price shock, and the global "stagflation" of the 1970s.[17] Keohane and others argued that international regimes and cooperation among

---

[15] Robert O. Keohane, *After Hegemony: Cooperation and Discord in the World Political Economy* (Princeton: Princeton University Press, 1984).

[16] Robert O. Keohane, "The Theory of Hegemonic Stability and Changes in International Economic Regimes, 1967–1977," in Ole Holsti et al., *Change in the International System* (Boulder, Colo.: Westview Press, 1980): 131–62.

[17] Steven Weber, "Institutions and Change" in Michael Doyle and John Ikenberry, eds., *New Thinking in International Relations* (Boulder, Colo.: Westview Press, 1997). The emphasis on regimes also grew out of the realization in the 1970s that international governance was not codeterminous with international organizations. Consult Friedrich Kratochwil and John Gerard Ruggie, "International Organization: A State of the Art on an Art of the State," *International Organization* 40, no. 4 (autumn 1986): 753–75.

the major economic powers would replace declining American leadership as the basis of the liberal international economic order. Thus, the political purpose of regime theory was, at least in part, to reassure Americans and others that a liberal international order would survive America's economic decline and the severe economic problems of the 1970s.

British scholar Susan Strange was the most outspoken critic of regime theory.[18] According to Strange, regime theory was at best a passing fad, and at worst a polemical device designed to legitimate America's continuing domination of the world economy. Strange and other critics alleged that such international regimes as those governing trade and monetary affairs had been economically, politically, and ideologically biased in America's favor, and that these regimes were put in place by American power, reflected American interests, and were not (as American regime theorists have argued) politically and economically neutral. Strange charged that many of the fundamental problems afflicting the world economy actually resulted from ill-conceived and predatory American economic policies rather than simply being symptoms of American economic decline.

Strange's foremost example of American culpability was the huge American demand in the 1980s and 1990s for international capital to finance America's federal budget and trade/payments deficit.[19] Through use of what she referred to as "structural power" (such as America's military, financial, and technological power), she alleged that the United States continued to run the world economy during that period and made a mess of it. Strange and other critics also alleged that the role of the dollar as the key international currency had permitted the United States to behave irresponsibly. More generally, Strange and other foreign critics charged that the American discipline of international political economy, and regime theory in particular, have been little more than efforts to defend America's continuing desire to reign economically and politically over the rest of the world. Whether or not we accept these criticisms, they should remind us that regimes and other social institutions are sometimes created to preserve inequalities as well as to improve coordination and overcome

---

[18] Susan Strange, "Cave! hic Dragones: A Critique of Regime Analysis," in Stephen D. Krasner, ed., *International Regimes*, 337–54. It is noteworthy that very few non-American scholars have been positively inclined toward regime theory or involved in its development. A major exception is Volker Rittberger, ed., *Regime Theory and International Relations* (New York: Oxford University Press, 1993).

[19] Susan Strange, *Casino Capitalism* (New York: Basil Blackwell, 1986); and Susan Strange, *Mad Money* (Manchester, U.K.: Manchester University Press, 1998).

other obstacles to mutually beneficial cooperation.[20] It is desirable to study such important issues as the origins of international regimes, the content, rules, and norms of international regimes, and the history of compliance by affected states, particularly in situations when a regime is perceived as being counter to a state's interests.

Origins

International regimes have developed in a number of different ways. Some have arisen spontaneously and do not involve conscious design; many of the informal rules governing markets are of this type. Others have resulted from international negotiations among states; the post–World War II Bretton Woods system of trade and monetary regimes, for example, was the result of international negotiations, primarily between the United States and Great Britain. Still other regimes have been imposed by powerful states on less powerful ones; the colonial systems of the nineteenth century are a notorious example. This section will concentrate upon regimes created through international negotiations, especially the Bretton Woods regimes for trade and monetary affairs that were the result of American leadership.

In creating the post–World War II regimes, the most important task for American leadership was to promote international cooperation. The United States undertook the leadership role, and other economic powers (Canada, Japan, and Western Europe) cooperated for economic, political, and ideological reasons. These allies believed that a liberal world economy would meet their economic interests and also solidify their alliance against the Soviet threat. In addition, cooperation was greatly facilitated by the fact that these nations shared an ideological commitment to a liberal international economy based on free trade and open markets.[21] All three factors—leadership, cooperation, and ideological consensus—were important to creation of the post–World War II liberal international economy.

[20] Andrew Schotter, *The Economic Theory of Social Institutions* (New York: Cambridge University Press, 1981), 26.

[21] The term "epistemic community," attributed to John Ruggie, has been given to the role of shared ideas or beliefs in promoting international cooperation. A useful discussion is Peter Haas, *Saving the Mediterranean* (New York: Columbia University Press, 1990). An important volume on the subject is Judith Goldstein and Robert O. Keohane, eds., *Ideas and Foreign Policy: Beliefs, Institutions, and Political Change* (Ithaca: Cornell University Press, 1993). Another important study is Judith Goldstein, *Ideas, Interests, and American Trade Policy* (Ithaca: Cornell University Press, 1993). While I agree that ideas are very important, they are important politically insofar as they are supported by the interests and power of important actors such as states or domestic political coalitions.

Content

The content of an international regime—the precise rules and decision-making techniques embodied in a particular regime—is determined by technological, economic, and political factors. An international regime could not function well if its rules were counter to scientific and technological considerations. Regimes governing international economic affairs must be based on sound economic principles and must be able to solve complex economic matters. The postwar international monetary regime based on fixed exchange rates, for example, had to solve such difficult technical problems as provision of international liquidity and creation of an adjustment mechanism for nations with balance of payments problems.

Economists, however, seldom agree on such complex issues; there are, for example, several competing theories on the determination of exchange rates. It is important to realize that the specific means chosen to solve a given economic problem may have significant consequences for individual states and/or may impinge on their national autonomy. In the early postwar monetary system, the central role of the U.S. dollar as a reserve and transaction currency greatly facilitated financing of American foreign policy. Thus, while the content of an international regime must be grounded on sound technical and economic considerations, it is important to recognize that regimes do produce political effects.

A number of regime theorists have a tendency to think of regimes as benign. Regime theory has emphasized the efficiency and efficacy of international cooperation and problem-solving and that regimes are instituted to achieve interstate cooperation and information sharing, to reduce transaction costs, and to solve common problems. While these goals do exist, it is also true, as some scholars of institutions point out, that institutions—and regimes—do create or preserve inequalities; regimes can also have a redistributive function.[22] History is replete with such examples as the carving-up of Africa at the Congress of Berlin (1878) and the post–World War I mandate system. The purpose, content, and actual consequences of every international regime must be closely examined; there should be no assumption that regimes are ipso facto of equal or mutual benefit to every participant.

[22] In his analysis of institutions and, by implication, regimes, Schotter, in his book *The Economic Theory of Institutions*, identifies four types of problems whose solutions lead to the creation of institutions: coordination problems, prisoner's dilemma–type games, cooperative-type games, and, most important for my present purpose, problems of inequality preservation.

Because international regimes frequently do have distributive consequences as well as implications for national autonomy, the rules, norms, and other factors embedded in regimes generally reflect the power and interests of the dominant power/s in the international system. Certainly, the liberal trade and monetary regimes following World War II promoted the economic and, I would emphasize, the political and security interests of the United States while also strengthening the anti-Soviet political alliance. Moreover, as American interests changed, the United States used its power to modify one or another of these regimes; the August 1971 Nixon decision to destroy the system of fixed exchange rates because he believed that it no longer suited American interests provided a particularly striking example of this type of behavior.

Nevertheless, it is unlikely that the regimes governing a liberal international economy do or will represent the interests of the dominant power/s alone and of no others. Liberal international regimes must satisfy the interests of all the major economic powers to at least some degree; if they do not, the regimes would neither function nor long survive. The major trading partners of the United States were satisfied with the postwar trade regime and, in fact, benefited economically from the regime more than did the United States. Although a liberal international economic order does reflect the interests of a dominant power, such a power cannot impose a liberal economic order on the rest of the world; ultimately, the regime must rest on international cooperation.

Compliance

Although some scholars deny, or at least minimize, the importance of the compliance issue, compliance with international regimes is a major problem, and it is important to understand the reasons for compliance or noncompliance.[23] The compliance or enforcement problem arises because there is no authoritative international government, because states frequently value highly their relative gains and national autonomy, and because there is a collective action problem in which individual actors are tempted to cheat and free ride. While the compliance problem may be of minor significance in many or even the majority of international regimes, when the rules and principles of

[23] Some scholars, for example, argue that as most states do comply with international regimes, compliance is not a serious problem. This position, that George W. Downs, David M. Rocke, and Peter N. Barsoom label the "managerial school," is criticized by these authors in their "Is the Good News About Compliance Good News About Cooperation?" *International Organization* 50, no. 3 (summer 1996): 379–406.

an international regime have significant distributive consequences for states and powerful domestic groups, or when they impinge significantly on the autonomy and security of states, the compliance problem becomes of overwhelming importance. Many of the international regimes governing the world economy, in fact, are of this latter type, because they do have important consequences for the distribution of global wealth and national autonomy.[24]

Scholars of international political economy have devoted considerable attention to possible solutions to this problem. An important proposed solution is based on the theory of iterative (or repeated) games and, in particular, on what game theorists call the Prisoner's Dilemma. Another is based on insights from the new institutionalism or "new economics of organization."[25] These approaches fall within the larger category of "theories of international cooperation." Most scholars of international political economy would accept the definition made popular by Robert Keohane that cooperation occurs "when actors adjust their behavior to the actual or anticipated preferences of others, through a process of policy coordination."[26] Although theories of cooperation may be helpful in explicating the nature and difficulties of the compliance problem, they do not really solve the problem.

The Prisoner's Dilemma is undoubtedly familiar to most readers of this book. Nevertheless, I shall provide a brief reminder: Two prison-

---

[24] The reasons why the distribution issue is such a major obstacle to international cooperation are discussed by James D. Morrow, "Modeling the Forms of International Cooperation: Distribution Versus Information," *International Organization* 48, no. 3 (summer 1994): 387–423. The formal treatment by Morrow and others of the distributive aspects of international cooperation have not been adequately integrated into the regime literature. I am indebted to George Downs for enlightening me on this scholarship.

[25] The "new institutionalism" is based largely on the research of Oliver Williamson and on the concept of transaction costs; that is, the costs of doing business. For a discussion of the relevance of this literature for IPE, consult Beth V. Yarbrough and Robert M. Yarbrough, "International Institutions and the New Economics of Organization," *International Organization* 44, no. 2 (spring 1990): 235–59. These ideas have been elaborated in their book, *Cooperation and Governance in International Trade: The Strategic Organizational Approach* (Princeton: Princeton University Press, 1992).

[26] Keohane, *After Hegemony*, 51–52. For a useful and extensive analysis of theories of cooperation, consult Helen Milner, "International Theories of Cooperation Among Nations: Strengths and Weaknesses," *World Politics* 44, no. 3 (April 1992): 466–96. Although the literature on game theory and international cooperation distinguishes among different types of problems, such as problems of coordination or of collaboration, I shall use "cooperation" to refer to all the varieties of international cooperation. For a valuable discussion of the issue, refer to Lisa L. Martin, "Interests, Power, and Multilateralism," *International Organization* 46, no. 4 (autumn 1992): 765–92.

ers are accused of a crime and held separately. If they both confess to the crime of which they are accused, they will both be punished. If neither confesses—that is, if in essence they cooperate with one another—they will both be punished, but less severely. However, if only one confesses (or defects) and the other does not confess, the latter will be punished more severely. Thus, although each has an incentive to cooperate with the other by not confessing, each also has an incentive to confess (defect). Uncertainty regarding what the other player will do could lead to a less than optimal outcome for both players.

This type of mixed motive game in which the players have a motive to cooperate and also a motive to defect is characteristic of almost every aspect of international politics and certainly of international economic affairs. Although the players would gain from cooperation, each might gain even more by defecting (cheating); yet both would lose if both cheat. For example, a nation might be able to increase its own relative gains in the international trading regime by exporting to other markets at the same time that it keeps its own markets closed; however, if others retaliate and close their markets, everyone would lose. In a monetary regime, a nation could increase its international competitiveness by unilaterally devaluing its own currency. However, if other countries simultaneously devalue their own currencies, everyone loses. Therefore, everyone is better off, at least in absolute terms, as a result of cooperation. Yet the possibility of increasing one's own relative gains by cheating or successfully "free-riding" always provides a powerful temptation in international affairs.[27]

A number of attempts have been made by economists and other scholars to solve the Prisoner's Dilemma. Proposed solutions entail methods or techniques designed to increase the likelihood that players will cooperate and not cheat; they include creation of norms of reciprocity, making each move in the game less distinct, and linking issues to one another. Such techniques attempt to lessen the incentive to cheat in a particular instance so that the players learn how to cooperate.[28] The most noteworthy effort to solve the Prisoner's Dilemma has been the concept of iterative games developed by Robert Axelrod and others.[29] This concept leads to the conclusion that, if a game is

[27] Bruno S. Frey has a valuable analysis of the "free-rider" problem and why international cooperation is so difficult in his *International Political Economics* (Oxford: Basil Blackwell, 1984), Chapter 7.

[28] An important discussion of this subject is Kenneth A. Oye, ed., *Cooperation under Anarchy* (Princeton: Princeton University Press, 1986), 2–24.

[29] Robert M. Axelrod, *The Evolution of Cooperation* (New York: Basic Books, 1984).

repeated over and over again and a participant pursues a "tit-for-tat" strategy in which cooperative moves are rewarded and uncooperative moves are punished, the participants in the game will learn to trust and cooperate with one another.[30]

The literature on the theory of repeated or iterative games has become extensive and has been subjected to intense theoretical criticism and defense. Although scrutiny of the theory has vastly increased our understanding of the compliance problem, this scholarly debate has not yet enabled us to predict when cooperation or defection from (cheating) a regime will in fact occur. The fundamental problem of uncertainty and hence of regime compliance has not yet been solved and probably never will be; a player can never be absolutely sure whether another player will cooperate or defect, and the costs of miscalculation could be extremely high. The absence of an adequate body of research on the actual functioning of specific regimes makes it impossible to be confident that regimes are of decisive importance in the behavior of states. In addition, a fundamental methodological problem makes it difficult to determine whether or not regimes actually make a difference in the conduct of international affairs. As one strong supporter of regime theory has stated, "Investigating the consequences of international regimes requires a counterfactual argument," that is, knowledge of what would happen if the regime did not exist.[31]

The "new economics of organization," or what some scholars prefer to label "neoinstitutionalism," has produced another important effort to solve the compliance problem. This theory of international cooperation has been described by George Downs and David Rocke as "a loose composite" of transaction-cost economics and noncooperative game theory.[32] According to new institutionalism, regimes can provide a solution to such problems as market inefficiencies, economic uncertainties, and market failures. However, as Downs and Rocke point out, this theory of international cooperation makes only a limited contribution to solution of the compliance problem, and

[30] Criticisms of Axelrod's approach to the cooperation problem include Joanne Gowa, "Anarchy, Egoism, and Third Images: The Evolution of Cooperation and International Relations," *International Organization* 40, no. 1 (winter 1986): 67–186; and David E. Spiro, "The State of Cooperation in Theories of State Cooperation: The Evolution of a Category Mistake." *Journal of International Affairs* 42, no. 1 (fall 1988): 205–25.

[31] Rittberger, ed., *Regime Theory and International Relations.*

[32] George W. Downs and David M. Rocke, *Optimal Imperfection? Domestic Uncertainty and Institutions in International Relations* (Princeton: Princeton University Press, 1995), 19.

compliance with international regimes ultimately rests on the domestic and, I would add, the foreign policy interests of individual states.

Despite its important insights into the functioning of the world economy, regime theory frequently sidesteps problems of national autonomy and interests. For example, every nation joining an international regime reserves the right to withdraw from the regime if its interests change. In addition, concerns over national autonomy place severe limits on the types of international regimes that are created. Even in the North Atlantic Treaty Organization (NATO), each member reserves the right not to come to the aid of another alliance member if the other is attacked.[33]

The increasing importance of social welfare in state behavior has not substantially changed matters, although many scholars of international political economy have suggested that it has. As James Mayall points out, international regimes have resulted in few, if any, sacrifices of domestic social welfare.[34] Despite much talk of international distributive justice, for example, voluntary sharing by one society of a substantial portion of its wealth with other societies is rare indeed. Foreign aid, for example, has never absorbed more than a small percentage of a nation's GDP, and with a few notable exceptions such aid has been and is given for national security or economic (rather than humanitarian) reasons. The modern welfare system has actually made states even more attentive to their own economic interests. The nationalistic nature of the modern welfare state is well demonstrated by the singular fact that every state severely restricts immigration, at least in part to restrict access to its welfare system.

While international regimes are useful to provide solutions to technical, economic, and other problems associated with the world economy, they also invariably affect the economic welfare, national security, and political autonomy of individual states. For this reason, states frequently attempt to manipulate regimes for their own parochial economic and political advantage. This concept of international regimes as both technical solution and arena of political struggle diverges from that held by many economists and liberal scholars of political economy that regimes are economically and politically neutral. The realist interpretation maintains that international regimes are neither above nor outside the struggle for power and advantage among states. Regimes are both a part and an object of a political

---

[33] James Mayall, *Nationalism and International Society* (New York: Cambridge University Press, 1990). In the case of NATO, every member has reserved the right whether or not to declare war if another member of the alliance is attacked.

[34] Ibid., Chapter 6.

struggle. As a consequence, if a regime is to be effective and its rules are to be enforced, it must also rest on a strong political base. Due to the central importance of distribution and autonomy issues to most nations, the compliance problem is unlikely to be resolved, and regime rules are unlikely to be enforced unless there is strong international leadership.

THEORY OF HEGEMONIC STABILITY

The theory of hegemonic stability, discussed below, in both its liberal and its realist versions, encountered a critical reception from a number of scholars.[35] The theory was attacked on theoretical, historical, and political grounds. The theoretical criticisms emphasized the possibility of a cooperative solution among nonhegemonic nations to the problems associated with creating and maintaining a liberal international economy.[36] Although it may be possible to create a stable liberal international order through cooperation but without a hegemon, this has never happened, and with no counterfactual example neither the theory nor its critics can be proved wrong. This problem, of course, is endemic in many areas of the social sciences. Some critics of the theory have tested it against late-nineteenth-century experience and found weaknesses in the theory.[37] Political criticisms have ranged from denunciations of the theory as a defense of or rationale for American policies to the opposite idea that the theory predicted the absolute decline of the United States. No proponent of hegemonic stability theory, at least to my knowledge, has been motivated to justify American behavior; to the contrary, most were very critical of the

[35] Several of the most important criticisms of the theory are John A. C. Conybeare, "Public Goods, Prisoner's Dilemmas and the International Political Economy," *International Studies Quarterly* 28, no. 1 (March 1984): 5–22; David A. Lake, "Leadership, Hegemony, and the International Economy: Naked Emperor or Tattered Monarch with Potential?" *International Studies Quarterly* 37, no. 4 (December 1993): 459–89; Duncan Snidel, "The Limits of Hegemonic Stability Theory," *International Organization* 39, no. 4 (autumn 1985): 579–614; and Helen V. Milner, *Interests, Institutions, and Information: Domestic Politics and International Relations* (Princeton: Princeton University Press, 1997), 24–25.

[36] For example, as I acknowledge above, the critics may be correct that significant international economic cooperation is possible without a hegemon *provided* that certain conditions exist, such as the number of players is small, international regimes exist, and "the shadow of the future" is long enough. However, this solution to the problem of international cooperation has never been tried.

[37] An example is Timothy J. McKeown, "Hegemonic Stability Theory and 19th Century Tariff Levels in Europe" *International Organization* 37, no. 1 (winter 1983): 73–91.

self-centered and irresponsible American behavior that began in the 1960s, if not earlier.[38]

A major reason for the criticisms of the theory by political scientists is that it was never adequately formulated. Indeed, the "theory" was more an intuitive idea based on a particular reading of history than a scientific theory. Because the theory was underdeveloped, it was open to both warranted and unwarranted criticisms. A number of critics, for example, interpreted the theory to mean that a dominant power is necessary to the emergence of a liberal international economy; they have gone on to make the point that Soviet hegemony did not create a liberal Soviet-dominated international economy. However, as I have emphasized in numerous writings, a liberal international economy requires a hegemon committed to liberal economic principles, as Great Britain was in the nineteenth century and the United States was in the twentieth century; the theory was never intended to suggest that a Soviet Union, Nazi Germany, or militaristic Japan would promote a liberal world economy. Moreover, despite the implied criticisms of some authors, the theory, at least in my opinion, posited that a hegemon is a *necessary* but *not a sufficient* condition for establishment of a liberal international economy. It is possible, as some critics have argued, that a hegemon's interests would be best served by an optimum tariff; yet, such an aggressive tactic would be a highly unlikely course of action for a strong liberal power such as Great Britain or the United States. Instead, the theory rests on the idea of international cooperation. Hegemony makes cooperation more feasible and is not, as some have suggested, opposed to cooperation.

The strongest support for the theory, or at least for the idea that strong leadership is necessary, has come from economists. This endorsement is rather amazing, because economists (with the notable exception of Kindleberger) are likely to argue that markets by themselves will manage the world economy. The most detailed and systematic empirical critique of HST by an economist is that of economic historian Barry Eichengreen (1989).[39] However, support for the theory was not the purpose avowed by Eichengreen; in fact, he believed

---

[38] Susan Strange criticized my argument that the irresponsible behavior of the United States was not due to America's relative economic decline. She was quite correct. See Susan Strange, "The Persistent Myth of Lost Hegemony," *International Organization* 41, no. 4 (1987): 259–74.

[39] Barry Eichengreen, "Hegemonic Stability Theories of the International Monetary System," in Richard N. Cooper et al., *Can Nations Agree?: Issues in International Economic Cooperation* (Washington, D.C.: Brookings Institution, 1989), 255–98.

that he had refuted the theory. Through examination of the historical record, Eichengreen tried to discover whether or not a hegemon had played a determining role in the rise and maintenance of an open world economy. He inquired specifically into the roles of Great Britain in the late nineteenth century and of the United States in the post–World War II era, particularly regarding the genesis and functioning of the international monetary system. Although he concluded that the record gave only modest support to the theory, his analysis actually supports its validity.

Eichengreen's lukewarm assessment of the theory appears to rest on the erroneous assumption that the hegemon must be an imperialistic power that imposes its will on other countries. His language suggests that he identifies hegemony with coercion and imposition of the hegemon's will on other countries. Throughout his analysis, he uses such terms as "dictating," "force," and "coerced" to describe the actions of the British and American hegemons. Yet, no proponent of the theory has used such language, but instead each has emphasized the essential leadership role of the hegemon in promoting international cooperation. In fact, Eichengreen's analysis itself confirms that the British and American hegemons "significantly influenced" the nature of the international monetary system through promotion of international cooperation. Without a hegemon, international cooperation in trade, monetary, and most other matters in international affairs becomes exceptionally difficult, if not impossible, to achieve.

Four years later (1993), Eichengreen again evaluated the theory of hegemonic stability from the perspective of historical experience.[40] Whereas his earlier analysis had focused on the international monetary system, this subsequent evaluation considered the international trading system. He stated that there was a positive association between hegemony and trade liberalization. Comparing the nineteenth century and post–World War II experiences, Eichengreen concluded that "the only example of successful multilateralism the historical record provides coincides with a period of exceptional economic dominance by a single power. And the growing difficulties of the GATT have coincided, of course, with US relative . . . economic decline." He then goes on to ask, "Why might this be?"

Eichengreen drew upon cartel theory to explain why a hegemon facilitates international cooperation: "Simple cartel theory suggests that it is possible to deter defection from a cartel containing many

---

[40] Barry Eichengreen, in Jaime De Melo and Arvind Panagariya, eds., *New Dimensions in Regional Integration* (New York: Cambridge University Press, 1995), 120–21.

members only when there is a dominant firm capable of acting as enforcer. In its absence, duopolies of, say, neighboring firms may be the most that monitoring and enforcement capabilities can support. This suggests that the growing prevalence of bilateralism is a corollary of the increasingly multipolar nature of the world economy."[41] Thus, Eichengreen has set forth a plausible explanation of why the decline of American leadership has contributed to the increasing importance of bilateral negotiations and regional arrangements in the world economy.

Other leading economists have also supported the validity of the theory. For example, Nobel Laureate Robert Mundell, a distinguished expert on international monetary and financial affairs, has pointed out that the stability of the international monetary system is dependent upon a dominant power. Other international economists such as Robert Baldwin and Swiss economist Bruno Frey have also written in support of the idea that a hegemon is necessary. Baldwin writes, for example, that the hegemonic role played by the United States increased the economic welfare of most non-Communist countries.[42] According to Frey, public choice theory suggests that it is impossible for public goods to be provided if there is no hegemon.[43]

One of the most interesting arguments supporting the necessity of a hegemon was set forth by Mancur Olson. Olson's views are especially apposite because of his innovative work on provision of collective goods and the fact that many critics of the theory cite his work to support their own criticisms. Commenting on provision of the collective good of free trade, Olson presents an ingenious theory based on domestic politics to explain why it is so difficult for a country to reduce trade barriers unilaterally and in the absence of external pressures exerted by a powerful state.[44] He then concludes, "Thus the world works better when there is a 'hegemonic' power—one that finds it in its own self-interest to see that various international collective goods are provided." He continues, "Naturally, the incentive a

[41] Eichengreen, in ibid., 121.

[42] Robert E. Baldwin, "Adapting the GATT to a More Regionalized World: A Political Economy Perspective," in Kym Anderson and Richard Blackhurst, *Regional Integration and the Global Trading System* (New York: St. Martin's Press, 1993), Chapter 18; Bruno S. Frey, *International Political Economics*.

[43] Frey, *International Political Economics*. According to Frey, Arrow's "impossibility theorem" demonstrates that with three countries and three goals, common or coordinated policies cannot be reached when each country has a different ordering of priorities. Leadership is required to break the deadlock

[44] Mancur Olson, in De Melo and Panagariya, eds., *New Dimensions in Regional Integration*, 122–27.

hegemonic power has to provide international collective goods diminishes as it becomes relatively less important in the world economy. In the United States, there has been a conspicuous resurgence of protectionist thinking, and a diminishing willingness of the country to provide foreign aid, as the American economy has come to encompass relatively less of the world economy."[45] From this perspective, the emergence of new industrial powers and new exporters of manufactured goods has resulted in increased American protectionist policies, beginning with the New Protectionism in the mid-1970s and with the shift to a greater emphasis on economic regionalism made manifest in the 1994 formation of the North American Free Trade Agreement.[46]

Lack of a counterfactual makes it impossible either to validate or refute the theory of hegemonic stability, but Eichengreen's empirical examination of the theory, the supportive commentary of other economists and political scientists, and the theoretical writings of Olson and others lend considerable support to its validity. For these reasons, even though the hegemonic stability theory (HST) does not provide a foolproof account of the eras of British and American leadership of the world economy, it does hold up quite well by the standards of the social sciences, including economics.

GOVERNANCE OF THE GLOBAL ECONOMY

Creation of effective international regimes and solutions to the compliance problem require both strong international leadership and an effective international governance structure. Regimes in themselves cannot provide governance structure because they lack the most critical component of governance—the power to enforce compliance. Regimes must rest instead on a political base established through leadership and cooperation. Although many liberal scholars consider the concepts of hegemony and of regimes to be incompatible or even opposed to one another, regimes governing economic affairs cannot function without a strong leader or hegemon. The theory of hegemonic stability posits that the leader or hegemon facilitates international cooperation and prevents defection from the rules of the regime through use of side payments (bribes), sanctions, and/or other means

[45] Ibid, 125.

[46] Robert E. Baldwin attributes the decline in U.S. support for a multilateral system and the shift to regionalism to the loss of hegemony. See Robert Baldwin, "Changes in the Global Trading System: A Response to Shifts in National Economic Power," in Dominick Salvatore, ed., *Protectionism and World Welfare* (New York: Cambridge University Press, 1993), Chapter 4.

but can seldom, if ever, coerce reluctant states to obey the rules of a liberal international economic order.

The American hegemon did indeed play a crucial role in establishing and managing the world economy following World War II; strong support and cooperation were provided by the Cold War allies of the United States. Moreover, as Downs and Rocke point out, regime compliance ultimately is dependent on domestic support. Post–World War II regimes rested on what John Ruggie called "the compromise of embedded liberalism," in which governments may and do intervene in their domestic economies to promote full employment but must also conform to internationally agreed-upon rules.[47] Postwar trade liberalization was politically acceptable because governments pursued policies to guarantee full employment and to compensate those harmed by the opening of national markets to international trade. Solution of the governance problem was, for decades, achieved through leadership, international cooperation, and domestic consensus.[48]

The idea that a liberal international economy requires strong political leadership by the dominant economic power was initially set forth by Charles Kindleberger in *The World In Depression, 1929–1939* (1973).[49] According to Kindleberger, the scope, depth, and duration of the Great Depression were more severe because there was no leader to carry out several tasks necessary for the world economy to function properly. Some of these tasks must be performed even in normal times; others are needed in a crisis. In normal times a leader must (1) maintain the flow of capital to poor countries, (2) provide some order in foreign exchange rates, at least among the key currencies, and (3) arrange for at least moderate coordination of macroeconomic policies among the leading economies. In times of crisis, the leader, in Kindleberger's words, must provide "open markets for distressed goods in depression and be a source of extra-supply when goods are tight, as in the oil crises of 1973 and 1979. The economic leader must also be a 'lender of last resort' in the event of a serious international financial

---

[47] John Gerard Ruggie, "International Regimes, Transactions, and Change: Embedded Liberalism in the Postwar Economic Order," in Stephen D. Krasner, ed., *International Regimes*, 195–231.

[48] Governance involves the establishment and operation of social institutions or sets of rules that guide the interaction of actors. This definition is set forth in Oran Young, ed., *Global Governance: Drawing Insights from the Environmental Experience* (Cambridge: MIT Press, 1997).

[49] Charles P. Kindleberger, *The World In Depression, 1929–1939* (Berkeley: University of California Press, 1973).

crisis. Lacking a leading country able and willing to discharge these functions, financial crises can be followed by prolonged depressions as happened in the 1930s. In short, the functions of the leader are capital lending, creation of a foreign-exchange regime, macroeconomic coordination, maintaining open markets, and being the 'lender of last resort.' "[50]

Stephen Krasner and I each appropriated Kindleberger's basic idea that a political leader was needed to create and manage an international liberal economy. However, each of us made several modifications that placed Kindleberger's insight within a state-centric intellectual framework of political analysis and thus fashioned a state-centric version of the theory of hegemonic stability. Both of us used the Greek word "hegemon" rather than "leader" to indicate that at times the leader had to exercise power to achieve its objective of establishing and managing a liberal world economy. A hegemon is defined as the leader of an alliance like that organized by Sparta to defeat the Persian invaders in ancient Greece or by the United States to defeat the Soviets. Whereas Kindleberger argued that the leader created a liberal international economy for both its own and cosmopolitan economic reasons, Krasner and I have both argued that the hegemon created a liberal international economy primarily to promote its own interests and its political/security interests in particular. Both of us have acknowledged that these security interests could also include the economic and military interests of allies.

When the United States played a central role in promoting an open and interdependent international economy (composed mainly of the United States and its allies) in order to strengthen the anti-Soviet alliance, America's motives were hardly altruistic. Nevertheless, despite the differences between Kindleberger's liberal version of the hegemonic stability theory and the Krasner/Gilpin state-centric version, both approaches maintain that provision of such international public goods as free trade and monetary stability requires a dominant power with an interest in a liberal world economy and a willingness to expend economic and political resources to achieve and maintain that goal.

The theory of hegemonic stability maintains that there can be no liberal international economy unless there is a leader that uses its resources and influence to establish and manage an international economy based on free trade, monetary stability, and freedom of cap-

---

[50] Charles P. Kindleberger, *The World Economy and National Finance in Historical Perspective* (Ann Arbor: University of Michigan Press, 1995), 62.

ital movement. The leader must also encourage other states to obey the rules and regimes governing international economic activities. The theory assumes that a liberal international economy requires that certain "public goods" will be promoted by the leader. A public good, as originally defined by Paul Samuelson, has the properties of "nonexcludability" (inclusiveness) and nonrivalrous consumption. This rather obtuse jargon means that any individual's consumption of a public good does not affect (decrease) consumption of the good by others, and that no one can be prevented from consuming the good whether or not he or she has paid for it. A lighthouse, of benefit to every ship whether or not the ship has contributed to the upkeep of the lighthouse, fulfills such criteria. In such a situation, individuals (and individual nations) have an incentive to free ride—to take advantage of the public good without paying for it—since no one can be excluded from enjoying the good. This means that public goods will generally be undersupplied because few actors will have an incentive to pay the costs of providing such goods.[51]

The public goods associated with a liberal international economy include an open trading system and a stable international monetary system. However, there are even greater tendencies toward free riding and for international public goods to be undersupplied within the international economy than in domestic affairs. This problem can, at least in theory, be overcome by a small group of cooperating states; however, I know of no example of this type of cooperation on such a large scale as the world economy. In practice, public goods have been and can be provided only by a leader (or hegemon) with an interest in supplying the good for all or in forcing others to share payment for the good.

A brief examination of the British and American eras of international leadership increases comprehension of the dynamics of the rise and erosion of a liberal world economy; both eras of economic liberalism required a hegemonic power. From the mid-nineteenth century to the outbreak of World War I, Great Britain led the efforts for trade liberalization and monetary stability; the United States has led the world economy since World War II.[52] The liberal world economy in

[51] For the case of international money, consult Paul De Grauwe, *International Money: Post-War Trends and Theories* (Oxford: Clarendon Press, 1989), 2

[52] My interest in the relationship between the structure of the international political system and the nature of the international economy was first aroused by my reading of E. H. Carr, *The Twenty Years' Crisis, 1919–1939: An Introduction to the Study of International Relations* (London: Macmillan, 1951). In this classic study of the collapse of the open world economy at the outbreak of World War I and the subsequent inabil-

the late nineteenth century was truly global and was generally characterized by nondiscrimination in trade, unrestricted capital movements, and a stable monetary system based on the gold standard. For decades the American system was composed only of the Free World; during the Cold War it was characterized by trade discrimination, by capital controls until the 1970s, and by monetary instability after 1971. Whereas the British promoted and inspired free trade by example and through a series of bilateral agreements, the United States has championed trade liberalization through multilateral negotiations within the GATT. Although there is disagreement on this subject, according to Joanne Gowa, security concerns did influence British trade policy.[53] Certainly, international security considerations—forging the Western alliance against the Soviet Union—played an extremely important role in America's promotion of free trade.[54] In the monetary realm, the Bank of England played a central role in management of the gold standard in the nineteenth-century system. However, even though the post–World War II international monetary system has been based on the dollar and subject to American influence, the Federal Reserve has had to share pride of place with the German Bundesbank and other powerful central banks.

British economic decline began in the late nineteenth century as other countries, especially Germany and the United States, industrialized; Britain responded with a gradual retrenchment of its global position and initiation of numerous measures to strengthen its security.[55] Although Great Britain modified a number of its economic policies, its huge dependence on trade forestalled a retreat into protectionism. Nevertheless, British leadership in trade liberalization did slacken,

---

ity of a weakened Great Britain to re-create a liberal international economy after the war, Carr demonstrated that a liberal world economy must rest on a dominant liberal power. Under the Pax Britannica, Great Britain used its power and influence to create an open world economy in which markets largely determined trade flows and economic outcomes. As the power of Great Britain waned in the latter decades of the century and finally collapsed in the interwar years, the fortunes of an open, liberal international economy suffered. In the absence of British leadership, the 1930s were characterized by economic conflicts among the great powers and the fragmentation of the world economy into spheres of influence dominated by one or another of these great powers.

[53] Gowa, *Allies, Adversaries, and International Trade.*

[54] From a strictly economic perspective, the United States after the war could have exploited its dominant economic position by imposing an optimum tariff on imports into its economy. Instead, it chose multilateralism, mainly for political reasons. One could say that the collective good provided by the American hegemon was the security of its allies.

[55] Robert Gilpin, *War and Change in World Politics* (New York: Cambridge University Press, 1981).

and by the 1930s Britain had retreated to a system of imperial preferences applied to the colonial empire and Commonwealth members.
As early as the mid-1970s, American political leaders, business interests, and scholars expressed strong concerns over the relative decline
and deindustrialization of the American economy caused by foreign
competition, principally from the Japanese. Such worries produced
the New Protectionism. As formal tariffs were reduced through trade
negotiations, the United States erected such nontariff barriers as those
embedded in the Multi-Fiber Agreement (1973), in which many
nations were assigned quotas; the United States also imposed "voluntary" export restraints on Japanese products. Responding to the ballooning American trade deficit, intensifying fears of deindustrialization, and rising protectionist pressures, the Reagan Administration in
the mid-1980s significantly modified America's commitment to multilateralism. It began to pursue a multitrack trade policy that has not
only deemphasized multilateral negotiations but also increased unilateralism and bilateralism (especially "managed trade" with Japan)
along with economic regionalism through the North American Free
Trade Agreement with Canada and Mexico.

Conclusion

Although the science of economics is a necessary foundation for comprehension of international political economy, this book focuses attention on the interaction of markets and political actors. Economics
alone is an inaccurate and insufficient tool for analysis of such vital
issues as the international distribution of wealth and economic activities, the effects of the world economy on national interests, and the
effectiveness of international regimes. This writer rejects the popular
idea that universal economic laws and powerful economic forces now
rule the global economy. Despite increasing economic globalization
and integration among national economies, it is still necessary to distinguish between national and international economies. Political
boundaries do and will divide the economies and economic policies
of one nation from those of another; political considerations also significantly influence and distinguish economic activities in one country
from the next. States, and other powerful actors as well, use their
power to influence economic activities to maximize their own economic and political interests.

New Economic Theories

A LTHOUGH NEOCLASSICAL economics is extremely useful in static analysis, it does not provide an adequate conceptual framework for the analysis and understanding of economic change and the dynamics of the global economy; for example, it cannot explain the exogenous factors such as changes in taste and technology that are important in understanding the long-term dynamics of an economy. Moreover, as Paul Krugman has observed, the neoclassical approach to economic affairs lacks both a temporal and a spatial dimension and assumes that economic activities take place in an abstract universe devoid of history and geography.[1] As a consequence, it can not adequately analyze the historical development or geographical structure of an economy. Most importantly, despite general agreement in the economics discipline on the significance of technological progress for economic change and long-term growth, neoclassical economics gives inadequate attention to technology and the sources of technological change. Neoclassical economics also ignores the importance of economic and other institutions.[2] Although economists acknowledge that nations must establish rules to govern economic activities, provide a favorable environment for private entrepreneurs, and assist in overcoming market failures, economic analysis gives short shrift to the role of governments and other institutions.

In recent years, a number of economists have developed new theories that help to compensate for the limitations specified above. As a group, these novel and still highly controversial theories—the new growth theory, the new economic geography, and the new trade theory—challenge such fundamental assumptions of neoclassical theory as perfect competition, constant returns to scale, and complete information. These new theories emphasize the importance of oligopolistic competition, economies of scale, and technological innovation, and they also incorporate historical processes, institutions, and spatial re-

[1] Paul R. Krugman, *Geography and Trade* (Cambridge: MIT Press, 1991).
[2] An important analysis of the importance of institutions is Richard R. Nelson and Sidney G. Winter, *An Evolutionary Theory of Economic Change* (Cambridge: Belknap Press of Harvard University, 1982).

lations. They facilitate understanding of a world economy characterized by discontinuities, disequilibria, and profound shifts over time in
the global distribution of wealth and hence of power. The world described by the new theories is one of simultaneous divergence and
convergence among national economies, one in which governments
can and do play a crucial role in economic affairs and in which technological innovation is a central feature. Although the new theories
have certainly not displaced conventional neoclassical economics,
they do challenge many of its assumptions and policy prescriptions,
and in some cases have led to modification of neoclassical principles.
For this writer, the new theories provide important insights into the
dynamics of both domestic and international economies.

Stressing the importance in economic affairs of history, geography,
and sociopolitical institutions, the new theories complement the insights and analytic techniques of a state-centric approach to political
economy. They do, of course, have limitations and do not provide us
with a complete understanding of economic change. As these new
theories either modify or complement mainstream neoclassical economics, I shall begin my discussion with an examination of several
important limitations of neoclassical economics as a tool for understanding the dynamics of the global economy.

CHANGE AND NEOCLASSICAL ECONOMICS

Because neoclassical economics does not consider history and geography when explaining economic affairs, it has limited applicability to
comprehension of the functioning of the economy over time and
across space. Indeed, neoclassical theory generally ignores the changes
in economic, political, and other social structures that inevitably result from economic growth. The discipline's focus on equilibrium actually inhibits understanding of the role of economic forces in the
evolution of the economy.

Neoclassical analyses provide neither a history of the economy nor
an explanation of its evolving nature. However, without a history of
the growth process and its effects on the power and interests of major
actors, it is hardly possible to understand the dynamics of the world
economy. Furthermore, neoclassical economics does not add a great
deal to comprehension of the geographic distribution of economic
activities within and across national economies, the evolution of trading patterns, or the spatial development of the economy. Although
neoclassical economists believe that the territorial distribution of eco-

nomic activities is of little consequence as long as every economy is behaving according to the law of comparative advantage, the question of which countries produce what—potato chips or computer chips—is of the utmost importance to groups, nations, and regions around the world. The geographic distribution of the international division of labor and the ways in which the spatial organization of economic activities change over time are among the most contentious issues in the world economy.

The failure of mainstream economists to give sufficient attention to technological innovation is an especially glaring limitation. In the traditional approach of neoclassical theory, there are several weaknesses: (1) Because technological advance is considered exogenous to the economic system, economists have developed no comprehensive explanation for it; (2) because economists consider technology to be a public good to which everyone has equal access, they do not adequately recognize the importance of monopolies of technology; and (3) because the theory of the production function assumes that economic actors have complete or certain knowledge of and access to available technology, economists frequently fail to integrate uncertainty into their writings.[3] Rather than technology being a public good equally available to all economic actors, in reality national differences in innovation and utilization of technology have become vital determinants of variations in national rates of economic growth, national competitiveness, and international trade patterns. Although there is some effort being made to incorporate a more realistic view of technology into neoclassical economics, such efforts have not gone far enough.

Many economists acknowledge that institutions (social, political, economic) do play a role in the outcome of economic activities; however, their emphasis on the market leads many, and maybe most, to ignore the significance of institutions. Even those who do take institutions seriously give little attention to their origins and functions. Explaining institutions as resulting from the attempts of rational individuals to maximize their interests, neoclassical institutionalists, for example, generally overlook the role of chance events and ideology in the origins of economic and other institutions. New insights provided by the concepts of path dependence and cumulative processes explain how historical accidents and nonrational events can have a

---

[3] Maurice Fitzgerald Scott, *A New View of Economic Growth* (Oxford: Clarendon Press, 1989), 72–74, 94.

powerful impact on the evolution of those institutions that shape economic affairs.[4] Although the new concepts attempt to overcome the inherent limitations of neoclassical theories, they have by no means overturned the basic theories or the assumptions of conventional economics.

WORLD VIEW OF THE NEW THEORIES

As Paul Krugman has argued, the new trade, growth, and other economic theories have profound implications for the analysis and functioning of the international economy. They provide a "world view of economics" very different from most of pre-1980 theory; they include increasing returns and imperfect competition, multiple equilibria, a crucial role for history, accident, and self-fulfilling prophecy. In this new and still controversial economic universe, there are arbitrary and accidental components that affect international economics.[5]

As a group, the new theories introduce both spatial and temporal dimensions into economic analysis, place technological innovation at the center of their analyses, and assign a prominent role in the economy to such institutions as national governments and corporations. The "new endogenous growth theory," "new economic geography," and "new strategic trade theory" have important implications for the study of international political economy.

Based on the fundamental behavioral assumption of neoclassical economics that society is composed of rational individuals whose primary purpose is to maximize their interests, these new theories depart from conventional neoclassical economics as they (1) assume that there are imperfect or oligopolistic markets, (2) emphasize the importance of technological innovation, and (3) utilize history or path dependence as an explanatory variable. Together, these novel theories remain highly controversial, and the evidence supporting them cannot be characterized (to use the language of economists) as "robust." With this caveat in mind, what are the common elements in the three theories that make them important for the study of international political economy?

Institutions, Scale Economies, and Imperfect Competition

All three theories—the new growth theory, the new economic geography, and the new trade theory—are based on the assumption of im-

[4] W. Brian Arthur, "Path Dependence in the Economy," *Scientific American* (February 1990): 92–99.
[5] Krugman, *Geography and Trade*, 8–9

perfect or oligopolistic competition in which markets are dominated by a few large firms. These new theories depict the economy as basically oligopolistic because of increasing returns to scale, cumulative processes, or some other market imperfections. They recognize the existence of powerful actors with some control over market forces. Indeed, especially in the leading technological sectors, a relatively small number of large firms, such as Siemens, Microsoft, and Matsushita, actually dominate the market.

The new theories have all been strongly influenced by research developments in the field of industrial organization. This research, which emphasizes the importance of scale economies and of imperfect competition in the organization of industrial sectors and the overall economy, challenges the assumption that all economic processes are characterized by constant returns and perfect competition. Conventional theory, for example, argues that if a firm doubles the input of both capital and labor, the output of the firm will only double and will, at some point, produce diminishing returns; this assumption places limits on an individual firm's capacity to dominate a market. If, on the other hand, scale economies and increasing returns to scale do exist, doubling both inputs would more than double the output and therefore would increase the firm's productivity. Consequently, in an industry characterized by increasing returns, a firm with a head start can increase its output and decrease its average costs much more rapidly than competitors just beginning production. Indeed, such a cost advantage could enable an existing domestic firm to establish a monopolistic market position; also, the region or nation in which such oligopolistic firms are located could itself grow more rapidly than other regions and nations. In time, the region/nation with oligopolistic firms could surpass and eventually dominate other regions or nations. In this way, the new theories have profound implications for the study of international political economy.

Technological Innovation

The new theories emphasize strongly the importance of technological developments for economic growth, the spatial location of economic activities, and international competitiveness. Technological innovation has become the primary determinant of economic growth in advanced economies and also of international competitiveness among industrialized economies. In fact, these new theories permit one to consider technology or knowledge as a separate factor of production. The growth rates of national economies, the patterns of international trade, and the overall structure of the international economy have

107

become increasingly dependent upon a nation's technological capabilities. The increased importance of technological innovation in turn has given every government a strong interest in the technological strength of its economy and has stimulated "technonationalism"—efforts by governments to prevent diffusion of their most important technologies. Competition among national economies for technological superiority has become a major feature of the international political economy.

History and Geography

The economic universe portrayed by the new theories is very different from that encountered in formal economic theories where the "economy" of neoclassical economists occupies neither time nor space and the equations that define the neoclassical economy and determine market equilibrium are solved simultaneously in a timeless void. What we noneconomists recognize as the economy—that is, a geographic space with a name like the American economy or the British economy—finds no place in formal economic theory. Neoclassical economists assume that the national economy is nothing more than a dimensionless point in space and the international economy is only a set of interconnected points.[6]

THE NEW THEORIES

The newer theories assume that history and geography are crucial to the definition of the nature and functioning of the economy, that the economic past largely determines the economic present, and that economic activities have a distinct spatial and hierarchical structure. They do not share the neoclassical assumption of an economic universe populated by powerless actors dispersed evenly throughout a timeless and dimensionless economic space.

Theory of Endogenous Growth

Possessing important implications for understanding the dynamics of the international political economy, the controversial "new growth theory" (or "theory of endogenous growth") was first set forth by Paul Romer (1986) and Robert Lucas (1988).[7] This theory leads to

[6] Ibid., 2.
[7] Paul M. Romer, "Increasing Returns and Long-Run Growth," *Journal of Political Economy* 94, no. 5 (October 1986): 1002–37; Robert E. Lucas Jr., "On the Mechanics of Economic Development," *Journal of Monetary Economics* 22, no. 1 (July 1988): 3–42.

conclusions that run counter to the ideas of conventional neoclassical economics regarding the role of the state in the economy, the institutional framework of economic activities, and the highly uneven distribution of wealth in the international economy. To appreciate the significance of the new growth theory, it is essential to review the neoclassical theory of long-term economic growth. These contradictory theories disagree on economic policies and the role for governments in economic affairs.

Background. The neoclassical explanation of long-term economic growth is based on formal economic models set forth by Robert Solow in the late 1950s;[8] almost all subsequent work on economic growth has been an elaboration of his pioneering ideas. He argued that economic growth is a product of capital accumulation, labor input, and technical progress.[9] His theory is based on the "neo-classical production function" in which the economic output of an economy is dependent on the quantity of capital and labor employed, and the theory of the production function itself is based on certain critical assumptions. It assumes that there are constant returns to scale and that if the amount of both capital and labor employed in producing a widget are doubled, the output will double; phrased differently, there are *no* increasing returns to scale. Another assumption is that marginal returns diminish over time, that if there is no additional technological progress, and if either the amount of capital is increased while the size of the work force remains stable or vice versa, successive additional investments will produce only decreasing gains in output (the law of diminishing returns).[10] Following this reasoning, economists conclude that the larger the capital stock in place, the smaller the benefit of each increment in capital investment.[11]

The neoclassical theory of economic growth concludes that economic growth, or the rate of growth in output, is a consequence of the rate of increase in labor input, the rate of growth of capital input, and the rate of technical progress, and that accumulation of the fac-

---

[8] The theories are discussed in Jeffrey D. Sachs and Felipe Larrain, *Macroeconomics in the Global Economy* (Englewood Cliffs, N.J.: Prentice-Hall, 1993), Chapter 18.

[9] Ibid., 555–56.

[10] Adam Szirmai, Bart Van Ark, and Dirk Pilat, eds., *Explaining Economic Growth* (Amsterdam: North Holland, 1993), 8.

[11] N. Gregory Mankiw, David Romer, and David N. Weil, "A Contribution to the Empirics of Economic Growth," *Quarterly Journal of Economics* 107, no. 2 (May 1992): 407–37.

tors of production accompanied by technical change accounts for the long-term growth of an economy.[12]

Over the long term, economic growth is dependent upon technological progress, which raises labor productivity and counters the inherent tendency toward diminishing returns.[13] Economists argue that a sustained increase in real GNP must be due either to an increase in the quantity of capital and labor used in production or due to more efficient use of these inputs (e.g., technical and/or organizational progress). Although empirical models of economic growth can determine the contribution of each cause to economic growth, they cannot explain the factors causing the growth of capital, labor, and/or technology.

Neoclassical growth theory leads to the conclusion that government policies can do little to accelerate the long-term rate of economic growth. That rate is determined by what Solow called the "steady state," which is defined as that point in economic growth when capital per worker reaches an equilibrium and remains unchanged. This means that any attempt to accelerate the growth rate of such an economy by increasing the savings rate or the amount of capital investment will have only a slight or transitory effect on the long-term rate of economic growth. A government-induced sustained increase in capital investment, for example, has only a temporary impact on the long-term growth rate. Although the ratio of capital to labor may increase, the marginal product of capital will decline and thus will reduce the effectiveness of the investment. While the government can do some things at the margin, such as increasing the national rate of savings or the supply of "effective" labor, such efforts will not have a major impact over the long term.[14]

Another important implication of the neoclassical growth theory for international affairs derives from the convergence theory or hypothesis. This hypothesis posits that labor productivity and per capita income levels of the relatively less developed countries should over the long run converge or catch up with those of the more developed countries.[15] Due to the technological gap between developed and less developed countries, LDCs can make large productivity gains by bor-

[12] Sachs and Larrain, *Macroeconomics in the Global Economy*, 556.

[13] Shahrokh Fardoust and Ashok Dhareshwar, *Long-Term Outlook for the World Economy: Issues and Projections for the 1990s*, International Economic Analysis Working Paper No. 372 (Washington, D.C.: World Bank, February 1990), 65.

[14] This discussion is based largely on Sachs and Larrain, *Macroeconomics in the Global Economy*.

[15] Fardoust and Dhareshwar, *Long-Term Outlook for the World Economy*, 72.

rowing technology from the technological leaders. Over time, the diffusion of capital, technology, and know-how from rich to poor will enable the less developed countries to increase their rates of economic growth both in absolute terms and in relation to the more advanced economies. Moreover, investment in poor countries should produce more rapid growth and greater increases in output than equivalent investment in rich countries; in the former, there will be higher marginal returns to inputs, while in the latter, marginal returns will decline. Thus, according to convergence theory, the rich will get rich more slowly and the poor will get richer more rapidly so they will gradually converge with one another and income inequalities between rich and poor countries will be eliminated.[16]

Limitations. An important criticism of the neoclassical growth theory focuses on its treatment of technology. Although the theory teaches that technological progress bears the primary responsibility for increases in per capita income over the long run, the theory does not explain the determinants of technological advance. Despite the central importance of technology as the ultimate determinant of long-term economic growth, the theory can explain neither economic change nor innovation.[17] The theory considers technological progress to be exogenous to economic growth and technology to be embodied in capital investment. Moreover, technology is considered a public good to which every firm anywhere in the world has access.

Furthermore, technology (unlike capital and labor) cannot be observed or measured directly, so it must be the residual (or "Solow residual") after the contributions of the other two factors to "total factor productivity" and to overall economic growth have been taken into account.[18] The term "residual," however, is quite misleading. Whereas 12 percent of the doubling of American productivity growth between 1909 and 1949 can be explained by the expansion of capital per worker, the residual or total factor productivity accounted for the other 88 percent increase. Some residual! As Sachs and Larrain have commented, the residual "is really a measure of our ignorance."[19] As a consequence, the neoclassical theory, based on factor accumulation,

[16] Walter Rostow, *Why the Poor Get Richer and the Rich Slow Down: Essays in the Marshallian Long Period* (Austin: University of Texas Press, 1980).

[17] Joseph Stiglitz, "Comments: Some Retrospective Views on Growth Theory," in Peter Diamond, ed., *Growth/Productivity/Unemployment: Essays to Celebrate Bob Solow's Birthday* (Cambridge: MIT Press, 1990), 50–68.

[18] Ibid., 556.

[19] Sachs and Larrain, *Macroeconomics in the Global Economy*, 556.

can explain only a small portion of what it purports to explain. For example, the theory cannot explain the persistently large gap in wealth between rich and poor countries.[20] Despite these serious limitations, and lacking any satisfactory alternative, the neoclassical theory is considered by most economists to be generally correct because it does what it is meant to do.[21]

Another criticism is that the original theory neglected human capital and knowledge skills. Work by Edward Denison and others demonstrated the crucial role of education in economic growth and hence the importance of investment in human capital.[22] Other studies have indicated that, due to positive investment externalities, investment in physical and human capital may contribute more to economic growth than the original neoclassical theory suggested; although investment improves the productivity of the investing firm, technological and other spillovers can also benefit other national firms and even the entire economy. For example, such positive externalities may explain why, since World War II, the return on capital investment in the industrialized countries has been much greater than neoclassical theory had predicted. Research in industrial organization, which emphasizes the importance of increasing returns to scale and the crucial role of research and development (R & D), has raised doubts about the basic assumptions of neoclassical growth theory. These ideas and others have been incorporated by Romer and Lucas into the new (endogenous) theory of economic growth.

The New Endogenous Growth Theory. Technological innovation and advances in knowledge are at the core of the differences between the neoclassical model and the new endogenous growth theory.[23] Whereas the neoclassical model builds on only two factors of production, (labor and capital), treats technology or knowledge as an exogenous factor, and assumes that progress in technology is produced by random scientific and technological breakthroughs, the new theory

[20] Maurice Obstfeld and Kenneth Rogoff, *Foundations of International Macroeconomics* (Cambridge: MIT Press, 1996), 473.

[21] Mankiw, Romer, and Weil, "A Contribution to the Empirics of Economic Growth."

[22] Cited in Sachs and Larrain, *Macroeconomics in the Global Economy*, 558.

[23] Many, if not most, of the central ideas in the new growth theory had been set forth earlier by other economists, including Joseph Schumpeter, Kenneth Arrow, Christopher Freeman, Richard Nelson, and Sidney Winter. A valuable history and critique of the theory is in Richard Nelson, "How New Is New Growth Theory?" *Challenge* 40, no. 5 (September/October 1997): 29–58. Nelson himself attributes much of the new thinking about economic growth to Moses Abramovitz.

incorporates technological progress and advances in knowledge as endogenous factors within the growth model. Technological advance is considered endogenous because technological innovations are the result of conscious investment decisions taken by entrepreneurs and individual firms. Firms are assumed to invest in research and development activities for the same reasons that they invest in other factors of production; that is, on the basis of the expected profitability of the investment. In effect, the new growth theory assumes that knowledge, technology, and/or "know-how" constitute a separate factor of production in addition to capital and labor.

The concept of knowledge or technology as a separate factor of production has important implications for understanding economic growth. Knowledge of how to do or make things can raise the productivity of the other two factors. Whereas knowledge and technology just happen in the neoclassical model, the new theory assumes that they result from conscious decisions and that technological advance is largely market-driven. Investment in capital and knowledge can stimulate and reinforce one another in a "virtuous circle" of cumulative causation so that acceleration in the rate of capital investment can raise the long-term growth in per capita income. In addition, whereas neoclassical growth theory is based on the assumption of constant returns to scale, the new theory is based on the existence of "economies of scale." Thus, whereas neoclassical theory predicts that the rate of long-term growth will decline because of diminishing returns, the new theory postulates that the possibility of increasing returns means that the growth rate need not decline.

The new growth theory is important because it permits or even encourages the use of government policies to increase the long-term rate of economic growth. Whereas neoclassical theory assumes that diminishing returns eventually place an upper limit on the returns to capital accumulation and hence on the long-term rate of economic growth, the new growth theory assumes that increasing returns to scale and positive investment economies can lead to an increased growth rate, especially in high-tech sectors. Whereas the neoclassical theory regards the savings rate as having only a modest effect on the long-term growth rate and technology as exogenous, endogenous growth theory suggests that government policies, through promotion of an increased national savings and investment rate and also increased support for R & D, can lead to a sustained higher rate of economic growth.

Romer makes several important points regarding the new growth theory:

(1) Investment in knowledge-creation and R & D activities by profit-seeking entrepreneurs is an important determinant of economic growth.

(2) While the results of R & D are partially captured or appropriated by the investing firm, some of the results are not captured but spill over and constitute public goods that can be exploited by other firms, thus stimulating economic and productivity growth throughout an economy.

(3) Nevertheless, most of the benefits of the new technology are captured by the investing firm and give it a competitive advantage over its rivals; this can lead to an oligopolistic market.

(4) Firms tend to underinvest in R & D, and governments should take appropriate actions to overcome this market failure.

(5) A nation's human capital and skills determine its long-term growth rate and its success in economic development.[24]

The new growth theory has many important implications for the nature of the economy and the status of neoclassical economics. The new theory is inconsistent with the fundamental assumption in neoclassical economics of perfect competition; that is, the belief that firms are "price-takers" because prices are determined by the market and firms cannot easily change the prices they charge. Although neoclassical theory assumes that if a firm should lower its price to increase its market share and should also increase its production, the increased output will not lead to economies of scale but only to lost profits; the new growth theory assumes that because increasing returns are possible, increasing output lowers unit costs and the firm can therefore increase its profit. And this means that the firm is a "price setter" rather than a "price-taker." To the extent that the new growth theory is correct, the market must be viewed as an imperfect or oligopolistic market rather than as a perfect one.

The new growth theory has engendered considerable controversy within the economics profession. Some critics charge that there is nothing especially novel about the new theory, asserting that its authors have merely codified in their model the technological innovation, monopolistic pricing, and increasing returns that have long been familiar to economists. Other critics argue that the traditional variables of growth such as capital investment and increases in the labor supply have far greater explanatory power than the new theory sug-

---

[24] Paul M. Romer, "Endogenous Technological Change," *Journal of Political Economy* 98, no. 5 (October 1990): S71.

gests.[25] Although Solow himself has praised the new growth theory, he believes that the theoretical foundations underlying the theory are simply not credible; the absence or presence of diminishing returns, he points out, is difficult to test. Arguing that the forces governing economic growth "are complex, mostly technological, and even a little mysterious," Solow has commented that economists are ignorant of the forces propelling the growth process and thus are incapable of providing governments with policy advice that would enable them to raise substantially the national rate of economic growth.[26] Perhaps, I would add, one cannot improve significantly on Keynes's attribution of economic growth to the existence of "animal spirits."

Despite the controversy surrounding the new growth theory, Elhanan Helpman's conclusion that it is an important complement to the neoclassical theory does appear warranted.[27] As he argues, few of the variations in economic growth among national economies are explained by the neoclassical formulation, which has been primarily concerned with capital accumulation. Romer and Lucas, on the other hand, rely on the proposition that "learning by doing" can result in decreasing costs and scale economies. They have applied this important idea to the accumulation of knowledge and human capital, and this, Helpman believes, may be their most important contribution. Romer and Lucas have taken the view that aggregate production exhibits increasing returns to scale, and they have noted that some of those returns accrue to a specific economic sector rather than just to an individual firm. The inability of a firm to monopolize all the results of its investment in R & D and the presence of spillovers mean that the social rate of return on such investment is more than twice the private rate of return. Thus, by combining imperfect competition or economies of scale with learning by doing and innovation, Helpman argues, Romer and Lucas have developed a model that helps explain long-term growth in per capita income.

The implications of the new theory for economic policy are very important. As Helpman suggests, the new theory means that public policy can significantly increase the rate of economic growth. In the new growth theory, technical progress is recognized as being profit-motivated, endogenous, and driven by the investment rate. The rate of innovation and hence of economic growth can be increased by

[25] N. Gregory Mankiw, "The Growth of Nations," Brookings Papers on Economic Activity No. 1 (Washington, D.C.: Brookings Institution, 1955).

[26] Robert Solow, IMF Survey, 16 December 1991, 378.

[27] Elhanan Helpman, "Endogenous Macroeconomic Growth Theory," European Economic Review 36, nos. 2/3 (April 1992): 237–67.

appropriate industrial and government policies that increase expenditures on knowledge creation, research and development, and such human capital formation as education and training. To the extent that government policies can facilitate creation of new knowledge and technology, there will be an effect on the distribution of wealth and power within the global economy. Some economists and political economists have applied the new economic theory to explain the rapid industrialization of the dynamic Pacific Asian economies.

Another important implication of the new growth theory is that political, economic, and other institutions—from governments to universities to corporations—can either hinder or facilitate technical advance and hence long-term economic growth. Differing from the neoclassical economics assertion that free markets tend to produce efficient outcomes, the new growth theory suggests that national economic structures, institutions, and public policies are major determinants of technological developments and economic growth. In fact, long before the new growth theory was formulated by Romer and Lucas, a number of economists and political economists had engaged in pioneering work on the determinants of innovative activities and the diffusion of technical knowledge in the production process. Among the most important contributors to an understanding of "national systems of innovation" are Christopher Freeman, Richard Nelson, and Keith Pavitt, whose writings have demonstrated the crucial role of technological advance in economic growth and the dynamics of economic systems.[28]

The new theory's emphasis on human capital as the key to economic growth weakens convergence theory, and this has significance for the nature and dynamics of the global economy. The new growth theory suggests that under some conditions, an initial advantage of one country over another in human capital will result in a permanent difference in income level between the countries. As Jeffrey Sachs and Felipe Larrain have pointed out, when human capital endowment is important, a rich country can maintain its lead indefinitely over poorer countries by generating sufficient new savings and investment.[29] According to the theory, the rich will get richer, the poor—unless they invest in human capital—will continue to lag behind, and the international economy will continue to be characterized by large

[28] Richard R. Nelson, *High Technology Policies: A Five-Nation Comparison* (Washington, D.C.: American Enterprise Institute, 1984); and Christopher Freeman, Raymond Poignanat, and Ingvar Svnnilson, *Science, Economic Growth, and Government Policy* (Paris: OECD, 1963).

[29] Sachs and Larrain, *Macroeconomics in the Global Economy*, 579–80.

inequalities among nations. Thus, the new growth theory implies that the uneven growth of national economies, rather than their convergence, is the characteristic pattern of the global economy.

To summarize, the new growth theory has important implications for political economy and for the structure of both international and domestic economies. It implies that the rate of economic growth in advanced economies need not decline, convergence between rich and poor is not automatic, imperfect or oligopolistic competition will appear in many industries (especially high-tech industries) due to increasing returns, and government policies can have a major and positive impact on an economy's long-term rate of economic growth. If, as the theory assumes, there are increasing returns to scale, economies do not inevitably reach a steady state of economic growth; rather, deliberate policy decisions by governments can encourage continued capital accumulation and result in a higher rate of self-sustaining economic growth.[30]

The New Economic Geography

Another new theory important to the study of international political economy (IPE) is "the new economic geography" (NEG).[31] The central question addressed by NEG is, Why do economic activities, especially in particular industries, tend to be heavily concentrated in certain geographic locations—cities or regions—and why do these concentrations generally persist over very long periods? Indeed, the existence and endurance of certain regional concentrations of economic activities provide a startling aspect of the geography of economic life. Regional economic clusters and their persistence cannot normally be explained by the neoclassical emphasis on factor endowments. Although the principle of comparative advantage argues that the location of an industry will be determined principally by factor endowments, factor endowments do not and cannot explain the location of many important industries. Although NEG does not deny the relevance of comparative advantage or the economics of location, it does argue that noneconomic factors, path dependence, chance, and cumulative processes frequently account for the origins and concen-

---

[30] Ibid., 571.

[31] This section is based on Krugman, *Geography and Trade*, and other writings by Krugman. Many of the key ideas on the spatial nature of economic activities have long been stressed by noneconomists, especially regional geographers. Two of Krugman's major contributions were to explain spatial concentrations through the use of a model based on economies of scale and to introduce these ideas into the mainstream of economics.

tration of manufacturing and many other economic activities in particular locations.[32]

The persistence of regional concentrations of economic activities or the core/periphery model of the structure of an economy has long been of great interest to Marxists, dependency theorists, and other scholars on the political left who attribute the core/periphery structure to capitalist imperialism and exploitation. While some conservative scholars have acknowledged the prevalence of the core/periphery structure, they have been unable to provide, or have been uninterested in providing, a satisfactory economic explanation of the universal tendency toward economic agglomeration. Although economic geographers have long been interested in the spatial organization of economic activities, their theories have unfortunately been ignored by economists and have not been incorporated into economics nor sufficiently integrated within the political economy literature. In the late twentieth century, some economists did attempt to explain the core/periphery structure of the economy through the new economic geography. Their explanation has considerable relevance for the study of IPE.[33]

According to NEG, the initial location and concentration of economic activities in a particular region is frequently a matter of mere chance or historical accident. However, once an industry or economic activity is established, cumulative forces and feedback mechanisms can lead to continued concentration of economic activities in that region for an extended period of time. Self-reinforcing processes mean that the evolution of a regional economy and its structure are largely determined by what Brian Arthur and Paul David have labeled the phenomenon of path dependence.[34] According to this simple but powerful idea, the historical past and cumulative processes largely deter-

---

[32] Most geographers undoubtedly characterize the new economic geography as the rediscovery of the wheel. Much that Krugman and others have written has already appeared in the literature of geography and is another example of the failure of economists to explore what historians and other social scientists have written. A valuable critique of the new economic geography by a geographer is Ron Martin, "The New 'Geographical' Turn in Economics," *Cambridge Journal of Economics* 23, no. 1 (January 1999): 65–91. A commentary on the slighting of geography by Krugman appears in *The Economist*, 13 March 1999, 92.

[33] The literature on core/periphery economic structures is extensive. A useful survey is in Arie Shachar and Sture Oberg, eds., *The World Economy and the Spatial Organization of Power* (Aldershot, U.K.: Avebury 1990).

[34] An important discussion of path dependence is in W. Brian Arthur, "Self-Reinforcing Mechanisms in Economics," in Philip W. Anderson, Kenneth J. Arrow, and David Pines, eds., *The Economy as an Evolving Complex System: The Proceedings of the Evolutionary Paths of the Global Workshop* (published for the Sante Fe Institute, Studies in the Sciences of Complexity, 1988), Vol. 5.

mine the choices available to a decision-maker and the context within which decisions are made. Path dependence thus implies that the economic universe—productive technologies, economic institutions, and the geographic distribution of economic activities—is largely the consequence of many minor random developments. Whereas conventional economics assumes that the magnitude of a cause determines the magnitude of its effect (i.e., there is a linear relationship between the two), path dependence analysis indicates that small, and even very small, causes can give rise to disproportionately large effects.

The important implications of path dependence for neoclassical theory may be illustrated by the theory of the production function. This theory, on which neoclassical growth theory is based, assumes that an entrepreneur selects from the range of available technologies. The rational entrepreneur will select the most efficient combination of factors of production and technological options. The key word here is "available." According to the path dependence idea, many of the technologies available to an entrepreneur are, like economic institutions, the result of random events and are not necessarily the most efficient. Indeed, especially in the area of advanced technologies or high-tech industries, some of the specific technologies available are not particularly efficient. Inferior and less efficient technologies can get locked in and be adopted rather than those that most technical experts would judge to be equal or even superior. An example is the complete victory of the Matsushita VHS standard for a VCR over Sony's equally good, if not superior, Betamax format. However, the most frequently cited example is the layout of the keyboard on a typewriter or a computer. The inefficient QWERTY layout was chosen because the keys of the first typewriters became jammed, and therefore the keyboard was deliberately redesigned to slow the speed of the typist; modern computers operating at nanosecond speeds retain this built-in inefficiency. However, my favorite example is even closer to my heart.

I am writing these lines on a Macintosh computer. It is well known that Macintosh users are fiercely loyal, and I include myself in this number. Any objective observer would have to grant that Macintosh hardware and software are far superior technically to their rivals in the Wintel world (of computers using the Windows operating system and the Intel chip).[35] Yet in the 1980s and 1990s the Macintosh share of the market deteriorated alarmingly, and the future of the company was in serious doubt. The principal reason for this decline does not

[35] "Wintel" refers to Intel computers using the Microsoft operating system.

lie in the technology or the intrinsic quality of the competing products, but in a number of serious marketing and other blunders made by successive Macintosh leaders. The personal computer (PC) gained a great advantage over the Macintosh due to huge economies of scale and decisively lower costs that could be credited in large part to Wintel's overwhelming share of the market; this meant that rational business persons equipping a company were much more likely to purchase Wintel computers than the superior and easier to use Mac.

Path dependence implies that a region or nation can have a dominant position in a particular industry simply for historical reasons. Industry concentration and a nation's trading patterns are not due to factor endowments alone, but may be due to the region's almost accidentally having achieved a head start in an industry. Such a head start has frequently enabled industries in a region to achieve economies of scale and to increase their efficiency through learning by doing, thus establishing and maintaining a decisive lead over potential rivals. There are many examples of industries or economic activities that cluster in a particular region due to an arbitrary event and the effects of path dependence; for example, the production of automobiles in Detroit and the computer industry in Silicon Valley.

The new economic geography substitutes imperfect competition for the neoclassical assumption of constant returns and perfect competition. NEG also assumes factor mobility and falling costs of transportation between the periphery and the core region. The interactions of increasing returns, decreasing transportation costs, and factor mobility can lead to further agglomeration or concentration of economic activities within the core region. Regions with a head start attract industries and economic activities from other regions; supply-and-demand factors reinforce one another, as suppliers want to concentrate near large markets and the concentration of suppliers in the region increases local demand.[36] As these various linkages, positive feedback mechanisms, and cumulative causation interact, over time an economic structure is created. This structure is composed of a dominant core, in which powerful oligopolistic firms are heavily concentrated, and a less developed and economically dependent periphery. The relatively self-sustaining core/periphery geographic structure characterizes all modern economic systems.[37]

---

[36] Krugman, *Geography and Trade*, 71.

[37] For a detailed discussion of the advantages of the core over the periphery, consult Alfred Weber, *Alfred Weber's Theory of the Location of Industry* (Chicago: University of Chicago Press, 1929).

Stated simply, a core/periphery structure is determined primarily by the interaction of scale economies and the costs of transportation.[38] If economies of scale were the only factors involved in the location of industry, one would expect that the world economy as a whole would be characterized by a single or just a few core/periphery structures. Instead, as we know, the world economy and even some large national economies have a number of core regions. This multiple core structure of the international economy is explained primarily by the cost of transportation; reductions in transportation costs tend to increase economic concentration, and increases in transportation costs have the opposite effect. However, additional forces are at work in determining the core/periphery structure. For example, such centrifugal (diffusion or decentralizing) forces as rising wages and land rents in the core encourage industries to move into the lower-cost periphery and thereby counter the centripetal (polarizing, agglomeration, or concentration) forces that pull economic activities inward toward the core. Also, every government engages in deliberate efforts to erect barriers or provide inducements that will make either the centripetal or the centrifugal forces work toward their own advantage. A notable example was Canada's National Policy, which utilized trade barriers to encourage American and other firms to invest in the Canadian economy and to thereby industrialize that country.

A nation that possesses one or more regional cores with strong industries can achieve an overwhelming and continuing competitive superiority over others. A region with a head start in the accumulation of knowledge often widens its productivity lead. The great effects of a head start motivate lagging nations to pursue particular industrial policies, including subsidies, erection of protectionist barriers, and other actions that may help them to catch up and to possess important core regions of their own. Possession of a core region is considered to be of immense political importance because it is associated with high wages, industrial power, and national autonomy.

The above model of regional concentration and diffusion is important to the nature and dynamics of the world economy. It implies that lowering trade or other economic barriers and the ensuing process of economic integration will create a core/periphery structure in which industry and other economic activities will migrate to the core region as barriers are decreased. In effect, increasing economic interdepen-

[38] As Krugman demonstrated in his *Geography and Trade,* the core/periphery structure is explained by the interplay of economic forces and historical developments. Also, see Paul Krugman and Maurice Obstfeld, *International Economics: Theory and Policy* 3d ed. (New York: HarperCollins, 1994), 184–85.

dence among national economies means that many economic activities will concentrate in a small number of regions populated by oligopolistic firms that enjoy economies of scale and/or lower transport and transactions costs. This process explains why uneven development of regions and nations characterizes both national and international economies. This tendency toward a core/periphery structure has profound implications for the future economic structure of Western Europe as internal barriers come down and progress is made toward creation of a single market.

In an increasingly integrated world economy in which core/periphery structures spread across national boundaries, the presence of core regions exclusively controlled by a single nation, and of a periphery composed of other nations, will necessarily lead to economic tensions and even political conflict between the dominant core economy and dependent peripheral economies. Escaping economic dependence and achieving political independence is an objective of every society. Core economies wish to maintain their dominant position, and peripheral economies wish to become core economies in their own right. The efforts of the dependent peripheral economies to escape domination by well-established regional cores, and the efforts of the cores themselves to maintain their dominant position, are crucial factors in the dynamics of the world economy. Thus, growing integration of the world economy has led to increasing efforts by individual nations, threatened regions within those nations, and such interstate regional alliances as the European Union to protect themselves against the centralizing forces of economic globalization. The new economic geography implies that the structure of strong core economies and dependent peripheries will continue to produce economic tensions and occasional political conflict.

Strategic Trade Theory

The new (strategic) trade theory is the culmination of several earlier developments that have modified conventional trade theory, which was based on factor endowments or comparative advantage and was developed in the early 1930s by Eli Heckscher and Bertil Ohlin. This Heckscher-Ohlin (or H-O) model of comparative costs or advantage postulated that a country would specialize in the production and export of those goods or services in which it had a cost advantage over other countries; the model was based on the familiar neoclassical assumptions.

Strategic trade theory (or STT) developed from economists' growing appreciation of imperfect competition, economies of scale, learning by doing, the importance of R & D, cumulative processes, and technological spillovers.[39] STT challenges the theoretical foundations of the economics profession's previously unequivocal commitment to free trade. In fact, the development of STT was stimulated by growing dissatisfaction with conventional trade theory's inability to explain trade patterns and by concern about the increasing trade problems of the United States, especially with Japan in the 1980s. The application to trade theory of novel methods associated with important theoretical advances in the field of industrial organization provided the means to develop an alternative to the H-O theory. Mathematical models of imperfect competition and game theoretic models had been incorporated into trade theory in the early 1980s by James Brander and Barbara Spencer (1983), theorists of industrial organization, and by the work of international trade theorists Avinash Dixit, Gene Grossman, and Paul Krugman.[40]

The theory of strategic trade provides a rationale for nations to use protectionist measures, for subsidies to particular industries, and for other forms of industrial policy to provide domestic firms with a decisive advantage in both home and world markets. Favored and protected firms can take advantage of increasing returns, cumulative processes, and the positive feedbacks associated with path dependence to increase their competitiveness in global markets.

The significance of strategic trade theory can be appreciated through consideration of the fundamental differences between perfect and imperfect competition. In those sectors where there is perfect competition (i.e., most of the economy), the behavior of one small firm cannot change the rules of the game, as it is too small to make a difference. This means that a small firm could not gain advantage through strategic behavior. However, if unit costs in certain industries continue to fall as output increases, output will expand and the number of firms in the market will decrease. Economies of scale in an industry mean that the market will support only one or just a few large firms; that is, such an industry will become oligopolistic, as happened in the automobile and computer sectors. Thus, the market will

---

[39] For an important collection of articles on imperfect competition and other aspects of these matters, see Gene M. Grossman, ed., *Imperfect Competition and International Trade* (Cambridge: MIT Press, 1992).

[40] James A. Brander and Barbara J. Spencer, "International R&D Rivalry and Industrial Strategy," *Review of Economic Studies* 50, no. 163 (October 1983): 707–22. An excellent discussion of these theoretical developments is in Paul R. Krugman, ed., *Strategic Trade Policy and the New International Economics* (Cambridge: MIT Press, 1986).

eventually be dominated by only a few firms, and this means that their behavior can make a difference and alter the decisions of other firms. If there is imperfect or oligopolistic competition in particular economic sectors, then monopoly rents or abnormally high profits can exist in that sector, and these rents or superprofits can be captured by a few firms or even by just one firm.[41]

The central idea of the new strategic trade theory (STT) is that firms and governments can behave strategically in imperfect global markets and thereby improve a country's balance of trade and national welfare. It assumes that some markets are characterized by imperfect or oligopolistic competition, and that this situation can create a strategic environment in which there is only a small number of players. Oligopolistic firms can and do consciously choose a course of action that anticipates the behavior of their competitors. If successful, this enables them to capture a much larger portion of the market than would be possible under conditions of perfect competition. Two of the most important strategies used to increase a firm's long-term domination of an oligopolistic market are dumping (selling below cost to drive out competitors in the product area) and preemption (making huge investments in productive capacity to deter others from entering the market).

Imperfect or oligopolisitc competition is most likely to occur in certain high-tech industries characterized by economies of scale and learning by doing. These include the aerospace, advanced materials, computer and semiconductor, and biochemical industries; these technologies, of course, are identified by all governments as the commanding heights of the information economy. Most of them are dual technologies, since they are of particular importance both to military weaponry and to economic competitiveness. Therefore, many nations consider it essential, for both commercial and security reasons, to take actions that will ensure that they have as strong a capability as possible in such technologies.

The device of preclusive investment provides an example of the application of strategic trade theory; in such a situation, investment by a domestic firm in a protected home market can give the firm an overwhelmingly competitive position within that economy, a position that can deter investment by other countries in that industrial sector. Government policies may provide a national firm with decisive advantages in global markets; indeed, Henry Rosovsky and other economists have argued that the strategy of "import protection in order to

---

[41] A monopoly rent is an excess return on a resource.

export" accounts in part for Japanese industrial success in the decades after World War II.[42] STT implies that a government can assist a firm to establish a monopolistic or oligopolistic position in world markets. For example, in a market capable of sustaining only a limited number of producers, a state subsidy to a domestic firm may deter foreign firms from entering the home or even foreign markets and thereby confer on subsidized firms a dominant or monopolistic position. Various strategic trade tactics have become important in the efforts of national governments to influence the location of industry worldwide.

STT clearly implies that governments should assist national firms in order to generate positive externalities (that is, technological spillovers) and also to shift profits from foreign firms to national firms.[43] Economists have long appreciated that a nation with sufficient market power could impose an optimum tariff and thereby shift the terms of trade in its favor.[44] By restricting imports and decreasing the demand for a product, a large economy may be able to cause the price of the imported good to fall. STT, however, goes much farther than optimum tariff theory in its recognition of a nation's ability to intervene effectively in trade matters and thus to gain disproportionately. A government's decision to support a domestic firm's plans to increase its productive capabilities (preemption) or to signal an intention to build excess productive capacity is an example of a strategic trade policy. By using a direct subsidy to a firm or by giving outright protection to a domestic industry, the government might deter foreign firms from entering a particular industrial sector. Since a minimum scale of production is necessary to achieve efficiency, especially in many high-tech industries, the advantage of being first (first-mover advantage) encourages a strategy of preemptive investment. Thus, government intervention through "preemption" or first strike becomes especially important in certain industrial sectors.

The new strategic trade theory departs from conventional trade theory in its assumption that certain economic sectors are more important than others for the overall economy and therefore warrant government support. The manufacturing industries, for example, are considered more valuable than service industries because manufacturing is characterized by higher rates of productivity growth; many be-

---

[42] Henry Rosovsky. "Trade, Japan, and the Year 2000," *New York Times*, 6 September 1985, Sec. 1.

[43] A frequently cited example is Airbus, an aircraft developed by a British-French consortium.

[44] An optimum tariff is one that improves a country's terms of trade to the detriment of its trading partners.

125

lieve that manufacturing also produces higher profits, higher value added, and higher wages. Some economic sectors, especially high-tech industries such as computers, semiconductors, and information processing, are particularly important because they generate spillovers and other positive externalities that benefit the entire economy. Because a new technology in one sector may have indirect benefits for firms in another sector, firms that do extensive research and development produce benefits that are valuable to many others. Indeed, a strategic industry may be defined as one that gives external benefits to the rest of the economy. However, because firms may not be able to capture or appropriate the results of their research and development activities, many will underinvest in these activities. Proponents of STT argue that such a market failure indicates that firms should be assisted through direct subsidy or import protection, particularly in high-tech industries that frequently raise the skill level of the labor force and thus increase human capital. If, as the proponents of strategic trade believe, such special industries exist, then free trade is not optimal and government intervention in trade matters can increase national welfare.

Strategic trade theory has become a highly controversial subject within the economics profession. Some critics argue that it is a clever, flawed, and pernicious idea that gives aid and comfort to proponents of trade protection. Others agree with this negative assessment but also make the point that the theory itself adds nothing really new to already discredited arguments favoring trade protection. Perhaps in response to severe denunciations of strategic trade theory by leading mainstream economists, some of the earliest and strongest proponents of STT have moderated their initial enthusiasm. Many economists consider it to be merely an intellectual game with no relevance to the real world of trade policy. Despite these criticisms and recantations, however, STT has had an important impact on government policy and has undoubtedly been a factor in the slowdown in the growth of world trade.

The neoclassical critique of strategic trade policy is that all industries, at least theoretically, are created equal; no economic sector is intrinsically more valuable than any other in terms of higher value added, higher wages, and so forth. The rate of productivity growth of an economic sector is considered the only real measure of its value and of its contribution to the nation's long-term economic welfare. A nation, therefore, should specialize in those economic sectors where high rates of productivity growth exist and where it has a comparative advantage. This sentiment was expressed in an often-employed statement attributed to Michael Boskin, chair of the Council of Economic Advisors in the Bush Administration (1989–1993) that "chips are chips" and that it is unimportant whether an economy produces one type of chip or the other. If a nation has a comparative advantage in potato chips but not in computer chips, then it should export the former and import the latter. Moreover, even if some economic activities may be intrinsically more valuable than others, critics of strategic trade policy argue that governments are incapable of picking winners and that any efforts to do so are very likely to be captured by special interests. Favoring one sector, the critics charge, would of necessity divert scarce resources and harm other sectors that might be even more valuable to the economy over the long term. Finally, the critics charge that subsidies and trade protection will only lead to foreign retaliation, and then everyone will lose.

What can be concluded about strategic trade theory and the industrial policy to which it provides intellectual support? The argument that shifting profits from one economy to another can occur has neither been proved nor disproved; it is quite difficult to assess whether or not government intervention in oligopolistic markets actually works, because economists lack reliable models of how oligopolists behave. However, the positive externalities argument for strategic trade policy and the arguments for the related industrial policy have support in the economics literature. Even though empirical evidence for the success of industrial policy is admittedly mixed, government support for particular industrial sectors has frequently been very successful in creating technologies in sectors that do spill over into the rest of the economy. Most importantly, there is strong evidence that government support for R & D has a very high payoff for the entire economy. Governments around the world certainly believe that support for high-tech industries produces a high economic return over the long term.

Conclusion

The new economic theories significantly enhance our understanding of the dynamics of the world economy and of the fundamental issues of international political economy regarding distribution of economic outcomes, states' efforts to retain their national autonomy, and conflict among states over the nature of international regimes. The process of economic growth, the concentration of economic activities in particular locations, and the diffusion of economic growth and economic activities to new regions are fundamental elements in the evolution of the world economy. Although market forces are central to these processes, such powerful actors as states and multinational firms constantly attempt to shape markets in ways that advance their own national or corporate interests. The new economic theories have led to recognition that interactions among economic/technological forces and powerful actors lead to shifts in the global distribution of economic activities, changes in comparative advantage and trading patterns among national economies, and ultimately, transformations in the international balance of economic and military power.

CHAPTER SIX

The Political Significance of the New Economic Theories

THE NEW economic theories have a number of significant implications for analysis of the world economy. Even though all three theories remain highly controversial within the economics profession, they nevertheless provide important insights into the nature and dynamics of international economic affairs, and they reinforce the state-centric interpretation of this book. In addition to emphasizing the central role of national governments in economic affairs, the theories emphasize the crucial nature of oligopolistic competition and the importance of technological innovation as determinants of international economic affairs.

NATIONAL GOVERNMENTS AND DOMESTIC ECONOMIES

Although every actor within the modern economy—whether a corporation, an interest group, or whatever—attempts to influence that economy, national governments and their policies are by far the most important determinants of the rules and institutions governing the market. Despite increasing globalization of economic activities, most such activity still takes place within the borders of individual states. Each state establishes limits that determine the movement of goods and other factors into and out of its economy, and through their laws, policies, and numerous interventions in the economy, governments attempt to manipulate and influence the market to benefit their own citizens (or at least some of their citizens) and to promote the national interests of that country. Every state, some more than others, attempts to use its power to influence market outcomes.

The new theories call attention to the importance of national governments and domestic economies within the world economy.[1] They

[1] The theories complement a similar change in scholarship in the field of international political economy, where the role of domestic factors has been given much greater attention in recent scholarship. A pioneering study on the interaction of domestic and international matters is Peter Gourevitch, *Politics in Hard Times: Comparative Responses to International Economic Crises* (Ithaca: Cornell University Press, 1986). An important analysis of the impact of domestic affairs on the international economy is Helen V. Milner, *Interests, Institutions, and Information: Domestic Politics and International Relations* (Princeton: Princeton University Press, 1997).

help explain continuing government intervention in the economy despite the apparent triumph of neoliberalism and increasing globalization. In a world where economic growth, the geographic location of industry, and comparative advantage are frequently produced by arbitrary decisions and cumulative processes, national governments have an almost overwhelming incentive to intervene in their domestic economies. Through industrial, strategic, and other interventionist policies, every nation, to one degree or another, does attempt to affect the international division of labor. There is growing concern within nation-states about which countries produce what and about the location of high-tech jobs and industries; this makes it unlikely that such crucial matters will be left solely to the interplay of market forces. National governments repeatedly attempt to use their political power and their position in the international political system to influence the international division of economic specialization as much as possible.

National leaders are reluctant to leave economic outcomes entirely up to market forces. This is reflected in the considerable differences among national economies regarding the relative importance of the state and the market in national economic structures and outcomes. Economic structures and institutions constitute what Nobel Laureate Douglass C. North has called "the incentive structure of a society," and are powerful determinants of economic performance.[2] Domestic structures also affect the interactions among national economies and between national and international economic affairs.

I shall use the term "national system of political economy" to refer to domestic structures and institutions that influence economic activities. The principal purposes of every national economy shape the defining characteristics of each system; these purposes may range from promotion of consumer welfare to creation and expansion of national power. The role of the state in the economy is a particularly important aspect of each national system; the differences among market economies range from the generally laissez-faire, noninterventionist stance of the United States government to the central role of the Japanese state in management of the economy. Yet, a third feature of a political economy is found in the mechanisms of corporate governance and private business practices; here again, the fragmented American business structure contrasts dramatically with the Japanese system of tightly integrated industrial groupings (the *keiretsu*).

The national system of innovation is another important aspect of a

[2] Douglass C. North, "Economic Performance Through Time," *American Economic Review* 84, no. 3 (June 1994): 359.

particular nation's political economy. When one speaks of a major technological advance or of a technological revolution, much more than nuts and bolts is involved. Many significant developments in technology involve a transformation in the organization of production and of the broader sociopolitical relationships in an economy.[3] Many important aspects of society must be changed in order to develop or take advantage of new technologies or production possibilities. Indeed, some writers use the term "techno-economic paradigm" to designate the whole range of economic and institutional transformations associated with a particular technological change.[4] Successive epochs of technological advance have entailed major transformations in economic behavior and in industrial organization. In today's digital or information age, the world economy is again experiencing a process of "creative destruction" from which new economic winners and losers will emerge, a process aptly described by Joseph Schumpeter as the dynamics of capitalism.

The new growth theory implies that political, economic, and other institutions—from governments to universities to corporations—can either hinder or facilitate technical advance, its adoption, and resultant long-term economic growth. While neoclassical economics maintains that free markets in themselves produce efficient outcomes, the new growth theory suggests that national and international economic structures and institutions are major determinants of technological developments and economic growth. In fact, long before Paul Romer and Robert Lucas set forth the new growth theory, a number of economists and political economists had conducted pioneering work on the determinants of innovative activities and the diffusion of technical knowledge in the production process. Christopher Freeman, Richard Nelson, and Keith Pavitt are among the most important contributors to an understanding of the resulting national systems of innovation.

Nathan Rosenberg and L. Birdzell Jr. have emphasized the crucial importance of the national system of innovation to technological progress in *How the West Grew Rich: The Economic Transformation of the Industrial World*.[5] They demonstrate that the economic growth

---

[3] For example, Japan's innovation of "lean production" was greatly facilitated by important aspects of the Japanese political economy, such as lifetime employment, long-term planning by both Japanese corporations and government, and the domination of the economy by large industrial groupings (*keiretsu*).

[4] Giovanni Dosi, Christopher Freeman, Richard Nelson, Gerald Silverberg, and Luc Soete, eds., *Technical Change and Economic Theory* (London: Pinter, 1988).

[5] Nathan Rosenberg and L. E. Birdzell Jr., *How the West Grew Rich: The Economic Transformation of the Industrial World* (New York: Basic Books, 1986).

131

and the technological success of the West have been due primarily to institutional innovations; the unique economic, political, and other institutions that have characterized the modern West have greatly facilitated technological advance, capital accumulation, and rapid economic growth. It was, Rosenberg and Birdzell point out, the freedom of individual entrepreneurs to experiment with novel institutions and economic arrangements that differentiated the West from other civilizations, and this freedom has been vital to the West's enormous economic success. Economic freedom created a powerful incentive for entrepreneurs to innovate, invest, and accumulate wealth.

Even though the modern state has been central to development of the national system of political economy and technological innovation, the state's role in fostering economic growth and international competitiveness has been largely neglected by neoclassical economics. The emphasis in neoclassical growth theory on factor accumulation is indeed appropriate, but it is only a first approximation to an explanation of the causes of a nation's growth. A particular society's possession of an institutional framework or national system of political economy that facilitates factor accumulation, technological innovation, and economic growth is crucial to its economic success. Those societies that adapt themselves to the requirements of economic growth and technological innovation in a particular epoch become the economic leaders of that epoch, and societies that do not or cannot adjust to such requirements fall behind.

OLIGOPOLY AND POWER IN ECONOMIC OUTCOMES

The economic universe of the new theories is populated by a few important economic actors and characterized by imperfect or oligopolistic competition.[6] In an oligopolistic market, power and strategy strongly affect economic outcomes; consequently, many international markets function differently from the predictions of conventional neoclassical economics. In the world of oligopolistic competition, powerful players can and frequently do use their market power to alter and manipulate the terms of exchange.[7] Indeed, powerful firms are frequently "price-setters" rather than "price-takers." In the neo-

---

[6] The significance of oligopolistic competition for economic theory is discussed in John R. Hicks, *The Crisis in Keynesian Economics* (Oxford: Basil Blackwell, 1974), 23–25.

[7] A collection of articles on the neglect of power in economic analysis is in Kurt W. Rothschild, ed., *Power in Economics: Selected Readings* (Harmondsworth, U.K.: Penguin Books, 1971).

classical world of perfect competition, the self-regulating market reigns and every economic situation has a single equilibrium solution. In an oligopolistic market, there are many possible rational economic outcomes, and power, strategy, and guile are important determinants of each economic outcome. Oligopolies profoundly change the nature and functioning of markets. As an old taunt in the economics profession says, "With oligopoly, anything can happen."[8]

Economists are obviously fully aware of the nature and importance of oligopolistic competition based on economies of scale. Alfred Marshall himself was cognizant of oligopoly but rejected its significance, perhaps because of its implications that increasing returns (and hence oligopoly) would make it theoretically possible for just one or a few firms to dominate an economy. As time has passed, the subject of oligopoly has been taken more seriously, and research in the field of industrial organization on oligopolistic markets has greatly extended understanding of the ways in which oligopolistic markets work. Yet it makes economists quite uncomfortable to recognize that oligopolies do exist.[9] The negative attitude of most economists toward the implications for economic analysis of oligopoly and economies of scale is conveyed in John Hicks's comment that increasing returns result in "the wreckage of the greater part of economic theory."[10] Clearly, there is good reason for economists to find oligopoly and imperfect competition distasteful. However, in political economy, oligopoly and imperfect competition are central concerns.

The world of oligopolistic competition is best comprehended through application of the theory of games (or simply game theory) set forth initially by John von Neumann and Oscar Morgenstern in their classic study, *The Theory of Games and Economic Behavior* (1944).[11] Game theory has become an extraordinarily complex and

---

[8] John Sutton, *Sunk Costs and Market Structure: Price Competition, Advertising, and the Evolution of Concentration* (Cambridge: MIT Press, 1991), xiii.

[9] For example, one important line of inquiry (that regarding contestable markets) appears to be motivated, at least in part, by a desire to mute the importance of oligopoly by suggesting that under certain conditions oligopolistic markets behave just like competitive markets. William J. Baumol, "Determinants of Industry Structure and Contestable Market Theory," in David Greenaway, Michael Bleaney, and Ian Stewart, eds., *Companion to Contemporary Economic Thought* (London: Routledge, 1991), Chapter 24; and William J. Baumol, John C. Panzar, and Robert Willig, with contributions by Elizabeth E. Bailey, Dietrich Fischer, and Herman Q. Quirmback, *Contestable Markets and the Theory of Industrial Structure* (New York: Harcourt Brace Jovanovich, 1982).

[10] John Hicks, quoted in W. Brian Arthur, "Increasing Returns and the New World of Business," *Harvard Business Review* (July-August 1996): 100–109.

[11] John von Neumann and Oskar Morgenstern, *The Theory of Games and Economic Behavior* (Princeton: Princeton University Press, 1944).

esoteric subject, but stated as simply as possible, the theory of games attempts to predict or explain outcomes of human interactions where the players are few in number and each player has a choice of alternative courses of action or strategies. Each individual's strategy is based in part on what that individual believes the strategy or strategies of the other player or players might be. Thus, game theory analyzes situations characterized by strategic uncertainty and interdependent decision-making. In other words, "I think that he thinks that I think . . ." ad infinitum.

According to game theory, each individual player chooses whatever strategy clearly maximizes gains or minimizes losses. The outcome of the game could be either losses or wins for either one or both of the players.[12] While in some cases the outcome of a strategic game can be predicted easily, this is not always the case. In a "Nash equilibrium" situation, the outcome *may* be predictable. Such a situation is defined as an array of strategies from which no player has an incentive to deviate.[13] In a Nash equilibrium where one array of strategic choices unquestionably dominates and is preferred by each player over all other possibilities, there can be only one outcome that will be satisfactory for both players. In other words, in such situations, oligopolistic competition may be indistinguishable from perfect competition. However, the real world of oligopoly is generally characterized by many situations in which a number of Nash equilibria are possible. This means that game theory is of little use in describing or predicting business behavior in situations of mutual interdependence.

The possibility of multiple equilibria has profound implications for both economics and political economy. Many, if not most, strategic situations in which firms and states find themselves do have many feasible equilibrium points or, in the jargon of the field, are said to have "multi-equilibria."[14] Instead of one obviously best array of strategies for both players, there are several possible arrays. In fact, there can be an infinite number of equilibria that promise to each cooperating player higher returns than would result from noncooperative behavior. In such situations, it is difficult and perhaps impossible to determine which array of strategies will be selected by the players. Thus, even in the case of cooperative players, it may be difficult to achieve a mutually satisfactory solution.

[12] The essence of game theory is discussed in Chapter 4.

[13] David M. Kreps, *Game Theory and Economic Modeling* (Oxford: Clarendon Press, 1990), 28.

[14] James D. Morrow, *Game Theory for Political Scientists* (Princeton: Princeton University Press, 1994), 306.

134

Regulations governing the market can significantly affect both the strategies available to market participants and also which Nash equilibrium will be chosen. Therefore, the rules or regimes can be or are important determinants of the outcome of economic activities.[15] Although liberals would argue that the rules and regimes can result from cooperative processes, more powerful actors frequently impose rules or regimes on other players in the market. Since the rules and institutions governing economic activities may reflect the interests of the powerful actors, market outcomes are profoundly affected by political, institutional, and other noneconomic factors; this is a subject central to the study of international political economy.

TECHNOLOGICAL INNOVATION

All the new theories of growth, economic location, and strategic trade accord an increasingly important role to technological change in determining the nature and dynamics of the world economy. Even though technological progress has always been acknowledged as an important factor in economic affairs, technology's scale, ubiquitous character, and rapid rate of advance are now reshaping every aspect of social, economic, and political affairs. As the twenty-first century begins, technological advances in computers and telecommunications are forcing nations to make major adjustments in their policies and economic structures. As we have already observed, technology has created a fluid world of scale economies and imperfect competition in which trade patterns, the location of economic activities, and growth rates are more arbitrary and dependent than in the past on the strategies of private firms and the policies of national governments. The increased importance of technological innovation in economic affairs has resulted in the following changes.

Technological Developments and International Competitiveness

Electronics-based design, manufacturing, and distribution have greatly reduced the time lapse between the innovation of a new product and its production and marketing, and this has facilitated rapid, flexible response to changes in demand.[16] Consequently, product diversification has increased and such activities as design, distribution, and service have gained importance as factors in competition. Moreover, the

---

[15] Kreps, *Game Theory and Economic Modeling*, 182.
[16] This discussion is based largely on Carl Dahlman, "The Third Industrial Revolution: Trends and Implications for Developing Countries" (April 1992), unpublished.

increased importance of these nonmanufacturing activities means that the importance of production costs in determining total costs has decreased; the result is that low-cost producers can lose some of their prior competitive advantage. Inputs of new materials and resource-saving processes also decrease the importance of traditional commodities in international trade, reduce commodity prices, and thus harm commodity producers around the world (including in the United States).

Organization of Production and Technological Innovation

The world economy is experiencing another phase of the industrial revolution that began in the latter part of the eighteenth century. The first phase, based on iron and steam power, was characterized by the rise of the factory system; these developments took place in Great Britain and led to the industrial and international preeminence of that nation. The second phase, beginning in the latter part of the nineteenth century and based on steel, petroleum, chemicals, electricity, and the internal combustion engine, occurred in the United States and, to a lesser extent, in Germany. This phase reached its highest development with the advent of the assembly line and mass production (labeled "Fordism" by many writers). Once again, the technological leader or leaders became the most powerful nation(s) in the world. And, as in the earlier phases of the industrial revolution, the dominant industrial nation used its power to reshape world affairs in its own economic and political interests. Furthermore, the economic expansion of the technological leader through trade and foreign investment imposed on other economies the choice of either adopting the new production methods or retreating behind protective barriers and inevitably falling behind in global economic competition.

Beginning in the 1970s, Japanese firms captured international leadership in one industrial sector after another, due in large part to their implementation of lean production techniques.[17] Various techniques associated with lean production—introduction of quality circles, reliance on just-in-time inventories (*kanban*) that save resources, and computerized automation—became central to the production process in Japan; these highly efficient techniques, pioneered at Toyota and associated with the technological and organizational revolution, diffused rapidly throughout Japanese industry. Later, these techniques

---

[17] The story of lean production and its advantages is told in James P. Womack, Daniel T. Jones, and Daniel Roos, *The Machine that Changed the World* (New York: Rawson Associates, 1990).

136

spread to other countries, but Japanese industry, with its ability to keep production costs low and the quality of its products high and to shift product mix much more rapidly than its competitors, took a decisive lead in manufacturing in many high-tech and other sectors. Indeed, Japanese superiority in manufacturing processes rather than in product innovation has been the key to Japan's outstanding export success. Even though many of Japan's most successful exports had been invented in the United States, Japan triumphed in manufacturing these products in high volume, at low cost, and with superior quality. After several years, however, as the Japanese system of lean production diffused to other countries, the overwhelming Japanese productive advantage decreased.[18] Indeed, during the 1990s, American corporations, through downsizing, heavy investments in computers, and development of new enterprises regained much of the competitiveness they had lost in the mid-1980s.

Globalization, Intensified Competition, and Transnational Alliances

Many developments in the 1990s increased the globalization of the world economy and also intensified international competition in a number of ways. Reduced transportation and communication costs contributed to growing globalization in the areas of trade, investment, and production. Gigantic multinational corporations became even more central to the management of trade and the organization of production around the world, and intrafirm or managed trade, rather than arms-length or market-based transactions, expanded to a much larger portion of international trade. Growing costs for research and development as well as the increasing importance of scale economies and the need for market access caused more and more firms to enter international markets to capture the returns on their investments. The ever-expanding scope of modern science and technology and the compression of time between innovation and commercialization provided yet another impetus for intercorporate alliances. Learning that no individual firm, nor even any single country, could take a commanding lead in every industry, more and more firms began to seek partners in other countries.

Technological Developments and the International Division of Labor

Technological developments affect significantly the comparative advantage of developed and developing countries; the impact is particu-

---

[18] David J. Jeremy, ed., *The Transfer of International Technology: Europe, Japan, and the USA in the Twentieth Century* (London: Edward Elgar, 1992).

larly notable in the rapid advances of the Pacific Asian electronics industry in the 1980s and early 1990s, where the effects of technological developments changed the international division of labor. In the final decades of the twentieth century, the developed countries, especially the United States, were becoming service economies, or "postindustrial societies," based on the creation, processing, and distribution of information. To speak of the United States as a service economy does not mean, as many Americans feared during the late 1980s, that the United States was becoming a nation of hamburger flippers; nor does it mean that services displace production of consumer and other types of goods. The advent of the service economy means that such services as information-based services are a growing input into the production of hard goods; these inputs make it possible to produce more and higher quality goods. The nature of manufacturing is changing and reducing employment in the traditional manufacturing sector at the same time that the volume of manufacturing output is increasing.[19] In the late nineteenth century, a similar transition occurred as the agriculture-based society shifted to a manufacturing-based society and industrialization transformed food production.

At the same time that the advanced industrial countries are becoming service-oriented economies, more traditional manufacturing is moving to the less developed countries of Pacific Asia and, to a lesser extent, to other parts of the world previously known as the Third World. Many developing nations shifted by the end of the century from being primarily commodity exporters to becoming exporters of manufactured goods. Unfortunately, however, this development was accompanied by increasing polarization between those rapidly industrializing economies that could take advantage of ongoing technological changes and the large majority of less developed countries that, for one reason or another, were unable to adjust to the technological revolution.

Restricted Access to Leading Technology

The new theories differ from neoclassical theory in the extent to which they assume that technological innovation can be appropriated or monopolized by an innovator. Neoclassical economics assumes that technology is a public good equally available to all firms; that is, that technical knowledge cannot easily be monopolized. Every firm

---

[19] Geza Feketskuty, *International Trade in Services: An Overview and Blueprint for Negotiations* (Cambridge, Mass.: An American Enterprise Institute/Ballinger Publication, 1988).

regardless of its size, nationality, or other features is believed to have an equal opportunity to appropriate and exploit the fruits of scientific and technical advance around the world. Thus, when a firm makes an investment decision, the neoclassical assumption is that it can incorporate "state-of-the-art" technology in its new plant and thereby be competitive in world markets.

The new growth, location, and trade theories assume, to the contrary, that technology can be and is being, at least temporarily, appropriated and monopolized by its innovators. Private firms and national governments can and do attempt to slow down the international diffusion of the most advanced technologies at a moment when achieving and maintaining control of technology and knowledge have become more and more important as factors in economic growth and international competitiveness. Thus, at the beginning of the twenty-first century, the technological leaders (Japan, the United States, and Western Europe) attempt to restrict transmission of their most advanced technologies to foreign competitors and to protect their intellectual property rights, especially from the encroachment of developing countries. Although an effort to safeguard intellectual property rights against piracy is proper in most cases, such efforts can lead to technonationalism and even denial of important medical technology to poor countries.[20]

Technological Leapfrogging

The new growth theory is based on the assumption that technological change is generally incremental within a well-established technological paradigm and that an oligopolistic firm can expect to maintain its lead over its rivals through continuous investment in established technology. This theory also suggests that technological leapfrogging can sometimes explain drastic reversals among firms and nations in their economic fortune and relative position, thus occasionally transforming the hierarchy of power and the structure of the international system. From time to time, one economy suddenly moves to a higher stage of technological development and productive efficiency. Such technological leapfrogging, especially when major powers are involved, can have profound and disturbing consequences for international economic and political affairs.[21] The new growth theory may

---

[20] Sylvia Ostry and Richard R. Nelson, *Techno-Nationalism and Techno-Globalism: Conflict and Cooperation* (Washington, D.C.: Brookings Institution, 1995).

[21] Elise S. Brezis, Paul R. Krugman, and Daniel Tsiddon, "Leapfrogging in International Competition: A Theory of Cycles in National Technological Leadership," *American Economic Review* 83, no. 5 (December 1993): 1211–19.

contribute not only to an understanding of the rise and decline of nations, but also to improved comprehension of the international political conflicts to which shifts in international status frequently give rise.

If technological advance is revolutionary, a technological leader may suddenly find itself at a decisive disadvantage and may even need to start anew and make substantial investments in the new technology. Whereas a technological leader with high wages and large investments in state-of-the-art technologies may have little or no incentive to take advantage of a newer revolutionary technology, a more technologically backward economy with no vested interest in the previously established technology and with cheaper labor and an undervalued currency is likely to view the new technology as a promising means to leap ahead of the leader. In times of normal incremental technological change, increasing returns to scale generally favor economic leaders. However, a new invention or a major technological breakthrough may favor the interests of a rising economy while disadvantaging those economic leaders who pay high wages and, as Mancur Olson has demonstrated, are also strongly influenced by vested interests that oppose adoption of new ideas.[22] In this way, success in one stage of economic development may create barriers to success in the next stage.

Intensified Competition for Technological Leadership

Historically, there has been a high correlation among technological, economic, and political leadership. The rise of particular nations to global preeminence—for example, Great Britain, the United States, Germany, and Japan—resulted from their ability to take advantage of the first and second Industrial Revolutions. As in those earlier revolutions, the latest technological revolution has given rise to intensified competition among national economies for leadership. In the late nineteenth century, the great powers struggled with one another over the commanding heights of mass production. At the close of the twentieth century and in the beginning of the twenty-first century, the battleground has been located among the high-tech industries of the computer and the information economies. This has produced an intensifying competition among the great economic powers for global supremacy in these technologies and, consequently, for dominant political power in the future.

[22] Mancur Olson Jr., *The Rise and Decline of Nations: Economic Growth, Stagflation, and Social Rigidities* (New Haven: Yale University Press, 1982).

Technological developments available at the turn of the century hold great promise that all economies could eventually benefit. These new technologies are so central to economic competitiveness and national power that the struggle to determine which nations will lead and which will follow in development and exploitation of these revolutionary technologies has been intensifying. Although recognition of the importance of the technologies has unleashed a competitive struggle among states for technological supremacy, it is highly unlikely that any nation will be able, in the early years of the twenty-first century, to achieve the commanding technological leads that Great Britain and the United States enjoyed in the nineteenth and twentieth centuries. The scope and expense of modern science and technology are simply too great for any one nation to acquire a monopoly position in every high-tech sector. Nevertheless, the competition will be fierce, because control over what have been called the "nerve centers" of the twenty-first century is at stake in this struggle.

Convergent and Divergent Economic Growth

The world economy portrayed by the new economic theories is characterized by both divergent and convergent economic growth among national economies and different regions within individual national economies. Despite the optimistic predictions flowing from the convergence theory of mainstream neoclassical economics, the growth process within and among national economies remains highly uneven. Although convergence has been taking place among the industrialized countries throughout the post–World War II era, few developing economies have converged with the developed economies despite the considerable progress that some have experienced. An important study by Robert Barro and Xavier Martin found that the prediction that convergence between rich and poor would occur has not been fulfilled; in fact, the growth rates of many countries are diverging from one another.[23] Government policies that encourage private entrepreneurship and national economic efficiency are important in determining that convergence rather than divergence will take place.

---

[23] Robert J. Barro and Xavier-Martin, "Convergence Across States and Regions" (Washington: Brookings Institution, Brookings Papers on Economic Activity 1, 1991), 107–58. These negative findings regarding convergence are supported by Mauruce Obstfeld and Kenneth Rogoff, *Foundations of International Marcroeconomics* (Cambridge: MIT Press, 1996), 454.

The low capacity of the societies in less developed countries to absorb the knowledge required for economic development has proved to be a particularly significant deficiency. As I have already pointed out, the availability of human capital and the ability to use knowledge are the most important determinants of economic development. Educational, institutional, and/or some other factors may provide reasons for the weakness of less developed countries in meeting the requirements for economic development.[24] As Moses Abramovitz has pointed out, convergence occurs only when national economies share a similar "social capacity." He was referring to the institutional and human components of a society that develop only slowly through educational and organizational responses to technological opportunity.[25] Unfortunately, few less developed countries possess such a capacity.

Differences in the level of social capacity among national economies leads to an international core/periphery structure in which strong concentrations of economic wealth and economic activities (the core economies) coexist with weaker or peripheral economies. Emergence of core economies and slower development of other economies results in an uneven evolution of the international economy. In the language of economics, economic development around the world is "lumpy," as development clusters in one region of the globe or another. While some nations and regions develop and become important components of the world economy, others remain stagnant or develop more slowly. Over time, however, new regional concentrations of economic activities arise and older developed regions decline, at least in relative terms.

The core/periphery structure is held together by mutual dependence; trade, investment, and other economic activities bind the core economy and peripheral economies. Yet, in almost all cases, the periphery is much more dependent on the core than vice versa. The core is the periphery's major source of capital and investment as well as being a large market for the exports of the periphery. The periphery is primarily a source of commodities (food, raw materials, etc.), lower valued exports, and in some cases, workers. In the language of

---

[24] Luc Soete and Bart Verspagen, "Technology and Growth: The Complex Dynamics of Catching Up, Falling Behind, and Taking Over," in Adam Szirmai, Bart Van Ark, and Dirk Pilat, eds., *Explaining Economic Growth* (Amsterdam: North Holland, 1993), 8.

[25] Moses Abramovitz first set forth his notion of social capacity in *Thinking About Growth and Other Essays on Economic Growth* (Cambridge: Cambridge University Press, 1989).

Hirschman, the core has power over the periphery because a rupture of their ties would be more costly to the latter than the former. Keohane and Nye (1977) had much the same point in mind when they distinguished between "sensitivity" and "vulnerability" interdependence.[26]

The global process of uneven economic development and the existence of core/periphery structures are the result of the interplay of opposed economic forces that successively create and undermine regional concentrations of industry and economic activity.[27] On the one hand are found forces of polarization or agglomeration that promote regional concentration of economic activities. These forces include economies of scale, the technological and other advantages gained by path dependence, and the cumulative process. In addition, externalities and the learning experience can give a region a powerful competitive advantage over other regions. For example, the ability of entrepreneurs within a region to take advantage of local technologies, knowledge spillovers, and economies of scale will enhance their competitiveness. In addition, a region may also possess the advantages of proximity to suppliers and customers and the linkages that develop among firms dealing in intermediate goods.[28] Then there are the opposed forces of spread and diffusion. The forces of dispersal that lead to development of new core economies include diffusion of technology from developed to industrializing economies, the exhaustion of valuable resources, increasing labor costs in the core/s, rising land costs, and such other diseconomies as urban congestion and rising taxation.

Whether the centrifugal forces concentrating economic activities or the centripetal forces dispersing them will prevail in a particular case is virtually impossible to predict; as with almost every economic question, the answer is, "It depends." It is impossible to know which economies will become core economies or which will be in the periphery over the long term. As Paul R. Krugman has pointed out, the organization of the world economy with respect to the location of

---

[26] These matters are discussed in Chapter 4.

[27] Prior to Krugman, a number of scholars such as Albert O. Hirschman and Gunnar Myrdal made important contributions to the study of the core/periphery formation. These writings are discussed in my book, *The Political Economy of International Relations* (Princeton: Princeton University Press, 1987). One important element missing from these earlier analyses, and emphasized by Krugman, is the role of economies of scale in the formation of core economies. A discussion of this earlier literature is Keith Chapman and David Walker, *Industrial Location. Principles and Policies* (Cambridge: Basil Blackwell, 1987).

[28] Anthony J. Venables, "Cities, Trade, and Economic Development," May 1999, unpublished.

particular industries, the concentration of wealth and economic activities in urban centers and core economies, and the uneven development of the globe and the unequal distribution of wealth among societies are, to a considerable degree, functions of chance, arbitrariness, and historical accident reinforced by increasing returns and cumulative processes.[29] Nevertheless, several generalizations on the global process of economic development can be extracted from the writings of economists on the new economic geography and other recent theories:

(1) The process of concentration or agglomeration divides the global economy into developed and less developed regions. Concentration of economic activities is particularly characteristic of manufacturing, as firms desire to be close to large markets and to suppliers of intermediate goods.
(2) Agglomeration is primarily confined to regions within individual developed economies. However, as trade and other barriers fall, uneven growth and a resulting core/periphery structure extend across national boundaries. Divergent growth rates rather than convergent rates are characteristic of the global economy.
(3) Economic development takes place sequentially and unevenly as clusters of economic activity spread from industrialized to industrializing countries.

While generally contributing to greater understanding of the dynamics of the world economy, the above generalizations lack certain key components that a comprehensive analysis should include. In the first place, Krugman's core/periphery model overlooks the economic, and especially the political, implications of that structure for the world economy. For example, a nation that possesses one or more regional cores with strong industries can achieve an overwhelming economic and competitive superiority over other nations. As economists point out, an economy with a head start in the accumulation of knowledge tends to widen its productivity lead. Actually, one implication of Paul Krugman's core/periphery formulation is that a hierarchical global economic and political structure will be created in which the core economy/economies possess the most important economic activities and the dependent periphery is where lower value-added economic activities are located. Such a situation inevitably becomes a major source of economic tension and even political conflict.

[29] Paul R. Krugman, *Geography and Trade* (Cambridge: MIT Press, 1991).

144

In the game of international economics, one vital national objective is to ensure possession of important core regions and leading industries. Because a head start is so very important, lagging nations are motivated to pursue such trade and industrial policies as subsidies to local businesses and erection of protectionist barriers in order to catch up with or leapfrog over the leading economy. Nations desire core regions because they are associated with high wages, economic power, and national autonomy. Almost every government engages in deliberate efforts to erect barriers to protect established industries or provide inducements to attract new industries. Policies of economic nationalism attempt to increase the probability that both the centripetal and centrifugal forces will work toward the nation's own advantage. A notable example of such an effort to redistribute industry and other economic activities to a nation's own advantage occurred when, in the last part of the nineteenth century, Canada put into place high trade barriers, subsidized a transcontinental railway, and took other actions to encourage foreign direct investment and to create an industrialized, united, and independent economy. This strategy of encouraging diffusion of industry to and within Canada met with considerable success.

Another significant implication of economic geography is that lowering trade and other economic barriers will lead to economic integration across national boundaries and to significant restructuring of national economies. As integration takes place, industry and other economic activities tend to migrate within the enlarged market. As displacements occur, existing core/periphery structures will be reconfigured and new structures will be formed. Increasing economic interdependence in the world economy or within a regionalized economy, such as the European Union or the North American Free Trade Agreement (NAFTA), will result in many economic activities shifting their geographic location. Yet it remains impossible to predict the overall result of this restructuring and whether industry will move to the periphery to take advantage of lower cost labor or will concentrate in the existing regional cores.[30]

The neoclassical characterization of a smooth evolution of the world economy is patently unrealistic. Indeed, as convergence among developed and developing economies takes place, conflict between

[30] Paul R. Krugman and Anthony J. Venables, "Integration and the Competitiveness of Peripheral Industries," in Christopher Bliss and Jorge Braga De Macedo, eds., *Unity with Diversity in the European Economy: The Community's Southern Frontier* (New York: Cambridge University Press, 1996), Chapter 3.

them invariably intensifies for several reasons.[31] In the first place, the rise of a new economic power decreases the relative economic share and international status of the dominant economy. A second and closely related effect is that this shift in economic wealth and technological capability causes an economy experiencing relative decline to be concerned over its national security. And, thirdly, as the rising power closes the economic/technological gap, it competes away the monopoly rents or superprofits of the more advanced economy. Under these circumstances, it is not surprising that declining powers have made scapegoats of rising powers and have charged that the latter have played the game unfairly; this happened in the late 1980s and early 1990s when Japan seemed to be displacing the United States as the world's dominant economic power.

There are several alternative strategies available to a declining economic power. The most drastic recourse is to use military power to remove the economic challenge and security threat posed by the rising power; fortunately, utilization of this option is rare and usually the result of serious political conflicts rather than of merely economic tensions. A second option is a retreat into trade protection (even though protectionism will most likely accelerate economic decline) or an attempt to weaken the rising economy. The third and most desirable response available to the challenged country is to take policy initiatives designed to rejuvenate its own flagging economy. This strategy of economic adjustment can mean letting the market work and/or implementing judicious interventionist policies to shift an economy away from those industries and economic activities in which it is losing comparative advantage and toward those in which it is gaining advantage. Frequently, a challenged economy pursues a combination of these strategies.

As the new theories suggest, a government can pursue specific macroeconomic and microeconomic policies to strengthen its economy. It can, for example, devalue its currency; although this choice may temporarily increase the competitiveness of the economy, it is at best a short-term strategy. A better strategy would be to take steps to increase the productivity of the economy. This can be done through improving market functioning. However, as the theory of strategic trade and the importance of technology suggest, the government can also take more direct actions. It is quite clear, for example, that gov-

---

[31] Staffan Burnenstam Linder, *The Pacific Century: Economic and Political Consequences of Asian-Pacific Dynamism* (Stanford: Stanford University Press, 1986), 90–94.

ernment support for basic scientific and technological R & D can produce large economic payoffs. In addition, the crucial role of skilled labor in economic development and international competition makes it imperative that governments actively promote education and worker training. As they respond to the process of uneven growth, governments do have choices.

Although the strategy of economic adjustment is certainly the preferable response to convergence and to relative economic decline, it is frequently the most difficult to carry out. As Mancur Olson argued in *The Rise and Decline of Nations* (1982), the balance of power within an economy tends to favor those groups whose interests lie with the status quo and therefore do not want to pay the costs of adjustment.[32] Because they know precisely what they may lose, threatened and entrenched economic sectors frequently put pressure on their governments for protection against the "unfair" trading and economic practices of rising competitors. In the contemporary world, a frequent response to convergence and other shifts in the global distribution of highly valued economic activities is to undertake or expand regional economic and political arrangements, such as the European Union and the North American Free Trade Agreement (NAFTA).

CONCLUSION

The new economic theories and their implications for the world economy lead me to conclude that governments and their policies are and will remain of crucial importance for the functioning of the international economy. Despite the increasing significance of the market and economic globalization, economic outcomes are determined not only by economic forces but also by governments and their policies. Yet, national societies differ fundamentally in the degree to which their governments play a meaningful role in the economy and in the ways in which they attempt to manage their economies.

---

[32] Olson, *The Rise and Decline of Nations*.

National Systems of Political Economy

M ANY PROFESSIONAL economists and scholars of international political economy (IPE), including myself, have given insufficient attention to the importance of domestic economies to the ways in which the world economy functions. Economists regard national economies as dimensionless points, while scholars of IPE have focused almost exclusively on the international political and economic system. While it was never justifiable to neglect the role of domestic factors in the study of international political economy, it has become increasingly obvious that the role of domestic economies and the differences among those economies have become significant determinants of international economic affairs. Thus, study of the different types of national economies or "national systems of political economy" and their significance for the global economy has become an important aspect of the study of international political economy.[1]

Several developments in the 1980s increased awareness of the importance of the differences among national political economies. The miserable economic performance of the socialist economies and of most less developed countries led many observers to appreciate the superiority of the market system. The extraordinary economic success of Japan and of the industrializing economies of Pacific Asia prior to the 1997 financial crisis led revisionist scholars to declare and others to worry that the capitalist developmental state model provided the best route to economic success. International economic conflicts intensified and led to charges that one country or another was not "playing fair," and the increasing integration of various national economies with others possessing differing economic structures and business practices increased awareness of the significance of these dif-

---

[1] The writings on comparative political economy are quite extensive. Examples include Peter A. Hall, *Governing the Economy: The Politics of State Intervention in Britain and France* (New York: Oxford University Press, 1986); and Gunter Heiduk, ed., *Technological Competition and Interdependence: The Search for Policy in the United States, West Germany, and Japan* (Seattle: University of Washington Press, 1990). A polemical but interesting work is Michel Albert, *Capitalism vs. Capitalism: How America's Obsession with Individual Achievement and Short-term Profit Has Led It to the Brink of Collapse* (New York: Four Walls Eight Windows, 1993).

ferences. As economic interdependence has progressed, national differences have more frequently become the subject of international negotiations and a factor in the growing movement toward economic regionalism.

In the 1980s and 1990s, there was some convergence among national economies, and the differences among them diminished in a number of important respects. Nevertheless, in the early years of the twenty-first century, fundamental differences among national economies remain important. This point is especially applicable to the American, German, and Japanese economies. These dominant economies not only influence the world economy, but they are also archetypes for many other economies. Whereas the American, British, and other "Anglo-Saxon" economies have much in common, the German economy shares many features with the corporatist-type economies of continental Europe, and the Japanese economy has, in certain respects, provided a model for the "developmental capitalist" economies of Pacific Asia.[2]

DIFFERENCES AMONG NATIONAL ECONOMIES

While national systems of political economy differ from one another in many important respects, differences in the following areas are worthy of particular attention: (1) the primary purposes of the economic activity of the nation, (2) the role of the state in the economy, and (3) the structure of the corporate sector and private business practices. Although every modern economy must promote the welfare of its citizens, different societies vary in the emphasis given to particular objectives; those objectives, which range from promoting consumer welfare to pursuit of national power, strongly influence and are influenced by such other features of a national economy as the role of the state in the economy and the structure of that economy. As for the role of the state in the economy, market economies include the generally laissez-faire, noninterventionist stance of the United States as well as the Japanese state's central role in the overall management of the economy. And the mechanisms of corporate governance and private business practices also differ; the relatively fragmented American business structure and the Japanese system of tightly integrated industrial groupings (the *keiretsu*) contrast dramatically with one another. Very different national systems of politi-

[2] Peter Katzenstein, *Corporatism and Change: Austria, Switzerland, and the Politics of Industry* (Ithaca: Cornell University Press, 1984).

cal economy result from the variations in the basic components of economies.

The purpose of economic activity in a particular country largely determines the role of the state in that economy. In those liberal societies where the welfare of the consumer and the autonomy of the market are emphasized, the role of the state tends to be minimal. Although liberal societies obviously differ in the extent to which they do pursue social welfare goals, the predominant responsibility of the state in these societies is to correct market failures and provide public goods. On the other hand, in those societies where more communal or collective purposes prevail, the role of the state is much more intrusive and interventionist in the economy. Thus, the role of such states can range from providing what the Japanese call "administrative guidance" to maintaining a command economy like that of the former Soviet Union.

The system of corporate governance and private business practices constitutes another important component of a national political economy. American, German, and Japanese corporations have differing systems of corporate governance, and they organize their economic activities (production, marketing, etc.) in varying ways. For example, whereas shareholders (stockholders) have an important role in the governance of American business, banks have played a more important role in both Japan and Germany. In addition, regarding business practices, whereas the largest American firms frequently invest and produce abroad, Japanese firms prefer to invest and produce at home. The policies of each government have also shaped the nature of business enterprise and business behavior through regulatory, industrial, and other policies; furthermore, some national differences in corporate structure and business practices, as Alfred Chandler has demonstrated, have evolved largely in response to economic and technological forces.[3]

The American System of Market-Oriented Capitalism

The American system of political economy is founded on the premise that the primary purpose of economic activity is to benefit consumers while maximizing wealth creation; the distribution of that wealth is of secondary importance. Despite numerous exceptions, the American economy does approach the neoclassical model of a competitive mar-

---

[3] Alfred D. Chandler, *Strategy and Structure: Chapters in the History of the Industrial Enterprise* (Cambridge: MIT Press, 1970).

ket economy in which individuals are assumed to maximize their own private interests (utility), and business corporations are expected to maximize profits. The American model, like the neoclassical model, rests on the assumption that markets are competitive and that, where they are not competitive, competition should be promoted through antitrust and other policies. Almost any economic activity is permitted unless explicitly forbidden, and the economy is assumed to be open to the outside world unless specifically closed. Emphasis on consumerism and wealth creation results in a powerful proconsumption bias and insensitivity, at least when compared with the Japanese and German models, to the social welfare impact of economic activities. Although Americans pride themselves on their pragmatism, the American economy is based upon the abstract theory of economic science to a greater degree than is any other economy.[4]

At the same time, however, the American economy is appropriately characterized as a system of managerial capitalism.[5] As Adolf Berle and Gardner Means pointed out in their classic study of American corporations, the economy was profoundly transformed by the late-nineteenth-century emergence of huge corporations and the accompanying shift from a proprietary capitalism to one dominated by large, oligopolistic corporations.[6] Management was separated from ownership, and the corporate elite virtually became a law unto itself. Subsequently, with the New Deal of the 1930s, the power balance shifted noticeably away from big business when a strong regulatory bureaucracy was established and organized labor was empowered; in effect, the neoclassical laissez-faire ideal was diluted by the notion that the federal government had a responsibility to promote economic equity and social welfare. The economic ideal of a self-regulating economy was further undermined by passage of the Full Employment Act of 1946 and the subsequent acceptance of the Keynesian idea that the federal government has a responsibility to maintain full employment through use of macroeconomic (fiscal and monetary) policies. Al-

---

[4] Excellent studies of the American political economy include John L. Campbell, J. Rogers Hollingsworth, and Leon N. Lindberg, eds., *Governance of the American Economy* (New York: Cambridge University Press, 1991); Frederic L. Pryor, *Economic Evolution and Structure: The Impact of Complexity on the U.S. Economic System* (New York: Cambridge University Press, 1996); and James E. Alt and K. Alec Crystall, *Political Economics* (Berkeley: University of California Press, 1983).

[5] This characterization of the American economy is based on William Lazonick, *Business Organization and the Myth of the Market Economy* (New York: Cambridge University Press, 1991).

[6] Adolf A. Berle and Gardner C. Means, *The Modern Corporation and Private Property* (New York: Macmillan, 1932).

151

though at the opening of the twenty-first century the federal government retains responsibility for full employment and social welfare, a significant retreat from this commitment began with the 1980 election of Ronald Reagan as President of the United States and the triumph of a more conservative economic ideology emphasizing free and unregulated markets.

Commitment to the welfare of individual consumers and the realities of corporate power have resulted in an unresolved tension between ideal and reality in American economic life. Whereas such consumer advocates as Ralph Nader want a strong role for the government in the economy to protect the consumer, American economists and many others react negatively to an activist government because of their belief that competition is the best protection for consumers except when there are market failures. In addition, there has been no persistent sense of business responsibility to society or to individual citizens. Japanese corporations have long been committed to the interests of their stakeholders, including labor and subcontractors, and German firms acknowledge their responsibility to society and are more accepting of the welfare state than are American firms. This explains why Japanese and German firms are much more reluctant to shift industrial production to other countries than are their American rivals. However, over time, the balance between the ideal and the reality of the American economy has shifted back and forth. In the 1980s, the election of Ronald Reagan as President and then his Administration's emphasis on the unfettered market diluted the welfare ideal of the earlier post–World War II era.

Economic Role of the State

The role of the American government in the economy is determined not only by the influence of the neoclassical model on American economic thinking but also by fundamental features of the American political system. Authority over the economy is divided among the executive, legislative, and judicial branches of the federal government and between the federal government and the fifty states. Whereas the Japanese Ministry of Finance has virtual monopoly power over the Japanese financial system, in the United States this responsibility is shared by the Treasury, the Federal Reserve, and several other powerful and independent federal agencies; furthermore, all of those agencies are strongly affected by actions of the legislative and judicial branches of government. In addition, the fifty states frequently contest the authority of the federal government over economic policy and implement important policies of their own.

Another restraining influence on the role of the American state in the economy is the tension between the private and public sectors. Not only does the adversarial relationship between government and business in the United States make cooperation very difficult, but their mutual suspicions are reflected in American politics. Whereas political conservatives reject, at least in principle, any strong role for the state in the economy, political liberals are fearful that private business interests will capture government programs in order to "feather their own nests," and this frequently produces political stalemate. At the same time, however, the fragmented structure of the American government and its many points of access make it easier for private interests to challenge government actions than it is in some other systems. These ideological, structural, and public versus private aspects of the American political economy have restricted greatly the capacity of the American government to develop a coherent and effective national economic strategy.

There is a major exception to the generally limited role of the American government in the economy in the area of macroeconomic policy-making. However, even in this area, the responsibility for macroeconomic policy, in actual practice, has been divided. The Congress and the executive branch are both responsible for fiscal policy, but control over monetary policy is vested in the Federal Reserve, and the "Fed" functions largely independently of the rest of the federal government. However, starting with the fiscal excesses of the Reagan Administration in the early 1980s and accumulation of an immense federal debt, the Congress and the executive branch deemphasized fiscal policy, and the Federal Reserve, with control over monetary policy, became the principal manager of the American economy.

The role of the federal government at the level of microeconomic policy is highly controversial. American society assumes that the government should establish a neutral environment for business and should not involve itself directly in business affairs. The primary responsibility of the government is believed to be the regulation of the economy, provision of public goods, and elimination of market failures. Notable examples are found in antitrust policies, regulation of pollution, and the safeguarding of public health. As Stephen G. Breyer and Richard B. Stewart point out in their authoritative text on administrative law and regulatory policy, the rationale for government intervention in the economy is to correct market failure as identified by economists. The unregulated market is treated as the norm, and advocates of government intervention must prove that such intervention is sometimes justifiable in order to achieve important public

153

objectives.[7] Market failures that may justify an active government role in the economy include monopoly power, negative externalities, and inadequate consumer information.

Industrial policy represents the greatest difference between the United States and other economies, except for Great Britain, another Anglo-Saxon economy.[8] Industrial policy refers to deliberate efforts by a government to determine the structure of the economy through such devices as financial subsidies, trade protection, or government procurement. Industrial policy may take the form either of sectoral policies of benefit to particular industrial or economic sectors or policies that benefit particular firms; in this way such policies differ from macroeconomic and general policies designed to improve the overall performance of the economy, policies such as federal support for education and R & D. Although Japan has actively promoted sector-specific policies throughout the economy, the United States has employed these policies in just a few areas, notably in agriculture and national defense. Although firm-specific policies are generally frowned upon in the United States as examples of "pork barrel politics," government policies in support of Chrysler and Harley David-son in years when they were threatened were considered successful firm-specific policies. However, as I shall note below, the United States in the 1980s took a major step toward establishing a national industrial policy.

The rationale or justification for industrial policy and associated interventionist activities is that some industrial sectors are more important than others for the overall economy. The industries selected are believed to create jobs of higher quality, like those in manufacturing, to produce technological or other spillovers (externalities) for the overall economy, and to have a high "value-added." These industries are frequently associated with national defense or are believed to produce a highly beneficial effect on the rest of the economy; the computer industry and other high-tech sectors provide examples of such industries. In general, however, the only justification for an industrial policy considered legitimate in the United States is to overcome a

[7] Stephen G. Breyer and Richard B. Stewart, *Administrative Law and Regulatory Policy* (Boston: Little, Brown, 1979).

[8] The literature on industrial policy is quite extensive. A good place to survey the subject is M. Donald Hancock, John Logue, and Bernt Schiller, eds., *Managing Modern Capitalism: Industrial Renewal and Workplace Democracy in the United States and Western Europe* (New York: Greenwood Press, 1991). An excellent and wide-ranging discussion of the subject is Keith Cowling and Roger Sugden, eds., *Current Issues in Industrial Economic Strategy* (New York: Manchester University Press, 1992).

market failure. In practice, most American economists, public officials, and business leaders are strongly opposed to industrial policy.
Their principal objection is that governments are incapable of picking
winners; many argue that politicians will support particular industries
for political ("pork barrel") reasons rather than for sound economic
reasons.[9] American economists argue that the structure and distribution of industries in the United States should be left entirely to the
market. This belief is supported by the assumption that all industries
are created equal and that there are no strategic sectors. Nevertheless,
despite the arguments against having an industrial policy in America,
such policies have developed in the areas of agriculture, national security, and research and development.

Corporate Governance and Private Business Practices

The American system of corporate governance and industrial structure parallels its political system. The governance and organization of
American business are characterized by fragmentation and an overall
lack of policy coordination. Indeed, the strong American antitrust
and competition policies are intended to prevent concentration of corporate power and direction. American business is much more constrained in its ability to share business information, to pool technological and other resources, and to develop joint strategies than are
its rivals. Many observers have charged that such restrictions disadvantage American firms in global competition.

Control of American business is also much more dispersed than in
Japan and Germany. Although American firms are much more responsive to shareholder concerns then are German and Japanese
firms, the largest shareholders in many of America's large corporations may own just 1 or 2 percent of the stock. In Japan, ownership
of 70 percent or more of the stock frequently resides in a cooperative
business grouping called a *keiretsu*. Also, industry and finance are
more completely separated from one another in the United States, and
in some instances this has meant higher capital costs than those enjoyed by foreign rivals. This also contributes to frequent conflicts between industry and finance, and these conflicts have been detrimental
to national policy-making. At the national level, the National Association of Manufacturers, Chamber of Commerce, and other business
organizations have no role commensurate with that of either the *kei-*

[9] A valuable and representative critique of industrial policy is Gene M. Grossman,
"Promoting New Industrial Activities: A Survey of Recent Arguments and Evidence"
(Princeton: Woodrow Wilson School, 1989).

155

danren (the organization representing Japanese big business) or the Federation of German Industries. Both the Japanese and German organizations can speak with a single strong voice and frequently do act on behalf of major business interests.

A fundamentally different conception of the corporation and its role in society underlies many of these contrasts between *shareholder* (stockholder) American capitalism and Japanese/German *stakeholder* capitalism. In the American system of shareholder capitalism, a firm's fundamental purpose is to make profits for its investors or shareholders; in principle, the firm has minimal obligations to employees and/ or to the communities in which its production facilities are located. Moreover, in the United States, a business corporation is regarded as a commodity that is bought and sold like any other commodity without regard for the social consequences of such transactions; waves of leveraged buyouts and corporate takeovers in the 1980s and 1990s were extreme examples of this mentality. In both Japan and Germany, on the other hand, the corporation is assumed to have a major responsibility toward its stakeholders (workers, subcontractors, etc.), and the interests of shareholders are given much less attention than in the American system; instead, firms are expected to promote larger social objectives. Japanese firms are expected to increase the power and independence of the Japanese nation and to promote social harmony; Germany also places a high premium on social welfare. American law is designed to ensure neutrality and fair play in the competitive market for corporate control. In Japan and Germany, profitability has been assigned less importance than economic stability. Moreover, German and Japanese policies are intended to limit hostile and foreign takeovers, and to control what Carl Kester has called "the global contest for corporate control."[10]

THE JAPANESE SYSTEM OF DEVELOPMENTAL CAPITALISM

G. C. Allen, the distinguished British authority on Japanese economic history, tells a story that provides an important insight into Japanese economic psychology. At the end of World War II, American occupation officials advised the Japanese that they should follow the theory of comparative advantage and hence concentrate on labor-intensive products in rebuilding their economy. Japan's economic and political elite, however, had quite different ideas and would have nothing to

---

[10] W. Carl Kester, *Japanese Takeovers: The Global Contest for Corporate Control* (Boston: Harvard Business School Press, 1991).

do with what they considered an American effort to relegate Japan to the low end of the economic and technological spectrum. Instead, the Japanese Ministry of International Trade and Industry (MITI) and other agencies of the Japanese economic high command set their sights on making vanquished Japan into the economic and technological equal, and perhaps even the superior, of the West. At the opening of the twenty-first century, this objective has remained the driving force of Japanese society.[11]

In the Japanese scheme of things, the economy is subordinate to the social and political objectives of society. As the distinguished Japanese economist Ryutaro Komiya has written, ever since the Meiji Restoration (1868), Japan's overriding goals have been "making the economy self-sufficient" and "catching up with the West."[12] In the pre–World War II years this ambition meant building a strong army and becoming an industrial power. Since its disastrous defeat in World War II, however, Japan has abandoned militarism and has focused on becoming a powerful industrial and technological nation, while also promoting internal social harmony among the Japanese people. There has been a concerted effort by the Japanese state to guide the evolution and functioning of their economy in order to pursue these sociopolitical objectives.[13]

These political goals have resulted in a national economic policy for Japan best characterized as neomercantilism; it involves state assistance, regulation, and protection of specific industrial sectors in order to increase their international competitiveness and attain the "commanding heights" of the global economy. This economic objective of achieving industrial and technological equality with other countries arose from Japan's experience as a late developer and also from its strong sense of economic and political vulnerability. Another very important source of this powerful economic drive is the Japanese

[11] Among the many important studies of the Japanese economy, several should be mentioned: Yasusuke Murakami, *An Anticlassical Political-Economic Analysis: A Vision for the Next Century*, ed. and trans. Kozo Yamamura (Stanford: Stanford University Press, 1996), is a brilliant interpretation of the distinctive nature of the Japanese economy; Takatoshi Ito, *The Japanese Economy* (Cambridge: MIT Press, 1992), is a very useful survey and analysis of the Japanese economy; Bai Gao, *Economic Ideology and Japanese Industrial Policy: Developmentalism from 1931 to 1965* (Cambridge: Cambridge University Press, 1997), is an outstanding history and evaluation of Japanese industrial policy.

[12] Ryutaro Komiya, *Industrial Policy in Japan* (Orlando, Fla.: Academic Press, 1988).

[13] Richard J. Samuels, *"Rich Nation, Strong Army": National Security and the Technological Transformation of Japan* (Ithaca: Cornell University Press, 1994).

157

people's overwhelming belief in their uniqueness, in the superiority of their culture, and in their manifest destiny to become a great power.

Many terms have been used to characterize the distinctive nature of the Japanese system of political economy: Shinto capitalism, developmental state capitalism, tribal capitalism, collective capitalism, welfare corporatism, competitive communism, network capitalism, companyism, producer capitalism, stakeholder capitalism, strategic capitalism, and, perhaps most famously or infamously, "Japan, Inc." Each of these labels connotes particularly important elements of the Japanese economic system, such as its overwhelming emphasis on economic development, the key role of large corporations in the organization of the economy and society, subordination of the individual to the group, primacy of the producer over the consumer, and the close cooperation among government, business, and labor. I believe that the term "developmental state capitalism" best captures the essence of the system, because this characterization conveys the idea that the state must play a central role in national economic development and in the competition with the West.

Despite the imperative of competition, the Japanese frequently subordinate pursuit of economic efficiency to social equity and domestic harmony.[14] Many aspects of the Japanese economy that puzzle foreigners are a consequence of a powerful commitment to domestic harmony; and "over-regulation" of the Japanese economy is motivated in part by a desire to protect the weak and defenseless. For example, the large redundant staffs in Japanese retail stores developed from an effort to employ many individuals who would otherwise be unemployed and discontented. This situation is also a major reason for the low level of productivity in nonmanufacturing sectors, and it accounts in part for Japan's resistance to foreign direct investment by more efficient foreign firms. The Japanese system of lifetime employment has also been utilized as a means to promote social peace; Japanese firms, unlike their American rivals, are very reluctant to "downsize" and lay off thousands of employees. At the opening of the twenty-first century, however, Japan's economic problems are causing this situation to change. Nevertheless, the commitments to political independence and social harmony are major factors in the Japanese state's determination to maintain firm control over the economy.

Economic Role of the State

Ever since the 1868 Meiji Restoration, the Japanese state has assumed the central role in the economy. Following Japan's defeat in World

[14] Frank Upham, *Law and Social Change in Postwar Japan* (Cambridge: Harvard University Press, 1987).

War II, the ruling tripartite alliance of government bureaucracies, the governing Liberal Democratic Party (LPD), and big business began to pursue vigorously the goal of catching up with the West. To this end, the elite pursued rapid industrialization through a strategy employing trade protection, export-led growth, and other policies. The Japanese people have supported this extensive interventionist role of the state and believe that the state has a legitimate and important economic function in promoting economic growth and international competitiveness. The government bureaucracy and the private sector, with the former frequently taking the lead, have consistently worked together for the collective good of Japanese society.

To attain the goal of rapid industrialization, the Japanese state supported, or even created, certain social characteristics, including an industrious and highly educated workforce. In many ways, the Japanese state created today's Japanese society.[15] Japan's postal savings institution fostered an extraordinarily high savings rate. Because of strict capital controls for much of the postwar era, the postal service was able, while paying depositors just a minimal rate of interest, to make these savings available for loans to Japanese firms; such financial assistance significantly reduced the cost of capital and contributed importantly to the rapid industrialization of the country and to international competitiveness. The Japanese state has also unfortunately played an important role in supporting social, political, and legal aspects of Japanese society that made it inhospitable to foreign direct investment and to the importation and consumption of foreign goods.[16] Fortunately, since the mid-1990s, this situation has been changing.

The unusual independence and power of the government bureaucracy accompanied by bureaucratic fragmentation within the government provide yet another distinctive aspect of the Japanese state that sets it apart. The economic and other bureaucracies of the government are virtually independent fiefdoms. With few major exceptions, each bureaucracy represents a particular segment of Japanese society and believes that it has a responsibility to promote the interests of that group. There are frequent disputes among agencies over policy and jurisdictional responsibility; these have increased as new technologies and economic developments have spread across the traditional functions of government agencies. Chalmers Johnson has made the

[15] The central role of the Japanese state in the formation of the Japanese economy and economic psychology has been demonstrated by Sheldon Garon, *Molding Japanese Minds: The State in Everyday Life* (Princeton: Princeton University Press, 1997).

[16] Edward J. Lincoln, *Japan's Unequal Trade* (Washington, D.C.: Brookings Institution, 1990).

159

point that the three major economic agencies responsible for foreign affairs frequently have differing foreign economic policies that conflict with those of the other agencies. Although bureaucratic struggles exist in every country, Japan does not have a powerful executive and therefore has no easy way to resolve such conflicts. In addition, the strong belief of the Japanese in consensus decision-making permits and even encourages stalemate and indecision. Indeed, during much of the postwar period the weak executive branch was of little consequence because of the agreement within the Japanese political elite on the path that all should follow. By the late 1990s, however, it became clear that the weakness of the Japanese executive had become a serious obstacle to Japan's ability to deal with its difficult economic and financial problems.

Another distinctive feature of Japanese society is that many "public" responsibilities have been assumed by the private sector. For example, private corporations carry a major responsibility for the social welfare of a substantial portion of the Japanese population. Whereas the American government delegates regulatory authority to quasi-autonomous public agencies, Japan delegates much of the responsibility for policing business activities to private business associations. This has been a highly pragmatic practice based on the close ties and mutual trust between private business and government. There is a particularly interesting example of this practice in the delegation of public functions in the privatizing of "law and order." One reason for the low level of street crime in Japan is that the *yakuza* (the Japanese Mafia) police the streets in exchange for police toleration of their businesses.

This practice of self-regulation and self-policing by business and other private associations is intended to provide social stability and ensure fairness. However, it does result in special treatment of particular groups, seemingly arbitrary decisions, and discriminatory behavior; this practice of self-regulation is also directly counter to the American concept of universal rules that apply equally to everyone regardless of status. Cultural differences in the definition of "fairness" have been a major source of American-Japanese economic tension that has, on occasion, erupted into open conflict. The Japanese practice of private associations assuming essentially public responsibilities has raised significant problems in the integration of Japan into the world economy. For cultural and other reasons, the Japanese find it virtually impossible to incorporate outsiders into the self-regulating associations that set the rules governing competitive behavior and other aspects of the conduct of business in Japan, while foreign com-

160

panies seeking entry into the Japanese market naturally regard the practice of self-regulation as discriminatory. The self-policing system, with its emphasis on "fairness" and on tailor-made rules enforced in self-regulatory associations, may conflict with the rules embodied in the World Trade Organization (WTO) and is thus an immense hurdle to be cleared to open the Japanese market and internationalize Japan more completely.

Industrial policy has been the most controversial aspect of the Japanese political economy.[17] As I have already noted, industrial policy refers to deliberate efforts of a government to guide and shape the overall structure of the economy. In the early postwar decades, the Japanese provided government support for favored industries, especially for high-tech industries, through trade protection, generous subsidies, and other means. The government also supported creation of cartels to help declining industries and to eliminate "excessive competition."[18] Through subsidies, provision of low-cost financing, and especially "administrative guidance" by bureaucrats, the Japanese state plays a major role in the economy.[19]

The effectiveness of Japanese industrial policy has been very controversial and a matter of intense debate. On one side are revisionist scholars and proponents of the developmental state who attribute Japan's success to its unique economic system and the government's powerful role in the economy. The opposing position is held by American and some Japanese economists, who emphasize Japan's market-conforming economic strategy.

Chalmers Johnson's *MITI and the Japanese Miracle: The Growth of Industrial Policy, 1925–1975* (1982), in which he credits Japan's Ministry of Trade and Investment (MITI) with having orchestrated postwar economic and technological success, is the most outstanding statement of the revisionist or developmental state position.[20] Accord-

[17] A useful and sympathetic treatment of Japanese industrial policy is Miyohei Shinohara, *Industrial Growth, Trade, and Dynamic Patterns in the Japanese Economy* (Tokyo: University of Tokyo Press, 1982). A wide-ranging discussion of Japanese industrial policy from several different perspectives is Hugh Patrick, ed., with the assistance of Larry Meissner, *Japan's High-Technology Industries: Lessons and Limitations of Industrial Policy* (Seattle: University of Washington Press, 1986).

[18] Jeffrey R. Bernstein, "Japanese Capitalism," in Thomas K. McCraw, ed., *Creating Modern Capitalism: How Entrepreneurs, Companies, and Countries Triumphed in Three Industrial Revolutions* (Cambridge: Harvard University Press, 1997).

[19] For a discussion of administrative guidance, consult Bernstein, "Japanese Capitalism," 479

[20] Chalmers Johnson, *MITI and the Japanese Miracle: The Growth of Industrial Policy, 1925–1975* (Stanford: Stanford University Press, 1982).

ing to Johnson, Japan is a capitalist developmental state rather than an American-style capitalist regulatory state. He credits MITI and other Japanese bureaucracies for Japan's outstanding postwar economic success. MITI and other agencies employed such techniques as import protection, government subsidies, and low-cost financing to promote rapid industrialization and development of the high-tech sectors. In the opinion of Johnson and other revisionists, the most important instrument of Japan's successful industrial policy was the device of administrative guidance, which was utilized to encourage and sometimes pressure private firms to invest in those industrial and high-tech sectors characterized by high value-added and favored by the government. In addition, Japan's export success has been due to its neomercantilist strategy of export-led economic growth.

On the other side of the debate, many American and some Japanese economists argue that Japanese economic success has been due to the fact that Japan pursued market-conforming economic policies and thus got the economic fundamentals correct.[21] They call attention to Japan's high savings and investment rate, superior management and entrepreneurship, and excellent system of education as bearing the primary responsibilities for Japan's success. In addition, the Ministry of Finance (MOF) has pursued stable and prudent macroeconomic policies. Explaining Japan's export success, many note that Japan, as a resource-poor and capital-skilled, labor-rich economy, has had a comparative advantage in manufacturing and industrial innovation.[22] According to this position, Japan's industrial policy had very little to do with its economic success and has even wasted resources.[23] Notable examples of failure are found in MITI's efforts to promote fifth-generation computers and a petrochemical industry. A more infamous example is provided by MITI's effort to prevent Honda from becoming an automobile producer, because MITI believed that Japan could not support another automobile company!

There is considerable evidence on both sides of this debate, but the outcome remains inconclusive because there is no counterfactual

[21] Hugh Patrick, *Asia's New Giant: How Japan's Economy Works* (Washington, D.C.: Brookings Institution, 1976); and Edward F. Denison and William K. Chung, *How Japan's Economy Grew So Fast: The Sources of Postwar Expansion* (Washington, D.C.: Brookings Institution, 1976).

[22] Gene M. Grossman, "Explaining Japan's Innovation and Trade: A Model of Quality Competition and Dynamic Comparative Advantage," *Bank of Japan, Monetary and Economic Studies* 8, no. 2 (September 1990): 75–100.

[23] A valuable assessment is provided by Daniel I. Okimoto, *Between MITI and the Market: Japanese Industrial Policy for High Technology* (Stanford: Stanford University Press, 1989).

experience to indicate whether Japan would have been more or less successful without government intervention.[24] Certainly, as critics charge, MITI made many mistakes and wasted resources. Yet several comments can be made in support of Japan's industrial policy. The government's support and protection of private firms in favored industrial sectors has been central to Japan's industrial policy. MITI and other Japanese economic bureaucracies' supportive policies were very important in enabling Japanese firms to close the technological gap with American and other Western high-tech industries. For example, Japanese competition (antitrust) policy encouraged the formation of the *keiretsu*, and by almost all accounts the *keiretsu* have been very important to Japan's industrial efficiency and international competitiveness.

In the early postwar years, the Japanese government selected a small number of powerful firms to be protected from both domestic and, especially, foreign competition; these protected firms were given tax credits and subsidies that enabled them to develop rapidly.[25] The government also supported technological developments through promotion of cooperative research programs and other means. Once the technology was fully developed, the government strongly encouraged domestic (but not foreign) competition to increase the firms' efficiency. This government support encouraged corporate strategies that emphasized profit-making at home and increased market share abroad. It is a mistake to assume, as some neoclassical economists do, that one can make a clear distinction between government policy and private initiatives in Japan.

The extensive use of "infant industry" protection has provided another key factor in the success produced by Japan's industrial policy.[26] Although it is undoubtedly correct, as American economists argue, that Japan and other governments have been largely unsuccessful in picking winners—that is, in selecting viable new industries—Japan has been very successful in protecting and supporting those sectors whose economic significance has been proved already in the United

[24] This point is made by Ryutaro Komiya, "Planning in Japan," in Morris Bornstein, ed., *Economic Planning: East and West* (Cambridge, Mass.: Ballinger, 1975). Moreover, as Komiya, one of Japan's most distinguished postwar international economists, points out elsewhere, Japan's industrial policy and its goals have changed considerably over the course of the postwar era: Komiya, "Industrial Policy in Japan," *Japanese Economics Studies* (summer 1986): 53–80.

[25] Ryuzo Sato, Rama Ramachandran, and Shunichi Tsutsui, "Protectionism and Growth of Japanese Competitiveness," in Dominick Salvatore, ed., *Protectionism and World Welfare* (New York: Cambridge University Press, 1993), Chapter 13.

[26] Ito, *The Japanese Economy.*

States and elsewhere: automobiles, consumer electronics, and scientific instruments.[27] Among the policies Japan has used to promote these infant industries have been the following:

(1) Taxation, financial, and other policies that encouraged extraordinarily high savings and investment rates.
(2) Fiscal and other policies that kept consumer prices high, corporate earnings up, and discouraged consumption, especially of foreign goods.
(3) Strategic trade policies and import restrictions that protected infant Japanese industries against both imported goods and establishment of subsidiaries of foreign firms.
(4) Government support for basic industries, such as steel, and for generic technology, like materials research.
(5) Competition (antitrust) and other policies favorable to the *keiretsu* and to interfirm cooperation.

Japanese industrial policy was most successful in the early postwar years when Japan was rebuilding its war-torn economy. However, as Japan closed the technology gap with the West and its firms became more powerful in their own right, Japan's industrial policy became considerably less significant in the development of the economy. Yet the population and the government continued to believe that the state should play a central or at least an important supportive role in the continuing industrial evolution of the economy.

Corporate Governance and Private Business Practices

The Japanese corporate system of industrial organization differs in several important respects from that of other industrialized economies.[28] Although its distinctive features have been undergoing important changes due to the maturing of the Japanese economy and to the economic stagnation in the late 1990s, fundamental differences remain between the Japanese and Western economic systems.[29] Three

---

[27] An excellent example of Japanese industrial policy has been the government's promotion of the Japanese automobile industries. During my several stays in Japan, I was impressed by the flawless condition of Japanese cars. A major reason, I was informed by Frank Upham, a New York University expert on Japanese law, was a set of government policies with respect to auto insurance and inspections that created strong incentives for Japanese consumers to purchase new cars. Then the consumers' replaced cars were shipped abroad to Southeast Asia and, in the 1990s, to Russia.

[28] Ryutaro Komiya, *The Japanese Economy: Trade, Industry, and Government* (Tokyo: University of Tokyo Press, 1990), Part II.

[29] Paul R. Krugman, *Trade with Japan: Has the Door Opened Wider?* (Chicago: University of Chicago Press, 1991).

of the most important differences are in the systems of industrial relations, of corporate finance, and of industrial organization. Although these elements are closely tied to one another and reinforce one another, it is useful to consider them independently.

The Japanese system of industrial relations has been characterized by a dual labor market. The core workers in Japan's large and highly competitive corporations such as Sony and Toyota, have enjoyed lifetime employment, have been paid on the basis of seniority, and have been considered stakeholders to whom Japanese firms have a social responsibility. Although the system has been strongly criticized and is being eroded by Japan's economic problems, one advantage of this system has been that, because lifetime workers are considered long-term assets, Japanese firms have a strong incentive to invest in laborers' skills. However, a major disadvantage of lifetime employment has been that it restricts the flexibility of Japanese firms and makes it difficult to reward younger and more valuable workers; it has also been nearly impossible to fire incompetent or redundant workers. On the other hand, the majority of workers, especially women and workers in smaller firms, have little job security and do not receive an equivalent share of the benefits of the system.

Whereas American firms tend to obtain the largest portion of their capital from the huge American stock market, Japanese firms rely on retained earnings and, most importantly, on an affiliated bank. Bank loans have generally been guaranteed by the government, either directly or at least implicitly. The Japanese banking system, including the government-run postal savings system, tight capital controls, and government macroeconomic policies have enabled Japanese firms to enjoy very low capital costs. As Kent Calder has shown, this financial system has been a crucial component in what he calls "Japan's strategic capitalism."[30]

Whereas American firms emphasize safeguarding both profitability and the interests of shareholders, Japanese firms have considered their primary responsibility to be toward a firm's stakeholders, and stakeholders include employees and subcontractors. American firms seek to maximize profits; Japanese firms have attempted to maximize sales and corporate growth. Differences like these led Alan Blinder, former member of the Federal Reserve, to question whether or not the Japanese economy was really capitalist![31]

---

[30] Kent E. Calder, *Strategic Capitalism: Private Business and Public Purpose in Japanese Finance* (Princeton: Princeton University Press, 1993).

[31] Alan S. Blinder, "More Like Them?" *American Prospect* 8 (winter 1992): 53.

The *keiretsu,* a business grouping or conglomerate whose members are bound together by the mutual trust and long-term relationships among a number of major firms, their suppliers, and their distribution networks, is a particularly important component of the Japanese corporate system.[32] At the heart of every *keiretsu* is a major bank (referred to in Japan as the main bank system) that supplies credit and plays a key role in the *keiretsu*'s economic strategy. Informal ties among member firms are reinforced by overlapping memberships on governing boards, mutual stock ownership, and other mechanisms. The purpose of these structures is to serve the interests of stakeholders rather than shareholders. There are horizontal *keiretsu,* enterprise groups such as Mitsui, Mitsubishi, and Sumitomo, that are composed of a few dozen members and include a large bank, manufacturing firms, and a distribution network along with other elements.[33] In addition, there are vertical *keiretsu* composed of a parent manufacturing company and a large network of long-standing subcontractors and suppliers of services. The approximately two dozen vertical *keiretsu* include leading Japanese manufacturing corporations in the automotive and consumer electronics industries, such as Toyota and Matsushita. Together, the vertical and horizontal *keiretsu* control much of Japanese business.

Dominant firms in a *keiretsu* may exploit and/or promote the strengths of their junior partners. For example, the parent firms work with their extensive stable of long-term and trusted subcontractors to increase the latter's technological capabilities and to improve the quality of the components supplied to the parent. The parent even shares exclusive information with its affiliates, and this greatly enhances the overall efficiency of the *keiretsu.* The extensive presence of the *keiretsu* in the Japanese economy thus has profound consequences for the nature of Japanese domestic and international economic competition and for the dynamics of the Japanese economy. Market share rather than profit maximization has been the principal driving force in Japanese corporate strategy; a large market share increases economies of scale and benefits the firm's stakeholders. Even

---

[32] Kester, *Japanese Takeovers.*

[33] The six or so horizontal *keiretsu* are the direct descendants of the prewar *zaibatsu* that the Occupation sought to destroy and thought they had. The principal characteristics of these groupings is that the members in each grouping hold one another's shares and have interlocking directorates. The presidents of member firms meet frequently to formulate strategy and decide upon joint policies. The members of the group also cooperate in financial matters, R & D activities, and marketing. Together, these six industrial groupings have a powerful presence in the Japanese economy.

though the Japanese economy is highly regulated, compartmentalized, and overprotected, this market is in fact extraordinarily competitive. For example, Japan has a number of automobile companies, whereas the United States has only three. Competition in Japan does tend to be oligopolistic and Schumpeterian; that is, it is based on technological innovation and is quality-driven rather than based on price competition; consumer prices are kept high by government policies to increase the profits of the corporate sector.

In his book on the governance of Japanese corporations, Carl Kester makes a convincing argument that the *keiretsu* is a highly efficient and rational mechanism for organizing economic activities, and its distinctive characteristics make it a formidable competitor in world markets.[34] Mutual trust, for example, substantially reduces transaction costs. Information exchange within the *keiretsu* decreases uncertainties and is conducive to innovative activities. Intragroup cross-shareholding protects members against hostile takeovers and significantly reduces the cost of capital.[35] The system is a mutual assistance society, and when a member firm gets into trouble, other members come to its rescue.

Corporate leadership's independence from outside shareholders permits the firm, unlike American management, to pursue a corporate strategy based on maximizing market share rather than short-term-profit maximization. As Ronald Dore has argued, the *keiretsu* contributes greatly to Japan's remarkable capacity to adjust to economic, technological, and other changes.[36] Certainly, no other country was as successful as Japan in adjusting to the two oil price rises of 1973–1974 and 1979–1980. Despite the troubles of the Japanese economy in the 1990s, the *keiretsu* has proved to be a successful innovator of new products and production techniques because of its immense internal resources and long-term perspective. The *keiretsu* mechanism has effectively joined the financial and other advantages of the large firm with the flexibility and innovative capabilities of the small firm.

Although (or perhaps because) the *keiretsu* is a highly effective means of industrial organization, it has been deeply resented by non-Japanese. One reason for this resentment is that the *keiretsu* is a closed system that excludes all outsiders. The term "outsider" includes not only non-Japanese firms, but any Japanese firm that is not

[34] Kester, *Japanese Takeovers*.

[35] Robert Zielinski and Nigel Holloway, *Unequal Equities: Power and Risk in Japan's Stock Market* (New York: Kodansha International, 1991).

[36] Ronald P. Dore, *Flexible Rigidities: Industrial Policy and Structural Adjustment in the Japanese Economy* (London: Athlone, 1986).

167

a member of the alliance of stakeholders who share the monopolistic rents generated by this oligopolistic form of business organization. The exclusive nature of the *keiretsu* system has significantly limited foreign firms' access to the Japanese market. The *keiretsu* also makes it extremely difficult for foreign firms to "take over" Japanese firms and gives Japanese firms a huge advantage in corporate expansion. Whereas the *keiretsu* firms can easily purchase a non-Japanese firm in order to acquire its technology or to gain market access, it has frequently been difficult for non-Japanese firms to purchase Japanese firms for the same purposes. Furthermore, the *keiretsu*'s control of distribution channels effectively shuts non-Japanese firms out of some Japanese markets. Although the situation is changing as this is written, non-Japanese still regard the *keiretsu* as a significant barrier to trade and foreign direct investment, while the Japanese, on the other hand, regard the *keiretsu* as a key element in their economic success. The problem of differential or asymmetrical access has been a major cause of conflict between Japan and its trading partners.

THE GERMAN SYSTEM OF "SOCIAL MARKET" CAPITALISM

The German economy has some characteristics similar to the American and some to the Japanese systems of political economy, but it is quite different from both in other ways.[37] On the one hand, Germany, like Japan, emphasizes exports and national savings and investment more than consumption.[38] However, Germany permits the market to function with considerable freedom; indeed, most states in Western Europe are significantly less interventionist than Japan. Furthermore, except for the medium-sized business sector (*Mittelstand*), the non-governmental sector of the German economy is highly oligopolistic and is dominated by alliances between major corporations and large private banks. The German system of political economy attempts to balance social concerns and market efficiency.[39] The German state

[37] This section draws from Philip Glouchevitch, *Juggernaut: The German Way of Business: Why It Is Transforming Europe—and the World* (New York: Simon and Schuster, 1992).

[38] Gunter Heiduk and Kozo Yamamura, eds., *Technological Competition and Interdependence: The Search for Policy in the United States, West Germany, and Japan* (Seattle: University of Washington Press, and Tokyo: University of Tokyo Press, 1990).

[39] The German system is representative of classical liberalism that emphasizes a free market and a strong welfare-oriented state. See Razeen Sally, *Classical Liberalism and International Economic Order: Studies in Theory and Intellectual History* (New York: Routledge, 1998).

and the private sector provide a highly developed system of social welfare.

The German national system of political economy is representative of the "corporatist" or "welfare state capitalism" of continental Europe, in which capital, organized labor, and government cooperate in management of the economy. This corporatist version of capitalism is characterized by greater representation of labor and the larger society in the governance of corporate affairs than in Anglo-Saxon shareholder capitalism.[40] Although the continental economies differ from one another in many respects, in all of them the state plays a strategic role in the economy. It is significant, especially in Germany, that major banks are vital to the provision of capital to industry. While, in many European countries, employee councils have some responsibility for running the company, in Germany labor has a particularly important role in corporate governance. Indeed, the "law of codetermination" mandates equal representation of employees and management on supervisory boards. Although the power of labor on these boards can be easily overstated, the system is a significant factor in Germany's postwar history of relatively smooth labor relations.

Ever since Chancellor Otto von Bismarck took the first important steps toward the modern welfare state in the late nineteenth century, the German state has assumed a major role in providing public welfare for every citizen. This national commitment to advance the overall welfare of the German people has rested on the extraordinary efficiency of German industry. In the modern era, pairing industrial efficiency with public welfare has been made manifest in the concept of the "social market." Germany emphasizes the values of domestic harmony and community. Worker benefits include a greatly reduced workweek, unemployment insurance, health care, and lengthy vacations. By one reckoning, the cost of benefits is equal to about 80 percent of a worker's take-home pay. The nation's high rate of productivity growth has enabled the German nation to provide these generous social welfare benefits, but these especially generous welfare programs have imposed a large burden on German business.

Economic Role of the State

The most important contribution of the German state to the economic success of their economy has been indirect. During the postwar era, the German federal government and the governments of the individual *Lander* (states) have created a stable and favorable environ-

---

[40] Katzenstein, *Corporatism and Change.*

169

ment for private enterprise. Their laws and regulations have success-fully encouraged a high savings rate, rapid capital accumulation, and economic growth. Germany has a highly developed system of codified law that reduces uncertainty and creates a stable business climate; the American common law tradition guides U.S. business, and the Japanese bureaucracy relies on administrative guidance.

At the core of the German system of political economy is their central bank, or Bundesbank. The Bundesbank's crucial role in the postwar German economy has been compared to that of the German General Staff in an earlier German domination of the Continent. Movement toward the European Economic and Monetary Union has further increased the powerful impact of the Bundesbank. Although the Bundesbank lacks the formal independence of the American Fed-eral Reserve, its actual independence and pervasive influence over the German economy have rested on the belief of the German public that the Bundesbank is the "defender of the mark" (euro) and the staunch opponent of dreaded inflation. Indeed, the Bundesbank did create the stable macroeconomic environment and low interest rates that have provided vital support to the postwar competitive success of German industry.

The role of the German state in the microeconomic aspects of the economy has been modest. The Germans, for example, have not had an activist industrial policy although, like other advanced industrial countries, the government has spent heavily on research and develop-ment. The German government, however, has not intervened signifi-cantly in the economy to shape its structure except in the support it has given through subsidies and protection to such dying industries as coal and shipbuilding and the state-owned businesses such as Luf-thansa and the Bundespost (mail and telecommunications). However, since the early 1990s, these sectors have increasingly been privatized. On the whole, the German economy is closer to the American mar-ket-oriented system than to the Japanese system of collective capi-talism.

Corporate Governance and Private Business Practices

The German system of corporate governance and industrial structure has noteworthy parallels to the Japanese system. As in Japan, power-ful national organizations such as the Bundesverband der Deutschen Industrie and the Deutscher Industrie-und Handelstag represent the interests of business in national affairs, and labor is also well orga-nized at the national level. IG. Metall, an organization that represents the auto and metal workers as well as other industries, can speak for

German labor in a way that the American Federation of Labor/Congress of Industrial Organizations cannot for American workers. Japanese organized labor, on the other hand, is fragmented into company unions and has almost no influence on either company or national affairs. The system of codetermination at the level of the firm has made German labor a partner, albeit a junior partner, in corporate governance.

German industrial organization has certain noteworthy features. One element is the prominent role played in the economy by medium-sized, privately owned firms, called the *Mittelstand.* Despite the international prominence given to Germany's large corporations, such as Siemens or Daimler-Benz, the *Mittelstand* constitute an important reason for German economic success. They are major exporters and are especially strong as suppliers of such intermediate goods as chemicals and machine tools. The second major component in German success is the publicly owned corporations whose shares are traded freely on the German stock market. Nevertheless, corporations such as these are much less important in the German economy than in the American economy. In fact, in the 1990s, there were only about six hundred fifty German companies listed on the stock market, and only about one hundred twenty were actively traded. The firms that are most important in the overall structure and governance of the German economy are the bank-linked corporations.

The integration of finance and industry has been a noteworthy feature of corporate governance in Germany. Although more informal than the Japanese *keiretsu,* long-term bank-corporate ties are a crucial element in the system. The major universal banks (i.e., those that perform all financial services) such as the Deutsche Bank and the Commerzbank are worthy of particular attention. Representatives of these banks and of the large German multinational corporations sit on one another's boards of supervisors. In important ways the system of cross-ownership and interlocking boards resembles the Japanese *keiretsu* with their integration of financial, industrial, and distribution activities; the system facilitates the sharing of vital information, provision of less expensive investment capital, and coordination of economic planning. Also, like the *keiretsu,* the system emphasizes long-term relationships based on negotiated prices and supply arrangements among corporations. However, German participants in these arrangements seek to advance the interests of their particular firm rather than those of the whole organizational alliance. It is important to note that as the German economy has globalized, the linkages between banks and industry have weakened.

171

Banking-industry ties have reduced conflict between industrial and financial interests over economic policy. Because of their pervasive financial power and their linkage with key industries, the major German banks play a central role in the governance of industry and in overall strategic planning for the German economy. While the German corporate world, like the Japanese, is closed, the German economy itself is open, and the German legal system and codified administrative procedures ensure that foreign businesses will be treated in a legally fair manner.

The powerful influence of German universal banks over the economy is primarily a function of the considerable freedom the banks enjoy to enter a great variety of business activities. Under the system of universal banking, German banks can participate in almost every conceivable financial activity, from commercial to investment to merchant banking. Until the 1990s, American commercial and investment banking, on the other hand, was restricted by the Glass-Steagal Act of the early 1930s. In this system, different activities have been conducted by different types of institutions, while German universal banks have had a hand in almost every facet of German financial and business affairs. For example, industrial financing is supplied principally through bank loans rather than through issuance of stock or commercial paper. The banks also own large portions of German companies, and the supervisory boards of German industry are frequently dominated by bankers. Industrial firms prize their ties with the banks because, in addition to ensuring lower cost capital, this arrangement has provided security against hostile takeovers and interfering shareholders.

The strategic role of banks and the close links between banks and industry in the German economy are largely the result of Germany's experience as a late industrializer. As Alexander Gerschenkron, and Thorstein Veblen before him, pointed out, the timing of industrialization is a key factor in determining the mechanism of capital accumulation and the overall structure of a nation's industrial system.[41] In contrast to Great Britain and the United States, where capital was initially accumulated largely in the hands of individual entrepreneurs, in Germany and other continental European countries there was relatively little capital in the hands of individuals. In these circumstances, the banks became the principal means of amassing sufficiently huge

---

[41] Alexander Gerschenkron, *Economic Backwardness in Historical Perspective: A Book of Essays* (Cambridge: Belknap Press of Harvard University Press, 1962); and Thorstein Veblen, *Imperial Germany and the Industrial Revolution* (New York: Macmillan, 1915).

amounts of investment capital to expedite industrialization and catch up with the industrial leaders. This historic linkage between finance and industry has continued in both Germany and Japan.

The most influential of the major German universal banks is, without question, the Deutsche Bank (DB). The DB's pivotal position in the German economy may be gauged by its holdings in the nation's major corporations; it has a substantial stake in Daimler-Benz, Germany's largest corporation, and it also has substantial holdings in Germany's leading insurance company (Allianz), its largest reinsurance company (Munich Re), and its major department store chain (Karstadt). The list of blue-chip companies in which DB has a large stake could easily be lengthened. In addition, members of the upper management of DB are on the supervisory boards of over one hundred fifty German corporations.

German government policies have supported and reinforced the position of Germany's major private banks in corporate governance. Corporate law has empowered banks by giving considerable rights to minority shareholders. For example, corporate law has required that 75 percent of the shareholders in a public corporation must approve any change in the corporation's capitalization and hence in the governing structure of a firm. This means that a bank with only a 26 percent share can block change. Since, in certain circumstances, the banks can also vote the shares of their account holders, this provides banks with considerable influence over corporate affairs.

The governing structure of German industry is affected by the German government's tolerance of the concentration of economic power, by horizontal cooperation, and by the linkages between finance and industry. Despite the fact that the American Occupation after World War II attempted to wipe out the German cartel tradition and to promote an antitrust mentality, this mentality remains relatively weak in Germany. The decision of the German government to permit Daimler-Benz to acquire Messerschmitt-Bölkow-Blohm, Germany's largest defense and aerospace firm, is an example of German tolerance of the concentration of economic power. (Subsequently, Daimler-Benz eliminated its interests in Messerschmitt-Bölkow-Blohm.)

German management is less restricted by shareholder concerns about annual returns on their investments than is American management. Freedom from outside scrutiny has unfortunately sometimes protected the incompetent, but it has enabled German management to pursue long-term plans. This situation began to change in the late 1990s, but previously, management independence had been greatly enhanced by the system of "dual boards." In Germany, there is both a supervisory board, comparable to the American board of directors, and a management board, composed of the chief executive and top management. While, in theory, the supervisory board is the superior body, in actual practice the management board, which is full-time and functions on the basis of consensus, is frequently dominant. This empowerment of management strengthens management's ability to make long-term strategic decisions.

The structure and governance of German industry is also significantly influenced by the negative German attitude toward corporate takeovers. The methods used to prevent hostile takeovers are legion: for instance, companies may simply stay private, stock may be distributed to increase resistance, blocking minorities may be employed, German corporate law can be utilized to discourage takeovers, and voting rights can be restricted. Whereas in the United States, corporate takeovers are defended as a blunt but effective means to guarantee high performance and to demonstrate the ultimate responsibility of management to the shareholders, in Germany takeovers have been regarded as destabilizing and destructive of important long-term business relationships. A number of American executives discovered this, to their chagrin, when they attempted to gain control of the Deutsche Bank. This attitude has made corporate takeovers and struggles over corporate governance rare in Germany, and German banks have seldom sold their stakes in German corporations. This situation, however, began to change in the late 1990s.

SIGNIFICANCE OF NATIONAL DIFFERENCES

This chapter has analyzed and compared the three national systems of political economy dominant at the beginning of the twenty-first century. The American system incorporates neoclassical precepts regarding the organization and functioning of an economy intended to maximize consumer satisfaction and facilitate adjustment to change. Many other countries consider the social costs of such an economy to be too high because of their impact on poverty and on those who lose through economic developments. The Japanese system places a high priority on social harmony and national power, but its critics consider that system to be inflexible, mercantilistic, and unresponsive to the concerns of other societies. The German emphasis on the social market has many of the virtues and vices of both the American and Japanese systems. Although each of these economies was experiencing important changes at the turn of the century, they remained distinctly different from one another, and their fundamental differences are significant for the nature and dynamics of the world economy.

The significance of the differences among national economies became more and more apparent in the late 1960s and 1970s as a consequence of the increasing interdependence of national economies. As economies became more integrated with one another, the domestic and international spheres became more closely linked to one another, and national policy makers became more and more concerned about the domestic economic structures and private economic practices of other societies that might affect the welfare of their own citizens and nations. As these national differences have become more significant, several questions have arisen: (1) Is one national system superior to the others, and should it therefore be the model for other economies? (2) Do national systems of political economy compete with one another in a "Darwinian struggle" for survival and dominance? and (3) Are systems of political economy converging?

Is One System Superior to the Others?

At one time or another during the postwar era, one or another national economy has been declared superior. In the 1970s, the German system of the Social Market was assigned credit for the postwar German "economic miracle"; as one enthusiastic writer stated, West Germany had become a juggernaut and a challenge to all other economies. In the 1980s, attention shifted to Japan, which was then enjoying a huge trade surplus and a rapid rate of economic growth; at that time, the Japanese system of state-led capitalism or developmental state capitalism became the envy of the rest of the world and the model to be emulated. Both Germany's and Japan's stakeholder capitalist systems were judged superior to America's shareholder (stockholder) capitalism, in part because the former were believed to free corporate leaders from short-term shareholder demands for higher dividends and thus to enable them to take a long-term view in their investment and other decisions. When Japan plunged into a serious financial crisis and recession in the 1990s, the prize for best performance went to the United States, whose economy was booming throughout much of the decade; American public officials, economists, and commentators announced that America's shareholder and free-market capitalism had proved superior to all others. The outstanding success of the American economy, many argued, was due to the fact that in the 1980s and 1990s the United States had created a novel type of economy based on a "New Economic Paradigm." The

175

rest of the world, Americans proclaimed, should adopt their model of deregulation, open markets, and minimal government intervention in the economy.

The claim that one economy is superior to others is difficult to assess. Nations differ greatly in their standards of judgment. Should one apply such criteria as the rate of economic growth, the extent of economic equality and social well-being, or perhaps what some have called a "misery index"? National values obviously differ on these matters. The French, for example, reject what they consider to be the ruthlessness of America's emphasis on the market and its insufficient attention to the problems of income inequality and economic insecurity. Many American observers, on the other hand, believe that the overly protective nature of the French state is largely responsible for France's economic troubles, especially its very high rate of unemployment. In short, an economic system strongly reflects the values of the society in which it is embedded and must be judged, at least to some extent, in terms of those values. The Japanese *keiretsu*, for example, would certainly be incompatible with American opposition to concentrations of economic power.

The most objective measures of national economic performance are an economy's rates of economic and productivity growth. However, even these measures have limitations. Productivity, particularly in those service industries that increasingly characterize the American and Western European economies, is difficult to measure. Another difficulty is that when an economy is beyond a certain level of economic development, its performance at any particular moment is more a function of the phase of the business cycle than of the economy's inherent features. Although economists and governments do not yet know how to manage an economy to avoid the business cycle, a government's use of macroeconomic policy obviously significantly influences national economic performance.

Despite the difficulties of the endeavor, the effort to determine whether particular economic arrangements are superior to others has engaged many scholars. Karl Marx, Joseph Schumpeter, and Alexander Gerschenkron have been among these scholars. One theme of these early writers as well as more recent commentators is that the stage or timing of economic development determines the nature and appropriateness of an economic system. Each stage in the evolution of technology and other aspects of capital accumulation is said to require a different form of economic and sociotechnological organization. Gerschenkron, for example, argued that the method of capital accumulation (by business enterprise, banking system, or state) was determined by the timing of economic development. Whereas Great Britain and the United States, as early industrializers, relied on capital accumulation by entrepreneurs and by shareholders, Germany and Japan as late starters emphasized accumulation by powerful banks, and the USSR and China as late, late developing countries depended on state-led capital accumulation.

A similar theme has been set forth by business economist Alfred Chandler (1977) and other scholars.[42] Each stage in the development of technology, this position argues, requires new and appropriate institutional arrangements. In fact, national institutional and societal restructuring is frequently necessary to take advantage of new technologies.[43] For example, it could be argued that the open and free-wheeling American economy is appropriate for the age of the Internet. Whether it is correct or not, this argument suggests that flexible and adaptable economic and other institutions are desirable. Another formulation of the evolving institutional requirements for economic success has been set forth by Robert Wade in his argument that, whereas the Japanese and East Asian economic model of state-led industrialization and capital accumulation is appropriate for economic takeoff, the American system of maximizing returns through the optimum allocation of the existing capital stock and national savings may be better suited to maintaining economic stability in an industrialized economy.[44]

Another approach to understanding superiority has been taken by Jeffrey Hart in his book *Rival Capitalists: International Competitiveness in the United States, Japan, and Western Europe* (1992). He argues that "variations in state-societal arrangements" determine the success and international competitiveness of national economies.[45] And Peter Katzenstein has made a strong case for the superior performance of corporatist small West European countries.[46] Although these ideas provide useful insights into the relationship of national

[42] Alfred D. Chandler Jr., *The Visible Hand: The Managerial Revolution in American Business* (Cambridge: Belknap Press of Harvard University Press, 1977).

[43] Carlotta Perez argues that an economy's institutions must be tuned to the dominant technologies of an era. See "Structural Change and Assimilation of New Technologies in the Economic and Social Systems," *Futures—The Journal of Forecasting and Planning* 15, no. 5 (October 1983): 357–75.

[44] Robert Wade, "The Asian Debt-and-Development Crisis of 1997: Causes and Consequences," *World Development* 26, no. 8 (August 1998): 1535–53.

[45] Jeffrey A. Hart, *Rival Capitalists: International Competitiveness in the United States, Japan, and Western Europe* (Ithaca: Cornell University Press, 1992).

[46] Peter Katzenstein, *Small States in World Markets: Industrial Policy in Europe* (Ithaca: Cornell University Press, 1985).

systems and economic success, economic performance is ultimately a function of many factors and cannot be completely explained by any particular institutional arrangement. Moreover, as the contributors to Suzanne Berger and Ronald Dore's edited book, *National Diversity and Global Capitalism: Domestic Institutions and the Pressures for National Convergence* (1996), amply demonstrate, different societies use different institutional arrangements to perform the same economic functions.[47] Although an economy may borrow "best practice" techniques and institutions from one another, as happened when the United States and others adopted Japan's system of lean production, there is no one-to-one correspondence across national economies between structure and function.

It is certain that some economic systems have failed miserably, notably the command economies of the former Soviet bloc, and this suggests that there are some minimal requirements for economic success. Nathan Rosenberg and L. E. Birdzell demonstrate, in *How the West Got Rich* (1986), that government policies and socioeconomic institutions must facilitate efficient, flexible, and innovative economic behavior.[48] Whether through an unfettered market mechanism or some form of state interventionism, a society must create incentives that encourage entrepreneurship, innovation, accumulation, and efficient use of the basic factors of production (especially through investment in capital and skilled labor). Society must also reward innovative activities and support the economy's ability to adjust to economic, technological, and other changes. However, such objectives as these can be fulfilled by differing economic institutions and practices.

The outstanding performance of the American economy in the 1990s and the dismal failure of many other economies convinced most Americans, as well as many others, that the American economy should be the model for the rest of the world. Throughout most of the decade, the United States enjoyed a high rate of economic growth, low unemployment, and low inflation, while Western Europe had a low rate of economic growth and a very high rate of unemployment. After the collapse of its bubble economy in the early 1990s, Japan entered a serious financial crisis and, somewhat later, a recession. Although the other Pacific Asian economies posted spectacular rates of

---

[47] Suzanne Berger and Ronald Dore, eds., *National Diversity and Global Capitalism: Domestic Institutions and the Pressures for National Convergence* (Ithaca: Cornell University Press, 1996).

[48] Nathan Rosenberg and L. E. Birdzell Jr., *How the West Got Rich: The Economic Transformation of the Industrial World* (New York: Basic Books, 1986).

economic growth throughout most of the 1990s, they were hit by a severe financial crisis and recession in the fall of 1997. The economic pace slackened in China, and the Russian economy was a disaster. Thus, for a period in the late 1990s, the United States was an economic oasis in a global economic desert.

American officials, business leaders, and popular commentators attributed the prolonged success of the American economy to fundamental changes that had occurred in the 1980s and the 1990s. Proponents of the "New American Economy" argued that the American economy had been transformed by several factors: deregulation, increased openness to the global economy, downsizing and restructuring of American corporations in the 1980s, and rapid technological advances (especially in the computer and information technologies) that increased national productivity. The globalization or openness of the American economy to imports kept prices down, decreased inflationary pressures, and hence permitted the Federal Reserve to pursue expansionary economic policies. Deregulation of the American economy made it better suited than its Japanese and European competitors to take advantage of the digital revolution. Some alleged that the productivity and international competitiveness of the American economy have significantly increased and surpassed the rest of the world. Many even proclaimed that the American economy had transcended the boom-and-bust business cycles of the past.

There is no dispute about the overall success of the American economy in the 1990s. Excellent management of the economy by the Federal Reserve as well as an upswing in the business cycle certainly played an important part in this success. However, it has not yet been demonstrated that the United States has created a superior economic model; indeed, good luck has played a role in American success. For example, the victory over inflation and consequent low interest rates can be attributed in large part to the fact that the rest of the world economy was in recession in the 1990s. Moreover, the American economy benefited greatly from a huge inflow of foreign capital that buoyed the stock market; indeed, by the late 1990s, America's national foreign debt had reached approximately $1 trillion. Economic expansion was also funded by the virtual elimination of personal savings and a huge buildup of consumer and corporate debt. Rapid economic expansion was accompanied by increasing income inequalities, job insecurity, and serious social problems. Despite the impressive achievements of the American economy in the 1990s, one must remember that it is dangerous to argue that the American or any other economic model is and will be, for all time, superior to others.

179

Do Nations Compete with One Another?[49]

The Clinton Administration assumed power believing that pursuit of a "competitiveness strategy" would restore the international competitiveness of the American economy. The United States, as the President told the American people, is "like a big corporation competing in the global marketplace." Clinton raised the competitiveness issue in response to America's huge trade deficit and to growing concern about the deindustrialization of the economy. The immense trade deficit with Japan alarmed the Administration and convinced many that the United States had become noncompetitive with Japan, especially in high-tech industries. The newly elected President created the National Economic Council in response to these concerns and charged it to develop a national strategy to deal with such problems.

About the same time, many West European leaders also began to express concern about the international competitiveness of Western Europe. In June 1993, Jacques Delors, then president of the European Commission, stated that the European economy's most basic problem was loss of international competitiveness. The fundamental reason for high unemployment, he proclaimed, was that Europeans were no longer competitive with the Americans and the Japanese, and the solution should be to increase competitiveness in high-tech industries. Other West Europeans have also spoken of the intense global economic struggle. Many political leaders and the general public began to believe that the economic well-being and even the political survival of Western Europe was at stake in this international struggle. Although both European and American concerns moderated in the late 1990s, concern over competitiveness continued to be very much alive.

The idea that nations qua nations are engaged in a zero-sum competition for market share and economic superiority is anathema to every mainstream economist. It was economist Paul Krugman who, in an article in the *Foreign Affairs* journal (1994), launched the attack on the Clinton Administration's competitiveness strategy and even on the very idea of national competitiveness.[50] Krugman previously had been a principal author of the theory of strategic trade and thus had inadvertently contributed to the intellectual rationale supporting the Administration's policies. In a series of books and articles, Krugman

---

[49] The question of whether national differences lead to economic and political conflicts is discussed in my book, *The Challenge of Global Capitalism: The World Economy in the 21st Century* (Princeton: Princeton University Press, 2000), Chapter 8.

[50] Paul R. Krugman, "Competitiveness: A Dangerous Obsession," *Foreign Affairs* 73, no. 2 (March/April 1994): 28–44.

subsequently moderated his former enthusiasm for strategic trade and argued that international economic competition takes place between individual business firms and not between national economies. Krugman and other American economists have noted, moreover, that since imports comprise just a small fraction of the American economy, the principal competitors for most American firms are other American firms. And interfirm competition is beneficial, because it rewards efficient producers, benefits the consumer, and leads to maximization of world wealth.

Whereas some individuals and governments believe that nations are engaged in a win-or-lose economic struggle, economists argue that free trade and international competition benefit everyone; indeed, according to the theory of comparative advantage, every nation has a comparative advantage in something and can therefore be a winner. The mercantilist or geoeconomics position of the Clinton Administration that emerged from belief in the win-or-lose struggle, Krugman correctly warned, would produce ill-conceived and reckless policies, including wasteful industrial policies and confrontational trade policies. Moreover, he warned that emphasis on competitiveness diverted attention from such fundamental problems as America's low savings rate and the declining skill level of an alarmingly large portion of the American workforce. Indeed, in the 1990s the United States found it necessary to import large numbers of engineers and scientists to staff its growing information economy.

As Krugman has pointed out, the most appropriate measure of an economy's performance is its productivity and not its balance of trade or of international payments.[51] The national level of productivity and the rate of productivity growth not only constitute the true measure of an economy's performance but also determine a nation's long-term well-being. For this reason, Krugman and other economists have no objection to the term "international competitiveness," provided that such thinking refers to national productivity and gives rise to improved government policies to increase national savings and investment in capital goods and in skilled labor.

It should be pointed out, however, that economic policies designed to increase a nation's rate of productivity growth do not necessarily have any effect on a nation's balance of foreign trade and international payments, although many noneconomists believe that there is a direct causal relationship. The trade balance and payments balance of an economy are determined principally by its savings/investment

---

[51] Productivity is a measure of the ratio of national output to national input.

181

ratio and by macroeconomic (fiscal and monetary) policies. Further-more, the productivity growth of one economy does not necessarily harm other economies and may even raise the economic welfare of others. For example, increased productivity of one economy can im-prove the economic welfare of its trading partners by making the former's exports less expensive. As a case in point, no one could deny that the high rate of productivity growth of the Japanese automotive and electronics industries has benefited American consumers enor-mously and has forced American firms to increase their own produc-tivity and competitiveness in price and quality.

Although nations may not compete with one another in a narrow economic sense, nations can be said to compete in a broader sense; that is, in their ability to manage their economic affairs effectively. At particular times, certain national economies are obviously superior in their ability to fashion and implement policies that promote eco-nomic and productivity growth. Beneficial economic policies encour-age savings, investment, and education, and also facilitate rapid ad-justment of the private sector to economic and technological change. Swedish economist Gunnar Eliasson stated that competitiveness can be defined as a nation's ability to renew itself. In this sense, competi-tiveness is ultimately the ability of a society to transform itself contin-uously in response to economic, political, and technological changes. The state and its policies must play a central role in transformation and adjustment; markets alone will not succeed. The state must ad-dress such issues as market failures and the provision of such public goods as R & D. Eliasson believes that competitiveness depends on the economy's flexibility both to adjust relative prices and to modify industrial structures by scrapping obsolete economic activities and thus releasing labor and capital to facilitate the development of viable new businesses. The capacity of an economy to transform itself is a crucial characteristic in the global struggle to determine which na-tions will develop a comparative advantage in those industries and economic activities most important to economic welfare and national power.[52]

The concept of the "competitive state" emerges from ideas ex-pressed by Eliasson and incorporates Krugman's argument that it is firms and not states that compete. The competitive state concept also incorporates the fact that firms are increasingly mobile as they seek

[52] Gunnar Eliasson, *The Knowledge Base of an Industrial Economy* (Stockholm: In-dustrial Institute for Economic and Social Research; distributed by Almqvist and Wik-sell International, 1988).

the most attractive locations in the global economy.[53] Moreover, it recognizes that governments cannot pick winners and that the choice of technologies must be left up to the private sector. According to this concept, however, governments should be active and should not leave matters to the market alone. As Vincent Cable has pointed out, a "competing nation" attempts to strengthen the position of its firms in the global economy and attract foreign investment through creation of a pool of highly educated, flexible workers, an efficient physical infrastructure, sound economic policies, and an attractive quality of life.[54] Such a competition strategy has been employed effectively by Singapore and has been adopted by Britain, Ireland, and other countries; Germany is also moving in this direction. However, another significant example of a successful competitive state is the United States. In 1980, for example, responding to fears of deindustrialization, the Congress passed the Bayh-Dole Act that, for the first time, permitted universities to patent the results of federally funded research and to license those results to private firms.[55] Subsequent legislation has strengthened this corporate-university alliance as a key element in America's competitive strategy in the area of high-tech industries. Many observers, however, do fear this could prove harmful to the universities over the long term.

CONVERGENCE, HARMONIZATION, OR MUTUAL RECOGNITION?

There are several possible solutions to problems engendered by national differences that have created obstacles to the smooth functioning and full development of the global economy. Differences could be eradicated or moderated either through the functioning of the market, as neoclassical *convergence* theory suggests, or through political negotiations to achieve *harmonization* of national practices. The convergence position requires patience, as it posits that national systems will converge through the operation of markets in which, over time, economic forces will cause nations to modify their economic structures and business practices. Harmonization, on the other hand, is based on international negotiations and reciprocity leading to elimi-

---

[53] The implications of this fact are developed by Robert Reich, *The Work of Nations: Preparing Ourselves for 21st Century Capitalism* (New York: Knopf, 1991).

[54] Vincent Cable, "The Diminished Nation-State: A Study in the Loss of Economic Power," in *What Future for the State? Daedalus* 124, no. 2 (spring 1995): 48–50.

[55] This development and its potential dangers is discussed by Eyal Press and Jennifer Washburn, "The Kept University," *Atlantic Monthly* 285, no. 3 (March 2000): 39–54.

nation of national differences; the negotiations between Japan and the United States over the Structural Impediments Initiative (SII) in the late 1980s is a prime example. Both methods of accommodation are slow, and the latter can be very confrontational. Still a third way to deal with national differences is by application of the principle of *mutual recognition*, in which nations agree to honor one another's economic and business practices. Indeed, mutual recognition has been central within the movement toward European and, to a lesser extent, North American regionalism.

Convergence

According to neoclassical convergence theory, economic interdependence will ultimately lead to a convergence in economic performance among national economies as rates of economic growth, productivity levels, and national incomes move toward one another. Many writers even argue that economic globalization necessarily forces convergence of the structural features of an economy and of private economic practices and that, therefore, national differences will disappear. These persons argue that intensification of global economic competition, expansion of trade and foreign direct investment, and interpenetration of national societies necessitate that societies adopt similar domestic institutions and economic practices. As other countries close the economic and technological gap with the more developed economies, the role of the market will become more central in each economy; then the policy prescriptions of neoclassical economics—economic openness, noninterventionism, and the like—will increasingly guide the economic activities of that society. Many American economists and public officials argue that the superior performance of the American economy in the 1990s and the weaknesses of the once-envied Japanese and other Pacific Asian economies have made the American economy and the free market the model for the world. Some observers even proclaim that the convergence process leads the world toward individualism and political democracy.

The neoclassical position assumes that national variations in economic performance are a function either of a catching-up process or of a country's failure to manage its economy according to the policy prescriptions of neoclassical economics. In this view, the outstanding economic success of Japan and the East Asian Newly Industrializing Countries (NICs) was caused by their having had the advantage of backwardness and their ability to apply the experience and technology of the more advanced economies when they mobilized national resources to expedite economic growth. Then, as countries develop,

184

they will inevitably converge toward the neoclassical model of a market economy. As these countries draw close to the more industrialized countries, their growth rates will slacken, and they will eventually settle down as more "normal" countries with more typical normal growth rates.

Since the end of World War II, there has indeed been convergence in economic performance among the more advanced economies. Convergence in productivity levels and other economic indicators has taken place between the United States and the other industrialized economies largely as a consequence of trade liberalization. However, the gap between rich and poor countries has actually widened except in the case of the East Asian and a few other industrializing economies. Some explain that most poor countries have failed to catch up because convergence can work only when political, social, and economic institutions are conducive to economic development and are supportive of inward flows of capital and technology; these conditions did exist in East Asia. The East Asian experience indicates that convergence between developed and less developed countries is not automatic, but, as Robert Barro has pointed out, requires an appropriate social and political infrastructure.[56]

Another possible reason why so many less developed countries have failed to catch up with the developed economies is supplied by the new growth theory. In that theory, an initial advantage of one country over another in human capital can and usually will result in a permanent difference in income level between the countries. This happens particularly when the differences in human capital are very large. Developed countries rich in human capital can sustain a much higher level of economic output than can less developed countries with a low level of human capital; thus, the former will be able to maintain a decisive lead indefinitely by generating more new savings and investment than the less developed economy can generate. Thus, even though poor countries may be gaining in wealth, the gap between them and the rich will continue.

If convergence in economic performance has been weak and uneven, what about convergence in economic institutions and business practices? With economic globalization, is the world gravitating toward the American free market model? It is certain that the increasing integration of national economies has encouraged societies to adopt particular institutions and practices proven especially successful else-

---

[56] Robert J. Barro, *Economic Growth and Convergence*, Occasional Papers No. 46 (San Francisco: International Center for Economic Growth, 1994).

where; the spread of the Japanese technique of lean production to the United States, Great Britain, and elsewhere exemplifies this phenomenon. But this does not necessarily lead to the conclusion that economic globalization has been homogenizing domestic economies. The only significant examination that I have found of whether or not institutional convergence has really occurred is in Berger and Dore's edited volume, *National Diversity and Global Capitalism*, mentioned earlier. In a number of case studies, the contributors to this excellent volume (all of whom are experts on one or another of the economies examined) seek to determine whether or not convergence of institutions and domestic practices has been occurring; the volume reaches the following conclusions:

(1) Despite some convergence in macroeconomic performance, very little convergence has taken place at the level of national institutions. National institutions tend to be "sticky" or, in the language of economics, "inelastic." Societal changes are usually very costly, strongly resisted, and exceedingly slow.
(2) Differing but equally effective systems of corporate and other institutions within national societies limit the need for convergence to achieve particular objectives.
(3) External pressures may require a response or outcome, but the character of the response is largely determined by domestic factors and is not limited to a unique or single response.
(4) Convergence of national institutions has been subject to international negotiations; it can seldom be identified as an automatic consequence of globalization.
(5) The domestic effects of globalization are largely determined by states themselves.

Despite this impressive study, evidence suggests that important changes in economic behavior and structure have been taking place in a number of countries and that these changes tend primarily toward the American model of shareholder capitalism. The two most notable examples of this development are Germany and Japan. Yet, one should not jump to the conclusion, at least not yet, that the German and Japanese economies are shedding their distinctive features.

The German system of stakeholder capitalism came under severe pressure in the 1990s. The unification of Germany in 1989 imposed a very high and continuing financial burden on the German economy; Germany has been required to pump substantial funds into the backward economy of the former East Germany. In addition, German industry has had to deal with high labor costs (both wages and welfare benefits) and with the costly effort to create a unified European currency. The tension between the costs of the overly generous German welfare state and the need for greater economic efficiency has constituted a serious problem and has encouraged German firms to establish production facilities in Eastern Europe, the United States, and elsewhere. Moreover, Germany for many years has had to contend with a chronic high rate of unemployment (over 10 percent). Most importantly, Germany has become increasingly aware that fundamental reforms are necessary if it is to meet the combined challenges of economic globalization, European economic integration, and the increasing importance of the Internet and information economy. The growing pressure to internationalize production and to significantly increase the capital available to German industry to further the development of high-tech industries has placed a severe strain on the German "Social Market" economy.

One of the central tasks of reforming and restructuring the German economy to bring it into the information age entails elimination, or at least significant weakening, of the close bank-industry alliances; these powerful alliances are held together by webs of cross-holdings and interlocking directorates. This system has a number of major negative consequences; it has tied up large amounts of capital in traditional industries and discouraged individual entrepreneurship. In order to transform itself into a high-tech information economy, Germany requires large amounts of capital to invest in new industries; such a need prompted the unprecedented decision of Daimler-Benz to list DaimlerChrysler on the New York Stock Exchange, a move that required the company to break with tradition and to open its books to outsiders. Similar remarkable changes are taking place in Germany itself in response to the growth of a shareholder mentality that is creating a more vigorous and innovative German economic system.

Several events in early 2000 signaled that a significant change in the bank-industry alliance was taking place. The first development was the bid of the British firm Vodafone AirTouch to acquire the German firm Mannesmann A.G. The initial reaction of the German government was to denounce the threatened hostile takeover as "anti-German" and contrary to German culture. Germany has always had a strong preference that German firms merge with other national firms and has opposed hostile takeovers. The intense opposition to hostile and cross-boundary mergers has been due to a corporate culture that favors consensus and the interests of such stakeholders as labor. In the past, a German bank would have stepped in and used its own capital to save the threatened German firm. When, in this

187

case, no rescue took place, this provided evidence that a fundamental feature of German economic culture was changing.

Another and even more important example of the profound change taking place in the German economy early in the year 2000 was the proposed merger of Deutsche and Dresdner banks engineered by the powerful insurance conglomerate Allianz A.G. Although the merger effort eventually failed, it did signal an important change in German economic culture. Such an initiative would have dismantled a key component of the bank-industrial system and led to the loss of many thousands of jobs, an event unheard of in Germany. This development in turn would have led to a major restructuring of a key segment of the German economy. Efforts to restructure German industry have been greatly facilitated by a new tax law that allows corporations to sell off their holdings and investments without paying capital gains taxes. The purpose of these sell-offs is to enable German banks and corporations to eliminate burdensome holdings and pave the way for the same type of corporate mergers, acquisitions, and takeovers as in the United States and elsewhere. As a result, Germany will be able to accelerate development of a more entrepreneurial and high-tech economy appropriate for the world of the Internet and information economy.

These developments will undoubtedly transform Germany and make it more of a "competing state." As German investors are demanding greater transparency in the management of German business and a much higher rate of return on their investments, the shift from stakeholder to shareholder capitalism will accelerate. Equity culture is spreading fast in Germany and the rest of Europe, and the number of shareholders is rapidly increasing. Yet, it is highly unlikely that the German "social market" economy will be wholly abandoned in favor of the American-style free-market economy. Although welfare programs will be trimmed in the interest of greater efficiency and flexibility, the welfare state is too ingrained in German mentality to be abandoned. In addition, the practice of codetermination has given German labor a powerful voice in German firms, and German unions have become so important in the overall economy that a Thatcher-Reagan type of conservative ideology is unlikely ever to sweep that country.

In Japan, the issue of institutional change has also become urgent. Throughout the 1990s, the Japanese system of political economy suffered one serious setback after another. In the early 1990s, major problems arose with the collapse of the inflated "bubble" economy and resulted in a severe banking crisis; Japan's banks found themselves with a huge burden of underperforming or bad loans. Subsequently, in the late 1990s, the East Asian economic crisis greatly aggravated Japan's economic slowdown and financial problems. In 1998, Japan lunged into its deepest recession since the end of World War II; moreover, in contrast to past crises, Japan's export-led growth strategy has been unable to reinvigorate the economy and, as these lines are written in the early spring of 2000, recession continues. At a more fundamental level, Japan's rapidly aging population, the overcapacity and low profitability of many export industries, and the overall low level of productivity outside the export sector portend severe economic troubles in the decades ahead.

These accumulating difficulties have caused many Japanese to accept the idea that a radical deregulation and restructuring of the Japanese political economy has become necessary. For example, Japan's Economic Planning Agency (EPA) published a report in 1995, *Toward the Revival of a Dynamic Economy*, in which it warned that Japan must either reform its economy or face long-term economic decline. Essential to any significant reform would be a shift from an export-led to a domestic-led growth strategy, opening of the economy to greatly increased amounts of manufactured imports and to foreign direct investment, and extensive deregulation of the economy. Such steps, some argue, would lead to a significant revival of the economy, increase overall productivity growth, and enable Japan to become more of a leader in the world economy. However, powerful resistance from the Japanese bureaucracy and from entrenched private interests, and the seeming indifference of the Japanese people, lead to doubt about the ability or willingness of Japanese political leaders to make truly significant reforms in the economy.

Nevertheless, Japan's national system of political economy has begun to change in a number of ways. The increased attention given to the Japanese consumer, the pervasive role of the Japanese state in the economy, and distinctive private business practices are changing. The system of lifetime employment and seniority-based pay is weakening because of recession and the increasing need in the information economy to reward the most valued younger workers; some firms have even been forced to lay off tens of thousands of workers. Under severe financial pressure, some *keiretsu* have begun to unravel as members have been forced to sell off their holdings in member firms. Corporate mergers and restructuring are still limited by Western standards, but are increasing; Renault's takeover of Nissan could never have occurred in the past. A significant increase in foreign direct investment and in the number of foreigners in the economy has taken

189

place. Younger Japanese have become much more entrepreneurial. Throughout the economy, an increasing emphasis on return to equity has caused firms to decrease their former concern with market share. The pressure for profitability and reform will increase as pension funds demand greater returns to support the growing population of the aged. High wages, production costs, and an overvalued yen are forcing Japanese firms to produce more and more goods in overseas plants.

The core of the Japanese industrial economy is the "main bank system." In the early postwar years, this system was very effective in collecting national savings and funneling them to the industrial members of the *keiretsu*. However, this system resulted in overly close banking-industry ties and led to major inefficiencies, corruption, and other abuses. The main bank system that once pumped capital into *keiretsu* regardless of risk has failed; it was this system that led to the colossal misallocation of capital that culminated in Japan's bubble economy. Largely as a consequence of the collapse of the bubble and the ensuing financial crisis, the main bank system has been under strain and has been undergoing major reforms. In addition, financial reforms of the late 1990s have increased competition, especially from American and other financial institutions, and have been forcing Japanese banks to become more prudent lenders and more profit-oriented in their practices. Nevertheless, powerful banks and the Ministry of Finance can be expected to remain major forces in the Japanese financial system.

Despite these impressive changes in Japan's political economy, there has been no significant alteration in such fundamental aspects of the economy as the political domination of the country by a conservative political, business, and bureaucratic elite; Japan's neomercantilist export-led growth strategy has not changed nor has the closed nature of the *keiretsu* been altered. Fundamental change will succeed only when and if Japan moves decisively in the direction of a more market-oriented economy. Such a transformation would require greatly expanded deregulation of the economy, and the Japanese economy is still the most regulated among industrialized countries. The overregulation of the economy by government bureaucracies has stifled innovation, discouraged entrepreneurship, and caused gross inefficiencies. Deregulation of the economy would stimulate entrepreneurship and increase productivity; it would also be an important step toward opening the Japanese market to imports, and this would further increase overall efficiency.

190

Meaningful deregulation of the Japanese economy will be extremely difficult to achieve. The power of domestic interests that seek protection and the emphasis on social harmony and safeguarding the weak have contributed to overregulation. Reform and deregulation would entail closing thousands of firms and putting hundreds of thousands of Japanese out of work; therefore, it is almost a certainty that public and vested interests will remain overwhelmingly opposed to such action. Moreover, as deregulation would weaken the power of the Ministry of Finance and other powerful bureaucracies, these agencies would also oppose any drastic reforms. It is instructive to note that the Japanese have a quite different concept of deregulation than does the United States. Whereas Americans interpret "deregulation" to mean the elimination of rules and regulators, the Japanese word for deregulation (*kisei kanwa*) means "relaxation of regulation" and not elimination.[57] Even though the rules may be changed, the Japanese bureaucracy will still attempt to regulate the system. Nevertheless, the task of regulation has become increasingly difficult as Japanese firms have become more powerful and as success in catching up with Western technology has led to a diminished role for central planning and bureaucratic control. As the Japanese are well aware, they must become technological innovators, and this requires some drastic changes in their society.

Most American economists and public officials believe that the solution to Japan's economic problems is to transform Japan into an American-type of free-market economy. However, the Japanese, like other Asians and most continental Europeans, are fearful of the possible consequences of adopting completely the American shareholder system. Most Japanese and Europeans reject the "Anglo-Saxonization" of the economy as a threat to social peace and, in the case of the Japanese, to economic/political independence. Japanese society, they fear, would be torn apart by the ruthlessness considered typical of the American economy and its toleration of high levels of economic insecurity and a large number of losers. For these reasons, Japan strongly resists conversion to the American economic model. More importantly, changing Japan into a Western-style economy would entail a fundamental shift in the relationships between individuals and society; there would have to be much greater emphasis on individualism, and some of the tight social bonds that are so characteristic of Japanese society would have to be weakened. These hurdles mean

[57] Bernstein, "Japanese Capitalism," 484.

191

that Japan is quite unlikely to become an American-type market economy.

Harmonization

Another possible solution to the problem posed by national differences is harmonization. Whereas the theory of economic convergence assumes that time and the market will lead to a blurring of national differences, the harmonization approach maintains that eradication of significant national differences should be an explicit goal of international negotiations. Many areas of government policies that lend themselves to harmonization already fall within the province of the World Trade Organization and other international institutions. The doctrine of national treatment embodied in the GATT/WTO, for example, prohibits discriminatory taxes and regulations to be applied to foreign firms. The Tokyo, Uruguay, and other GATT Rounds of trade negotiations have resolved many vexing issues that arise from cultural, historic, and government regulatory traditions. All these achievements, however, are only a small step toward a solution of the problem.

The first major effort toward negotiated harmonization of national differences was made in the Tokyo Round of trade negotiations; by the mid-1980s the concept of reciprocity, or more pointedly, "specific reciprocity," had become the principal mechanism employed to achieve greater harmonization among national systems of political economy. Under the GATT and, to a lesser extent, under the WTO system, general reciprocity had been the rule; nations would make broad concessions to trading partners in exchange for other broad concessions. Underlying this negotiating tactic was an assumption that, over time, concessions from one country to another would balance out, and everyone would benefit from a more open international economy. Rightly or wrongly, by the mid-1980s the United States and Western Europe believed that general reciprocity was working too slowly; the United States in particular believed that its trading partners (read especially Japan) had failed to carry out the agreements to which they had committed themselves. Therefore, in place of general reciprocity, the United States and Western Europe resorted to a policy of specific reciprocity under which these nations would not make any concessions and might even withdraw prior concessions if the other party did not fulfill its side of the agreement; this position was the rationale for the 1990s American policy of "managed trade" toward Japan, in which the United States demanded a percentage of the Japanese market in automobiles and other products in exchange for Japanese access to the American market. Needless to say, Japan and other countries that have been the object of such treatment have deeply resented it and regard specific reciprocity as an unwarranted interference in their domestic affairs. Whatever the merits of specific reciprocity, it is one tool for dealing with the increasingly important clash between national systems of political economy and the threat that these national differences pose to maintenance of an open world economy.

The most contentious issues lie outside the jurisdiction of international organizations, and governments everywhere prefer that no international organization should have the authority to enact, enforce, or prescribe universal rules or regulations for conducting business. Every government prefers to leave such matters in its own hands. At the same time, however, every government (and certainly every business firm) would like those government regulations, economic structures, and private business practices that constrain the activities of its own firms in foreign markets to be eliminated. This objective of transforming the regulations and business practices of foreign governments has been aggressively pursued by the United States and, to a lesser extent, by Western Europe.

Competition policy is one critically important policy area that lies outside the jurisdiction of existing international institutions and that has become a source of increasing friction. Economists concerned with competition policy refer to restrictive business practices that pose an obstacle to economic growth, trade expansion, and other economic goals. Competition policy applies to those domestic economic policies and regulations that determine legal or legitimate forms of business behavior and practices; such policies have become significant points of contention between the United States and the developmental states of East Asia. The antitrust tradition that attempts to prevent collusive business practices and concentration of corporate power is the essence of competition policy in the United States, and it facilitates entry into the American economy by foreign firms. Japanese and South Korean competition policies, on the other hand, not only tolerate but actually encourage concentration of corporate power in the form of the *keiretsu* and the *chaebol*. Although both these institutions are troubled at the opening of the twenty-first century, it is unlikely that they will be dismantled in the name of increased openness and competition.

Can harmonization and the policy of specific reciprocity work rapidly and effectively enough to overcome the political problems raised by national differences? Successive American Administrations have

193

believed that the process of economic convergence and reliance on multilateral negotiations to overcome problems of policy, structural, and behavioral differences work much too slowly. Many reason that the United States and its more open and competitive economy suffer from efforts to pursue goals in this fashion. Thus, Americans have supported a policy of enforced harmonization, and where this tactic has failed, of protectionism. As has already been mentioned, the most notable or infamous example of this approach was the prolonged and acrimonious Structural Impediments Initiative (SII) negotiations between Japan and the United States. These negotiations, in which the United States sought to transform important aspects of the Japanese economy, achieved little and left a bitter residue in Japan.

Mutual Recognition

The most simple approach to the problem of national differences is mutual recognition. According to this principle, every nation should accept the legitimacy of the rules by which other nations manage their economies. For example, a multinational firm establishing a subsidiary in another economy should be free to behave as it does in its own economy. This approach has been adopted by the European Union. Except in a few basic areas such as health and national standards, the members of the Union have agreed to permit businesses to operate throughout Western Europe in accordance with the laws and regulations of their home country. Thus, the subsidiary of a German corporation doing business in France would be governed principally by German law; nevertheless, more and more business regulations are being formulated in Brussels.

The fundamental question, of course, is whether or not the principle of mutual recognition is applicable to other parts of the world. The principle is particularly well suited to Western Europe for a number of reasons. Continental Europe inherited the Roman and Napoleonic legal and administrative traditions, and, as Peter Katzenstein has pointed out, the nations of continental Europe share a concept of the limited state; that is, the state is regarded as an impartial and independent entity separate from society but responsible for creating a favorable and impartial environment for private business. Economic and cultural differences among the European nations are minor when compared to those in any other regions of the globe. Also, during the postwar era the processes of deregulation, privatization, and liberalization have reduced the role of the state in the economy and harmonized to a considerable degree the economic structures and business practices across the Continent. Both the historic traditions and other

194

developments in Western Europe have facilitated adoption of the principle of mutual recognition as an expeditious means to promote the economic unification of the Continent.

Needless to say, the conditions that exist in Western Europe do not exist anywhere else in the world. Within the North American Free Trade Agreement area, although the United States and Canada are very close in almost every aspect of national life, there is an enormous gap between these countries and Mexico in many respects; the principle of mutual recognition is hardly applicable to NAFTA or to relations between North and South America. The economic, cultural, and political diversity in the Asia/Pacific area is even more striking. The principle of mutual recognition cannot serve as a means toward the economic and political integration of that region and certainly cannot provide the basis for a resolution of differences between the West and these rising economic powers. At the heart of the problems is the fact that economic and political affairs are intimately joined to one another. It is therefore difficult to isolate the economy from the polity so that the former may function according to the principles of neoclassical economics. Moreover, if one incorporates religion as a vitally important element in many of these states, as it is in the Middle East, application of the principle of mutual recognition as a solution to the problem of national differences becomes totally out of the question.

CONCLUSION

In the early years following the end of the Cold War, there was a prevalent belief that the clash between capitalism and communism would be replaced by a clash between rival forms of capitalism. This belief, at least thus far, has been proved wrong. Yet it is obvious that increasing interdependence of national economies has made legal, policy, and structural differences among national societies both more important and frequently also a source of tension and occasional political conflict. Differing national systems of political economy constitute a serious obstacle to the movement toward an even more open multilateral global economy. Differences in such matters as competition policy, business practices, and corporate structures have become major concerns of international trade and other negotiations.

CHAPTER EIGHT

The Trading System

ECONOMISTS OF every persuasion are convinced that free trade is superior to trade protection.[1] In fact, they consider free trade to be the best policy for a country even if all other countries should practice trade protection, arguing that if other countries resort to trade protection, the economy that remained open would still gain more from cheaper imports than it would lose in denied export markets. Despite this powerful inclination within the economics profession to favor free trade and open markets, trade protection has never totally disappeared; and indeed, during the past two centuries, restricted trade has been a pervasive feature of the world economy. As economic historian Paul Bairoch has pointed out, free trade has historically been the exception and protectionism the rule.[2] Although nations want to take advantage of foreign markets, they are frequently unwilling to open their own economies. Nations and domestic interests alike fear a world in which market forces rule and relative prices determine the patterns and distribution of the gains from trade. Throughout modern history, trade has been regarded either as an international public good from which everyone benefits or a battleground in which there are winners and losers.[3] Even though the argument for free trade is powerful, trade protectionism continuously resurfaces in new guises.[4]

The classic era of free trade and international laissez-faire lasted less than three decades, from the repeal of the Corn Laws (1846) to approximately the 1870s, when protectionist tariffs increased. From the latter decades of the nineteenth century to the years immediately

[1] This chapter draws from Chapter 3 of my book, *The Challenge of Global Capitalism: The World Economy in the 21st Century* (Princeton: Princeton University Press, 2000).

[2] Paul Bairoch, *Economics and World History: Myths and Paradoxes* (New York: Harvester Wheatsheaf, 1993), 16.

[3] John Dunn quoted in Vincent Cable, "The Diminished Nation-State: A Study in the Loss of Economic Power," in *What Future for the State? Daedalus* 124, no. 2 (spring 1995): 25.

[4] A valuable history of the debate over free trade is Douglas A. Irwin, *Against the Tide: An Intellectual History of Free Trade* (Princeton: Princeton University Press, 1996).

following World War II, trade protection grew steadily and became increasingly prevalent up to and during the Great Depression of the 1930s. Following World War II, the world again experienced an era of trade liberalization and expansion, largely as a consequence of successive rounds of trade negotiations carried out under the auspices of the General Agreement on Tariffs and Trade (GATT) and strongly supported by American leadership. International trade grew even more rapidly than did national economies. Consequently international trade integrated national economies more closely with one another. In the mid-1970s, global stagflation, the New Protectionism, and other developments slowed and, in some cases, reversed this liberalization trend.[5] The United States was particularly guilty of New Protectionism in its use of such nontariff barriers as "voluntary export restraints" to keep out Japanese and other imports.

Major steps were taken toward further trade liberalization with new rounds of trade negotiations, and particularly with the successful completion of the Uruguay Round of trade negotiations (1993). The Uruguay Round created the World Trade Organization (WTO) to replace the increasingly obsolescent GATT. However, new threats also surfaced in the form of managed trade, economic regionalism, and a new trade agenda dealing with such problems as "fair" labor standards and environmental protection. Tension between free trade and trade protection has continued, and the future of a free-trade regime remains precarious.

At the opening of the twenty-first century, the free-trade regime is threatened by intellectual, economic, and political developments. The shift from "comparative" to "competitive" advantage as the basis of trade, the implications of the new strategic trade theory, and other developments have undermined the theoretical or intellectual arguments for trade liberalization. Increasing trade penetration into domestic economies and national affairs has forced recognition of such complex problems as formulation of definitions of "fair and legitimate" economic behavior; that which is considered "fair" in one society may be considered "unfair" in another. Trade issues have become focused on culture, national sovereignty, and other complex issues that are not easily amenable to bargaining and compromise solutions. In addition, political opposition to trade liberalization has grown among many groups concerned about worker welfare, the environment, and human rights. Many less developed nations now believe

[5] H. Richard Friman, *Patchwork Protectionism: Textile Trade Policy in the United States, Japan, and West Germany* (Ithaca: Cornell University Press, 1990).

that the trading system functions to their disadvantage. It is particularly noteworthy that the three major trading powers—the United States, Western Europe, and Japan—became convinced that the political costs of lowering certain trade barriers in response to demands from one or another major power had become unacceptable. These several obstacles to further trade liberalization reached a crisis point at the November 1999 meeting of the WTO in Seattle.

THE DEBATE OVER FREE TRADE

The liberal doctrine of free trade is based on the principles of the market system formulated by classical economists. Adam Smith and David Ricardo argued that removing the impediments to the free movement of goods would permit national specialization and facilitate optimal utilization of the world's scarce resources. Trade liberalization would lead to efficient trade patterns determined by the principle of comparative advantage; that is, by relative factor prices (of land, capital, and labor). Adoption of the principle of comparative advantage or comparative cost would ensure that a country would achieve greater economic welfare through participation in foreign trade than through trade protection. Underlying this liberal commitment to free trade is the belief that the purpose of economic activity is to benefit the consumer and maximize global wealth. Free trade also maximizes consumer choice, reduces prices, and facilitates efficient use of the world's scarce resources. From this perspective, the primary purpose of exports is to pay for imports rather than to enhance the power of the state.

According to its advocates, trade liberalization produces a number of specific benefits. In the first place, trade liberalization increases competition in domestic markets, and thereby undermines anticompetitive practices, lowers prices, increases consumer choice, and increases national efficiency. In addition, free trade increases both national and global wealth by enabling countries to specialize and to export those goods and services in which they have a comparative advantage while importing those goods and services in which they lack comparative advantage. Free trade also encourages the international spread of technology and know-how around the globe and thus provides developing economies with the opportunity to catch up in income and productivity with more advanced economies. Last, but not least, free trade and the international cooperation that it entails increase the prospects of world peace.

Ever since Adam Smith's attack on mercantilism in *The Wealth of Nations* (1776), economists have rejected trade protection because of its high costs to an economy, and there are many empirical studies strongly criticizing trade barriers.[6] For example, a study by Gary Clyde Hufbauer and Kimberly Ann Elliot, published in 1994, in the context of the bitter controversy over the ratification of the North American Free Trade Agreement (NAFTA), found that past protection of twenty-one American industries had actually saved few jobs and that the cost to consumers had been approximately $170,000 per job saved! The equivalent figure for Japan is $600,000. While one may quarrel with the precision of these figures, it is indisputable that trade protection constitutes a heavy burden on an economy.[7]

Trade protection also has a negative impact on income distribution. A tariff or other restrictive measure creates economic or monopoly rents and shifts income from consumers and nonprotected sectors to the protected sectors of the economy. American restrictions in the late 1980s on the importation of flat panels and memory chips for computers provide an excellent example of the cost to American consumers and the harm done to other industries by protection of one particular industry. In this example, import restrictions raised costs for American computer makers and thus made them less competitive; restrictions on importation of flat panels led Apple Computer to shift production of its then popular Powerbook computer overseas. Paradoxically, some types of import protection can even shift income from domestic consumers and producers to foreign producers. A notable example was the imposition of voluntary export restraints on Japanese automobile imports into the United States in the early 1980s. This action proved very advantageous for the Japanese automobile industry at the same time that it decreased the competitive stimulus to the American automobile industry. Finally, one of the most serious dangers of trade restrictions is that they tend to protect declining noncompetitive industries.

The one important exception to economists' universal belief in the superiority of free trade over trade protection is the protection of infant industries.[8] Many economists, I believe, accept the argument first set forth by Alexander Hamilton that nourishing infant industries

---

[6] Adam Smith, *An Inquiry into the Nature and Causes of the Wealth of Nations* (New York: Modern Library, 1937 [1776]).

[7] Gary Clyde Hufbauer and Kimberly Ann Elliot, *Costs of Protection in the United States* (Washington, D.C.: Institute for International Economics, 1994).

[8] Another alternative to free trade is the imposition of an optimum tariff. Under certain circumstances, a large country can impose a trade barrier that improves its terms of trade to the disadvantage of its trading partners. However, the gains will probably be too small to warrant the risk to the trading system and political consequences.

can provide an acceptable rationale for trade protection. An infant industry is one that, if protected from international competition, will become sufficiently strong and competitive to enable it to survive when protection is eventually removed. A major problem with infant-industry protection, however, is that protection too frequently becomes permanent. Another important problem is that no theoretical or other means exists to determine whether or not a particular infant industry, if protected, could eventually achieve a competitive position in world markets. Only a trial-and-error process can determine the long-term competitiveness of a protected industry. Nevertheless, as I pointed out in chapter seven, most successes attributed to industrial policy and strategic trade policy are really examples of successful infant-industry protection.

From eighteenth-century mercantilists to present-day protectionists, advocates of trade protection have desired to achieve certain political, economic, and other objectives more than the economic benefits for the entire society of free trade. However, the specific objectives sought by protectionists have varied over time and space. Economic nationalists regard trade protection as a tool of state creation and statecraft; for example, a trade surplus is considered beneficial for national security. Many representatives of less developed countries believe that trade with industrialized countries is a form of imperialism; they fear that free trade benefits only the developed economy and leads to dependence of the less developed countries on the developed ones. Opponents of free trade in developing economies also include advocates of the "developmental state" who believe that the state rather than free markets should have the principal role in the process of economic development. In developed economies, proponents of trade protection reject free trade and other forms of globalization as threats to jobs, wages, and domestic social welfare; organized labor in industrialized countries increasingly advocates protection against imports from low-wage economies with inadequate labor standards. In recent decades, more and more environmentalists have denounced trade as a threat to the environment. Many liberals (in the American sense of the word) have come to believe that trade violates human rights and encourages child labor. Unfortunately, the forces in developed countries that are opposed to free trade, especially in the United States, gained considerable momentum in the 1990s.

The most systematic economic rationale for economic nationalism and trade protection was provided by Friedrich List, a German who fled to the United States in the middle of the nineteenth century to avoid political persecution. Strongly influenced by Alexander Hamilton's protectionist ideas, List argued in his *National System of Political Economy* (1841) that every industrial nation has pursued and should pursue protectionist policies in order to safeguard its infant industries.[9] List maintained that once their industries were strong enough to withstand international competition, these countries lowered their trade barriers, proclaimed the virtues of free trade, and then sought to get other countries to lower their barriers. Free trade, List believed, was the policy of the strong. If one were to translate List's ideas into modern parlance, one would say that every successful industrial power at some point in its history has carried out an activist industrial policy.[10]

At the beginning of the twenty-first century, many trade protectionists advocate promotion through national industrial policies of high-tech and certain other favored sectors in order to build the nation's industrial strength and increase its competitiveness. They believe that the state should guide and shape the overall industrial and technological structure of the society through trade protection, industrial policy, and other forms of government intervention. In addition to such high-tech industries as computers and electronics, economic nationalists also favor support for more traditional manufacturing industries such as the automobile and other mass-production industries characterized by high value-added and high wages. Although in its efforts to catch up with the West, Japan has conspicuously and aggressively pursued an industrial policy, industrial policies have also been employed by the United States, Western Europe, and many developing economies to promote industries believed important for national security and economic development.

Economists have strongly disputed the alleged benefits of trade protection.[11] Trade protection, they point out, reduces both national and international economic efficiency by preventing countries from exporting those goods and services in which they have a comparative advantage and from importing those goods and services in which they lack comparative advantage. Protection also decreases the incentive of firms to innovate and thus climb the technological ladder; it also discourages shifting national resources to their most profitable use.

[9] Friedrich List, *The National System of Political Economy* (New York: Longmans, Green, 1928; first published in 1841).

[10] Support for List's position comes from Paul Bairoch, *Economics and World History: Myths and Paradoxes*, Chapter 4.

[11] An outstanding critique of protectionist arguments for protection is W. Max Corden, *Trade Policy and Economic Welfare* (Oxford: Clarendon Press, 1974).

As David Hume (1711–1776) demonstrated, protectionism decreases exports over the long term. Although erecting trade barriers can improve exports temporarily, this improvement causes the value of the currency to rise, thus undercutting competitiveness; protectionism can also increase the cost of inputs, and that decreases competitiveness over the long term. The protectionist argument that competition from low-wage economies lowers wages and causes unemployment in industrialized economies is rejected by most economists; they point out that the principal cause of the economic plight of unskilled workers in the developed economies is the rapid technological change caused by the computer and the information economy, both of which favor highly skilled workers. The major consequence of protectionism, economists argue, is redistribution of national income from consumers to protected producer interests. Finally, trade protection invites retaliation from other countries, and this means that everyone will lose.

Despite economists' arguments supporting trade liberalization, trade protectionism persists, and its advocates too frequently succeed. Endogenous trade theory explains the success of protectionism by calling attention to the fact that the political process generally favors special interests desiring protection rather than general consumer interests. Whereas the benefits of free trade diffuse across a society, the benefits of protection are concentrated in a few groups of producers. This situation provides motivation for producers to organize in order to influence public policy and thus gain protection.[12] As the *Wall Street Journal* has quipped, "The first rule of trade agreements is that the benefits are widely dispersed, the costs are very concentrated, and the losers are very vocal."[13]

TRADE AND THE ECONOMY

Not only is the debate over free trade inconclusive, but also there are several misunderstandings regarding what trade does and does not do, and these misunderstandings have fueled protectionist rhetoric. They have also contributed to negative attitudes in the United States and elsewhere about economic globalization and its alleged consequences for the economy.

[12] On the political economy of trade, consult John S. Odell and Thomas D. Willett, eds., *International Trade Policy: Gains from Exchange between Economics and Political Science* (Ann Arbor: University of Michigan Press, 1990).

[13] *Wall Street Journal*, 6 December 1999, A1.

One pernicious misunderstanding in the United States at the opening of the twenty-first century is the idea that a nation's trade deficit is due to the "unfair trade practices" of a country's trading partners. Obviously, some countries do cheat and gain temporary advantage in trade. However, a chronic trade deficit like the one the United States experienced during much of the last quarter of the twentieth century was due to macroeconomic factors and not to cheating by trading partners. The trade/payments balance of a country is a result of a nation's spending patterns and is due, in particular, to the difference between national savings and domestic investment. A country with a high savings rate relative to its investment rate will have a trade/payments surplus. On the other hand, a nation with a savings rate that is low relative to its investment rate will have a trade/payments deficit. The behavior of a nation's trading partner does not affect the former's trade/payments balance. In the 1980s and 1990s, the huge and persistent trade/payments deficit of the United States was due primarily to the low rate of American savings. Nevertheless, incorrectly blaming Japan for the deficit, in the early 1990s the Clinton Administration launched an aggressive attack on Japan as an unfair trader.[14]

Another and equally unfortunate misunderstanding is the belief that imports from low-wage developing countries are responsible for increasing wage inequality in the United States and for unemployment in Western Europe. Most economists agree on the facts regarding income inequality in the United States. Late in the twentieth century, income inequality increased significantly. Between the end of World War II and 1973, rapid economic and high productivity growth did raise income uniformly for Americans of all income brackets, and incomes approximately doubled. Between 1973 and the mid-1990s, however, the pace of income growth slowed and income inequality increased. Whereas median family income increased 10 percent between 1973 and 1999, income in the highest bracket (95th percentile) grew more than a third while income in the lowest income grouping (20th percentile) remained virtually unchanged, especially for women. The real earnings of many low-wage and middle-class workers stagnated or experienced only modest gains, while the wealthier 20 percent of American families gained greatly. In brief, after the 1970s, the standard of living of many American workers grew very slowly, while income inequality increased considerably.

[14] This subject is discussed in Gilpin, *The Challenge of Global Capitalism*, Chapter 8.

A large number of Americans, particularly organized labor, blame manufactured and other imports from low-wage economies for income inequality and job insecurity and demand restrictions on imports. Protectionists like Ross Perot and Patrick Buchanan have asked how an American worker earning $20 or more an hour could possibly compete against billions of Chinese, Indians, Indonesians, and Bangladeshi earning less than $.20 an hour! This unfair competition from low-wage countries, many proclaim, has been rapidly advancing up the technological ladder so that it is harming a growing number of white-collar workers; India, for example, has become a world-class center of data processing and software development. Globalization has also increased immigration of workers from poorer countries into the advanced industrial countries, workers who then "take jobs away" from local workers. Therefore, many critics of globalization charge that increased trade flows, "run-away" plants of American multinational firms, and immigration are responsible for the deteriorating economic plight of more and more workers in the United States.

Most American economists have disputed these charges and attributed almost all of the relative decline in the wages of low-skilled American workers to technological changes within the American economy itself. Technological advances such as the computer and information economy, they have argued, significantly decreased the demand for low-skilled workers and greatly increased the demand for skilled, especially college-educated, workers. Furthermore, these economists have noted that the relatively small trade flows between the United States and low-wage economies cannot possibly explain the roughly 30 percent difference in wages between skilled/college-educated and unskilled workers in America. Instead, this decline in the wages of low-skilled workers has been due to such technological developments as automation, lean production techniques, and computerization.

At the beginning of the twenty-first century, advanced economies are rapidly shifting from unskilled, blue-collar, labor-intensive industries to service industries and to greater reliance on skilled labor in manufacturing as well as in other aspects of economic life. This structural change parallels the shift from agriculture to manufacturing in the late nineteenth century when, as agriculture became more mechanized, superfluous farm workers migrated from the land to the factory. In the late 1990s, many of the tasks formerly performed by unskilled and less skilled workers were being carried out by computers and automated processes. The new service- and knowledge-based industries require more highly skilled workers than in the past, and this means that the demand for unskilled workers has declined dramatically throughout the American economy. The semiskilled assembly-line worker in Detroit or Cleveland who once commanded a high wage in the automobile and other mass-production industries is indeed becoming superfluous in the information economy.

British economist Adrian Wood disagrees with this consensus among economists and points out that competition from low-wage countries has stimulated labor-saving technological change in the United States and thereby reduced the demand for low-wage labor.[15] Although, viewed from this perspective, some of the effects on wages attributed to technological changes can be attributed to trade competition from low-wage economies, it is highly doubtful that imports from low-wage economies are as significant as opponents of globalization have claimed. It is certain that trade protection is not a wise solution to the problems of stagnant wages, income inequality, and job insecurity. The solution lies in job-training programs and other programs to aid adjustment to rapidly changing economic and technological developments.

In the 1990s the issue of trade and unemployment became important in both Western Europe and the United States. In Europe, a high rate of long-term or structural unemployment had emerged in the 1970s, particularly in southern Europe, France, and even Germany. The overall rate of unemployment in Western Europe in the 1990s had reached approximately 10 to 12 percent, more than twice that of the United States. In some countries the rate climbed over 20 percent! Not surprisingly, it became almost an article of faith among business, political, and intellectual leaders that imports from low-wage economies were responsible for this situation. In the United States, the issue became inflamed during the debate over the ratification of the North American Free Trade Agreement (NAFTA). Some political leaders, especially Perot and Buchanan, along with organized labor, proclaimed that the agreement would result in the loss of millions of American jobs. The Clinton Administration, after considerable vacillation, maintained that the agreement would create "jobs, jobs, jobs." Both positions were wrong.

A country's unemployment rate is determined principally by its macroeconomic policies. Through fiscal and monetary policies, the developed countries in Western Europe and the United States can,

---

[15] Adrian Wood, *North-South Trade, Employment, and Inequality: Changing Fortunes in a Skill-Driven World* (Oxford: Clarendon Press, 1994).

within certain limits, manage a nation's rate of unemployment. In a well-functioning economy, trade does not decrease or increase unemployment. While NAFTA has not affected the number of jobs in the American economy, it has redistributed jobs from one economic sector or region of the country to others. In Western Europe, the high rate of unemployment has been a consequence of several factors: inflexible labor markets, overly generous welfare programs that discourage expanded employment, and highly restrictive macroeconomic policies associated with meeting the requirements for nations to join the European Monetary Union. Domestic factors and not international trade have been the major causes of Western Europe's high level of chronic unemployment.

Trade, however, does create losers as well as winners in the areas of both wages and employment. Economic sectors in which a nation possesses or wins a comparative advantage gain from trade, while sectors in which a nation loses comparative advantage suffer. As losers frequently feel the pain more acutely than winners feel the gain, both ethical and political reasons make it necessary that national policy assist or compensate workers and others harmed by trade liberalization. In any case, the worst response a nation can make to inevitable shifts in comparative advantage is to close itself off from the stimulus of trade competition.

REVISIONS OF CONVENTIONAL TRADE THEORY

Since its development in the early 1930s by Eli Heckscher and Bertil Ohlin, the factor endowments or factor proportions model has been accepted as the standard explanation of international trade. The Heckscher-Ohlin (or H-O) model of comparative costs or advantage postulates that a country will specialize in the production and export of those products in which it has a cost advantage over other countries. This theory is based on assumptions of constant returns to scale, universal availability of production technologies, and determination of a country's comparative advantage and trade pattern by its factor endowments.[16] This theory implies that:

(1) A country will export those products that are intensive in its abundant factor; that is, a capital-rich country will export capital-intensive goods.

[16] This section draws on Ronald Rogowski's highly innovative paper entitled, "How Economies-of-Scale Trade Affects Domestic Politics,." Center for International Relations, Working Papers No. 13, May 1997, University of California, Los Angeles.

(2) Trade will benefit the owners of locally abundant factors and harm owners of the scarce factors. Thus, although all countries will benefit in absolute terms, there will be important distributive consequences that will favor either capital or labor in trading countries (Stopler-Samuelson Theorem).

(3) Trade in factors (capital or labor) and trade in goods will have the same effect and can fully substitute for one another (Mundell equivalency).

(4) Under certain circumstances, trade in goods will over time equalize the return (wages to labor and profits to capital) for each factor of production (Factor-Price Equalization Theorem).

The basic problem with the H-O model or theory is that actual trading patterns frequently differ from what the theory predicts. A notable example is found in intraindustry trade among countries with similar factor endowments. Indeed, most trade among industrialized countries takes place largely in the same product sectors; for example, the United States both exports to and imports from other industrialized countries. As a consequence of the efforts by economists to explain this and other departures from the H-O theory, the concept of comparative advantage has been made increasingly elastic. Some economists regard actual trade patterns as resulting from many factors other than natural endowments, factors including historical accidents, government policies, and cumulative causation. Moreover, the standard H-O theory itself has been modified and expanded to include such important factors as human capital (skilled labor), "learning by doing," technological innovation, and especially economies of scale. Revisions have so transformed the original H-O model that some economists now argue that the theory of international trade is not much more than an eclectic enumeration of the many factors that determine comparative advantage and trade flows.

However, it is very difficult to incorporate these newly recognized factors into a formal model, and because there is no satisfactory alternative model, economists continue to support the standard H-O theory of trade based on factor endowments. As Richard Caves and Ronald Jones have argued, the Heckscher-Ohlin theory, with its emphasis on factor endowments, is still largely valid.[17] Moreover, as economists argue, national specialization and the benefits of a territorial division of labor remain valid concepts that are of overwhelming

---

[17] Richard Caves and Ronald Jones, quoted in David B. Yoffie and Benjamin Gomes-Casseres, *International Trade and Competition: Cases and Notes in Strategy and Management*, 2d ed. (New York: McGraw-Hill, 1994), 8.

importance for the efficient use of the world's scarce resources. True! But this generalization does not explain or determine which country will produce what, and nation-states will always be very reluctant to leave that decision entirely up to the market.

Concept of Human Capital

An especially important modification of trade theory followed Wassily Leontief's discovery of the Leontief Paradox.[18] In his research, Leontief discovered that the United States had a comparative advantage in exporting labor-intensive goods, especially agricultural products and other commodities. This empirical finding ran counter to the prediction that the United States as a capital-rich country would have a comparative advantage in capital-intensive goods. According to the Stopler-Samuelson theorem, derived from conventional trade theory, a country will export goods produced by its most abundant factor of production and import goods made by its least abundant factor. The paradox or anomaly that Leontief found in American exports was eventually resolved by introduction of the concepts of "human capital" and of economies of scale into both trade theory and the neoclassical theory of economic growth.[19] Recognition of the importance and effect of investment in training, education, and know-how in the United States, and of the resulting increase in the skills and productivity of American workers, explained the Leontief Paradox. While the idea of human capital considerably enriched and extended our understanding of international trade, it did make the original H-O theory less rigorous or, as economists would say, less robust.

Rise of Intraindustry Trade

Since the reconstruction of Western Europe and the freeing of trade through successive GATT negotiations, most trade has taken place, contrary to the H-O theory, between countries with similar factor endowments; most exports of industrialized economies go to other industrialized countries. Such *intra*industry trade entails an economy's exporting and importing goods in the same economic sectors (as in exportation of one type of automobile and importation of another type). *Inter*industry trade, on the other hand, entails exporting and importing goods in very different economic sectors, such as exporting manufactured goods and importing raw materials. Intraindustry trade

---

[18] Wassily W. Leontief, "Domestic Production and Foreign Trade: The American Capital Position Reexamined," *Economia Internazionale* 7, no. 1 (1954): 3–32.

[19] William A. Kerr and Nicholas Perdikis, *The Economics of International Business* (London: Chapman and Hall, 1995), 24–26.

has been a prominent feature of north-north trade, whereas interindustry trade has tended to characterize north-south trade. How can this type of trade among advanced industrialized economies be explained?

The Heckscher-Ohlin model predicts that most trade should take place among countries with *dissimilar* endowments and that intraindustry trade should not even exist. If comparative advantage and trade patterns are determined by fixed endowments and relative prices, why should the industrial countries in effect be "taking in one another's laundry"? This anomaly can be explained by differing national tastes, product differentiation, and economies of scale. Americans, for example, traditionally like big cars, and Europeans, small ones; Americans have tended to possess a comparative advantage in the former and Europeans in the latter. Yet, there is a market in the United States for small European cars and vice versa. Since the importance of intraindustry trade was recognized, the Heckscher-Ohlin model has been applied primarily to trade between developed and less developed countries and not to the intraindustry trade based on product differentiation and scale economies that is characteristic among industrial countries.

However, here another anomaly is encountered. Japan, during most of the latter half of the twentieth century, imported a remarkably small share of the manufactured goods that it consumes. Unlike Western European and U.S. trade, only a small portion of Japanese trade has been intraindustry trade—that is, a two-way flow of trade within particular industries. For example, whereas Japan was the world's largest exporter of automobiles for many years, its imports of automobiles and auto parts were negligible. Instead, even in the 1990s, the pattern of Japanese trade continued to be largely *interindustry* trade; Japan was importing mainly food, fuel, and raw materials and exporting mainly motor vehicles and other manufactures. While this unique Japanese trading pattern began to change in the final years of the twentieth century, it had long been a major source of economic conflict between Japan and its trading partners.

Integration of International Trade and Foreign Investment

Another important development in the postwar era has been the increasing integration of international trade and foreign direct investment (FDI) by multinational corporations (MNCs). When capital in the form of portfolio investment became increasingly mobile across borders in the late nineteenth century, economists assumed that international capital movements were due to differences among countries in rates of return and in investment risk. When foreign direct investment—for example, the establishment of a production facility by a firm of one nationality within another economy—became an increasingly important feature of the international economy, economists assumed that FDI, like portfolio investment, was due to differences in interest rates and that exports and foreign production were, in essence, perfect substitutes for one another. This acceptance of the Mundell equivalency continues to pervade economists' attitudes toward FDI. Recently, a number of economists have begun to rethink the nature and significance of foreign direct investment and have applied industrial organization theory to the behavior of multinational firms and the determination of international trade patterns.

The increasingly important role of the MNC in the world economy has resulted in a significant movement toward internationalization of both services and industrial production. Organization of service industries and of manufacturing on a regional or global basis has greatly affected the trading system. A substantial proportion of world trade now takes place as *intrafirm* transfers at prices set by the firms and as part of global corporate strategies. By the 1990s, this type of managed trade had become a prominent feature in the international economy. In the late 1990s, over 50 percent of American and Japanese trade was intrafirm trade. The resulting trade patterns frequently do not conform to conventional trade theory based on traditional concepts of comparative advantage.

There is intense disagreement on the implications of FDI's increasing importance for international trade and for the international distribution of wealth and economic activities. Assuming that investment and its trade effects are just another application of the law of comparative advantage, many if not most economists believe that FDI has only marginal implications for patterns of trade and that its distributive effects are primarily domestic. Many noneconomists, however, believe that FDI and the activities of multinational corporations have an immense impact on patterns of international trade and on the distribution of wealth—and, I shall add—power. In addition, whereas most business economists believe that the MNC is above politics and facilitates the rational organization and utilization of the world's scarce resources to everyone's benefit, critics believe that MNCs pursue their own private interests (and/or those of their home countries) to the detriment of everyone else.

From Comparative to Competitive Advantage

Another important intellectual development that has undermined the H-O theory of international trade is a shift among economists from emphasizing "comparative" to emphasizing "competitive" advantage, especially in high-tech sectors. International competitiveness and trade patterns frequently result from arbitrary specialization based on increasing returns rather than from efforts to take advantage of fundamental national differences in resources or factor endowment.[20] This new thinking about the arbitrary or accidental nature of international specialization and competitiveness emphasizes the increasing importance of technology in determining trade patterns.[21] The increasing importance of technology and of economies of scale has become an important factor in corporate and national economic strategies.

In 1966, Raymond Vernon's product cycle theory of foreign direct investment incorporated technology into trade theory; his work foreshadowed later writings on the importance of technological innovation for trade and investment patterns.[22] According to Vernon, American FDI in the 1960s could be explained primarily as a result of America's competitive advantage in product innovation and of the desire of American firms to deter or forestall the rise of foreign competitors.

Additional influential work on the broad subject of the shift from comparative to competitive advantage has been produced by Michael Porter, a professor at Harvard University's Business School. Through his extensive research, Porter has attempted to explain why the firms of some countries have been more competitive in specific industrial sectors than the firms of other countries.[23] The United States, for example, has been very strong in aircraft, while Japan has had an advantage in consumer electronics and automobiles. Through his detailed and extensive empirical studies of the trading patterns of several countries, Porter found determinants of such patterns, at least among industrialized countries.

The central finding of Porter's research was that the internal characteristics of a national economy (including what I have identified as the national system of political economy) affect the environment of

---

[20] Krugman, *Geography and Trade* (Cambridge: MIT Press, 1991), 7.

[21] Robert M. Solow, "Growth Theory," in David Greenaway, Michael Bleaney, and Ian Stewart, eds., *Companion to Contemporary Economic Thought* (London: Routledge, 1991), 407.

[22] Raymond Vernon, *Sovereignty at Bay* (New York: Basic Books, 1971); and Vernon, "International Investment and International Trade in the Product Cycle," *Quarterly Journal of Economics* 80, no. 2 (May 1966): 190–207.

[23] Michael E. Porter, *The Competitive Advantage of Nations* (New York: Free Press, 1990).

domestic firms in ways that either facilitate or obstruct development of competitive advantage in certain industries. According to Porter, several aspects of a national economy are particularly important: the national culture and its influence on the purpose of economic activities, the status of capital and labor, the nature of effective demand, the condition of supporting industries, and the industrial structure of the economy. These several factors, Porter argues, determine domestic competitive conditions, and those conditions in turn influence the international competitiveness of particular sectors of the economy.

Using specific industrial sectors as the units of analysis rather than the individual firm or the national economy as a whole, Porter demonstrates that an economy with a competitive advantage in a particular sector invariably has several strong firms in that sector. Intense domestic competition among these oligopolistic firms confers on them their strong competitive position in international markets. Thus, for Porter, the competitive advantage of Japanese firms in automobiles and consumer electronics is explained by the supercompetitiveness of the domestic market. This supercompetition in Japan has been concentrated on winning market share rather than profit maximization, and is carried out primarily through product innovation, application of technology to productive processes, and great attention to quality control rather than through the price competition characteristic of American firms. Intense oligopolistic competition at the domestic level, Porter concluded, provided a better explanation of the international competitiveness of Japanese firms in certain sectors than did any other factor, certainly more than possible corporate collusion or government interventionist policies.

As a good economist, Porter eschews the importance of the nation itself as a factor in international competitiveness. However, in fact Porter is talking about the importance of differences in national policies as an explanation of international competitiveness. Although it was not his intention, Porter actually demonstrates that national governments *do* play an important role in helping or thwarting the efforts of firms to create competitive advantage. Government policies can and do support or hinder the supply-and-demand factors affecting the success of particular sectors. Furthermore, governments can protect infant industries from international competition until they are strong enough to compete on their own, and they can also foster technological innovation through support for R & D, assist domestic firms to gain access to foreign technology, and protect proprietary knowledge from foreign competitors. In short, a government can take a long-term perspective and establish policies that foster a favorable domestic environment for those sectors most likely to be competitive in international markets.

As he substitutes the term "competitive advantage" for the traditional emphasis of neoclassical economics on "comparative advantage," Porter's research strongly supports the idea that advantage in international trade, at least in high-tech industries, can be and is created by deliberate corporate and national policies. Comparative or competitive advantage results from deliberate corporate decisions and government policy choices rather than appearing as a gift from Mother Nature. If international competitiveness is indeed increasingly based on technological developments, learning by doing, and economies of scale, then individual firms are ultimately responsible for creating or failing to create competitive advantage, but governments can and do have an important and even decisive role in promoting their own national firms in international markets.

Mainstream economists have been hesitant to acknowledge the increased importance of such factors as technology and learning by doing in the determination of trade patterns.[24] Nevertheless, the fundamental idea that comparative or competitive advantage is largely arbitrary and a product of human intervention rather than a fixed gift of nature is accepted by growing numbers of mainstream economists.[25] Introducing the concept of "knowledge capital" as a determinant of economic growth and international competitiveness, Grossman and Helpman argue that comparative advantage results from natural endowments supported by experience.[26] Moreover, they emphasize that nations with a headstart in a particular technology tend to strengthen their position over time, and that technologically deficit nations, especially small nations, may find it impossible to ever catch up.[27] As the idea of path dependence teaches us, productivity increases

---

[24] Despite the importance of Michael Porter's pioneering empirical studies, his ideas appear to have had almost no impact on the American economics profession, perhaps because the work is largely empirical and the findings cannot be expressed in a formal model.

[25] Gene M. Grossman and Elhanan Helpman, "Trade, Innovation, and Growth," *American Economic Review* 80, no. 2 (May 1990): 86.

[26] Gene M. Grossman and Elhanan Helpman, "Comparative Advantage and Long-Run Growth," *American Economic Review* 80, no. 4 (September 1994): 796–815.

[27] Gene M. Grossman and Elhanan Helpman, "Hysteresis in the Trade Pattern," in Wilfred J. Ethier, Elhanan Helpman, and J. Peter Neary, eds., *Theory, Policy and Dynamics in International Trade: Essays in Honor of Ronald W. Jones* (New York: Cambridge University Press, 1993), 288. The term "hysteresis" is used by economists to mean that an economic outcome has been determined by historical factors. This is a rare concession to the role of history in economic outcomes.

with cumulative experience and is determined to a considerable degree by the initial pattern of specialization.

These important considerations that "international comparative advantage in the production of and sale of high-technology goods . . . . must be struggled for and earned through superior technological innovativeness" has significantly intensified what F. M. Scherer has labeled "international high-technological competition."[28] The drive for technological superiority has notably increased the receptivity of governments to the "new trade theory."

New Trade Theory

The most important and certainly the most controversial development challenging the conventional theory of international trade is the "new trade theory," more commonly known as "strategic trade theory" (STT). Therefore, I repeat here much of my earlier discussion of strategic trade theory. Strategic trade theory is the culmination of earlier challenges to conventional trade theory because it incorporates a growing appreciation of imperfect competition, economies of scale, economies of scope, learning by doing, the importance of R & D, and the role of technological spillovers. STT is significant because it challenges the theoretical foundations of the economics profession's unequivocal commitment to free trade. In fact, STT originated with the development of new analytical tools and growing dissatisfaction with conventional trade theory and its inability to explain the increasing trade problems of the United States, especially with respect to Japan in the 1980s.[29] The application to trade theory of novel methods associated with important theoretical advances in the field of industrial organization provided the means to develop an alternative to the H-O model. Mathematical models of imperfect competition and game theoretic models were first incorporated into trade theory in the early 1980s by James Brander and Barbara Spencer (1983), two theorists of industrial organization.[30] Before I consider the theory, however, I will discuss oligopolistic competition briefly.

[28] F. M. Scherer, *International High-Technology Competition* (Cambridge: Harvard University Press, 1992), 5.

[29] David B. Yoffie and Benjamin Gomes-Casseres, *International Trade and Competition: Cases and Notes in Strategy and Management*, 2nd ed. (New York: McGraw-Hill, 1994), 5–17.

[30] James A. Brander and Barbara J. Spencer, "International R & D Rivalry and Industrial Strategy," *Review of Economic Studies* 50 (1983): 707–22.

Under conditions of perfect competition, strategic behavior is not possible because the behavior of one or just a few firms cannot significantly change market conditions for other firms. However, if unit costs in certain industries do continue to fall as output increases (economies of scale), the total output of firms will expand but the number of firms will decrease. Economies of scale in an industry mean that the market will support only one or just a few large firms; that is, the industry will become oligopolistic, and the market will eventually be dominated by a few firms. This would permit the behavior of one firm to make a difference and to alter the decisions of other firms. If imperfect or oligopolistic competition exists, then monopoly rents or abnormally high profits can exist in that economic sector; the resultant rents or superprofits could then be captured by a small number of firms or even by one firm. Individual firms, then, may well pursue corporate strategies to increase their profits or economic rents.

Oligopolistic firms can and do consciously choose a course of action that anticipates the behavior of their competitors. If successful, such action enables them to capture a much larger share of the market than would be the case under conditions of perfect competition. For example, oligopolistic firms can and do follow strategies in which they adjust their own prices and output in order to alter the prices and output of competitor firms. Two of the most important strategies used to increase a firm's long-term domination of an oligopolistic market are *dumping* (selling below cost to drive out competitors in the product area) and *preemption* (through huge investment in productive capacity to deter other entrants into the market).

Imperfect or oligopolisitc competition is most likely found in certain high-tech industries characterized by economies of scale and learning by doing. The sectors most likely to become oligopolistic include computers, semiconductors, and biotechnology; these technologies, of course, are identified by most governments as the "commanding heights" of the information economy. Many are dual technologies, because they are very important to both military weaponry and to economic competitiveness. Many countries consider it essential for both commercial and security reasons to take actions that will ensure a strong presence in some or all of these sectors. The importance of a head start in these industries encourages firms to pursue a "first-mover" strategy so that cumulative processes and path dependence will strengthen their market position.

The theory of strategic trade takes the existence of imperfect or oligopolistic competition one step further and suggests that a government can take specific actions to help its own oligopolistic firms. Government policies can assist national firms to generate *positive externalities* (e.g., technological spillovers) and to *shift profits* from foreign firms to national firms. Economists have long appreciated that a nation with sufficient market power could enact an optimum tariff and thereby shift the terms of trade in its favor. By restricting imports and decreasing the demand for a product, a large economy may be able to cause the price of the imported good to fall. Strategic trade theory, however, goes much farther than optimum trade theory in recognizing the capacity of a nation to intervene effectively in trade matters and thus to gain disproportionately. A government's decision to support a domestic firm's plans to increase its productive capabilities (preemption) or even to signal intention to build excess productive capacity exemplifies a strategic trade policy. Through use of a direct subsidy to a firm or outright protection of a domestic industry, the government might deter foreign firms from entering a particular industrial sector. Since a minimum scale of production is necessary to achieve efficiency, especially in many high-tech industries, the advantage of being first ("first-mover advantage") encourages a strategy of preemptive investment.

Strategic trade theory departs from conventional trade theory in its assumption that certain economic sectors are more important than others for the overall economy and therefore warrant government support. Manufacturing industries, for example, are considered more valuable than service industries because manufacturing has traditionally been characterized by higher rates of productivity growth and has produced higher profits, higher value-added, and higher wages. Some economic sectors, especially such high-tech industries as computers, semiconductors, and information processing, are particularly important because they generate spillovers and positive externalities that benefit the entire economy. Because a new technology in one sector may have indirect benefits for firms in another sector, firms that do extensive research and development are valuable to many others. However, because firms may not be able to capture or appropriate the results of their research and development activities, many will underinvest in these activities. Proponents of strategic trade theory argue that such a market failure indicates that firms should be assisted through direct subsidy or import protection, particularly in high-tech industries, which frequently raise the skill level of the labor force and thus increase human capital. If, as the proponents of strategic trade believe, such special industries do exist, then free trade is not optimal, and government intervention in trade matters can increase national welfare.

216

Strategic trade theory has become a highly controversial subject within the economics profession. Some critics argue that strategic trade theory is a clever, flawed, and pernicious idea that gives aid and comfort to proponents of trade protectionism. Other opponents of the theory agree with this negative assessment and maintain that the theory itself adds nothing really new to dubious arguments favoring trade protection. Perhaps in response to the severe denunciations of strategic trade theory by leading mainstream economists, some of its earliest and strongest proponents have moderated their initial enthusiasm. Many economists consider STT to be an intellectual game with no relevance to the real world of trade policy. Despite these criticisms and recantations, however, strategic trade theory has had an important impact on government policy and has undoubtedly been a factor in the slowdown in the growth of world trade.

What can be concluded about strategic trade theory and the industrial policy to which it provides intellectual support? The case for *profit shifting* from one economy to another has neither been proved nor disproved; it is difficult to assess whether or not government intervention in oligopolistic markets actually works, because economists lack adequate models of the ways in which oligopolistic firms really behave, and because the effects of trade policy in oligopolistic industries can depend to a critical degree on that behavior. The *positive externalities* argument for strategic trade policy and its first cousin, industrial policy, have strong support in the literature. Even though empirical evidence for the success of industrial policy is admittedly mixed, government support for particular industrial sectors has frequently been very successful in creating technologies that spill over into the rest of economy. Most importantly, there is strong evidence that government support for broad-scale R & D produces a very high payoff for the entire economy. Certainly, governments around the world believe that providing support for high-tech industries is a highly productive investment over the long term.

POSTWAR TRADE REGIME

The post-World War II trading system was born in conflict between American and British negotiators at the Bretton Woods Conference (1944). Reflecting their industrial supremacy, US negotiators wanted free trade and open foreign markets as soon as possible. Although the British were also committed to the principle of free trade, they were extremely concerned over the "dollar shortage," possible loss of domestic economic autonomy to pursue a full employment policy, and

217

a number of related issues. The eventual compromise agreement to create the International Trade Organization (ITO) left many issues unresolved.

In 1948, the United States and its principal economic partners created the General Agreement on Tarriffs and Trade (GATT) to promote "freer and fairer" trade, primarily through negotiated reductions of formal tariffs. When the ITO was turned down by the U.S. Senate in 1950, the GATT became the world's principal trade organization. The GATT is a fixed-rule trading system, and such a rule-based system is quite different from managed or "results-oriented" trade that sets quantitative targets or outcomes. The GATT was also based on the principle of multilateralism; trade rules were extended without discrimination to all members of the GATT; unilateralism, bilateralism, and trading blocs were prohibited except in unusual cases. Another feature of the system was the principle of overall or general reciprocity; that is, trade liberalization and rules were to be determined by mutual balanced concessions. A system of specific reciprocity, on the other hand, requires that quite specific rather than general concessions must be made. The GATT also incorporated provisions for the impartial adjudication of disputes.[31] Although the principles of the GATT trade regime were significantly qualified by escape clauses and exceptions, its creation was a major accomplishment, and it has facilitated extremely important reductions in trade barriers.

The GATT proved remarkably successful in fostering trade liberalization and providing a framework for trade discussions. However, in contrast to the abandoned ITO, its authority and the scope of its responsibilities were severely limited; it was essentially a negotiating forum rather than a true international organization, and it had no rule-making authority. Moreover, it lacked an adequate dispute-settlement mechanism, and its jurisdiction applied primarily to manufactured goods. The GATT did not have authority to deal with agriculture, services, intellectual property rights, or foreign direct investment; nor did the GATT have sufficient authority to deal with customs unions and other preferential trading arrangements. Its power to resolve trade disputes was also highly circumscribed. Successive American Administrations and other governments became increasingly cognizant of the GATT's inherent limitations, and following the Uruguay Round, they incorporated it in 1995 within the World Trade Organization (WTO), whose responsibilities and au-

[31] Jagdish Bhagwati, *The World Trading System at Risk* (Princeton: Princeton University Press, 1991).

thority are much broader and which is a full-fledged international organization rather than merely an international secretariat (like the GATT).

The GATT, and later, the WTO, served the important political purpose of facilitating the reduction of trade barriers. The principle of comparative advantage indicates that a nation would increase its gains by opening its market to foreign goods; also, an open economy would enjoy lower prices, consumer choice, and greater national efficiency. Nevertheless, because potential losers would strongly oppose lifting trade barriers, proponents of free trade have to confront a mercantilist attitude that believes exports are good and imports are bad. This attitude is revealed when trade agreements are characterized as "concessions" to a foreign government. Because of this prevalent attitude, and for other political reasons, negotiated reductions of trade barriers based on the principle of reciprocity are necessary. The political logic of the GATT/WTO is that because liberalization harms certain interests that will inevitably oppose trade liberalization, it is necessary to liberalize in a coordinated way with concession for concession, thus making it easier to defeat protectionists. Once trade barriers have been lowered, a framework of agreements makes it quite difficult to raise them again.

The GATT, despite the limitations of its mandate and its cumbersome organizational structure, was important for many years in reducing barriers to international trade and in helping to establish rules to reduce trade conflict. The GATT provided a rule-based regime of trade liberalization founded on the principles of nondiscrimination, unconditional reciprocity, and transparency (for example, use of formal tariffs and publication of trade regulations); as trade relations constitute a Prisoner's Dilemma situation, unambiguous rules are required to forestall conflict.[32] Trade rules were determined and trade barriers were reduced through multilateral negotiations among GATT members. In effect, GATT members agreed to establish regulations lowering trade barriers and then let markets determine trade patterns; member states pledged not to resort to managed or results-oriented trade that set import quotas for particular products. Under GATT, markets were opened and new rules established by international negotiations; agreements were based on compromise or unconditional reciprocity rather than on unilateral actions by the strong or by specific reciprocity. GATT's goal was an open multilateralism; that

<hr />

[32] Avinash K. Dixit, *The Making of Economic Policy: A Transaction-Cost Politics Perspective* (Cambridge: MIT Press, 1996), 124.

is, the agreement provided for extension of negotiated trade rules to all members of the GATT without discrimination. However, candidates for membership did have to meet certain criteria and agree to obey its rules. The founders of the GATT wanted a steady progression toward an open world economy, with no return to the cycle of retaliation and counterretaliation that had characterized the 1930s.

The postwar period witnessed a number of agreements to lower tariff barriers. A significant shift in negotiations took place during the Kennedy Round (1964–1967). That Round, initiated by the United States as a response to growing concern over the possible trade diversion or discrimination consequences of the European Economic Community, substituted general reciprocity for the prior product-by-product approach to tariff cuts (specific reciprocity). GATT members agreed to reduce tariffs on particular products by certain percentages and made trade-offs across economic sectors. The Round resulted in a reduction of trade barriers on manufactures of approximately 33 percent and in a number of basic reforms, including regulation of "dumping" practices. In addition, preferential treatment was given to exports from less developed countries (LDCs).

The next major initiative to liberalize trade was the Tokyo Round (1973–1979), which, after years of bitter fighting, proved far more comprehensive than earlier efforts. It included significant tariff cuts on most industrial products, liberalization of agricultural trade, and reduction of nontariff barriers. In addition, the industrial countries pledged to pay greater attention to LDC demands for special treatment of their exports. However, the most important task of the Tokyo Round was to fashion codes of conduct to deal with unfair trade practices. To this end, the negotiations prohibited export subsidies and eliminated some discrimination in public procurement. However, that Round did not resolve the serious American-European dispute over agriculture, satisfy the LDCs, or stop the noxious proliferation of nontariff barriers that occurred as a consequence of the New Protectionism that had commenced in the 1970s.[33]

Nevertheless, trade-liberalizing agreements did enable international trade to grow rapidly. Substantial expansion of trade meant that imports penetrated more deeply and trade became a much more important component in domestic economies. In fact, in some European Economic Community countries, exports soared. And even the domestic markets of the United States and Japan were internationalized

[33] European Union agricultural subsidies are approximately $324 per acre in contrast to $34 per acre in the United States. *Burlington Free Press*, 12 December 1999, 3A.

to a significant extent. It is particularly noteworthy that Japanese imports soon included a growing percentage of manufactured goods. Meanwhile, GATT membership greatly expanded over the years, and growing trade flows created a highly interdependent international economy, despite the 1970s slowdown.

THE URUGUAY ROUND AND WORLD TRADE ORGANIZATION

By the mid-1980s, the Bretton Woods trade regime was no longer adequate to deal with a highly integrated world economy characterized by oligopolistic competition, scale economies, and dynamic comparative advantage. In addition, the New Protectionism of the 1970s had led to the erection of numerous nontariff barriers, such as quotas and government subsidies.[34] Moreover, the character of trade itself was changing and outgrowing the rules and trading regime of the early postwar era. Trade became closely intertwined with the global activities of multinational firms, and trade in both services and manufactures expanded rapidly; trade among industrialized countries became the most prominent feature of the trading system. In the 1980s, the "new regionalism," especially acceleration of the movement toward European integration, was recognized as a threat to the multilateral trading system. And at least from the early 1980s, the United States pressured its West European and other trading partners for a new round of trade negotiations to strengthen the multilateral trading system. Eventually, this American pressure overcame European and other resistance, and the Uruguay Round of trade negotiations was launched at Punta del Este, Uruguay, in 1986, resulting in intense negotiations until its conclusion in 1993.

The treaty produced by the Uruguay Round, which came into force on January 1, 1995, reduced tariffs on manufactured goods and lowered trade barriers in a number of important areas.[35] At the same time

[34] The New Protectionism, as distinct from the "old" protectionism, was characterized by hidden trade barriers, a shift from rules to discretion, and a return to bilateralism. See W. M. Corden, *The Revival of Protectionism* (New York: Group of Thirty, 1984).

[35] A detailed and optimistic assessment of the Uruguay Round is found in Ernest H. Preeg, *Traders in a Brave New World: The Uruguay Round and the Future of the International Trading System* (Chicago: University of Chicago Press, 1995). John Whalley and Colleen Hamilton, on the other hand, believe that the success of the Round was greatly overstated, especially with respect to new rules governing antidumping practices, subsidies, and other areas of agreement that were quite modest. Nor, they point out, did it do much for services or FDI. See Whalley and Hamilton, *The Trading System After the Uruguay Round* (Washington, D.C.: Institute for International Economics, 1996).

221

that formal tariffs on merchandise goods were reduced to a very low level, the Uruguay Round decreased or eliminated many import quotas and subsidies. The agreement's twenty-nine separate accords also reduced trade barriers and for the first time extended trade rules to a number of areas that included agriculture, textiles, services, intellectual property rights, and foreign investment. By one estimate, by the year 2002 the agreement should increase world welfare by approximately $270 billion. While many economists and public officials praised the agreement, others emphasized the modesty of its gains. However, the long-term effects of these achievements remain in doubt. Speaking of the agreement, John Jackson, a leading expert on trade law, stated that the "devil is in the details."[36]

The Uruguay Round's most significant accomplishment was the creation of the World Trade Organization (WTO). In doing this, the Round took an important step toward completion of the framework of international institutions that had originally been proposed at Bretton Woods (1944). Although the WTO incorporated the GATT along with many of its rules and practices, the legal mandate and institutional structure of the WTO were designed to enable it to play a much more important role than the GATT had played in governance of international commerce. The WTO has more extensive and more binding rules. Moreover, the WTO has, in effect, the primary responsibility to facilitate international economic cooperation in trade liberalization and to fill in the many details omitted in the 22,000-page Uruguay Treaty. That Agreement establishing the WTO expanded and entrenched the GATT principle that trade should be governed by multilateral rules rather than by unilateral actions or bilateral negotiations.

The World Trade Organization (WTO) is, in essence, an American creation. The WTO's predecessor, the General Agreement on Tariffs and Trade (GATT) had served well America's fading mass-production economy, but it did not serve the emerging economy equally well. As a consequence of economic and technological developments prior to

[36] The sheer magnitude of the agreement is extraordinary. As John Jackson has commented, the Uruguay Round negotiations were undoubtedly the most extensive ever carried out by any international organization. The agreement contained 22,000 pages and weighed 385 pounds! Although the agreement did not achieve many of the objectives sought by the United States, which had proposed the negotiations, it was an impressive achievement nevertheless. See John H. Jackson, in Peter B. Kenen, ed., *Managing the World Economy: Fifty Years After Bretton Woods* (Washington, D.C.: Institute for International Economics, 1994), 132f.

the Reagan Administration, the United States had become an increasingly service-oriented and high-tech economy. Therefore, in a major effort to reduce trade barriers, the Uruguay Round was initiated by the Reagan Administration and later was supported by the Bush Administration and, after much vacillation, by the Clinton Administration as well.

Although the WTO was not given as extensive rule-making authority as some desired, it does have much more authority than the GATT. The GATT dispute-settlement mechanism was incorporated in the WTO, reformed, and greatly strengthened by elimination of such basic flaws as long delays in the proceedings of dispute panels, the ability of disputants to block proceedings, and the frequent failure of members to implement decisions. The agreement also established a new appellate body to oversee the work of the dispute panels. Most importantly—and controversially—the WTO was empowered to levy fines on countries that refused to accept a decision of the dispute panel.

The institutional structure of the trade regime also changed significantly. Whereas the GATT had been a trade accord supported by a secretariat, the WTO is a membership organization that increases the legal coherence among its wide-ranging rights and obligations and establishes a permanent forum for negotiations. Biennial ministerial meetings should increase political guidance to the institution. The Uruguay Round also created a trade-policy-review mechanism to monitor member countries. With over 130 members, however, the WTO's ability to carry out its assigned responsibilities is subject to doubt.

Despite the impressive achievements of the Uruguay Round in reducing trade barriers, many vexing issues were left unresolved. Trade in certain areas such as agriculture, textiles, and shipping continues to be highly protected. The failure to reduce tariffs on agriculture and textiles was and continues to be especially vexing because lower tariffs would greatly benefit LDCs. Trade barriers are still high in most developing countries, especially with respect to services, and developed countries continue to restrict imports of automobiles, steel, textiles, consumer electronics, and agricultural products. Completion of the Uruguay Round's so-called "built-in" agenda is crucial, and the many issues unresolved at the close of the negotiations remain problematic at this writing. In addition, since the end of the Uruguay Round, a number of new and extremely difficult issues have surfaced, including labor standards, the environment, and human rights. Even

223

more ominous, American public opinion has become more skeptical of the costs and benefits of trade, and by the late 1990s the WTO and trade liberalization were clearly on the defensive.

NEW THREATS TO AN OPEN TRADING SYSTEM

In order to deal with the many issues left unresolved in the Uruguay Round and eliminate the many barriers that continue to restrict free trade, in 1999 the WTO prepared to launch a Millennium Round of trade negotiations. The proposed round was very ambitious, and the following issues were among the important matters to be considered:

(1) Further reduction of trade barriers on industrial products.
(2) Reductions of barriers, particularly high tariffs in less developed countries, to trade in services, including information technology, financial services, and telecommunications.
(3) Reduction of fishing subsidies that promote over-fishing.
(4) Simplification of customs procedures.
(5) Increasing transparency in government procurement of goods and services.
(6) Granting duty-free access to ADC markets for the poorest countries.
(7) Extension of the interim agreement not to impose customs duties on Internet transactions or e-commerce.
(8) Paving the way for agreement on foreign investment and competition policy.[37]
(9) Reviewing WTO antidumping and antisubsidy rules to curb abuse of these otherwise legitimate trade rules.
(10) Reviewing problems in implementing existing ("built-in") agreements on textiles, intellectual property protection, and investment rules.
(11) Establishing a forum involving the World Trade Organization, International Labor Organization, and United Nations Conference on Trade and Development (UNCTAD), as well as other organizations to discuss links among trade, economic development, and labor questions.

The Millennium Round, where these important and highly controversial trade issues were to be negotiated, was to be launched in November 1999 at a WTO trade ministers meeting in Seattle, Washing-

---

[37] The purpose of international competition policy or what Americans call "antitrust" policy is to set the terms on which global business is conducted.

ton. Unfortunately, strong differences among member governments, especially among the three major economic powers, along with turmoil in the streets, resulted in near chaos and the collapse of that conference. Launching of the Millenium Round therefore had to be delayed.

The New Trade Agenda

As the volume of world trade expanded and trade penetrated more and more deeply into national societies, it became increasingly entwined with politically sensitive matters and came into conflict with powerful domestic interests, especially in the United States. This development has produced the "new trade agenda," which includes such highly controversial issues as labor standards, human rights, the environment, and national sovereignty. Although some proponents of the new trade agenda are unalterably opposed to free trade and are even outright protectionists—and large parts of American organized labor provide a prime example of those who want free trade only on their own parochial terms—most advocates of one or another of the issues on the new trade agenda want radical changes in the WTO that would, most experts believe, greatly weaken the trade regime. Examination of the new trade agenda and the intense political controversy surrounding various items reveals serious threats to the trade regime that will be difficult to overcome.[38]

The issues of "fair" labor standards, human rights, and environmental protection center mainly on the question of whether these important and politically sensitive issues should be treated together with conventional trade issues or in a different venue. On the one hand, powerful groups, especially in the United States and Western Europe, believe strongly that these matters should be incorporated into the international trade regime, and that trade liberalization should be made subordinate to achievement of the particular specific objectives of their varying political agendas. On the other hand, most economists, governments, and business groups are strongly opposed to integrating these issues into international trade negotiations, fearing that, however well intended some groups are, the important issues of labor standards, human rights, and environmental protection will be and are being exploited by outright protectionists. Indeed, the stalemate generated by these possibly irreconcilable positions led to

[38] These matters are discussed in I. M. Destler and Peter J. Balint, *The New Politics of American Trade: Trade, Labor, and the Environment* (Washington, D.C.: Institute for International Economics, 1999).

225

the defeat in 1997 of President Clinton's request for "fast track" authority that could have greatly facilitated negotiation of trade agreements.

In the United States, the opposition of environmentalists to the trade regime had become intense by the late 1990s.[39] This opposition was inflamed by two controversial decisions of the trade dispute settlement mechanism. The first was a 1991 GATT ruling against the American ban on importing tuna caught by methods that killed dolphins; the second was another trade ruling in 1998 against an American law intended to protect sea turtles. The dolphin issue illustrates the difficulties created when environmental issues and trade matters intersect. The case arose from a Mexican accusation that the American law protecting dolphins discriminated against Mexican fishermen. The GATT based its ruling on the established principle that governments should not discriminate on the basis of the ways in which a good is produced. This principle had been accepted because such an extension of GATT authority to cover productive processes would have required it to probe deeply into sensitive domestic matters, and few countries would tolerate such an extension of authority. In addition, the American law had been poorly drafted and did indeed discriminate against Mexican fishermen. Moreover, the law had been passed without adequate discussions of the issue with Mexico. A different approach might have met the desires of both environmentalists and those who feared that environmental laws would be used as protectionist devices.

American environmentalist critics of the trade regime fall into two major camps, one of which accepts the principle of free trade but believes that environmental protection should be incorporated into trade negotiations and be given equal if not a higher priority than trade liberalization. This group also believes that the WTO and its dispute-settlement mechanism should become more open to the public. The other and more radical position opposes free trade as a threat to the environment and rejects the WTO as an instrument of powerful corporate interests; this latter group agrees with American neoisolationist conservatives that the WTO constitutes an infringement of American sovereignty. Together, the environmentalists have become a formidable force in the political struggle over trade.

Although few economists or other advocates of trade liberalization challenge the importance of protecting the environment, most have

---

[39] Daniel C. Esty, *Greening the GATT: Trade, Environment, and the Future* (Washington, D.C.: Institute for International Economics, 1994).

strongly opposed integration of trade liberalization with environmental protection. There is great concern that environmental regulations could and would be used to promote trade protection. Many are also seriously concerned that trade measures designed to protect the environment would shift the domain of trade negotiations from products to industrial processes. Yet, environmentalists are rightly concerned because trade negotiations and the trade regime do give priority to commercial interests over the environment, and there is indeed reason to worry that trade negotiations could lead to a *downward* harmonization of environmental standards. As both trade liberalization and environmental protection are desirable objectives, work toward both goals must continue through international negotiations.

The issues initially raised by environmentalists in Seattle are serious and must be addressed by national governments. Yet, with a few particularly important exceptions such as global warming and pollution of the oceans, almost every environmental issue can be most effectively dealt with on a domestic or regional basis. The serious problems of nuclear and other hazardous wastes, water contamination, air pollution, toxic dumps, and carbon dioxide (CO_2) emissions have little or nothing to do with international trade. One of the most vehement groups of protesters in Seattle consisted of opponents of logging and especially of "clear cutting." That problem is primarily the result of high government subsidies to timber companies (as in Alaska) and to forest destruction caused by land-hungry farmers and the national development strategies in many less developed countries (LDCs). Even though the primary responsibility for overcutting belongs to national governments, environmentalists have made the WTO the whipping boy in this matter and many others. Moreover, even when environmental issues do relate to international trade (as does happen in ocean oil spills and in trade in endangered species), the WTO does not have either the authority or the power to deal with such matters. These pressing matters can be dealt with effectively in such other ways as international conventions; this did happen in the international agreement on safety rules for genetically modified foods.[40]

The issue of labor standards has become a major impediment to trade liberalization, especially in the United States where it has been raised forcefully by organized labor and, to a lesser extent, by human rights advocates genuinely concerned over child labor in less developed countries, and in China in particular. Actually, a disproportion-

---

[40] Although this agreement was hardly perfect, it permits countries to bar imports of genetically modified foods. *New York Times*, 30 January 2000, A1.

ate number of the street protesters in Seattle were union members mobilized by the American AFL-CIO, whose president, John Sweeney, rejoiced at the collapse of the meeting. The International Labor Organization (ILO) has established labor standards, but most advocates of labor standards and opponents of child labor believe that that organization is much too ineffective to deal with these issues; moreover, the United States and a number of other countries have not even ratified all of the ILO's standards. Although some advocates of labor standards and of prohibitions against child labor are genuinely concerned over the oppressive conditions of labor in many countries, others use the issue as a protectionist device. Suspicion that American unions are more interested in keeping LDC exports out of the United States than they are in helping LDC workers is reinforced by the following episode: in early 2000, the United States agreed to increase Cambodia's quota of textiles imported into the United States in exchange for the latter's agreement to improve labor standards, including raising wages substantially. Under the agreement, Cambodian textile workers would have earned $40 per month (compared to $20 per month for Cambodian university professors). However, implementation of this agreement was blocked by American unions.[41]

Most economists, businesses, and national governments also reject the idea that labor standards and human rights should be incorporated into trade negotiations. Economists are concerned that consideration of labor standards in trade negotiations would unduly complicate the already horrendous task of achieving agreement on trade liberalization and would provide a convenient and effective rationale for protectionist measures against low-wage economies. Developing countries have strongly denounced efforts to impose "Western" standards on them. They have reason to believe that such proposals are motivated by protectionist interests and would be used to reduce their comparative advantage based on low-wage labor and provision of only minimum welfare benefits.

The closely related issues of labor standards, human rights, and child labor are legitimate and need to be addressed. Furthermore, some countries are undoubtedly guilty of "social dumping"; that is, of competing through denying workers fundamental rights and decent working conditions. However, remedying the problem will be extraordinarily difficult. As almost every LDC is strongly opposed to incorporating labor standards and human rights into the WTO, the effort to do so would be likely to destroy the effectiveness of the

---

[41] *Wall Street Journal*, 28 February 2000, A1.

organization. It is particularly ironic that many of the protestors at Seattle who denounced the rulings of the WTO as an infringement of American sovereignty also advocated that the WTO impose labor and human rights standards on delinquent LDCs! Needless to say, it will be difficult indeed to reconcile the positions of those who desire and those who oppose incorporation of workers' rights into the trade regime.

Ultimately, the solution to the associated problems of labor standards, human rights, and child labor must be provided through a combination of education and economic development. In general, those countries with the highest labor and environmental standards and those that have respect for human rights are the most developed countries, countries in which there is great wealth and a strong and concerned middle class. In societies with low income per capita, where parents frequently need the wages of their children, outside intervention like trade sanctions is unlikely to succeed.[42] In the short term, the best solution is to exert organized consumer pressure against those firms and countries that violate decent labor standards, human rights, and child labor. For example, according to the *New York Times*'s Thomas Friedman, following the GATT ruling against the American law banning tuna caught with nets that also catch dolphins, consumer pressures in the United States forced firms and the fishermen they deal with to change their practices; soon many brands carried the label "dolphin safe."[43] While such a method of dealing with a problem would fail to satisfy the AFL-CIO and others, there is some evidence that suggests that this technique has been used successfully with certain issues.

One of the most disturbing aspects of the new trade agenda is that the WTO and other international economic institutions have come under heated attack by an unholy alliance of environmentalists and human rights advocates, protectionist trade unions, and ultraconservative neoisolationists. As in the vehement protests surrounding the WTO's November 1999 meeting in Seattle and the April 2000 protests in Washington, the WTO and other international agencies have become lightning rods for concerned and frustrated groups around the globe who want the world to be different from its present unfortunate state. The impossible and contradictory demands of the Seattle protesters ranged from abolishing the WTO altogether, because it is

---

[42] Economists such as Jeffrey Sachs and Paul R. Krugman have pointed out that the important issue in many LDCs is whether there will be enough jobs.

[43] Thomas Friedman, *New York Times*, 8 December 1999, A31.

undemocratic and infringes on American sovereignty, to demands that it actively intervene in the sovereign affairs of nations to eliminate such destructive practices as forest clear-cutting and pollution of streams, lakes, and rivers. The World Trade Organization, the World Bank, and the International Monetary Fund have become the symbols of globalization for all those groups and individuals who blame globalization for their own and the world's problems.

International economic institutions have certainly made a number of serious mistakes. The controversial role of the IMF in the East Asian financial crisis is a prime example. The World Bank also has funded many questionable projects in poor countries. The WTO may have erred in certain of its decisions. Reforms that will make these institutions more accountable and sensitive to noneconomic matters are required. Yet, the wholesale attack on these institutions by the political left and right is unwarranted. It is wrong, for example, to blame these institutions for failures to achieve debt relief for poor countries, to open ADC markets to LDC exports, and to prevent the environmental damage caused by development projects supported by the World Bank. The responsibility for these failures lies with national governments. Debt relief was thwarted by the refusal of the rich industrial nations to appropriate the funds required to make debt relief possible. Opening the American market to more LDC goods has been resisted by labor unions and other powerful interests. Prevention of the environmental damage caused by large development projects in less developed countries has seldom been a priority for the LDCs themselves. If these and other problems of the global economy are to be resolved, protesters should direct their attention to the national governments that are ultimately responsible.

The argument that the WTO violates American sovereignty and somehow has been imposed on the United States is particularly disturbing. The WTO was created by a treaty sponsored by President Reagan, has been endorsed by Presidents Bush and Clinton, and was ratified by a two-thirds vote of the United States Senate. Under the American Constitution, a ratified international treaty becomes part of the law of the land and is incorporated into the definition of American sovereignty. The United States and other members have delegated to the WTO the responsibility to enforce existing trade agreements. It is not, as critics charge, a supergovernment that can legislate new laws. A dispute panel's interpretation of a trade law obviously can have a significant effect on trade regulations, but the WTO cannot force a country to do anything against its will. Moreover, interna-

230

tional law permits a nation to abrogate a treaty if it believes that the
treaty no longer serves its national interest.

Disarray Among Major Economic Powers

Although the Seattle street protestors attracted the most attention at
the November 1999 WTO meeting, responsibility for the abysmal
failure of that meeting belongs to the major economic powers, and to
the Clinton Administration in particular. For domestic political reasons, President Clinton tried to force the conference to include the
issue of "labor standards" on the agenda of future trade negotiations.
His irresponsible reference in a newspaper interview to the imposition
of economic sanctions on countries that did not meet certain labor
standards was especially noxious to developing countries, who quite
correctly viewed the President's motives as protectionist. Another factor in the breakdown of the negotiations was the inexperience of the
newly appointed WTO Director-General Mike Moore. Still other factors were the lack of adequate preparation for the meeting, lack of
an agreed-upon agenda, the unwieldiness of a meeting composed of
135 member-nations, and the "brusque chairmanship" of Charlene
Barshefsky, head of the U.S. delegation.[44]

The unwillingness of the major economic powers, especially the
United States and the European Union (EU), to contemplate serious
trade liberalization was also critical in the Seattle fiasco. Each major
economic power had a different agenda that conflicted with others
and precluded a successful outcome. High on the Clinton Administration's formal agenda were such issues as elimination of European agricultural subsidies and protection of intellectual property rights.
However, at the conference, President Clinton subordinated this formal agenda to the issue of labor standards. Furthermore, the Clinton
Administration refused to discuss the outrage in Japan and other
countries over the Administration's extensive and improper use of the
WTO's antidumping provision as a protectionist device.[45] The Administration also opposed the European Union's (EU's) strong desire
to put competition policy on the agenda and instead supported a nar-

[44] Ms. Barshefsky insisted on chairing the meeting with what many delegates charged
was an abrasive and domineering style. Poorer members, for example, complained that
they were excluded from "behind closed doors" meetings where important decisions
were made.
[45] Under both GATT and WTO rules, a country can impose duties on goods being
dumped on the world market. Both the United States and Western Europe have grossly
misused this safeguard provision for purely protectionist purposes.

row agenda favoring American export interests—financial services, information technology, aircraft, and agriculture—while demonstrating little concern for the welfare of American consumers.

At Seattle, both the Japanese and the West Europeans, also for domestic political reasons, adamantly opposed opening their economies to agricultural imports. In the EU, protection of agriculture through large subsidies to farmers is considered essential to the achievement of European economic and political integration. In Japan, the ruling Liberal Democratic Party, needing the votes of rural Japanese, opposed opening its market to imports of rice and other agricultural imports. The inability of the major economic powers to find compromises to these fundamental differences doomed the conference to failure. For all three major participants, domestic political objectives took precedence over trade liberalization.

The prospects for a major breakthrough in trade negotiations are not especially promising. Trade barriers in a number of important sectors such as textiles and agriculture may have declined, but only to a level that is politically acceptable to powerful constituencies. Moreover, both in the United States and in Western Europe, public opinion has grown increasingly worried about the impact of imports, especially from low-wage economies. In addition to obstacles to further liberalization raised by the industrialized countries, the industrializing countries have also become increasingly disillusioned with opening their markets. Experience of the East Asian economic crisis has increased the concerns of many about the dangers of opening their economies.[46] Reenergizing the process of trade liberalization will require strong political leadership.

CONCLUSION

The trade regime was one of the most important achievements of the latter half of the twentieth century. The eight GATT rounds of trade negotiations, beginning with the Kennedy Round in the early 1960s, reduced tariffs in industrialized countries to less than 4 percent on average, one-tenth of what they had been in the 1940s; quotas were reduced, and many subsidies were reduced or eliminated. There are estimates that lowered trade barriers have put an additional $1000 annually into the pockets of American consumers. The economies of less developed countries have also gained greatly as these countries

[46] David Woods, "The Seattle Fiasco," *Braudel Papers*, No. 24, (São Paulo, Brazil: Braudel Institute, 2000), 1.

have reduced their own trade barriers. Despite intense controversy over some of its decisions, the WTO dispute mechanism thus far has worked well. The number of GATT/WTO members has increased from twenty-three to one hundred thirty-five, and about thirty additional states wish to join in 2000. The shift around the world since the 1980s to more market-oriented economic policies is indicated by all these developments. However, as trade has expanded and penetrated more deeply into domestic economies and the trade agenda has broadened significantly, trade has come into conflict with powerful local interests and has thus become increasingly controversial. The clash between the forces of economic globalization and domestic concerns has triggered a backlash against globalization that threatens to undermine the political foundations of the trade regime.

The International Monetary System

IN THE DECADES immediately following World War II, monetary and financial affairs were in general isolated from one another.[1] The international monetary system based on fixed but adjustable exchange rates was generally isolated from international finance, with little interaction between the two. In fact, there was really no international financial system as we now conceive it, because almost every country maintained capital controls. This relatively simple situation began to unravel in the 1960s with the emergence of the Eurodollar market.[2] The first oil crisis in 1973 and the subsequent huge financial surplus of the Organization of Petroleum Exporting Countries (OPEC) changed this situation and led to creation of an international financial system. This then led to the integration of international money and international finance. For the first time in the postwar era, the international monetary system and international finance interacted and influenced one another.

Whereas the purpose of the international monetary system is to facilitate transactions in what economists call the "real" economy (trade, manufacturing, etc.), the purpose of the financial system is to provide the investment capital required for economic activities and development around the globe. Both the efficiency and the well-being of the world economy are profoundly affected by the success or failure of one or another of the two systems. However, the close ties of the international monetary system and international finance in the contemporary era have made the tasks of both systems much more difficult. As flows of international capital and foreign investment are conducted in money, changes in exchange rates—that is, in the value of particular currencies—inevitably change the value of an investment. If one buys dollars to invest in the United States and the value

---

[1] This chapter draws from Robert Gilpin, *The Challenge of Global Capitalism* (Princeton: Princeton University Press, 2000), Chapter 4.

[2] The Eurodollar market consists of foreign currencies, especially dollars, on deposit in West European and other international banks. The origins of the Eurodollar market lay principally in the desire of American banks to escape Regulation Q, which set an upper limit on interest charges. An additional factor in the rise of the Eurodollar market was hard currency deposits of the Soviet Union in European banks.

of the dollar falls, then the value of the investment is that much less. Similarly, international flows of foreign capital can cause a currency to appreciate (rise in value), as happened to the dollar in the early 1980s and during much of the 1990s. Erratic exchange rates can discourage trade and foreign investment, and international financial flows, in turn, can cause erratic exchange rates. Both the international monetary system and the international financial system are vulnerable, and disturbances in either or both systems can cause international economic turmoil, like that in East Asia during the late 1990s.

Although the monetary and financial aspects of the world economy are intimately linked, one can separate them for analytic purposes. This chapter concentrates on the international monetary system, and the following chapter, on international finance. There has been no stable and satisfactory international monetary system since the breakdown of the system of fixed exchange rates in the early 1970s. Reform of the monetary system involves complex technical issues, and every possible solution to technical matters carries important implications for the distribution of wealth both among and within national economies, and for the welfare of individual states. Prospects for a stable and integrated international monetary system will remain clouded until and unless these difficult technical and political matters can be resolved.

The Postwar International Monetary System

The post–World War II international monetary system was designed in 1944, and its fundamental principle was that exchange rates should be fixed in order to avoid the "beggar-thy-neighbor" policies of the 1930s and the ensuing economic anarchy. The International Monetary Fund (IMF) created at that time was intended to achieve this goal and to provide monetary reserves sufficient to enable member governments to maintain the exchange rates for their currencies at predetermined values. The IMF was designed to use contributions from member countries and to offer reserve credits to states with international payments problems. In addition, the monetary system had to anchor its members' monetary policies to some objective standard in order to prevent global inflation or devaluation. Stabilization of a monetary system can be achieved by tying every currency to a "nonmonetary" asset (gold being the asset of choice), by coordinating national monetary policies, or by following a leader whose past policies promise that it will provide the desired degree of economic stability in the future. Although all three methods were in fact employed in the early postwar years, the monetary policies of member states were anchored by tying every currency to the dollar, which in turn was tied to gold; the major powers also informally coordinated their economic policies.

The postwar monetary system of fixed rates, which lasted until the early 1970s, proved extraordinarily successful. Designed to provide both domestic policy autonomy and international monetary stability, the system in effect provided a compromise between the rigid gold standard of the late nineteenth century, under which governments had very little ability to manage their own economies, and the monetary anarchy of the 1930s, when governments had too much license to engage in competitive devaluations and other destructive practices. To achieve both autonomy and stability, the system was based on the following principles: fixed or pegged exchange rates along with sufficient flexibility to enable individual states to deal with extraordinary situations (including pursuit of full employment), reliable reserve credit in the event of an international payments problem, and agreement among member countries to peg their currencies to the dollar at $35 an ounce in gold. The International Monetary Fund was responsible for managing the system through approval of exchange rate adjustment in the event of a fundamental disequilibrium in a nation's balance of payments; the IMF could also make its monetary reserves available to deficit countries. These principles governed the system quite successfully for nearly three decades.

The ways in which the system actually functioned, however, did not fulfill the intentions and expectations of its founders. A significant difference was that, although the IMF had been assigned responsibility for maintaining reserves, in practice the buildup in dollar reserves held by member governments actually achieved this goal, and the American dollar became the foundation of the international monetary system in this way. Cooperation among the United States and its allies, and the passive U.S. attitude toward the dollar's exchange rate before 1971, made IMF actions in this area unnecessary. In the early postwar era, members also followed U.S. policy preferences, and they were reassured that this would provide stability to the system. However, by the time of the Vietnam War in the 1960s, the United States had ceased to pursue price stability, and inflation acceleration caused by that war eventually led the Nixon Administration to abandon the fixed-rate system in August 1971. Yet, even then, the United States and the dollar remained central to the system.

The key role of the dollar in the international monetary system facilitated the American alliance system and functioning of the world economy; the international role of the dollar as both a reserve and a transaction currency became a cornerstone of America's global economic and political position. Because, for political as well as for economic reasons, America's major allies and economic partners were willing to hold dollars, the international role of the dollar conferred on the United States the right of "seigniorage"; this means that the provider of the currency for an economy, in this case the international economy, enjoys certain privileges. As President Charles de DeGaulle of France bitterly complained in the 1960s, the "hegemony of the dollar" conferred "extravagant privileges" on the United States, because it alone could simply print dollars to fight foreign wars, could buy up French and other businesses, and could go deeply into debt without fearing negative consequences.

Nevertheless, there was a fundamental contradiction at the heart of this dollar-based system. While the huge outflow of American dollars to finance the rebuilding of Western Europe and Japan and the American military buildup during both the Korean and Vietnam Wars helped solve certain problems, this outflow of dollars meant that the United States would one day be unable to redeem in gold, and at the agreed price of $35 per ounce, those dollars held by private investors and foreign governments. Robert Triffin, in a series of writings, predicted that confidence in the dollar would be undermined as the American balance of payments shifted from a surplus to a deficit.[3] This problem did become acute late in the 1960s when escalation of the Vietnam War and its inflationary consequences caused deterioration in international confidence in the value of the dollar. As that confidence declined, the foundations of the Bretton Woods System of fixed rates began to erode.

Decreased confidence in the dollar also led to intensifying speculation in gold, and this was followed by futile attempts to find ways to recreate confidence in the system. For example, in the late 1960s, Special Drawing Rights (SDRs) were created by the IMF as a new reserve asset, although they were never utilized extensively. However, as Benjamin Cohen has convincingly argued, it was only when a political solution was devised that maintenance of the dominant position of the dollar was ensured.[4] America's Cold War allies, fearing that collapse of the dollar would force the United States to withdraw its forces from overseas and to retreat into political isolation, agreed to

---

[3] Robert Triffin, *Gold and the Dollar Crisis: The Future of Convertibility* (New Haven: Yale University Press, 1960).

[4] Benjamin J. Cohen, *Organizing the World's Money: The Political Economy of International Monetary Relations* (New York: Basic Books, 1977).

237

continue to hold overvalued dollars. The dollar was also bolstered for a period of time because such export-oriented economies as West Germany and, at a later date, Japan, wanted to retain access to the lucrative American market and therefore supported the high dollar. However, as soaring inflation undercut the value of the dollar, a more fundamental economic solution was needed.

THE END OF FIXED EXCHANGE RATES

In the early 1970s, the deteriorating position of the dollar became the central issue in the world economy. Escalation of the Vietnam War and the simultaneous launching of the Great Society Program by the Johnson Administration (1963–1969) had caused the global rate of inflation to accelerate and to threaten the value of the dollar. The U.S. government, attempting to hide the financial cost of the Vietnam War from the American people, refused to increase taxes and chose instead to pay for its warfare and welfare policies through inflationary macroeconomic policies. The succeeding Nixon Administration (1969–1974) compounded the problem of inflation. In addition, the Federal Reserve threw caution to the wind as it stimulated the economy, a move that critics labeled a blatant attempt to reelect Nixon. Subsequent intensification of speculative attacks on the overvalued dollar and ballooning of the American trade/payments deficit resulted in the Nixon Administration's decision on August 15, 1971, to force devaluation of the dollar.

To achieve the goal of a devalued dollar and to overcome the opposition of foreign export interests, the United States announced that it would no longer redeem dollars for gold. Simultaneously, to force other countries to appreciate their currencies, the Administration imposed a 10 percent surcharge on imports into the American economy and announced that the surcharge would be removed only after a satisfactory devaluation of the dollar had been achieved. Following bitter denunciations of this unilateral American action, especially by West Europeans, and after intense negotiations, the dollar was indeed substantially devalued by the Smithsonian Agreement of December 1971, in which other countries agreed to appreciate their currencies. The international monetary system was thus changed, at least de facto, from one based on fixed exchange rates to one based on flexible rates. In this way the postwar system of fixed exchange rates had become a casualty of reckless American policies, high inflation, and increasing international mobility of capital.

238

Subsequent efforts of an international committee to develop a new system of stable exchange rates failed. The overwhelming problems posed by increased capital mobility, along with fundamental differences between the United States and Western Europe over any new system, made agreement impossible. As a consequence of this impasse, the major industrial powers accepted economic reality at the Jamaica Conference (1976) and instituted flexible rates. I describe this situation as a "nonsystem" because there were no generally recognized rules to guide the flexible rates or any other decisions on international monetary affairs.

THE FINANCIAL REVOLUTION AND MONETARY AFFAIRS

The shift from a system of fixed to flexible exchange rates generated an intense debate in the economics profession. The majority of economists, certainly at least the majority of American economists, expected that this shift would be beneficial for the world economy. They believed that the combination of fixed rates and increasing economic interdependence through trade, investment, and monetary flows had imposed severe constraints on national economic policy and thereby had decreased the ability of individual governments to pursue macroeconomic policies that would promote full employment and other economic benefits. Economists believed that a system of flexible rates would delink national economies from one another and thus permit every government to pursue those economic policies best suited to its own national circumstances.

A minority of economists, however, strongly disagreed with this optimistic assessment and was very concerned about the potentially inflationary and destabilizing consequences of delinking the international monetary system from the anchor of gold or some other commodity. If the system were not anchored to an objective standard, the value of money and the stability of prices, they reasoned, would henceforth rest entirely on the discretion of individual governments. Believing that governments were not to be trusted to pursue stable economic policies, they worried that governments would behave so irresponsibly that inflation and monetary instability would soon disrupt the world economy.

The majority of economists remained convinced that their colleagues' fears of inflation and instability were unfounded. However, the unanticipated "financial revolution" of the mid-1970s and its consequences proved that the optimism of the majority of economists had been unfounded. Growth of the Eurodollar market and overseas

239

expansion of American banks in the 1960s had resulted in the emergence of an international financial market. Then, in the 1970s, development of the new international financial system accelerated following deregulation of domestic financial systems, removal of capital controls in a number of countries, and the greatly increased size and velocity of global financial flows, an increase made possible by modern communications and new financial techniques and instruments. Moreover, the huge OPEC monetary surplus following the first oil crisis, and the need to recycle those funds, proved important in the development of the international financial market. Before the end of the 1970s, the scale and velocity of international financial flows had expanded enormously and had truly transformed the international economic system.

Integration of global financial markets and increased monetary and financial interdependence of national economies had a significant impact on domestic as well as international economics. Financial market integration means that the macroeconomic policies of one country have a significant impact on the economic welfare of other countries. For example, if country A raises its interest rates to decrease domestic inflationary pressures, those higher rates will attract capital from other countries with lower interest rates, and the resulting increase in country A's money supply then contributes to the inflationary pressures that higher interest rates were intended to counter. Simultaneously economic activity is reduced in the economies from which the capital flows. Integration of national financial markets actually reduced macroeconomic policy autonomy. Despite the shift to flexible exchange rates, domestic and international economic spheres became even more closely linked to one another because of financial market integration.

Another unanticipated consequence of the financial revolution has been that international financial flows have become an important determinant of exchange rates, at least in the short term. This situation has greatly increased exchange rate volatility, especially between the dollar and other major currencies (the Japanese yen and the German mark). By the end of the 1970s, international financial flows dwarfed trade flows by a ratio of about 25:1; the size of the flows also contributed greatly to volatility. The tendency of exchange rates to "overshoot" in response to financial flows has proved important in producing fluctuations; that is, the exchange rate tends to make large swings up and down rather than find a new and stable equilibrium, and such overshooting causes a disequilibrium in currency values and hence increases exchange rate volatility. This situation has made it difficult for markets to move smoothly from one equilibrium exchange rate to the next and for anyone to know what the equilibrium exchange rate should be.

Since fixed rates were eliminated, economists and public officials have debated heatedly whether or not exchange rate volatility has produced negative consequences for the real economy through its impact on trade flows, business activity, and economic growth. Some economists believe that volatile rates may have contributed to development of the New Protectionism in the mid-1970s. Many economists now believe that the world should return to a system of fixed rates because of the high costs of exchange rate volatility.

Freeing financial markets facilitated reorganization and transformation of international business. Increased integration of national financial markets encouraged creation of a single, globally integrated market for corporation ownership and such corporate takeover activities as the late-1990s merger of Chrysler and Daimler-Benz. Although, in Japan, government regulations and the system of corporate groupings or *keiretsu* have made foreign takeovers very difficult, elsewhere there has been a huge increase in acquisitions and alliances by multinational corporations since the mid-1970s.

The substantial increase in international interdependence has also had a profound impact on domestic economic policy. Economic interdependence considerably reduced the capacity of many countries to pursue full-employment policies, and this in turn undermined the domestic consensus supporting an open world economy. Increased interdependence also has integrated such once-isolated policy issues as trade flows and exchange rate determination, thus immensely complicating the task of managing the world economy and raising important questions about the adequacy of the rules governing international economic affairs.

With these several developments, the Bretton Woods rule-based international monetary system was replaced by a shaky political agreement among the dominant economic powers (G-7); this change made the central bankers of the major economic powers de facto managers of the international monetary system. What soon became known as the "reference range" system was based on the cooperative, and sometimes not so cooperative, efforts of central bankers and finance ministers to stabilize currency values. As time went by, however, this cooperative mechanism became less and less satisfactory, and many proposals have been put forth to reform the nonsystem and to return to a rule-based system, or at least to a more satisfactory arrangement based on cooperation among the major economic powers. Lacking a satisfactory solution to the problem of unstable exchange rates, and frustrated by what they considered to be irresponsible American macroeconomic policies, West Europeans sought to isolate themselves from American actions through creation of the European Monetary System (EMS) and the accompanying Exchange Rate Mechanism (ERM). This European initiative became a further important step in the development of regional arrangements within the international monetary system. Despite these setbacks, efforts to strengthen international monetary affairs have continued.

EMBEDDED TECHNICAL AND POLITICAL ISSUES

Although an efficient international monetary system benefits every country, serious political and economic difficulties almost invariably impede creation or reform of an international monetary system. Every solution to technical problems has important distributive consequences that affect differently both various nations and powerful domestic constituencies; strong reactions can be evoked because some may lose more or benefit less than others from any new monetary arrangement. During the early postwar years, both the United States and its trading partners were upset over the asymmetries of the dollar-based system. Many Europeans objected to the economic and political privileges bestowed on the United States, and the United States, as the reserve-currency country, fretted increasingly over its inability to reduce its trade deficit by devaluing the dollar. Eventually, President Nixon in August 1971 "solved" American concerns about asymmetry by forcing appreciation of other currencies.

The creation and/or reform of an international monetary system involves highly complex technical issues. The formal models and mathematical techniques of economists that are required to deal with monetary and financial matters are beyond the technical competence of most noneconomists, and even beyond many economists; yet the international monetary system is of intense concern and importance to national governments and private economic interests. The mechanisms responsible for the system's efficient functioning—adjustment, liquidity creation, and confidence-building measures—produce a differential impact on the national interests of various countries and also on the interests of powerful groups within economies. Technical mechanisms are seldom politically neutral; they affect the economic welfare, political autonomy, and even the international prestige of individual states, and they also have an impact on the interests of capital, labor, and other domestic groups. Every state wants an efficient and well-functioning international monetary system. However, individual states and powerful domestic groups may disagree strongly on specific matters, such as currency values and the precise mechanisms employed to solve technical problems.

The distributive consequences of solutions to technical problems are illustrated by the liquidity issue, which is closely tied to the issue of seigniorage; that is, the economic benefits accruing to the country whose currency is used as the basis of the international monetary system. Solutions to the adjustment problem determine whether deficit or surplus countries must pay the high costs of reestablishing a balance-of-payments equilibrium. The nature of the international monetary system also has important implications for such different constituencies as tradeable/nontradeable sectors, labor and/or capital, and industry/finance.

Political differences mean that a well-functioning monetary system requires strong leadership by a nation or group of nations with an interest in maintaining the system. The leader(s) must assume the initiative in solving highly technical problems as well as providing and managing the key currency used for maintaining reserves, carrying out economic transactions, and providing liquidity. Furthermore, the leader should be the "lender of last resort" and from time to time should provide financial assistance to countries experiencing severe financial problems. Although this leadership role could, in theory, be provided by two or more nations or even by an international organization, leadership has historically been provided by a dominant economic and military power; for example, Great Britain in the late nineteenth century and the United States following World War II. Not surprisingly, the rules governing the international monetary system have in general reflected the interests of the leading economic powers.

The Belgian economist Paul DeGrauwe has pointed out that economists differ fundamentally with one another over almost every aspect of international monetary affairs, from determination of currency values to the virtues of fixed versus floating rates; this makes explication of economists' views on this matter quite challenging.[5] Particularly since the early 1970s, the area of international monetary affairs has been the focus of intense controversy. Although professional books and journals have been filled with proposals to reform the regime, few proposals have been implemented, and the monetary system's inherent problems and contradictions remain unresolved.

---

[5] Paul DeGrauwe, *International Money: Post-War Trends and Theories* (Oxford: Clarendon Press, 1989).

Economists' theories about the varied and complex aspects of the international monetary regime have usually followed rather than preceded events that they attempt to explain. Indeed, many theories regarding monetary affairs have been merely ex-post-facto explanations of important developments that economists had failed to predict. Such theoretical and policy differences among experts increase the difficulties of finding solutions to the problems.

Adjustment

An international monetary regime must determine the method by which national economies will restore equilibrium (i.e., reduce a deficit or a surplus) in their international accounts (balance of payments), and an efficient international monetary system should minimize the costs of making adjustments. Every adjustment policy results in economic costs, and some methods of adjustment are considerably more costly for individual economies and for the overall world economy than are others.

A country with an imbalance in its international payments may pursue such short-term expedients as drawing down its national reserves (a deficit country) or adding to its national reserves (a surplus country). However, with few exceptions, a deficit country cannot continue drawing down its reserves for very long, and eventually the debtor country must take measures to eliminate the cause of the imbalance. On the other hand, a surplus country, like the United States for much of the twentieth century and Japan at the end of the century, can continue to add to its reserves for a very long time, a practice that irritates its trading partners. Both deficit and surplus countries employ additional methods to overcome payments imbalances. One such method is to change the exchange rate by devaluing the currency (a deficit country) or appreciating it (a surplus country). Another method is to make changes in macroeconomic policy; that is, to shift to deflationary (a deficit country) or expansionary (a surplus country) economic policies.

Some currencies will inevitably get out of line with one another. Many nations live beyond their means and pursue inflationary policies; others, like Japan during most of the second half of the twentieth century, desire a continuous payments surplus and therefore choose to live below their means (a deflationary policy). Such national differences in inflation/deflation rates will cause currency values to change; some method acceptable to all must be available to bring currencies back into equilibrium. And, of course, for every deficit country, there must be surplus elsewhere. While either the deficit or surplus country (or both) could make adjustments, under the Bretton Woods System it was generally assumed that the burden of adjustment rested with the deficit country. However, the deficit country can and frequently does take actions to impose the costs of adjustment on the surplus country. For example, the United States has attempted, with some modest success, to impose the burden of adjustment on Japan through policies intended to eliminate the American-Japanese trade/payments imbalance.

Adjustment, for a deficit country, means that it must reduce its standard of living or at least reduce the rate of increase in that standard, achieve a long-term reduction in national income and/or reduce employment levels. The rules governing the international monetary system will determine the approved methods of making such an adjustment. However, regardless of the choices available, transition from "high living" to "living within one's means" must necessarily impose a real cost on the deficit country, and the precise manner in which adjustment occurs will also impose costs on other countries. For example, the deflationary consequences of the East Asian financial crisis harmed many American exporters. It is clear that all countries would like to shift as many adjustment costs as possible to others and away from themselves. Working out the distribution of the costs of adjustment among deficit and surplus nations is at the heart of solving the adjustment problem.

For a deficit country living beyond its means, both currency devaluation and/or deflation of the economy are painful, because the former entails a drop in national income and the latter, a rise in unemployment. For a surplus country, currency appreciation is painful for its export industries but beneficial for its importers and consumers; on the other hand, macroeconomic stimulus of the economy carries the risk of inflation. How much better it would be, therefore, to transfer the adjustment costs to one's trading partners! As mentioned above, a case in point is the long-simmering economic clash between the deficit United States and the surplus Japan. From the 1980s onward, the United States resisted deflationary policies that would reduce its trade deficit but would also mean a decline in the American standard of living. Meanwhile, Japan resisted an appreciation of the yen that would harm its export industries, and Japanese agreement at the Plaza Conference (September 22, 1985) to appreciate the yen was achieved only after intense American pressures. Since solution of the adjustment problem impinges on the interests of states and of powerful interests within states, adjustment mechanisms do and will reflect the interests of powerful states and groups.

Liquidity

An efficient international monetary system must also provide international liquidity. Participating countries must have financial reserves sufficient to meet balance-of-payments deficits caused by such economic shocks to the system as the sudden increase in the price of petroleum in 1973 or by persistent use of such unwise policies as an inflationary macroeconomic policy or maintenance of an overvalued currency. Reserves are important because they enable a deficit country to finance, at least for a short period, a payments disequilibrium and to increase the time and options available to the country as it seeks a longer-term solution to its deficit problem. A country can also use reserves to delay a possibly costly devaluation of its currency. A nation's reserves (like any other form of money) are also a store of value; they may include gold, convertible foreign currencies, or deposits with the International Monetary Fund.

While provision of optimal international liquidity facilitates the world economy's functioning, neither underprovision nor overprovision is desirable. Underprovision may be recessionary and overprovision, inflationary. Under the gold standard during the last decades of the nineteenth century, there was underprovision of reserves, and while the gold standard was a very stable system, this system frequently resulted in high levels of unemployment and depressed wages. On the other hand, during the early post–World War II era of the dollar standard, overprovision of reserves by the United States meant a high level of inflation that eventually led to the breakdown of the Bretton Woods monetary system of fixed rates. With economists and governments disagreeing about the rules that should govern international reserves, the rule of the strong has generally prevailed and the dominant powers have had a significant impact, at least over the shortterm, on maintaining the level of international liquidity to accord with their own economic and political interests.

Seigniorage is an important aspect of liquidity creation. Not only is national prestige enhanced when a nation's currency is selected as the most important currency, but seigniorage can also be a major source of increased income to the nation, particularly to its banking system. In addition, seigniorage can increase the economic and political autonomy of the country because that country is freed, at least for a time, from balance-of-payments constraints. On the other hand, seigniorage has associated costs; for example, the nation with the right of seigniorage usually has to pay interest to other countries holding assets denominated in its currency. To maintain seigniorage also means that a country must avoid actions that undermine confidence in the value of its currency. Moreover, the country supplying the key currency may find it difficult to devalue its currency, as happened to the United States in the early 1970s.

Increased national income and national autonomy or freedom of action are important benefits of seigniorage. The banking system of a country supplying an international currency enjoys both economies of scale and other cost advantages over its competitors simply because most international reserves and transactions are held in its national currency. Under the gold standard in the late nineteenth century, British sterling was the key currency, and London financial institutions enjoyed high profits as the center of the international monetary system. Following World War I, London and sterling were challenged by New York and the dollar, and the profits from seigniorage began to flow to the United States and its banking system. It remains to be seen whether or not the euro of the European Union and a European city or cities will appropriate financial and monetary leadership in the twenty-first century.

Seigniorage also confers greater freedom from economic restraints on the key-currency country and, hence, more autonomy than other countries enjoy. Throughout the Cold War, the capacity of the United States to fight foreign wars, maintain troops abroad, and finance its foreign policy was largely dependent on the willingness of its allies to hold American dollars and dollar-denominated assets. Even after the Cold War, the role of the dollar as the world's key currency permitted the United States to live far beyond its means for years and thus to become the world's foremost debtor nation. Other countries, by holding dollars, actually gave the United States interest-free loans. As the American debt has been denominated in dollars, this debt burden could be inflated away, and devaluation of the dollar in the 1990s did indeed reduce the debt owed by the United States while simultaneously imposing heavy costs on Japanese and other lenders. Nevertheless, the United States will continue to enjoy the privileges of seigniorage as long as there is no acceptable alternative and holders of dollars or dollar-denominated assets maintain confidence in the dollar.

Confidence

A stable international monetary system is also dependent on solution of the confidence (credibility) problem; other countries must have confidence that the reserve-currency country will not pursue inflationary policies leading to devaluation of their own reserves. If they lose confidence, other countries will shift the composition of their

247

reserves. A shift can also occur because of changes in the interest rate paid on assets denominated in a currency or because of changes in exchange risk or in concerns about inflation. A reserve-currency country must pay an attractive interest rate on assets denominated in its currency, and it must also take confidence-building measures to convince private and public holders of its currency that its currency will continue to be convertible into other sound assets and will not lose value because of inflation or changes in exchange rates. Confidence-building measures can be quite costly.

DEVISING AN INTERNATIONAL MONETARY SYSTEM

Differing subjective judgments and interests among public officials and intense disagreements among economists about the appropriate applicable economic model or theory add complications to the development or modification of a monetary system. There are intellectual and theoretical disagreements among economists and public officials about many possible solutions to the technical issues embedded in a monetary system. Economists, for example, even disagree about the economic model to apply to determination of exchange rates, and there are trade-offs among desirable but mutually exclusive goals. A choice, one that is primarily political, must be made.

At the heart of the difficulties in finding solutions to exchange rate instability is the fact that national economies have very different rates of inflation and/or price instability. Whereas some governments place a high value on price stability, others prefer to pursue expansionary and frequently inflationary policies to reduce unemployment or stimulate economic growth. Germany and Japan, having given priority to price stability throughout the postwar era, have followed strong antiinflationary policies while the United States, at least until the late 1970s, pursued mild to highly inflationary policies.

The problem of devising a stable and politically acceptable international monetary system is further compounded by the inevitable trade-offs among the following equally desirable goals: fixed exchange rates, national independence in monetary policy, and capital mobility. These three goals are referred to by economists as a *trilemma*, or as the *"irreconcilable trinity."* Nations may want stable exchange rates to reduce economic uncertainty, but they may also desire discretionary monetary policy in order to promote economic growth and steer their economies between recession and inflation. In addition, governments may want freedom of capital movements to facilitate the conduct of trade, foreign investment, and other international business activities.[6]

Unfortunately, no international monetary and financial system can accommodate all three of these desirable goals (fixed exchange rates, national independence in monetary policy, and capital mobility), although it can incorporate at most two of these objectives. For example, a system of fixed and stable exchange rates such as the Bretton Woods System, along with some latitude for independent monetary policies, is incompatible with freedom of capital movement because capital flows could undermine both fixed exchange rates and independent monetary policies. A system with fixed exchange rates and independent macroeconomic policies promotes economic stability and enables a government to deal with unemployment. However, such a system sacrifices freedom of capital movement, one of the most important goals of international capitalism. A system of fixed rates and freedom of capital movements would be incompatible with an independent monetary policy.

Different countries and domestic interest groups prefer to emphasize one or another of these goals. In the late 1990s the United States, for example, preferred independent monetary policy and freedom of capital movements, and thereby sacrificed stable exchange rates. The members of the European Community, on the other hand, preferred relatively fixed rates. Some countries, notably Malaysia and China, placed a high value on macroeconomic independence and have imposed controls on capital movements. Specific economic interests also differ in their preferences. Whereas export businesses have a strong interest in the exchange rate, domestic-oriented businesses place a higher priority on national policy autonomy. Investors prefer freedom of capital movements, whereas labor tends to be opposed to such movement, unless of course it means inward rather than outward investment. As national situations and interests differ, there is no one solution to the trilemma that would be satisfactory for all.

Many economic conservatives argue that the first major effort to resolve the problem was the most successful; that is, creation of the classical gold standard under British leadership in the latter decades of the nineteenth century. Under that system of "golden fetters" (to

---

[6] The Mundell-Fleming model, developed in the 1960s by Robert Mundell and John Fleming, integrates international capital flows with other factors determining demand and output. This development created what has become known as open-economy macroeconomics in contrast to the domestic orientation of most economists in the 1960s. This theoretical development is set forth in Robert A. Mundell, *International Economics* (New York: Macmillan, 1968).

use the title of Barry Eichengreen's important book on the subject), there was indeed international monetary stability, but governments had little control over their own economies, and the domestic economy frequently suffered as a result.[7] The collapse of the gold standard at the outbreak of World War I resulted in a situation in which governments had too much license over economic policy; the 1930s and 1940s were an era of economic anarchy, competitive devaluations, and "beggar-thy-neighbor" policies that lasted until the Bretton Woods System was created at the end of World War II. The Bretton Woods System, based on fixed exchange rates and supervised by the International Monetary Fund, continued until officially terminated in the mid-1970s. The subsequent volatility and unpredictability of exchange rates produced by the more recent "nonsystem" have led to many proposals to reform the international monetary regime.

REFORM OF INTERNATIONAL MONETARY AFFAIRS

In 1930, John Maynard Keynes set forth the ideal objective of an international monetary system:

This, then, is the dilemma of an international monetary system—to preserve the advantages of the stability of local currencies of the system in terms of the international standard, and to preserve at the same time an adequate local autonomy for each member over its domestic rate of interest and its volume of foreign lending.[8]

After the breakdown of the system of fixed exchange rates in the 1970s, the international monetary system strayed far from the Keynes ideal. The "reference range" system, which replaced the system of fixed rates, is actually a "nonsystem" of floating exchange rates in which international monetary affairs are not governed by rules or understandings about such factors as rate adjustment or liquidity creation. Or, to put it another way, there is no regime for international monetary affairs; instead, under the reference range nonsystem, the central banks and finance ministers of the three dominant monetary powers—the United States, Germany, and Japan—cooperate to keep their exchange rates aligned or to change them in an orderly fashion. However, in this nonsystem, erratic American macroeconomic poli-

---

[7] Barry J. Eichengreen, *Golden Fetters: The Gold Standard and the Great Depression, 1919–1939* (New York: Oxford University Press, 1992).

[8] John Maynard Keynes, *A Treatise on Money: The Applied Theory of Money.* (Cambridge: Cambridge University Press, 1971; first published in 1930), 272.

cies and huge trade deficits have caused large exchange rate fluctuations and have seriously vexed America's trading partners.

The reference range nonsystem represents the triumph of the central bankers. Stability of the international monetary system has rested mainly on informal cooperation among the American Federal Reserve, the German Bundesbank (replaced in 1999 by the Central European Bank), and the Bank of Japan, which have intervened in currency markets to protect the integrity of the system, prevent financial instability, and stabilize exchange rates through secret agreements and sporadic intervention in the market. After the disturbing experience of hyperflation in the 1970s, interbank cooperation has also been employed to suppress inflationary tendencies. However, many critics, especially on the political left, have denounced this international alliance of conservative bankers as the cause of high unemployment and even of the global economic crisis of the late 1990s.

Many economists believe that this system of informal cooperation among central bankers and finance ministers is the best possible solution to the problems of the international monetary system. They reject the contention that fluctuating exchange rates have a negative impact on economic affairs and argue that, if this should happen, exchange rate volatility could be managed through currency hedging and other techniques. Other economists and central bankers, on the other hand, believe that the present nonsystem should be replaced by a rule-based monetary system or more institutionalized cooperation. A serious problem, they point out, is that there are radical fluctuations in exchange rates that cause uncertainty and thereby inhibit trade and investment; exchange rate uncertainty also is alleged to encourage such regional monetary arrangements as the European Monetary Union.[9] Many economists and public officials who worry about this and other weaknesses in the reference range system believe that a fundamental reform of the international monetary system is urgently needed.

Since the collapse of the Bretton Woods System of fixed rates, the issue of fixed versus flexible exchange rates has been central to all questions of international monetary reform. At the heart of this debate are the "irreconcilable trinity" and the difficult choices it poses for national governments. In general, economists prefer flexible rates in order to facilitate international capital movements and adjustments

---

[9] Whether fluctuations in currency values are actually harmful is a matter of debate among economists. For a discussion of the issue, consult Ronald I. McKinnon and K. C. Fung, "Floating Exchange Rates and the New Interbloc Protectionism: Tariffs versus Quotas," in Dominick Salvatore, ed., *Protectionism and World Welfare* (New York: Cambridge University Press, 1993), 10.

251

in the real economy made necessary by economic shocks. Central bankers and a minority of economists prefer fixed rates in order to ensure price stability. A number of conservative economists and others prefer a return to the nineteenth-century gold standard, as it would eliminate government control over monetary affairs and prevent inflation. Most economists reject this proposal because it would also eliminate the ability of governments to manage their economies in the case of recession or an economic shock. Whether one prefers the macroeconomic independence that comes with flexible rates or the microeconomic benefits that accompany stable exchange rates is at the core of this debate.

Arguments for More Stable Exchange Rates

Advocates of a return to more stable exchange rates assert that the experiment with flexible (floating) rates has failed and that flexible rates have resulted in excessive currency and price volatility, destabilizing international capital flows, and inflationary economic policies. Excessive exchange rate volatility increases uncertainty and risk in both international trade and foreign investment and thus impedes international economic integration. Some experts also argue that volatility of currency values has decreased the effectiveness of the price mechanism and of the principle of comparative advantage as tools in international trade and foreign investment decision-making.

Erratic swings in the three major currencies have occurred within a period as short as one or two years; swings in which some currency values have varied by as much as 30 to 40 percent. For example, the dollar's value moved from 250 yen in 1985 to 79 yen in 1995, back up to 148 yen in 1998, and then down again to 105 in early 2000.[10] The resulting uncertainty in relative prices made it almost impossible to calculate relative costs and comparative advantage, calculations needed for a market economy to function efficiently. From such experiences some have concluded that floating rates impose high costs in economic growth and in the efficient allocation of economic resources, even arguing that unstable exchange rates have contributed to trade protectionism. These individuals believe that fixed rates, on the other hand, provide international discipline over inflationary monetary policy, reduce uncertainty that interferes with trade and investment, and thereby facilitate competition based on comparative advantage and efficient capital flows.

---

[10] Robert Mundell, "Threat to Prosperity," *Wall Street Journal*, 30 March 2000, A30.

Proponents of more stable exchange rates are fully aware that economic and political developments have made impossible a return to the type of pegged-rate system laid down at Bretton Woods. These individuals advocate, instead, a compromise between greater international stability and provision of some flexibility for the policies of individual governments. Many are concerned because governments need to be able to respond to economic shocks and other developments through various schemes based on the idea of a contingent exchange rate target; the schemes have such labels as "pegged but adjustable exchange rates," "crawling peg," "managed floating rates," "adjustable peg," and "exchange rate target zones." Whatever the exact formulation, Nobel Laureate Robert Mundell believes that a more stable international monetary system requires close cooperation among the three major currencies.[11] As such cooperation would entail restraints on American economic policy, its political prospects are not promising.

Arguments for Flexible Exchange Rates

Fixed (stable) exchange rates are very costly to maintain in a world with huge international financial flows. These financial flows have become the principal determinant of exchange rates, a role previously played by trade flows. Therefore, unless a country is willing either to shut itself off from international investment or to give up the possibility of an independent macroeconomic policy (two of the components of the "irreconcilable trinity"), it must accept flexible (floating) rates. A system of flexible exchange rates provides the least costly means for economies to adjust to external shocks, like the 1973 rise in oil prices. Proponents of flexible rates argue that when a government faces a balance of payments disequilibrium, it is far better to devalue its currency than to deflate its economy or resort to capital controls. The value of a currency should be free to change so that other more important values, or "real" variables such as wages and employment, need not change. Indeed, the flexible rates in existence in 1973 made the necessary adjustments easier than they would have been if there had been fixed rates, which, during the oil crisis, would have forced countries to adjust to the price rise either through severe deflation or capital controls.

Advocates of floating rates argue that they are inherently desirable because the value of a currency acts as a balancing mechanism for the rest of the economy, and because flexible rates protect and cushion an

[11] Ibid.

economy from disturbances originating in the international economy. While there may be some problems of uncertainty and inflation associated with flexible rates, reliance on fixed rates to avoid such problems makes adjustment both more costly and more difficult. Many argue, moreover, that the costs of floating rates have been greatly exaggerated; they point out that the problem of monetary uncertainty can be reduced by private firms' "hedging" in the foreign exchange market.

Monetary expert Barry Eichengreen argues that economic and political changes have made a return to a system of fixed rates impossible.[12] One change is the institutionalized structure of labor markets associated with the welfare state, a development that seriously restricts the fluidity with which prices and wages can adjust to economic shocks. Another important change is the increasingly politicized environment in which domestic monetary policy must be formulated; politicization of macroeconomic policy in almost every democratic country has eroded the credibility of government policies and the commitment of monetary authorities to pursue noninflationary monetary policy. As the twenty-first century opened, few governments could be relied upon to maintain long-term robust or steadfast monetary policy. The most important change is the greatly increased mobility of capital movements around the world that has been encouraged by deregulation of capital markets, technological developments, and new financial instruments, all of which have also greatly limited governmental ability to contain market pressures.

Eichengreen argues that these economic and political changes have restricted possible international monetary arrangements to either (1) an international monetary system based on freely floating exchange rates, or (2) monetary unification among groups of countries to enable creation of single currency areas managed by regional central banks. Freely floating exchange rates would be a step away from an integrated, rule-based world economy, as such an arrangement could have few, if any, rules governing such technical matters as exchange rate adjustment and liquidity creation. Under such a monetary arrangement, an individual nation could intervene in the market to guide the floating rate of its currency but could not set and hold to a targeted value. Therefore, the means to guarantee a stable international monetary system, Eichengreen has argued, is complete monetary integration; that is, creation of a single currency managed by a

---

[12] Barry J. Eichengreen, *International Monetary Arrangements for the 21st Century* (Washington, D.C.: Brookings Institution, 1994).

central bank. However, as the twenty-first century opened, the only effort to achieve monetary unity was that in Western Europe.

Many economists and public officials believe that Eichengreen's analysis is much too pessimistic, and few are willing to give up the search for an effective means to stabilize exchange rates through an international monetary authority, international policy cooperation, or some other mechanism. However, many would undoubtedly agree that an effective governance mechanism must soon be devised to manage international monetary affairs in order to avoid the real danger that the monetary system will disintegrate either into monetary anarchy similar to the 1930s or will fragment into regional arrangements based on such dominant regional currencies as the American dollar, the euro, or the Japanese yen. A stable international monetary system must rest on the cooperation of the major economic powers, a situation that has not been easy either to establish or to maintain.

UNITY OR FRAGMENTATION OF THE MONETARY SYSTEM?

Creation of the European Monetary System (EMS) and the common currency (euro) pose a serious threat to the unity of the international monetary system. There is considerable interest and disagreement among public officials, economists, and political pundits on both sides of the Atlantic Ocean and in other parts of the globe concerning the implications of the euro for the dollar and the international economy in general. The most important questions are whether or not the euro will displace the dollar as the world's principal currency, what the consequences for the United States would be if it did, and how the euro would affect the functioning and management of the international monetary and economic system. The large number of economic and political unknowns surrounding the euro make it impossible to provide any conclusive answers to these and other relevant questions. Nevertheless, these issues are of such moment for the future of the global economy that they must be addressed, even if only tentatively.

Throughout the postwar era, the international role of the dollar has been an important feature of the world economy. Somewhere between 40 and 60 percent of international financial transactions are denominated in dollars. For decades the dollar has also been the world's principal reserve currency; in 1996, the dollar accounted for approximately two-thirds of the world's foreign exchange reserves. The possibility that the euro will replace the international role of the dollar as a transaction and reserve currency has become extremely important, particularly for the United States and its financial commu-

255

nity. In Western Europe, many believe that eventually the euro will, to a significant degree, displace the dollar. On the other hand, most American economists believe that the euro is unlikely to displace the dollar. They believe, moreover, that if a shift from the dollar to the euro should occur, it would happen very slowly over a lengthy period and thus give the United States sufficient time to make such necessary adjustments as elimination of its huge trade/payments deficit.

Most American economists expect that the continuing international role of the dollar will depend more on the strength of the American economy than on anything else, and that the importance of the dollar to international financial markets will be determined primarily by the international competitiveness of the American financial system. The euro, according to this position, could replace the dollar only if West Europeans create an integrated and efficient financial market. Many doubt that this will happen for some time. Thus, American officials and economists tend to discount the possibility that the international reign of the dollar will be undermined by the euro, at least in the foreseeable future.

If the euro were to replace the dollar as the world's key currency, there would be important implications for both private American financial interests and the American government. The success of the euro could have a large negative impact on American banks and financial institutions because a large volume of transactions in a currency leads to economies of scale and decreased transaction costs. The larger the volume of currency transactions in a particular country's currency, the greater the profits and competitiveness enjoyed by the banks and financial institutions of that country. If the euro were to replace the dollar as a reserve or transaction currency, then the benefits of scale and lower transaction costs would be transferred from American to European financial institutions. By one estimate, the portfolio switch from the dollar to the euro could be as large as $1 trillion.

The international role of the dollar has conferred a number of economic and political benefits on the United States, and if the dollar were to lose its status as the world's key currency, the United States would forfeit these benefits. The international demand for dollars has meant that the United States has been able to finance its huge and continuing trade/payments deficits since the early 1980s at a minimal cost. In effect, the United States government has been able to assume that other countries would automatically finance its trade/payments deficit because others, needing dollars to conduct their international business, did not demand high interest rates. Moreover, the United

States has been able to borrow in its own currency and thus avoid exchange-rate risks. Many of the dollars in circulation are overseas in the hands of non-Americans; this so-called "dollar overhang" of about $265 billion is the equivalent of an interest-free loan to the United States that some have estimated to be worth about $13 billion in annual interest payments. In addition, American prestige is certainly enhanced by the international role of the dollar.

Many West European leaders believe that the euro will greatly strengthen their political position vis-à-vis the United States in international economic negotiations. The euro could eliminate the nearly automatic financing of the American balance of payments deficit and limit the considerable financial freedom the United States has had to pursue its independent economic and foreign policies. In addition, a successful euro could undercut Japan's ambition to have the yen play a much larger role as an international currency. In a global economy composed of three major currencies, the Japanese fear that the yen could become the "odd man out." Growing concern about such a possibility has, in fact, stimulated Japan to propose a global "currency triumvirate" of the dollar, the euro, and the yen, an arrangement that would be managed by the three major economic powers.

The real or even the perceived threat that the euro could displace the dollar could trigger a serious conflict between Western Europe and the United States—and possibly Japan as well, thus creating a three-way struggle. If a struggle were to erupt between the dollar and the euro similar to the earlier struggle for supremacy between the dollar and sterling in the 1920s and 1930s, considerable economic and political costs could be incurred by such a transatlantic conflict. The united international monetary system could fragment into regional blocs centered on the euro, the dollar, and, possibly, the yen. At the beginning of the twenty-first century, a number of smaller countries were considering whether to tie their currencies to the currency of their dominant trading partner.

The possibility of the development of currency blocs arises from the belief that currency blocs would reduce exchange rate risk among member countries, as is happening in Western Europe; such a change would be especially important for countries that trade heavily with one another and was a major reason for creation of the Economic and Monetary Union (EMU).[13] A common currency could also en-

---

[13] Zanny Minton Beddoes, "From EMU to AMU?: The Case for Regional Currencies," *Foreign Affairs* 78, no. 4 (July/August 1999): 8–13.

courage a low rate of inflation among member countries, provided that the leading country maintained a low inflation rate; this was the case in the Exchange Rate Mechanism, where West Germany was the leading economy. The major economic disadvantage of a currency bloc or union is loss of national independence in macroeconomic policy-making. However, the most serious risk in currency blocs is that they could intensify the already strained political relations among the United States, Japan, and Western Europe.

FEW OR MANY NATIONAL CURRENCIES?

Another possible threat to a unified global monetary system arises from "dollarization" of national currencies. The term "dollarization" refers to the decision of a less developed country to tie its currency closely to the dollar or to accept the dollar as its currency; Argentina has chosen the first option and Panama and Ecuador, the second. More broadly, dollarization refers to the use by one country of any major currency, including the euro or the yen. For a less developed country, the purpose of dollarization would be to stabilize its currency and exchange rate and to dampen inflation; dollarization would also reassure investors that, in the event of a crisis, they would be compensated in a hard currency. A number of American policymakers believe that the use of dollars by LDCs would strengthen the dollar against the euro.

Advocates of dollarization allege that, in the era of globalization and massive financial transactions across national borders, a world with more than one hundred currencies is grossly inefficient and cannot possibly continue over the long term.[14] Dollarization would result in a reduction of transaction costs, and this makes dollarization, like fixed rates and a regional currency, very attractive to business executives. The financial and exchange rate crises of the late 1990s revealed the vulnerability of weaker currencies. By tying these currencies to stronger currencies, dollarization would stabilize and protect from market instabilities the weaker currencies of less developed countries. Nevertheless, despite the apparent attractiveness of dollarization, many economists believe that it would actually prove harmful to less developed countries.

[14] Ricardo Hausmann, "Should There Be Five Currencies or One Hundred and Five?" *Foreign Policy*, no. 116 (fall 1999): 65–79.

The arguments for and against dollarization are similar to those for and against fixed exchange rates and regional currencies.[15] Dollarization enforces fiscal and monetary discipline on the less developed country and reduces monetary uncertainty. These restraints discourage irresponsible macroeconomic policies. Moreover, dollarization, like a fixed exchange rate, reduces uncertainty and transaction costs. Most importantly, dollarization would reduce currency speculation and the likelihood of financial crises and of competitive devaluations.

Although dollarization could be very important, most economists believe that its possible benefits are far outweighed by the advantages of flexible exchange rates. Arguments against dollarization and for a flexible exchange rate emphasize that the exchange rate functions as a safeguard for the real economy. In effect, an exchange rate appreciation or depreciation acts as a shock absorber. For example, a drop in demand for an economy's exports can lead to slower economic growth and increased unemployment. It would then be possible, of course, to permit wages to fall. However, the reduction of wages across an economy is a long and politically difficult process. A more simple solution would be to depreciate the currency, and this in turn would decrease the price of the country's exports and increase demand, thereby benefiting the economy. One should recall, however, that what is good for a major country may not be good for a smaller economy. For example, an LDC whose currency is tied to the dollar may wish to stimulate its economy, whereas the United States may not wish to do so. Stimulus of the LDC economy would lead to a reduction of its dollar reserves and eventually cause the expansion of its economy to stop. In effect, the LDC ties its monetary policy and management of its economy to the larger country's policies if it adopts dollarization.

CONCLUSION

Despite economists' justified skepticism of dollarization and a drastic reduction in the number of national currencies, it seems inevitable that over the long term, smaller economies will link their currencies closely to their major trading partners. By the end of the twentieth century, LDCs were already tying their currencies to the dollar, euro, or yen. However, this slow-moving development does not necessarily

[15] Jeffrey Sachs and Felipe Larrain, "Why Dollarization Is More Straitjacket Than Salvation," *Foreign Policy*, no. 116 (fall 1999): 80–92.

mean either that three currency blocs will emerge or that the global economy will fracture. Nevertheless, the possibility that currency blocs may emerge makes clear the need for improvements in policy and monetary cooperation among the United States, Japan, and Western Europe. In the meanwhile, public officials, central bankers, and economists should and do continue to search for a compromise that would achieve Keynes's stated objective for an international monetary system: that is, international currency stability along with domestic policy flexibility. Although the economics literature is replete with schemes to achieve these dual goals, this can happen only if political cooperation among the major economic powers is achieved first.

CHAPTER TEN

The International Financial System

T HE "FINANCIAL REVOLUTION" of the 1970s was a major development in the postwar international economy.[1] Removal of capital controls by leading economies and the consequent freedom of capital movement resulted in increased integration of national capital
markets and creation of a global financial system. Emergence of an
international financial market has greatly facilitated efficient use of
the world's scarce capital resources and has enabled capital-poor
LDCs to borrow funds for economic development. On the other
hand, international capital flows have increased the instability of the
international economy. The international financial system itself is inherently unstable and subject to serious crises. Despite its importance,
the nature and the extent of the global integration of financial matters
are poorly understood outside the economics and financial communities.

PARTIAL GLOBALIZATION OF INTERNATIONAL FINANCE

International finance is the one area to which the term "economic
globalization" clearly applies. Globalization of finance has become a
crucial and distinctive feature of the world economy. The international movement of capital has integrated economies around the
world. The daily turnover in currency exchanges increased from $15
billion in 1973 to $1.2 trillion in 1995; the equity and bond markets
also grew and became more global. The ability to move billions of
dollars from one economy to another at the push of a button has
transformed international finance and increased its impact on both
international and domestic economies. However, it is important to
place these developments, like other aspects of economic globalization, in proper perspective.

Despite the impressive numbers that describe the international financial system, in relative terms the volume of financial flows at the
beginning of the twenty-first century is still not equal to the interna-

---

[1] This chapter draws from Chapter 5 of Gilpin, *The Challenge of Global Capitalism*
(Princeton: Princeton University Press, 2000).

tional flow of capital at the end of the nineteenth century. Prior to World War I, for example, the British invested approximately one-half of their savings abroad. Between 1880 and 1913, British capital exports averaged 5 percent of GNP and at their peak reached almost 10 percent of GNP. In contrast, although the world marveled at Japanese capital export in the 1980s and early 1990s, Japan actually exported only the equivalent of 2 to 3 percent of its GNP. We should also remember that pre–World War I British investments were largely in railroads, port facilities, and other infrastructure that provided physical foundations for the highly interdependent international economy developing at that time. Without substantial British overseas investment in the United States and other "lands of recent settlement," these countries would not have developed at the rate they did achieve. Today, a substantial portion of international capital flows are short-term (six months or so) and highly speculative, and there is controversy concerning the extent to which they actually contribute to world economic development.

Although internationalization of finance has become an important feature of the global economy, the international financial system continues to be largely nationally based and consists of closely interconnected, discrete national financial systems. Some countries, such as Japan and China, even retain controls on capital flows. Moreover, in the prosaic language of economics, finance is still characterized by a powerful "home bias" effect. Investors tend to invest in their home economies rather than to maintain internationally based investment portfolios. In the 1990s, for example, 94 percent of the stocks in the American stock market and 98 percent of the stocks in the Japanese stock market were domestically owned, and Japanese financial markets were closely regulated by the powerful Ministry of Finance. However, one should note that the "home bias" tendency may be lessening even though the world is still characterized by national financial markets.

An important study by Martin Feldstein and Charles Horioka found that increased freedom of capital movement has not integrated international finance as much as many believe.[2] If the world were really integrated in financial matters, then national savings rates and investment rates would no longer be closely correlated, and interest rates around the world would be more nearly equal. If capital were fully mobile, investment in a particular country would depend on the

---

[2] Martin Feldstein and C. Horioka, "Domestic Savings and International Capital Flows," *Economic Journal* 90 (1980): 311–19.

investment opportunities in that economy and would not be highly correlated with the savings rate in that nation. The fact is, however, that savings and investment are closely correlated; high-saving countries, such as Japan, tend to be high-investing countries, and vice versa for low-saving countries. The United States is a major exception to this generalization in that domestic investment significantly exceeds national savings and is dependent on foreign borrowing. Moreover, in a perfectly integrated international financial system, the cost of capital, discounting the risk factor, would be approximately equal everywhere; instead, significant national differences in capital costs remain characteristic of the world economy.

Despite these caveats, the globalization of finance is a reality, and it does have profound consequences for the international economy. The absolute size, the high velocity, and the global scope of financial movements have been very important in the postwar period. In particular, the increased importance of speculative, short-term investments by financiers such as George Soros, by "hedge funds" in emerging markets, and by international banks have significantly increased the vulnerability of the international financial system and the world economy more generally; speculative funds amount to hundreds of billions of dollars. Many economists and public officials believe that these short-term, speculative flows increasingly threaten the stability of the global economy and should therefore be regulated.

Financial crises are a recurrent feature of the international economy. Even prior to the 1997 East Asian crisis, the postwar international economy had experienced several serious crises; three were especially important. The first resulted from the debt problems of many less developed countries in the late 1970s and early 1980s; a number of LDCs in Latin America and elsewhere had borrowed heavily from commercial banks in the mid-1970s and were thus highly vulnerable to the global recession of the late 1970s. The second was the 1992–1993 collapse of the European Rate Mechanism that forced Great Britain to withdraw from the effort to create a common European currency and resulted in fragmentation of the movement toward monetary unity. The third crisis was the collapse of the Mexican peso in 1994–1995, which threatened to precipitate a general financial crisis throughout Latin America; only the quick intervention of the Clinton Administration averted such a crisis.

These earlier crises were concentrated in particular regions, did not threaten the larger international economy, and were managed relatively easily, at least when compared to the East Asian financial crisis of 1997. That crisis was vastly different. The end-of-the-century crisis

263

began in the most economically robust region of the world, its consequences were truly devastating for that region, and the crisis eventually spilled over into the larger global economy. It is reasonable to say that the crisis resulted, at least in part, from globalization and transformations in modern finance; huge short-term investments in the region by international banks and financiers made these countries highly vulnerable to sudden swings in investor preferences. Nevertheless, as I have argued elsewhere, the risky policies undertaken by governments in the region must assume much of the blame.[3] The severity of the crisis led many to believe that international financial movements must be made subject to some regulatory mechanism.

NATURE OF FINANCIAL CRISES

Recurrent financial crises cause one to question the rationality of markets and to ask how rational actors can become caught up over and over again in investment booms or manias that almost invariably result in financial panics and crises. Or, to put the matter another way, if economic actors are rational, as economists assume them to be, how can one account for the frequent utter irrationality of financial markets? As Charles Kindleberger has written, over the past several centuries the world economy has been subject to a series of financial "manias, panics, and crashes" (to use the title of his book) that have shaken international capitalism.[4] Some economists have even argued that economic and institutional changes have made serious financial crises impossible, and that if crises were to occur, they would be caused by unique historical circumstances and would certainly not be caused by the inherent workings of the capitalist system. Given such attitudes in the profession, it is not surprising that few economists anticipated the East Asian or global financial turmoil.

The generally dismissive attitude of professional economists to the dangerous and destabilizing consequences of international financial crises has been challenged by Hyman Minsky, a maverick economist hardly at the forefront of the discipline. In a series of articles spanning a number of years, Minsky set forth what he called "the financial instability" theory of financial crises.[5] According to his theory, finan-

---

[3] Gilpin, *The Challenge of Global Capitalism*, Chapter 5.

[4] Charles P. Kindleberger, *Manias, Panics, and Crashes: A History of Financial Crises* (New York: Basic Books, 1979).

[5] This discussion of Minsky's theory of financial crises is based on Kindleberger's *Manias, Panics, and Crashes: A History of Financial Crises*. Minsky's writings on the subject can be found in Hyman P. Minsky, *Can "It" Happen Again?: Essays on Instability and Finance* (Armonk, NY: M. E. Sharpe, 1982).

cial crises are an inherent and inevitable feature of the capitalist system, and they follow a discernible and predictable course. The events leading up to a financial crisis begin with what he calls a "displacement," or an external shock to the economy; this external shock, which must be large and pervasive, can take such different forms as the start of a war, a bumper or a failed crop, or innovation and diffusion of an important new technology. If large and pervasive enough, the external/exogenous shock increases the profit opportunities in at least one important economic sector while simultaneously reducing economic opportunities in other areas. In response to a shift in profit opportunities, a number of businesses with adequate financial resources or lines of credit rush into the new area and abandon existing areas. If the new opportunities turn out to be sufficiently profitable, an investment boom or mania begins.

Rapid and substantial expansion of credit is a key aspect of an investment boom; this greatly expands the total money supply. Even though, as Minsky points out, bank credit is notoriously unstable, an investment boom is fueled as well by personal and business funds used to finance the speculative boom and thereby add further to the money supply and expansionary activity. In time, the urge to speculate drives up the price of the sought-after goods or financial assets. The price rise in turn creates new profit opportunities and draws more investors into the market. This self-reinforcing or cumulative process causes both profits and investments to rise rapidly. During this "euphoria" stage, to use Minsky's apt word, speculation on price increases becomes yet another important factor driving up the market. More and more investors, lusting after the rewards of rising prices and profits, forsake normal considerations of rational investment behavior and invest in what by its very nature is a highly risky market. This irrational development is the "mania" or "bubble" phase of the boom. As the mania phase accelerates, prices and the velocity of speculative monies increase.

At some point along this path of speculation, a few insiders, believing that the market has reached its peak, begin to convert their inflated assets into money or "quality" investments. As more and more speculators realize that the "game" is about over and begin to sell their assets, the race to get out of risky overvalued assets quickens and eventually turns into a stampede toward quality and safety. The specific event or market signal that triggers the rout and eventually causes a financial panic may be a bank failure, a corporate bankruptcy, or any number of untoward events. As investors rush out of the market, prices fall, bankruptcies increase, and the speculative

265

"bubble" eventually bursts, causing prices to collapse. Panic follows as investors desperately try to save what they can. Banks frequently cease lending, and this causes a "credit crunch"; a recession or even a depression may follow. Eventually, the panic ceases through one means or another, the economy recovers, and the market returns to an equilibrium, having paid an enormous price.

Economists, with a few notable exceptions, reject Minsky's model of financial crises because they believe no general model of financial crises can be formulated, as every crisis is either unique or of a very particular type for which a specific model is required. They consider every financial crisis to be a historical accident not amenable to general theorizing. A further criticism is that Minsky's model of financial crises assumes that such crises are generated by uncertainty, speculation, and instability—and economists assume rationality and brush away such awkward aspects of economic behavior. Nobel Laureate Milton Friedman, for example, has even proclaimed that because economic actors are at all times rational, speculation cannot occur in a market economy. In fact, he argues that what most of us call "speculation" is the effort of investors to protect themselves from the irrational actions of governments. Minsky, on the other hand, considered irrationality ("euphoria") and financial crises inherent features of modern capitalism. In Kindleberger's formulation, even if one were to assume the rationality of the individual investor, the historical record demonstrates over and over that even markets themselves sometimes behave in irrational ways and that "mob psychology" provides the best explanation of financial manias. Although individuals may be rational, financial speculation is a herd phenomenon in which the seemingly rational actions of many individuals lead to irrational outcomes.

Although Kindleberger is reluctant to declare that financial crises are an inherent feature of domestic capitalism, he asserts that they are inherent in international capitalism. He argues that Minsky's model is applicable to the realm of international finance, where one finds those essential features of an international financial crisis that were set forth by Minsky. Risky speculation, monetary (credit) expansion, a rise in the price of desired assets, a sudden and unexpectedly sharp fall in the price of the assets, and a rush into money or quality investments are endemic in the international pursuit of high profits by international investors. The East Asian financial crisis and subsequent global financial turmoil did indeed closely follow Minsky's model. Speculative investment in emerging markets by international banks and highly leveraged hedge funds fueled the mania and the investment bubble, until the collapse of the Thai baht on July 2, 1997, signaled the end of the East Asian "miracle." Somewhat over a year later, in mid-August 1998, devaluation of the Russian ruble and other bad news from Russia triggered global financial turmoil.

THE EAST ASIAN FINANCIAL CRISIS

In the summer of 1997, East Asian economies suffered a devastating blow. Economies that only four years earlier had been hailed by the World Bank as exemplars of "pragmatic orthodoxy" and as "remarkably successful in creating and sustaining macroeconomic stability" experienced the worst economic collapse of any countries since the 1930s and were declared victims of their own irresponsible ways! Beginning in Thailand in early July, the crisis spread rapidly up the East Asian coast and engulfed every nation in Southeast and East Asia. It had previously been unthinkable, given modern economic knowledge, that a financial crisis of this magnitude could occur. In fact, no one had predicted the crisis. In retrospect, however, a crisis of some sort appears to have been inevitable, given all the things that could and did go wrong in the months preceding it. In the language of social science, the East Asian financial crisis was overdetermined. If one cause had not plunged the East Asian economies into crisis, there were half a dozen others that might have done so.

The East Asian economic crisis made more credible to many people the charge that economic globalization has significantly increased international economic instability and has been harmful to domestic societies. It is certainly undeniable that the economic plight of East Asia attests to the ability of international financial markets to wreak havoc on domestic economies. However, imprudent domestic economic policies were as important as global economic forces in making these economies highly vulnerable to sudden shifts in international financial flows. Many of the allegedly negative effects of economic globalization are actually due either to poor economic management by governments or to developments that have nothing whatsoever to do with economic globalization. The victims in these situations have generally been small economies. The United States has run a trade/payments deficit for approximately three decades without unleashing any dire consequences! While large states with large markets and resources may be able to defy economic forces for a long time, such a privilege is rarely accorded to small states, especially small states with such reckless policies as borrowing "short" and lending "long"; that

267

is, those who finance long-term development and risky projects with short maturity funds.

It is extraordinary that there is no mechanism to regulate international finance. Even though the world economy experienced three major financial crises in the 1990s—the 1992–1993 crisis of the ERM, the 1994–1995 Mexican/Latin American crisis, and, beginning in 1997, the East Asian crisis—efforts to create effective regulations governing international capital flows and financial matters have not made much progress. A number of scholars, including Paul Kindleberger, Susan Strange, and James Tobin note that the international financial system is the weakest link in the chain of the international economy and that international finance should be regulated effectively. Financial markets, these scholars have argued, are too subject to irrational manias and crises and cannot police themselves. In such a situation, it is quite unfair to blame the East Asian crisis solely on the forces of economic globalization and on "wicked" Western speculators like George Soros.

Although destabilized financial markets will eventually return to an equilibrium, the crises can impose an unacceptably heavy cost on innocent bystanders and on the larger world economy. For this reason, scholars such as Kindleberger, Strange, and Tobin advocated establishment of international regulations or a formal regime to govern financial markets. For example, Tobin and others have proposed an international tax to discourage financial speculation, especially in short-term investments. Others, such as George Soros, go farther and argue that creation of an international central bank and true "lender of last resort" should be at the heart of a mechanism to govern international finance; that is, an authority should be created to function internationally as central banks do domestically. Then, when a government finds itself in trouble, the international bank could step in to rescue it. It is not necessary to say that the prospects of establishing such an international central bank are quite remote, at least under the political conditions of the early twenty-first century!

In the late summer of 1998, the East Asian economic crisis spilled over into the global economy, setting the stage for what President Clinton declared the worst economic crisis in fifty years. The Russian government's devaluation of the ruble against the German mark by about 40 percent in late August triggered the globalization of the crisis. The Clinton Administration, for political reasons, had bet heavily on "saving" Russia and had pressured the IMF to loan Russia tens of billions of dollars, many of which were subsequently squandered and funneled to private Russian accounts in foreign banks. Investors and governments around the world panicked as they witnessed a major nuclear power reneging on its agreements and facing economic/political chaos. Worried that other countries would also default, investors searching for safe havens in the early fall of 1998 began to withdraw funds from LDCs. Declining corporate profits and investor panic led to a precipitous fall of the American and other stock markets (October 31, 1998). The threat that the Long-Term Management Fund would collapse greatly deepened the crisis. These events in turn set off a serious credit crunch that further slowed global economic growth. Late that fall, some estimated that approximately one-third of the world economy was in recession; the United States alone was still experiencing economic growth. With the depression in East Asia and recession in much of the rest of the world, commodity prices fell considerably, and this caused economic distress in many commodity-exporting sectors, including American agriculture.

American officials had become concerned in the early fall that the financial crisis would continue to spread and had focused much of their attention on Brazil. Brazil possessed many of the characteristics of a developing economy in serious trouble, including a huge budget deficit and sizable international debt. The country's uncertain fiscal situation was accompanied by a heavy capital outflow and put severe pressure on the Brazilian real. The Clinton Administration feared that financial collapse in Brazil, a major importer of American products, would seriously damage the American economy and accelerate turmoil throughout the world. As the troubles of the global economy continued to unfold, the Administration took action. In a well-publicized speech in mid-September to the New York Council on Foreign Relations, the President proposed that all the major economic powers stimulate their own economies in order to restore global economic growth; he also proposed that the major economic powers should meet at the time of the next IMF/World Bank meeting in October and should then develop a longer-term solution to the problem of global financial instability.

These Clinton initiatives were given a cool reception. Every central bank ignored the suggestion that interest rates be cut in order to stimulate global growth. Nevertheless, on October 15, the Federal Reserve, motivated primarily by concerns about the American economy, did cut interest rates; it did so twice more before the end of November. These important moves restored investor confidence and succeeded in reinvigorating the American economy. The other major economic powers had agreed, although without enthusiasm, to Clinton's proposal that they meet, and that meeting took place during the annual joint meeting of the IMF and World Bank (WB) that was held in Washington in late October.

269

At the IMF-WB meetings, President Clinton set forth proposals for a "new international financial architecture" to contain the spreading economic crisis and prevent future crises. The Administration also hoped to forestall efforts by other governments (mainly Western Europe and Japan) to impose new restrictions on international capital flows. The President's proposals were considered at the October 30 meeting of the major economic powers, and several important decisions were reached. The G-7, assuming that if investors were fully aware of risky situations, they would not repeat the mistakes made in Mexico (1994–1995) and in East Asia, agreed that much greater transparency of financial conditions in every country was crucial to prevention of future financial crises. In addition, the G-7 called for much tighter international standards for accounting and for bank regulation.

The most important G-7 decision was to accept Clinton's proposal that the IMF should establish a $90 billion contingency fund to provide countries with emergency financial assistance; the fund would help only those countries already carrying out economic reforms and those whose economic "fundamentals" were basically sound. Before a crisis actually occurred, this would enable the IMF to intervene in order to shore up the country's financial defenses of its currency by providing adequate liquidity and thereby preventing financial panic. When it made this proposal, the Clinton Administration had Brazil in mind, as Brazil required a huge infusion of foreign capital to keep its economy afloat. Following a bruising but ultimately successful battle in the Congress over replenishment of IMF funds, much of which had previously been squandered in Russia, in November the IMF offered Brazil a large assistance package of over $40 billion and attached a precondition that the Brazilian economy be significantly overhauled. In early 1999, having failed to improve its economic performance, Brazil suffered a major economic crisis.

As important as the G-7 decisions had been, they failed to quell the intense controversy over reform and regulation of the international financial system. By early 2000, a number of proposals had been formulated to deal with destabilizing international financial flows; current proposals range from creation of a worldwide central bank to imposition of an international tax on financial transfers across national boundaries (called the "Tobin tax").[6] Some experts believe that

---

[6] An excellent discussion of international financial reform is Barry J. Eichengreen, *Toward a New International Financial Architecture: A Practical Post-Asian Agenda* (Washington, D.C.: Institute for International Economics, 1999). Also, Council on Foreign Relations, *Safeguarding Prosperity in a Global Financial System: The Future International Financial Architecture*, Report of an Independent Task Force (New York: Council on Foreign Relations, 1999).

self-imposed national restrictions on both financial inflows and out-flows are necessary. A number of governments such as Japan, China, Malaysia, and Chile have, in fact, instituted controls on financial flows. The European Union, too, has begun consideration of some regional regulations on capital flows.

Controversy over Regulation of International Finance

With the global financial turmoil of the late 1990s, the economics profession and many governments became concerned about and deeply divided over international finance and regulation of interna-tional capital/investment flows. Many American economists believed, and certainly the Clinton Administration did, that international fi-nancial flows perform a crucially important role, and that such flows should be free from government regulation. Most economists also believe that the financial system should ensure that capital moves from economies with surplus savings to those where investment op-portunities exceed local savings—that capital should be free to move toward those places and activities where it will be used most effec-tively and will thereby increase efficient utilization of the world's scarce capital resources. The prevailing opinion in the United States is that markets rather than governments or international organizations should govern the international financial system. At least since the time of the Reagan Administration, the United States government has strongly believed that American financial interests benefit greatly from freedom of capital movements, and it has made a concerted effort to open foreign economies to those investments. The Clinton Administration, led first by Treasury Secretary Robert Rubin and Deputy Secretary Lawrence Summers, and later by Summers as Trea-sury Secretary, enthusiastically carried this effort forward.

However, the East Asian financial crisis caused some American economists and many governments concern about the frequently dev-astating impact of international financial movements. A number of prominent economists in the United States and elsewhere challenged the value of unrestricted international capital flows, arguing that al-though it has been amply demonstrated that international trade bene-fits the global economy, the benefits of free capital movements have not been adequately demonstrated. On the other hand, the costs to the international economy of frequent financial crises have become painfully obvious. Indeed, as Kindleberger has shown, international financial history does record constantly recurring speculative manias, panics, and crises. Therefore, many have concluded that international

271

financial matters should not be left entirely up to the free play of market forces, but that some rules or mechanisms to regulate international capital movements should be devised.

Unfortunately, economists disagree over the cost and desirability of international financial flows. Although they agree on the virtues of trade liberalization, no comparable agreement exists with respect to capital flows and whether or not they should be regulated. It is worth noting, for example, that six of America's most distinguished economists—Jagdish Bhagwati, Stanley Fischer, Milton Friedman, Paul Krugman, Jeffrey Sachs, and Joseph Stiglitz—have disagreed with one another vehemently, and not always in a friendly spirit, regarding analysis of the East Asian financial crisis and the policies that should be pursued to prevent future crises. While some believe that governance of the international financial system should be left entirely up to the market, other economists and the IMF favor freedom of capital movements along with greater IMF surveillance over both domestic and international financial matters. A number of countries, including Japan, Germany, and France, believe that greater international controls are required over monetary and financial matters.

Reliance on the Market

Those economists who believe that a completely open and unregulated international financial system is the only realistic way to deal with the problems resulting from international financial flows also believe that any other approach necessarily raises the problem of "moral hazard." Moral hazard would be a problem, because if lenders and borrowers were to believe that the IMF or another official agency would rescue them from their folly, they would be encouraged to engage in reckless behavior; indeed, this had happened in the East Asia financial crisis. On the other hand, an unregulated financial market would itself punish investors and borrowers who failed to pursue prudent economic behavior. If international investors realized that no one would rescue them if they got into trouble, they would become more cautious with their investments.

Milton Friedman, Walter Wriston, George Schultz, and William Simon, all of whom wanted reliance on the market, believed that the IMF was ineffective and obsolete and should be abolished. Friedman considers the IMF's role in the world economy to exemplify bureaucratic self-aggrandizement. The IMF, Friedman points out, had originally been created to supervise the system of fixed exchange rates that was ended by President Nixon in 1971. The IMF then found a new function as an economic consulting agency for countries in trouble, offering money in exchange for promises of reforms. In Friedman's opinion, this interventionism by the IMF encouraged countries to continue to pursue unwise and unsustainable economic policies (moral hazard). Russia's failure to take the hard decisions required to salvage its devastated economy, he believes, was a classic example of IMF encouragement of irresponsible behavior.

For Friedman and fellow conservatives, the IMF's response to the Mexican crisis of 1994–1995 represented a quantum jump in the IMF's counterproductive interventionism. Mexico was bailed out by an aid package of $50 billion put together by the IMF, the United States, and other countries. Friedman has asserted that the IMF money actually ended up in the hands of such foreign entities as American banks that had foolishly lent money to Mexico, and that Mexico itself was left in recession and saddled with higher prices. However, the Mexican crisis had a longer term and even more serious consequence because it fueled the East Asian crisis by encouraging investors to again make risky investments. Drawn by high returns and assured that the IMF would bail them out if the exchange rate broke down and governments defaulted, investors poured money into the emerging markets of East Asia. In effect, the IMF and its provision of insurance against currency risk subsidized private banks and investors, a clear example of inducing moral hazard; that is, encouraging undesirable and/or counterproductive behaviors. This chain of reasoning led Friedman and others to conclude that the solution to financial instability must be through elimination of IMF-induced moral hazard.

The market-oriented position rests on the assumption that investors are rational and will not invest in risky ventures if they know that they will not be bailed out. Therefore, elimination of moral hazard also eliminates the problem of serious international financial crises. Although this conclusion may be correct, no such approach has ever been tried, and there is no empirical evidence to support such a daring policy experiment. Indeed, available evidence leads this writer to conclude that investors are *not* consistently rational, that they *do* get caught up in what Minsky called "euphorias," and that, when the speculative bubble bursts, many innocent people get hurt. This causes most governments to be unwilling to risk leaving financial matters entirely "up to the market;" indeed, many governments have even installed mechanisms at the domestic level to protect their citizens from financial instability.

Strengthening the IMF

Others believe that the solution to the problem of international financial instability can be found in strengthening the regulatory role of the IMF. Proponents of this position, especially the Clinton Ad-

273

ministration and the IMF, believe that liberalization of capital movements should be a primary purpose of the IMF. While agreeing with the market approach about the beneficial nature of unrestricted international capital flows, they believe that a greater supervisory role by the IMF and other reforms are necessary. Indeed, the IMF has already taken a number of important initiatives to create a regime for international finance. Most importantly, the IMF charter has been amended to give it greater jurisdiction over financial matters. As IMF's first deputy managing director Stanley Fischer has stated, the amendment is intended "to enable the Fund to promote the orderly liberalization of capital movements." He has also noted, however, that achievement of this goal requires continuous and reliable information on the financial conditions in potentially risky economies, development of an effective surveillance system to monitor such economies, and greater authority for the IMF to act as the "lender of last resort."[7]

The following paragraphs discuss some of the major proposed reforms to strengthen the role of the IMF in preventing financial crises.

Greater Transparency and Improved Information-Gathering. The 1994–1995 Mexican crisis was made worse by the poor information about Mexican financial conditions supplied by the Mexican Government to the IMF and investors. For example, the size of both Mexico's financial reserves and its external debt were kept secret. In 1996, lessons learned from this experience did lead to increased IMF data gathering and dissemination. Nevertheless, some experts have asserted that even the improved system of data gathering proved inadequate when it did not forestall the 1997 East Asian financial crisis. Although more reliable information on the financial conditions of developing economies could be an important safeguard against reckless investing, governments do wish to keep financial data secret in order to increase their leverage with foreign investors, and this raises a major hurdle. The predicament is made worse because governments also wish to keep their financial condition secret in order to strengthen their relative position in the intensifying competition for capital imports. The 1997 East Asian crisis, however, did strengthen the belief that greater openness about the financial conditions in many countries is required.

Codes of Conduct and Better Surveillance. The IMF has placed much greater emphasis on developing codes of conduct regarding "good

---

[7] The purpose of the "lender of last resort" is to pump money into an economy whose banking system is suffering from a "liquidity problem." The term "liquidity problem" is explained below in note 9.

practice" in financial affairs in order to increase discipline at the international level. Among other changes, this effort requires upgrading of the Basle Accord (1988) regulating international bank practices.[8] In addition, improved surveillance and monitoring of specific economies for such potential dangers as high budget deficits and high rates of inflation may suggest potential financial troubles. However, even if a country is warned of impending problems, it may not act to forestall them, and the IMF remains powerless to force such action. Nor would it be proper for the IMF to warn investors about potential problems in a particular country.

Lender of Last Resort. In a world of increasing capital flows and growing numbers of borrowers, it is inevitable that individual countries will occasionally experience serious financial troubles and require international assistance in the form of a large infusion of money to prevent a liquidity or even an insolvency problem.[9] Many believe that the IMF should perform the role of lender of last resort; however, the IMF is seriously limited in this capacity because, unlike a true central bank, the IMF cannot create money; also, its cumbersome governing mechanism prevents it from acting quickly in a crisis. In addition, assumption of the lender-of-last-resort role raises the problem that the larger the IMF's resources, the greater the risk that it will encourage moral hazard.

Strengthening the IMF in order to promote freedom of capital movements and prevent financial crises has been an important objective of the United States. American commitment to promarket ideology, powerful financial interests to which the U.S. Treasury is highly responsive, and a general belief that America has a strong comparative advantage in financial services have been reflected in U.S. efforts to keep economies open to international finance. However, the controversy in 1998 over America's $18 billion contribution to the IMF illustrates that the Clinton Administration's effort (backed by export

---

[8] "Basle" refers to the International Bank for Settlements in Basle, Switzerland, which sets standards for international banks. The Basle Accord of 15 July 1988 established international harmonization of regulations regarding the capital adequacy or reserve requirements of international banks. The agreement was the result of an American initiative in response to American banking interests. American proponents of the agreement believed that foreign banks had an unfair advantage because of their relatively low reserves requirements. Despite strong opposition from other countries, American pressure for the accord eventually won.

[9] A "liquidity" crisis exists when an otherwise sound economy has a temporary cash-flow problem. An "insolvency" crisis exists when an economy has severe economic problems and cannot repay its debts without making major economic reforms.

interests) to strengthen the IMF's role in preventing financial crises had many opponents; that Congressional and public controversy raised serious questions about the ability of the United States to lead in fashioning a "new international financial architecture."

Regulation of International Finance

A number of economists and governments favor some controls over international capital movements. Agreement that short-term capital flows should be regulated appears strong. James Tobin and other American economists, for example, have proposed a tax on short-term capital flows, and Paul Krugman has argued that countries in financial difficulty should consider capital controls. The French, German, and Japanese governments have raised the possibility of other measures to tame large swings in global financial markets and in currency values. They have also proposed that the European Union, Japan, and the United States should manage exchange rates and keep them within specific bands or target zones in order to stabilize the global economy. However, the United States has strongly objected to delegating decisions over interest rates and other aspects of its own economy to any international authority; it prefers to rely on the market.

The differences between the United States and its principal economic partners over currency and financial matters were the subject of the annual meeting of the G-7 finance ministers and central bankers in February 1999, where creation of a mechanism to regulate international finance was the principal issue discussed. On one side of the debate were the German, French, and Japanese governments favoring increased controls; many European and Japanese officials wanted to control hedge funds in particular. On the other side were the United States and U.S. and other central bankers who strongly opposed an international authority and preferred to leave matters to national governments and central bankers. The differences between the United States and the other economic powers partially reflect ideological positions on market functioning, but they also reflect the relative competitiveness of American financial institutions as well as their political strength within the United States. Eventually, agreement was reached that a "financial stability forum" composed of national currency regulators meeting twice a year to consult and consider ways to improve the quality of financial information would be created. The difficulties experienced by the G-7 in efforts to agree on reforms of international financial affairs do not augur well for the future stability of the global economy.

276

The underlying motive of the West Europeans and the Japanese in their advocacy of greater controls over international finance is, at least in part, political. The West Europeans would very much like to diminish the American role in international monetary and financial matters in order to minimize the potential negative impact of American policies on Europe. The European Union would like to restrict the independence of American macroeconomic policy. Japan has encouraged greater use of the yen in international transactions and would like to distance the Asia-Pacific region from the international use of the dollar.

CONCLUSION

Freeing capital and integrating financial markets around the world have had several important consequences for the global economy. Freedom of capital movements has complicated and, some believe, reduced macroeconomic policy autonomy and the ability of individual governments to control their own economies.[10] International financial flows have also become an important determinant, and many economists believe they are *the* most important determinant of exchange rates (at least in the short term) and a cause of erratic movements in currency values. Movement toward a single, globally integrated market for corporation ownership has resulted from increased financial flows, and this has greatly facilitated corporate mergers and takeovers across national boundaries and the integration of the world economy by multinational firms. Altogether, the reemergence of international finance has increased interdependence of trade, monetary, and other aspects of the international economy. The need to mesh these formerly separate domains of international economic affairs has complicated the task of managing the world economy.

---

[10] A dramatic example of how international financial flows have constrained domestic economic policy was the disastrous attempt of the French socialist government of François Mitterrand in the early 1980s to stimulate the laggard French economy. Capital flight forced the French government to rein in its expansionary economic policies. This instructive episode is analyzed from quite different perspectives by Michael Loriaux, *France After Hegemony: International Change and Financial Reform* (Ithaca: Cornell University Press, 1991); and Paulette Kurzer, *Business and Banking: Political Change and Economic Integration in Western Europe* (Ithaca: Cornell University Press, 1993).

The State and the Multinationals

THE IMPORTANCE of the multinational corporation (MNC) is a key feature of globalization of the world economy.[1] However, opinions differ greatly over the significance for domestic and international economic affairs of the globalization of corporate activities. Some commentators believe that the multinational corporation has broken free from its home economy and has become a powerful independent force determining both international economic and political affairs. Others reject this position and believe that the multinational corporation remains a creature of its home economy.

Although there are many more technical definitions of a multinational firm, this chapter refers simply to a firm of a particular nationality with partially or wholly owned subsidiaries within at least one other national economy. Tens of thousands of MNCs with numerous subsidiaries conduct business around the world. Such firms expand overseas primarily through foreign direct investment (FDI), whose purpose is to achieve partial or complete control over marketing, production, or other facilities in another economy; such investments may be in services, manufacturing, or commodities. FDI can entail either the purchase of existing businesses or the building of new facilities (called "greenfield" investment). Overseas expansion is frequently accompanied by mergers, takeovers, or intercorporate alliances with firms of other nationalities.[2] Whereas the purpose of portfolio investment is to obtain a financial return on the investment, FDI, as well as alliances, mergers, and similar ventures, are usually part of an international corporate strategy to establish a permanent position in another economy.

In one sense, multinational firms have existed for a very long time. The Dutch East India Company, the Massachusetts Bay Company, and other companies of merchant-adventurers were forerunners of today's MNCs like IBM, Sony, and Daimler-Chrysler. These earlier

---

[1] Sylvia Ostry, *A New Regime for Foreign Direct Investment* (Washington, D.C.: Group of Thirty, 1997), 5.

[2] Benjamin Gomes-Casseres, *The Alliance Revolution: The New Shape of Business Rivalry* (Cambridge: Harvard University Press, 1996).

transnational firms, however, were far more powerful than contemporary MNCs are; they commanded armies and fleets, had their own foreign policies, and controlled vast expanses of territory: the sub-Asian continent (India, Pakistan, and Bangladesh), the East Indies (Indonesia), and South Africa. Modern MNCs are much more modest. Another major difference between those early transnational firms and today's is that the former were principally interested in agricultural products and extractive industries in particular regions of the world, whereas major firms in the early twenty-first century are principally involved in manufacturing, retailing, and services, tend to operate on a regional or worldwide basis, and usually pursue an international corporate strategy. It is particularly significant that, whereas the earlier firms frequently exploited and subjugated native peoples, today's MNCs, with some exceptions, are important sources of the capital and technology required for economic development of the less developed countries.

EXPLANATIONS OF FDI AND THE MNC

Despite the importance of multinational corporations in the functioning of the international economy, neoclassical economists have remarkably little to say about them. The indifference of mainstream economists to the MNC means that the student of the MNC must turn for an understanding of these firms to the writings of radical economists, business economists, and political economists—groups of scholars with a long-term interest in multinational firms and their impact.

Mainstream Economists and the MNC

The indifference of most neoclassical economists to the multinational corporation despite its importance in the global economy can be explained in various ways.[3] Their strong belief in the primacy of markets causes those economists to discount the importance of institutions; they believe that a firm's behavior is determined almost entirely by market signals and that, therefore, the nationality of the firm and whether it is operating domestically or internationally are of slight importance. Furthermore, the Mundell equivalency, accepted by most economists, holds that international transfer of the factors of produc-

---

[3] A survey of the economics literature on the subject can be found in Gene M. Grossman, ed., *Imperfect Competition and International Trade* (Cambridge: MIT Press, 1994), 9–10.

tion (capital, technology, etc.) through foreign direct investment (FDI) produces consequences for the real-world equivalent to those from the international flow of goods. In other words, from the economist's perspective, trade and investment are perfect substitutes for one another. Economics also teaches that trade precedes investment rather than vice versa. The location of economic activities around the world and patterns of trade are determined by the theory of location and the principle of comparative advantage; production will be located where it is most efficient. An economist might argue that FDI is an indirect route to economic specialization based on the distribution of productive factors.

Also, methodological obstacles have prevented economists from formulating a generally accepted theory to explain FDI and the MNC. MNCs are primarily oligopolistic firms and function in imperfect markets, and as has already been noted, there is no satisfactory formal model to account for all types of oligopolistic behavior. Lack of a general model encourages ambiguous and contradictory attitudes among economists toward multinational firms. A major reason why neoclassical economics has been unable to provide a general theoretical explanation for the MNC and FDI is that the MNC is largely a product of market imperfections and unique corporate experiences. For example, IBM manufactures in a number of countries so as to maintain good political relations with host governments rather than for strictly economic reasons. Some market imperfections are created by national governments through such policies as trade protection and industrial policy; in fact, a government sometimes creates market imperfections to encourage foreign MNCs to invest in their economies. A notable example is the erection of trade barriers and the provision of "tax breaks" to encourage FDI. Without such imperfections, a firm might find it more efficient to export its products from its home economy or to license its technology to a foreign firm.

The ambiguous attitude of professional economists toward the MNC is illustrated in Paul Krugman's writings. On the one hand, he has taken the conventional position that MNCs are not a significant factor in the international economy; indeed, he and coauthor Maurice Obstfeld have written in their textbook on international economics (1994) that the effects of FDI on global distribution of economic activities and other economic outcomes cannot be distinguished from those of international trade.[4] The principal effect of FDI, they argue,

---

[4] Paul R. Krugman and Maurice Obstfeld, *International Economics: Theory and Practice*, 3d ed. (New York: HarperCollins, 1994), 162.

is on the domestic distribution of income; that is, between capital and labor. On the other hand, Krugman argues in many of his other writings that the oligopolistic nature of international business is significant for trade patterns and the location of economic activities. For example, because oligopolistic firms engage in strategic behavior, an MNC's decision whether to export a product from its home market or to invest abroad in order to service a foreign market will strongly affect the location of economic activities and the rates of economic growth around the world. In this fashion, the activities of MNCs can have a profound impact on international economic affairs. MNCs are not merely substitutes for trade; indeed they attempt to extend their power and control over foreign economies. It is clear that multinational firms desire not only to earn immediate profits, but also to change and influence the rules or regimes governing trade and international competition in order to improve their long-term position.

Fortunately, the traditional indifference of economists to MNCS has begun to change in response to a number of theoretical developments, as well as the undeniable importance of the MNC in the world economy. Theoretical advances in industrial organization and strategic trade theory, as well as growing appreciation of the significance of technological innovation for comparative advantage, have made economists more aware of MNC importance. For example, the MNC has been acknowledged as a means to reduce transaction costs; it may be cheaper to organize vertically through FDI than by market transactions. The research of Harvard economist Richard Caves has stressed the importance of "appropriability"; that is, of a firm's ability to maintain control of a valuable asset such as a trademark or technology.[5] Nevertheless, even though mainstream economists have become somewhat more sympathetic to the idea that MNCs do behave differently from non-MNCs and have a particularly important role in the world economy, a cursory examination of current economics syllabi and textbooks confirms that economists do not yet consider the MNC an important aspect of the world economy.

Business Economists and the MNC

Business economists have long had a strong interest in the wellsprings of corporate behavior, an interest strongly influenced by the pioneering scholarship of Alfred Chandler.[6] Beginning in the 1960s, interest

---

[5] Richard E. Caves, *Multinational Enterprises and Economic Analysis* (Cambridge: Harvard University Press, 1982).

[6] Alfred D. Chandler, *Strategy and Structure: Chapters in the History of the Industrial Enterprise* (Cambridge: MIT Press, 1970).

in corporations has been extended to firms operating internationally. Research on the MNC has been pursued almost exclusively by American and British business economists with a liberal commitment toward the overwhelming benefits of FDI to both home and host countries. Scholarship on this matter has been overwhelmingly empirical and has seldom been informed by economic or other types of social theory. Because this writer cannot do justice to the huge volume of writings that have paralleled and interpreted the several stages in the development of the MNC, I shall focus on just a few important contributions to illustrate the essence and evolution of this scholarship.

An early important contribution was the influential pioneering work of Raymond Vernon. Vernon's product cycle model of FDI stressed the importance of economic and technological leadership and provided an important insight into the overseas expansion of American MNCs in the 1960s. Another valuable contribution to the subject was made by British business economist John Dunning, who, along with others, attempted to provide a general explanation of the MNC; the result was the eclectic theory of FDI that accounted in large part for the second stage of the MNC's evolution. The most recent explanation is generally identified with Michael Porter's extensive and almost encyclopedic empirical research on the firm as a strategic player in the game of international economic competition.

Vernon's Product Cycle Theory. The crux of Vernon's product cycle theory, as set forth in *Sovereignty at Bay* (1971), was that every product follows a life cycle from innovation through maturity to decline to eventual obsolescence.[7] American firms, Vernon argued, had a comparative advantage in product innovation due to the huge size of the American market (the demand side) and to American superiority in research and development (the supply side). During the initial phase of the product cycle, firms export new products from their home industrial base, but in time a number of changes associated with the maturing of the product, such as standardization of production techniques, diffusion abroad of industrial know-how, and creation of significant foreign demand for the product, stimulate the entry of foreign imitators into the market. To deter foreign firms from entering the market and undercutting their monopoly position, the original firms establish production facilities in other economies. Thus, according to Vernon's product cycle theory, foreign direct investment

---

[7] Raymond Vernon, *Sovereignty at Bay* (New York: Basic Books 1971).

is principally a device used by firms to preempt foreign competition and to maintain their monopoly rents.

Vernon's theory, which assumed that there were large gaps in wealth and technology between the United States and other countries, helped to explain the overseas expansion of American firms in the 1960s. As such gaps disappeared in the 1970s, the relevance of his theory to the behavior of American firms declined. Furthermore, product cycle theory could not account for the subsequent expansion abroad of European and Japanese firms and the firms of many other nations. Other business economists' explanations of these new developments include such specific and general factors as the erection of trade barriers, the importance of market proximity, the decline in transportation costs, and the problem of currency fluctuation. The "eclectic" theory, primarily associated with John Dunning and the Reading school, was the most systematic effort to incorporate the many developments during this second stage in MNC evolution into a coherent general explanation of the MNC and FDI.[8]

Dunning's and the Reading School's Eclectic Theory. The eclectic theory of the MNC, developed by John Dunning and the Reading School (named after the University of Reading, England), provides important insights into the MNC, as it emphasizes technology as a factor in MNC development. Revolutionary advances in communications and transportation have made it technically possible for businesses to organize and manage services and production systems on a global basis. In effect, technological advances have greatly reduced the transaction and other costs of internationalizing. However, the eclectic theory is hardly a theory at all, at least not a theory that mainstream economists would acknowledge; rather it is a collection of ideas gathered from many sources and much research on the MNC. Dunning and his Reading colleagues believe these ideas provide a comprehensive understanding of the MNC. While Dunning's integration of various ideas and insights into the nature and behavior of the MNC is generally nontheoretical, it is nevertheless quite valuable. However, the usefulness of the eclectic theory is most relevant for understanding a particular stage in the evolution of the MNC; subsequent changes in the MNC have necessitated newer explanations for their behavior.

---

[8] The writings of John N. Dunning on the MNC are voluminous. One place to start is Dunning, *Explaining International Production* (London: Unwin Hyman, 1988). In addition to Dunning, other members of the Reading School include Peter J. Buckley and Mark C. Casson.

283

Work by Michael Porter and others builds on and incorporates the core of Dunning's eclectic explanation.

According to Dunning's eclectic theory, the unique nature and extraordinary economic success of the MNC are due to particular characteristics that give the MNC important advantages over purely domestic corporations. These advantages are ownership, location, and, most importantly, internalization, a concept that was also extensively developed by Richard Caves, one of few mainstream economists to seriously consider FDI and the MNC.[9] These oligopolistic firms usually possess some proprietary or firm-specific advantage that they want to exploit rather than lose to a rival firm; such an internal advantage may be a trademark or possession of a particular technology. Although some of the most important MNCs are not high-tech, it is not coincidental that many MNCs predominate in industries characterized by extensive and expensive research and development activities. Obviously, such firms are anxious to appropriate for themselves all the results of their R & D efforts.

As Caves has pointed out, FDI's advantages in ownership and internalization explain why firms are willing to assume its high costs and risks. Although in most cases it would be far more efficient to export from existing plants in the home economy than through production abroad, Caves argues that maintaining within their own control such monopolistic advantages as a trademark or know-how gives firms market power and the ability to extract rents. This internalization objective can best be achieved through FDI and the creation in other economies of subsidiaries that are owned by the parent firm. Oligopolistic firms attempt to keep firm-specific advantages within the secure confines of the firm and out of the hands of rival firms through the establishment of "greenfield" plants or the acquisition of wholly owned foreign subsidiaries over which they have exclusive control.

Many such firms also possess locational advantages, because MNCs have access to factors of production around the world and can, therefore, employ such country-specific advantages as access to low-cost skilled labor or to other special local resources. Considered in terms of the Heckscher-Ohlin model of international trade, these firms can exploit the comparative advantages possessed by other economies, and such flexibility can give them a considerable advantage over purely domestic firms. Moreover, even though the firm's home economy may be losing comparative advantage in its particular industrial sector, the MNC itself can maintain its presence in the in-

[9] Caves, *Multinational Enterprises and Economic Analysis*.

dustry through FDI in economies gaining comparative advantage within that industry.

Other factors have been important to the success of the MNC, including deregulation of markets and services around the world. Certainly, deregulation and integration of financial markets have facilitated foreign direct investment. The continuing shift in comparative advantage in many traditional and other industrial sectors to low-wage industrializing economies has also been a factor determining MNC strategy. And particularly among Japanese firms, a desire to leap over trade barriers and to reduce growing trade friction has also contributed to FDI expansion. Yet another relatively important consideration has been the corporate ideology spread by numerous business consultants and other prophets of the global corporation that firms must learn to "manage across borders" and become truly global if they are to survive in the new global economy.

Porter's Strategic Theory. Another noteworthy interpretation of the MNC has emerged from the research of Michael Porter at the Harvard School of Business. Porter's *Competitive Advantage of Nations* (1990) and his numerous other writings argue that the MNC has entered an era of strategic management.[10] Porter assumes that international business is characterized by a "value chain" of activities ranging from extraction to production to marketing. The individual firm must decide which and how many of these activities it wishes to pursue and in what locations around the globe. These decisions in turn depend on the overall competitive strategy of the firm. Following the lead of Alfred Chandler in his classic contributions to business studies,[11] Porter argues that the firm's strategy determines its structure and its location of economic activities throughout the world economy. In the development of his theory of strategic management, Porter follows the eclectic theory's definition of the inherent advantages possessed by MNCs. But the overwhelming advantage of the MNC over domestic firms, according to Porter, is that it provides access to a wide array of possible strategies through which it can "tap into the value chain." In contrast to a domestic firm, a multinational firm can carry out its activities at the most efficient location for each particular activity anywhere in the world. Because the firm pursues its strategy and integrates its activities across national borders, many analysts

[10] The references to Porter in this chapter are based on Michael E. Porter, *The Competitive Advantage of Nations* (New York: Free Press, 1990).

[11] Chandler, *Strategy and Structure.*

prefer to use the term "transnational" rather than "multinational" corporation.

The essence of strategic management is that the transnational firm has available to it more extensive options and techniques than do even the largest domestic firms. These mechanisms include not only FDI, but also strategic alliances, outsourcing component production and licensing technologies. These corporate activities create international complexes or networks of corporate relations with the parent MNC in its home economy. Through modern information technologies and monopoly of information resources, the multinational corporation can become dominant over both its domestic and international competitors. Needless to say, such a depiction of a firm's strategy, structure, and activities has evolved far beyond that portrayed in Vernon's product cycle model or even in Dunning's eclectic theory. These transnational firms have become worldwide institutions coordinating economic activities that are located in many countries.

Political Economists and the MNC

There are two distinctive bodies of writings by political economists on the multinational corporation: the radical (or quasi-Marxist) critique and the state-centric interpretation.

Marxist or Radical Theories. Stephen Hymer's innovative ideas present the most systematic critique of the MNC.[12] Hymer, trained as a technical economist at the mecca of neoclassical economics (the Department of Economics at the Massachusetts Institute of Technology), has contributed to the subject both as an economist and a radical political thinker, but I am primarily concerned with his latter work. At the time of Hymer's writings in the early 1960s, economists scarcely distinguished between foreign direct investment and foreign portfolio investment. Instead, they assumed that FDI, like portfolio investment, could be explained primarily by differences in interest rates between home and host economies. Hymer showed, on the other hand, that FDI was fundamentally different from portfolio investment and could be explained as part of a firm's expansionist strategy and by its desire to control productive or other facilities in foreign countries. Economic, political, and technological developments in the post-

---

[12] Stephen Hymer first set forth his ideas in his 1960 doctoral dissertation, "The International Operations of National Firms: A Study of Direct Investment," which was not published until 1976 by the MIT Press.

286

war world had made overseas expansion of American corporations possible and even necessary. At the time of Hymer's writings, American corporations were rapidly expanding in the Western Hemisphere, the Middle East, and Western Europe. Anticipating both the subsequent application of industrial organization theory to the study of the MNC and the eclectic theory, Hymer argued that American firms invested abroad to exploit and preserve some firm-specific or monopolistic advantage.

Despite the potential importance of Hymer's scholarship, it made little impression on the economics profession. Unfortunately, Hymer's death at a young age meant that he had no opportunity to develop and defend his ideas. Hymer's ideas were neglected, at least in part, because his innovative thinking was too far ahead of the rest of the economics profession. Only years later did insights from industrial organization theory vindicate at least some aspects of his thinking. Another possible reason, however, for economists' neglect of Hymer's theories is that Hymer was a Marxist, and although economists deny that his Marxism posed a problem, I find this denial difficult to accept. Whatever the truth of the matter, it is the Marxist aspect of Hymer's innovative approach that is of interest at the moment.

In his Marxist or quasi-Marxist theory of the MNC, Hymer set forth, or at least foreshadowed, many (if not most) of the ideas that we now associate with radical critiques of the MNC. He believed that monopoly capitalism is driven by two fundamental laws. He believed the first law of international capitalism to be the law of increasing firm size: that as firms grow in size and scope, they expand both within and across national borders, creating a hierarchical core/periphery structure and international division of labor around the world. At the core of this international structure are the advanced capitalist economies, while the periphery is composed of dependent and exploited less developed economies.

Hymer's second law is the law of uneven development. He argued that due to their large size, considerable mobility, and monopolistic power, the MNCs exercise control over and exploit the whole world to their own advantage. These corporate activities produce a world economy composed of the exploiting wealthy societies of the north and the exploited impoverished societies of the south. Or, in language also used by dependency theorists, the development of the capitalist north and the underdevelopment of the peripheral south are integral and complementary aspects of international capitalism in the age of

287

the MNC.[13] Almost all the subsequent writings by radical scholars are in large part just variations on Hymer's provocative ideas.[14] This generalization also applies to many of those protesting the multinational corporation at the time of the WTO meetings in Seattle in 1999 and the IMF/World Bank meetings in Washington in 2000, even though the protestors doubtless were unaware of Hymer's theories.

State-centric Interpretation. State-centric writings on the multinational corporation assert that the rise and success of the MNC in the modern world could have happened only within a favorable international political environment. They maintain that despite the several theories of business economists, the MNC cannot be explained solely in terms of market forces and/or corporate strategies.[15] While economic factors are obviously important for the emergence and success of MNCs, they could not exist without a favorable international political environment created by a dominant power whose economic and security interests favor an open and liberal international economy. Just as the Pax Britannica provided a favorable international environment for the overseas expansion of British firms and investors in the late nineteenth century, so American leadership following World War II provided a similarly favorable international environment for the overseas expansion of American and other capitalist firms in the post–World War II era. In the 1980s and 1990s, the United States, Western Europe, and Japan all had an interest in maintaining and even strengthening international conditions that favored MNCs. State-centric writers believe that if the consensus and cooperation of the major capitalist powers were to break down, the predominant role of the MNC in the world economy would gradually diminish.

The state-centric position also assumes that multinational firms are essentially national firms competing with one another around the world. Proponents of this position argue that these firms are closely attached to and ultimately dependent on their respective home economies. As Paul Doremus and his colleagues point out in their excellent book, *The Myth of the Global Corporation* (1998), each MNC is a

---

[13] Among the more innovative and influential extensions of Hymer's early work is Robert Cox, *Production, Power, and World Order: Social Forces in the Making of History* (New York: Columbia University Press, 1987).

[14] For example, see William Greider, *One World, Ready or Not: The Manic Logic of Global Capitalism* (New York: Simon and Schuster, 1997).

[15] This is the thesis of my book *U.S. Power and the Multinational Corporation: The Political Economy of Foreign Direct Investment* (New York: Basic Books, 1975).

distinctive product of its home base and reflects its social, economic, and political values.[16] Despite the hyperbole of corporate executives and business consultants that MNCs have shorn themselves of national coloration and become stateless enterprises, MNCs are actually deeply embedded in and very much a product of the history, culture, and economic systems of their home societies.

THE MULTINATIONALS AND THE INTERNATIONAL ECONOMY

The world's largest MNCs account for approximately four-fifths of world industrial output while typically employing two-thirds of their work force at home; they are not nearly as footloose as many critics charge.[17] Foreign direct investment (FDI) has been growing at a rapid rate. Between 1985 and 1990, FDI grew at an average rate of 30 percent a year, an amount four times the growth of world output and three times the growth rate of trade. FDI has in fact become a major determinant of trade patterns. The annual flow of FDI has doubled since 1992 to nearly $350 billion. Intrafirm trade—that is, trade among subsidiaries of the same firm—accounted for one-third of American exports and two-fifths of U.S. imported goods in 1994. About one-half of the trade between Japan and the United States is actually intrafirm trade. This intrafirm trade takes place at transfer prices set by the firms themselves and within a global corporate strategy that does not necessarily conform to the conventional trade theory based on traditional concepts of comparative advantage. Evidence suggests that these trends will continue and could even accelerate.

The gross statistics, however, hide noteworthy aspects of FDI and of other activities of MNCs. Despite much talk of corporate globalization, FDI is actually highly concentrated and is distributed unevenly around the world. Although FDI has grown rapidly in developing countries, most FDI has been placed in the United States and Europe, while only a small percentage of U.S. foreign direct investment has gone to developing countries. This concentration of FDI is due to the simple fact that the United States and Europe are at present the world's largest markets. Nevertheless, throughout most of the 1990s, FDI in less developed countries (LDCs) grew at about 15 percent annually. However, FDI in LDCs has been highly uneven and concentrated in a small number of countries, including a few in

---

[16] Paul N. Doremus, William W. Keller, Louis W. Pauly, and Simon Reich, *The Myth of the Global Corporation* (Princeton: Princeton University Press, 1998).

[17] *The Economist,* 29 January 2000, 21.

Latin America, especially Brazil and Mexico, and in the emerging markets of East and Southeast Asia. The largest LDC recipient of FDI has been China. Between 1991 and 1995, foreign direct investment placed in the United States amounted to $198.5 billion; in China, $114.3 billion; and in Mexico, only $32 billion. The emerging markets were attractive, at least prior to the 1997 financial crisis, due to their rapid economic growth, their market-oriented policies, and their cheap labor. One should note, however, that the least developed countries in Africa and elsewhere have received a pitifully small percentage of the total amount invested in the developing world. Need it be said that this skewed distribution does not fit the image of globalization!

The increasing importance of MNCs has profoundly altered the structure and functioning of the global economy. These giant firms and their global strategies have become major determinants of trade flows and of the location of industries and other economic activities. Most FDI is in capital and technology-intensive sectors. These firms have become central in the expansion of technology flows to both industrialized and industrializing economies and therefore are important in determining the economic, political, and social welfare of many nations. Controlling much of the world's investment capital, technology, and access to global markets, such firms have become major players not only in international economic but in international political affairs as well, and this has triggered a backlash in many countries.

According to DeAnne Julius, one of the world's most knowledgeable experts on the MNC, the huge expansion of FDI, intercorporate alliances, and intrafirm trade throughout the 1980s and 1990s reached a level where "a qualitatively different set of linkages" among advanced economies was created; some have estimated that more than twenty thousand corporate alliances were formed in the years 1996–1998.[18] The growing importance of FDI and intercorporate cooperation means that the world economy has reached a "takeoff" point comparable to that wrought by the great expansion of international trade in the late 1940s and the subsequent emergence of the highly interdependent international trading system. The growth in FDI and in the activities of multinational corporations of many nationalities has linked nations more tightly to one another, and this has further affected the global economy.

---

[18] DeAnne Julius, *Global Companies and Public Policy: The Growing Challenge of Foreign Direct Investment* (London: Pinter, 1990).

The role of MNCs in the world economy remains highly controversial. Critics charge that foreign direct investment and the internationalization of production are transforming the nature of international economic and political affairs in ways that undermine the nation-state and integrate national economies. Impersonal market forces and corporate strategies are believed to dominate the nature and dynamics of the international economic and political system. While Kenichi Ohmae and many others may believe such a development to be highly beneficial for mankind, others regard the MNC as an exploitative imperium stalking the world. These critics believe that giant firms, answerable only to themselves, are integrating societies into an amorphous mass in which individuals and groups lose control over their own lives and are subjugated to firms' exploitative activities. The world, these critics charge, is coming under the sway of a ruthless capitalist imperialism where the only concern is the bottom line.

Many and perhaps most professional economists (with the important exception of business economists), on the other hand, discount the significance of multinational firms in the functioning of the world economy. The neoclassical interpretation acknowledges that large oligopolistic firms may be politically important and may also affect the distribution of income within national economies. However, these economists deny that the investment, marketing, and other economic activities of these firms around the world have any great impact on the "real" economy of international trade, location of economic activities, or national rates of economic or productivity growth. In neoclassical economics, the global location of economic activities and patterns of international trade are determined according to location theory and the principle of comparative advantage.

Both extreme positions are exaggerations. Critics exaggerate the evils of the MNCs and their role in the world economy. Although some MNCs do exploit and damage the world, the MNC as an institution is beneficial to many peoples worldwide; it is, for example, a major source of capital and technology for economic development. On the other hand, the proponents of the MNCs exaggerate their importance and overstate the internationalization of services and production. The nation-state remains the predominant actor in international economic affairs, and domestic economies are still the most important feature of the world economy. Although some convergence has been occurring, national societies retain their essential characteristics and are not becoming part of any homogenized amorphous mass. In an era of oligopolistic competition and rapid technological innovation, location theory and the conventional theory of compara-

291

tive advantage cannot tell the whole story of what is happening in the world economy. Multinational firms and their investment activities are important parts of the explanation.

INCREASED REGIONALIZATION OF SERVICES AND MANUFACTURING

One of the most important recent developments in the world economy has been the internationalization of services and of industrial production, a development facilitated by falling costs for communication and transportation that have enabled firms to integrate production and other activities around the globe. Continuing restructuring of services and manufacturing was extremely important in the nature of the world economy as it entered the new millennium. Nevertheless, the importance of this development is frequently misunderstood and exaggerated. Whereas FDI in the year 2000 is only a small part of the total domestic investment of the rich countries, in the decade prior to 1914, British capitalists invested almost as much abroad as at home, and the European stock of FDI was higher in 1914 than it is relatively in the twenty-first century. Furthermore, contrary to the oft-stated opinion that MNCs have "globalized" technology and put their own firms everywhere on an equal footing, nothing could be farther from the truth. For reasons internal to the firms themselves, and because of conditions prevailing in many developing countries, technology tends to diffuse from industrialized to industrializing countries relatively slowly.[19]

Moreover, internationalization of services and production is highly concentrated among the major powers and within particular regions; one estimate made in the mid-1990s was that 85 percent of all foreign investment takes place among the members of the Triad (United States, Western Europe, and Japan).[20] The multinational firms of the three major economic powers have been concentrating their FDI in their respective backyards and fashioning regionalized production and service networks. American FDI has been shifting away from East and Southeast Asia toward Mexico. Whereas American firms relied previously on East and Southeast Asia as sources for components, outsourcing has recently been shifting toward Mexico; although be-

---

[19] This is the conclusion of Keith Pavitt in summarizing the pathbreaking work on technology policy and innovation carried out at the University of Sussex's Science Policy Research Unit.

[20] Robert Boyer and Daniel Drache, *States Against Markets: The Limits of Globalization* (New York: Routledge, 1996), 2.

cause of China's very low wage labor and vast potential as a market, China has been an exception to this trend. Japanese firms prefer East Asian subcontractors, and most of their manufactured imports have come from this region. Germany, for economic and political reasons, and to take advantage of East Europe's highly skilled and lower-cost labor, has been investing heavily in Eastern Europe, especially Poland, the Czech Republic, and Hungary. Evidence thus suggests that regionalism as well as globalism characterizes the strategies of multinational firms. While economic competition and financial markets have become increasingly global, production and services are increasingly regional.[21]

The trend toward regionalization of investment, services, and production can be explained in several ways. New methods of production and management, such as "lean production" and flexible manufacturing, encourage regionalization; both techniques require highly trained and motivated workforces that can be utilized more fully and with less risk at the regional than at the global level. Indeed, the need to move to low-wage areas has been greatly reduced as the share of unskilled labor in production has fallen dramatically since the 1970s. Regional concentration also facilitates scale economies in production. Another consideration is that regional production networks enable firms to be closer to their principal customers; this factor will become even more important as regional markets continue to develop in Western Europe and North America. Cultural affinities may also play a part in this trend. Furthermore, regionalization of production can insulate economies throughout the region from trade wars and currency fluctuations. For these and other reasons, the movement toward regionalization of production will continue within North America, Pacific Asia, and Western Europe and is likely to strengthen in Latin America and elsewhere.

The increased importance of regionalization in the world economy raises some disturbing possibilities. The trend toward regionalization could lead to weakening of the post–World War II movement toward trade liberalization. While the MNCs of the major economic powers continue to pursue global strategies and to invest in one another's economies (with the exception caused by Japan's relatively low level of inward FDI), they are also concentrating their own FDI in neighboring countries. Creation of regional rather than global production and sourcing networks has become a notable trend. If the movement

---

[21] Charles Oman, *Globalization and Regionalization: The Challenges for Developing Countries* (Paris: Development Centre of the OECD, 1994).

toward globalization should be slowed by increased regionalization of services and production, the open global economy could suffer a setback; this would have serious negative consequences for countries that were not members of a regional arrangement. And in the year 2000, most less developed economies lie outside the emerging regional blocs.

DEBATE OVER THE MNC AND THE NATION-STATE

There are divergent views of the MNCs' role in the world economy and of their relationship to their home economies. On the one hand are some who believe that the MNCs' increasing importance in the organization and management of the international economy constitutes a transformation of global economic and political affairs. For them, globalization of production and the central role of the multinational firm in the world economy represent the triumph of market forces and economic rationality over the anachronistic nation-state and a politically fragmented international economy. On the other hand, the state-centric position argues that the extent and impact of globalization are greatly overstated and that the nation-state continues to set the rules that MNCs must follow. In this debate, the importance of multinational corporations is really not at issue, and few observers other than economists deny their significance. Powerful corporations, their far-flung subsidiaries, and their global alliances, as John Stopford and Susan Strange have demonstrated in their book *Rival States, Rival Firms* (1991), have, for more than a decade, been recognized as major features of contemporary international affairs.[22] However, arguments continue regarding the extent to which these corporate giants have affected the nature and organization of the international economy and the relative significance of the nation-state in its functioning.

MNCs have certainly introduced changes in the global economy. As firms have increased their presence in foreign markets, some distancing from their home economies has taken place and their national identities have been attenuated; yet, the greater part of a firm's production, R & D, and activity remains in the home economy. It is also true that the huge expansion of intrafirm trade has changed the meaning of imports and exports. If, for example, the overseas sales of

---

[22] John M. Stopford and Susan Strange, with John S. Henley, *Rival States, Rival Firms: Competition for World Market Shares* (New York: Cambridge University Press, 1991).

American subsidiaries are taken into account, then the United States has had a large trade *surplus* for many years. The increased international mobility of firms has encouraged national governments to pursue aggressive policies to attract FDI.

The Global Firms and the Borderless Global Economy

Kenichi Ohmae, the Japanese business consultant, is a strong proponent of the thesis that the MNC has become a powerful independent actor rivaling and even outstripping the nation-state in importance. In his book, *The Borderless World*, he argues that the global (i.e., stateless) firm is a natural response to a borderless world economy characterized by homogeneous consumer tastes.[23] The ongoing process of economic globalization, Ohmae contends, has transformed the very nature of the multinational corporation itself. In his view, the early multinational corporation treated foreign operations as appendages used to manufacture products that had been designed and engineered back home; in such a situation, the chain of command and the nationality of the firm were clear. However, Ohmae is convinced that the nature of the firm has changed drastically due to extensive outsourcing and integration of production and other corporate activities on a global basis. The transnational firms of the 1990s, he believes, have become truly global corporations that are stateless and independent of their national origins. Corporate planning, for example, is now more and more likely to be conceived in global rather than national terms. Even ownership itself has become unclear as equity-sharing, joint ventures, and corporate alliances unite firms across national borders. Ohmae and many others argue that the world's corporations are shedding their national identities and becoming true citizens of the world as they make their production and other decisions without special reference to their home country.

Those who agree with Ohmae maintain that alliances and linkages among global corporations across national boundaries have led to the home economy's loss of significance in the competitive success of the firm. Instead, Ohmae argues, the most important firms must have a strong base in all three members of the Triad—North America, Western Europe, and Japan. Firms need foreign partners to obtain market access or to share the increasing costs of research and product development. The increasing importance of scale economies and the escalating costs of R & D, as well as the rapid pace, scope, and cost of

---

[23] Kenichi Ohmae, *The Borderless World: Power and Strategy in the Interlinked Economy* (New York: HarperBusiness, 1990).

modern technology, all encourage the growth of corporate alliances within and across national borders.

Ohmae and others argue that international corporate alliances have undermined the significance of national boundaries and created transnational links that override national political differences. Although corporate alliances can be identified in all industries, they are especially important in such high-tech sectors as aerospace, electronics, and automobiles, which are characterized by costly research-and-development activities, large economies of scale, and a high risk of failure. The rapid pace of technological change, the huge costs involved in technological innovation, and protectionist regional arrangements mean that even the largest firms need foreign partners with which they can share technology and other resources as well as gain access to protected markets. According to this formulation, there is international competition between industrial complexes composed of major corporations rather than between individual firms, and therefore a firm's international standing depends on the relationships that it has been able to establish with other firms.

The process of economic globalization, according to this position, has several important consequences for the overall world economy. Some allege that within the Triad itself, there is a trend toward economic convergence; many believe that the production, financial, and technological structures of the leading economies are following a common pattern. Also, the ups and downs of Triad economies are viewed as synchronous, moving together through business cycles and having common economic policies. Growing trade, investment, and technology flows within the Triad have drawn the major economies closer together, and the global firm has become both a cause of and a response to the increasing integration of the world economy.

The global economy populated by these firms has been described by former Clinton Administration Labor Secretary Robert Reich as a seamless web in which there no longer are any purely national economies, corporations, or products.[24] In a world where components may be made in several countries, assembled in another, and sold in yet a third, the nationality of a particular firm or good has become almost impossible to identify and, moreover, has become irrelevant. Reich and others have contended, therefore, that traditional measurements of trade and payments balances have lost significance. Reich has argued that even though the United States had a substantial trade and

---

[24] Robert Reich, *The Work of Nations: Preparing Ourselves for the 21st Century Capitalism* (New York: Knopf, 1991).

payments deficit in the 1980s and 1990s, this deficit was offset by a surplus in foreign production and sales by the subsidiaries of American multinational corporations.

The considerable increase in the internationalization of business in the 1990s gives support to those who argue that globalization has triumphed. One-half or more of the products manufactured in the United States contain one or more components produced elsewhere, and in some cases it is difficult to classify the nationality of the product: Are the Honda Accords, many of which are made in the United States, an American or a Japanese car? One-half of all imports and exports in the world economy are estimated to be transactions between parent corporations and subsidiaries. Although many more statistics and anecdotes could be cited to support the triumph of globalization, I maintain that multinational, transnational, or, if you prefer, global firms are still national firms conducting international business.

MNCs and the Nation-State

In an opposed view, MNCs are considered products of their home economy. Both industrial production and service industries are believed to be primarily nation-based.[25] Although it is true that the total volume of goods produced overseas by American firms had increased significantly to around 20 percent of total production by the end of the century, in the early twenty-first century the remaining 80 percent of the American economy was still largely insulated from the world economy. With few exceptions, a firm's primary market is still its home market, and the policies of home governments weigh more heavily in the decisions of the firm than do those of host governments. Moreover, it is important to remember that foreign markets are also national markets and that corporate strategies must be geared to other national markets and to the policies of host governments.[26] In addition, internationalization of services and production are occurring on a regional basis more frequently, especially in Europe and North America. And the policies and organizations of emerging regional blocs tend to reflect the economic and political interests of their dominant member states.

[25] See Razeen Sally, "Multinational Enterprises, Political Economy and Institutional Theory: Domestic Embeddedness in the Context of Internationalization," *Review of International Political Economy* 1, no. 1 (spring 1994): 161–92.

[26] Stephen Thomsen and Stephen Woolcock, *Direct Investment and European Integration: Competition Among Firms and Nations* (London: Royal Institute of International Affairs, 1993).

An excellent exposition of the state-centric position can be found in *Multinationals and the Myth of Globalization*, by Doremus et al., mentioned earlier (see footnote 16). This careful study, which examines the behavior of American, German, and Japanese multinationals across a broad range of industrial sectors and activities, successfully challenges the argument that technological, economic, and other transnational forces are leading to a convergence of state policies, domestic economic structures, and MNC behavior. Instead, the authors find that the domestic structure and economic ideology of the home economy continue to affect powerfully the strategies and activities of MNCs. They illustrate many significant differences among the firms of the three dominant economies and note that these differences can be explained by domestic factors, such as the historical experience of the country, differing economic ideologies, the structure of the economy, and the internal mechanisms of corporate governance. Although such firm-specific factors as the firm's industrial sector and the characteristics of its products obviously affect the firm's behavior, the authors convincingly demonstrate that, in the most fundamental areas of corporate strategy, the domestic roots of firms usually remain decisive determinants of their behavior.

Many basic differences in corporate strategy and behavior reflect national institutional structures, economic policies, and social priorities. The United States has tended to take a laissez-faire attitude toward business, except when an especially strong case can be made for government intervention. Germany, on the other hand, with its concept of the "social market" and labor/management partnership, has traditionally placed a greater emphasis on the social or community responsibilities of the firm. Japan has placed a high priority on maintaining a strong indigenous industrial base and preserving core elements of the system of lifetime employment. The resulting behavioral differences among American, German, and Japanese firms can be found in such core aspects of corporate behavior as patterns of strategic investment, intrafirm trade, research and development, corporate governance, and long-term corporate financing. American firms are more likely than German or Japanese firms to conduct basic R & D in other countries; they also are much more likely to invest abroad. National differences are reflected, too, in the levels of intrafirm trade. Whereas American firms are characterized by only a moderate level of intrafirm trade, German firms have a higher level, and Japanese firms have a very high level. This brief list of national differences could be expanded considerably; however, there have been many changes in national traditions, and there is a modest trend toward convergence in corporate behavior and structure.

Arguing that the nation-state is still the principal actor in international economic affairs, proponents of the state-centric position assert that multinational corporations are simply national firms with foreign operations and that, with few exceptions, these firms remain deeply embedded in their national societies. Their boards of directors and corporate management are composed predominantly of nationals, and corporate leaders are responsible to stockholders or stakeholders who are also overwhelmingly nationals. Even though this situation is changing, relatively few firms have foreign nationals as corporate directors or members of top management. Furthermore, control over corporate finances is normally retained in the home country. The key elements of research and development are also still retained in the home economy. The strategy of the firm is influenced strongly by home-country policies and other local considerations; despite some common factors such as the importance of outsourcing to reduce costs, corporate strategies are not converging toward a common pattern. And every government in one way or another promotes the interests of its own national firms. In short, at the turn of the century, there are no truly stateless global corporations, and it will undoubtedly be decades before some do emerge if they do so at all.

There is no question that intercorporate alliances have gained great importance in the organization and functioning of international business, but the significance of this development can easily be and has been overstated. Alliances among corporations of different nationalities have created valuable crossnational or transnational ties, yet intercorporate alliances are notoriously unstable. About 40 percent of these alliances last only about four years. Their fragility or inherent weakness is because, while corporate alliances may provide for cooperation in such specific areas as research on a particular technology, or cooperation in a particular market, the firms frequently continue to be fierce rivals outside the realm of the agreement. Corporate alliances are driven by a firm's desire to increase its market share; thus, when situations change, the interest of the corporation in the alliance may well change also. Indeed, corporate alliances far removed from commercialization are likely to fare better than other alliances. All in all, corporate alliances are matters of power and interest and are just as fragile as alliances among states.

In *The Competitive Advantage of Nations*, Michael Porter demonstrates that the national economy remains the predominant economic entity in the global economy. In his analysis, the home base of a multinational firm is the central determinant of the firm's international competitiveness. Multinational firms are and must continue to be national firms, he argues, because their competitive advantage is created in and must be maintained in their home economy. Porter argues that the world economy is organized in clusters of industrial excellence that are nation-based. The competitiveness of these national clusters, such as the strength of Japanese firms in automotive products or of American firms in computers, is determined by local factors and national policies. National specialization, strong national firms in particular industries, and differentials in national wealth all indicate the continued importance of national economies.

Although American academics, American corporate leaders, and Japanese business consultants may propagandize the idea of the global corporation, Japanese business and the Japanese government have definitely not accepted the idea that corporations have shed their nationality and become stateless. The giant Japanese electronics conglomerate Matsushita is and always will be Japanese; the task of the Japanese Ministry of International Trade and Industry (MITI) is and always will be to promote the interests of Matsushita and other Japanese corporations. Indeed, the well-being of these corporations is considered identical to the well-being of Japanese society. While Americans may ridicule the remark of then Defense Secretary "Engine Charlie" Wilson that "what is good for General Motors is good for the country," the Japanese really do believe that what is good for Matsushita or Toyota is good for Japan. Japanese society considers the overseas sales of *Japanese* products and the market share of *Japanese* firms to be very important. Nor are the concepts of the global corporation and the seamless world economy very appealing to those West Europeans who are attempting to create a unified European economy and strong European corporations that will compete effectively against their American and Japanese rivals.

AN INTERNATIONAL REGIME FOR FDI AND MNCs

In light of the increased significance of the MNC in every facet of the global economy, it is remarkable that there are no international rules to govern FDI, not even any that are comparable to those affecting international trade and monetary affairs. There are national, bilateral, regional, and multinational agreements on MNCs and FDI, but no overall comprehensive agreement. Although the Uruguay Round moved toward establishment of such rules, it fell far short of establishing a satisfactory regime to regulate FDI. Many economists believe that an investment regime is unnecessary because markets will discipline errant states and firms. Perhaps! But this is asking too much of markets. There is evidence to the contrary, that an international agreement governing MNCs and FDI is desirable. Such an agreement could "lock in" the trend toward liberalization of national policies affecting FDI, eliminate distortions caused by governmental "beggar-thy-neighbor" policies, and reduce conflicts among states and multinational firms.

Canadian trade negotiator Sylvia Ostry has suggested that a satisfactory international investment regime would have to embody several characteristics, including the rights of establishment, national treatment, and nondiscrimination.[27] The right of establishment means that firms of every nationality have the right to invest anywhere in the world. The principle of national treatment requires that national governments must treat the subsidiaries of foreign firms as if they were their own. In addition, countries should not discriminate against the firms of particular countries; this provision makes it necessary that national policies governing inward-FDI should be transparent. An investment regime would also have to deal with the fact that every country restricts or limits investment in certain economic sectors, such as finance, culture, and national security. Another task would be to determine which types of national restrictions are legitimate and which should be prohibited. Although these objectives are reasonable, the political obstacles to incorporating them into an international investment regime are formidable.

Several important initiatives have been launched to govern MNCs and FDI, but none have advanced very far by the beginning of the twenty-first century. FDI impinges directly on national economies and can infringe on national values and economic independence. For this reason, states, especially less developed countries (LDCs), are reluctant to surrender jurisdiction in these matters to an international body. They fear domination by the huge corporations of the United States and other industrialized economies. Moreover, the very fact that MNCs operate across two or more national jurisdictions makes the task of framing an international regime extraordinarily difficult. An investment regime would have to address such sensitive issues as taxation of foreign investment, transfer pricing (the prices charged by one subsidiary to another), and governmental use of financial and other questionable inducements to attract foreign investment. A par-

---

[27] Sylvia Ostry, *A New Regime for Foreign Direct Investment* (Washington, D.C.: Group of Thirty, 1997).

ticularly vexing problem for America's trading partners is the extra-territorial application of American law, not just to the foreign affiliates of American firms, but also to those of foreign corporations. For example, the Helms-Burton Act punishes foreign firms that deal with Cuba and is an especially infamous example of American efforts to impose its own laws and policies on other countries. LDCs and other smaller states want protection against the concentration of power represented by the MNCs, while corporations want guarantees against capricious actions by states; there is understandable distrust on both sides.

Do Global Corporations Pose a Threat?

The large size of MNCs, their market power, and their pursuit of global strategies have raised fears in many groups and countries that they will become subjugated to and exploited by MNC globalization of production and services. These concerns are not groundless, as MNCs do represent huge concentrations of economic and, frequently, political power. In the 1980s and 1990s, a massive expansion of corporate power took place in the United States, Western Europe, and elsewhere. This merger wave was due to a number of factors: the spectacular American stock market that has given some large firms the capital to take over others, deregulation and the weakening of antitrust policy, and new communications and other technologies that enable firms to oversee larger operations and enjoy greatly increased economies of scale.

Increasing concentration of power among media, entertainment, and telecommunications firms has been one of the most disturbing consequences of the merger movement and corporate aggrandizement.[28] Two prominent examples of such concentration are the merger of America Online, Inc., with Time Warner in January 2000 and Vodafone AirTouch's acquisition of Mannesmann A.G. The trend toward larger and larger firms in the media sector emerges from the logic of digital business itself. Although competition is fierce and uncertainties are great in these sectors, established firms enjoy economies of scale and find it easy to expand because the cost of replication of digits is relatively minuscule. Thus, once these firms whose expertise and competitiveness lies in the manipulation of digits establish

[28] Despite the antitrust action against Microsoft, the Clinton Administration was very tolerant toward the rapid and extensive merger movement in the United States. Secretary of the Treasury Summers and others argued that competition in the American economy is robust as globalization has more than offset the negative effects of mergers and reduced the pricing power of big firms. In addition, economies of scale and increased efficiency achieved by mergers are believed to help consumers.

themselves, it is not costly to expand to incorporate other digital or would-be digital firms (such as Time Warner). In this way, economies of scale in e-commerce appear to lead to massive scale in corporate structure. Although the United States has been the forerunner of this development, similar restructuring has begun in Western Europe.

Paradoxically, corporate globalization is associated with both increased scale and increased competition. Although many fear increased scale, the benefits of increased competition are enormous, whether or not they are appreciated. Consider, for example, the benefits to the American consumer and economy as a whole from Japanese exports and investments. Japanese exports to the United States have meant that the American consumer has enjoyed a much wider range of goods of high quality and lower price. The American economy as a whole has also benefited from Japanese FDI and introduction of such Japanese production techniques as lean production. Would the American consumer and overall economy really have been better off if barriers to imports and investment had kept out Sony and Honda? I doubt it very much. Consumers and the overall economy in less developed countries also benefit from FDI, and so do workers. It is important to note that, in general, MNCs pay higher wages, create more jobs than do domestic firms, and have higher labor standards; and the economy gains capital and technology from the MNCs. This means that MNCs can be particularly important to LDCs, especially to those where agriculture is predominant. MNCs in Turkey, for example, pay 124 percent of average Turkish wages.[29]

Maintenance of a strong regulatory system and encouragement of firms of many nationalities to invest and compete in the local market can provide an effective response to the dangers of corporate power. Despite these and other safeguards, a global economy populated by powerful multinational firms is a daunting prospect, especially for the firms and governments of small, poor countries. There is a great temptation to close national borders to imports and to foreign direct investment. However, such a response to the increasingly integrated global economy could be extremely costly. Without access to foreign capital and technology, economic development would be very difficult or even impossible; as Nobel Laureate Arthur Lewis, from the Third World himself (Barbados), has pointed out, developing countries must have large infusions of outside capital to build the costly physical infrastructure required for their economic development.[30] Debt forgiveness, foreign aid, and technical assistance could help

[29] *The Economist*, 29 January 2000, 21.
[30] W. Arthur Lewis, *The Evolution of the International Economic Order* (Princeton: Princeton University Press, 1978).

303

close the rich-poor gap, but these measures are hardly enough. Although for many, globalization is a threat, it is also part of the solution to underdevelopment; the industrial success of the emerging markets of East Asia exemplify the importance of trade, foreign investment, and technology imports.

The argument that small countries cannot compete in the world of the strong is nonsense and is contradicted by experience. Tiny Finland has established itself as a leader in wireless telephony (Nokia) and other high-tech industries. Israel is a world leader in many technological developments. Ireland has reversed a century and a half of economic stagnation by making itself an attractive site for investment by high-tech firms. Among industrializing and less developed countries, India has become a major international player in computer software. Taiwan has a flourishing semiconductor and computer industry, and Singapore and Hong Kong have outstanding records of economic success. However, if an LDC is to join this league of small but very successful countries, it must have an honest and competent government, invest heavily in education at all levels, respect international property rights, encourage entrepreneurship, support a diversified and excellent national program of R & D, and pursue sound macroeconomic policies. A nation that is unwilling to assume these crucial responsibilities is quite unlikely to succeed in the global economy and risks domination by foreign firms. Unfortunately, too many less developed and postcommunist economies are at serious risk.

CONCLUSION

The role of the MNC has grown increasingly important in the integration and organization of the global economy. Yet, it is important to appreciate that most economic activities are still overwhelmingly nationally based. Moreover, the prevailing idea that MNCs are destined to rule the global economy may turn out to be quite misleading. The global economy rests and must continue to rest on a secure social and political foundation, and there is no guarantee that this foundation will survive in the decades ahead. As the economic historian William Parker reminds us, in the late nineteenth century the international capitalist system began to break down because of a mismatch between new large-scale capitalist firms and the interests of many Europeans.[31] Today, this sober analysis would have to be expanded to include a global economy composed of diverse cultures and interests.

[31] William N. Parker, "Capitalistic Organization and National Response: Social Dynamics in the Age of Schumpeter," in Richard H. Day and Gunnar Eliasson, eds., *The Dynamics of Market Economies* (Amsterdam: North-Holland, 1986), 351.

The State and Economic Development

THE HERCULEAN task of raising the great mass of humanity from poverty to acceptable levels of economic welfare is one of the most difficult tasks facing the world economy.[1] There is intense disagreement among economists, public officials, and other experts over the best ways to achieve this goal. Indeed, there is not even a generally accepted commitment to accord priority to economic development. Early attempts by India and other less developed countries (LDCs) to make economic development an explicit objective of the postwar world economy at the 1944 Bretton Woods Conference were rejected by the United States and other industrialized countries.[2] The World Bank, the International Monetary Fund, and regimes governing the world economy were established primarily to serve the interests of the dominant powers. Although industrialized countries have subsequently provided technical and financial assistance and given trade preferences, they have continued to resist LDC demands for a development regime.

Among both scholars and public officials, there are strong disagreements regarding the relative importance of the state and the market in economic development; these disagreements have been central to the conflict between the developed and the less developed countries.[3] Throughout much of the postwar era, a debate has raged between the neoclassical proponents of reliance on the market and the proponents of state intervention. In the early postwar period (1945–1970), development economics, which emphasized the role of the state, was preeminent. Development economists argued that developing countries required an activist government; moreover, they believed that the in-

---

[1] A sweeping study of why some nations have become rich and most others have remained poor is David S. Landes, *The Wealth and Poverty of Nations: Why Some Are So Poor and Some So Rich* (New York: W. W. Norton, 1989).

[2] This discussion is based on Harold James's magisterial history of the IMF: *International Monetary Cooperation Since Bretton Woods* (Washington, D.C.: International Monetary Fund; New York: Oxford University Press, 1996).

[3] A very useful history of the debate over the best route to development is John Rapley, *Understanding Development: Theory and Practice in the Third World* (Boulder, CO: Lynne Rienner, 1996).

ternational community should play a central role in LDC development. Then, during the 1970s and 1980s, the neoclassical belief in the free market triumphed both in academia and in international institutions, and the ideology of "neoliberalism" and the doctrine of "structural adjustment" became dominant in the International Monetary Fund and the World Bank.[4]

In the late 1980s and early 1990s, the "theory of the developmental state" arose to challenge neoliberalism. Differing with the policy prescriptions of neoliberalism but consistent with development economics, the theory of the developmental state emphasized that the state should play the central role in economic development. The controversy between proponents of the "developmental state" and of neoliberalism has focused on differing interpretations of the rapid and extraordinary economic success of the Newly Industrializing Countries (NIEs) of East and Southeast Asia. Neoliberalism argues that the success of these economies has been due to their reliance on the market and the minimal role of the state in the economy. The theory of the developmental state, on the other hand, credits the central role of the state for the rapid industrialization of the East Asian economies. This position gained many adherents among noneconomist scholars of economic development. Then, in 1997, the East Asian financial crisis shifted the weight of the argument to the neoliberal emphasis on the importance of the market and the dangers of state intervention in the economy. Proponents of the developmental state strongly disputed this assessment and argued that the crisis was caused by international economic and political pressures. And so the debate continues. To a significant degree, the fate of the great mass of mankind located in LDCs will be affected by whether the state-centric or market-centric approach to economic development is ultimately dominant. To understand the nature of this crucial debate about the best path to economic development, one must begin at its origins in the early post–World War II era.

THE RISE AND DEMISE OF DEVELOPMENT ECONOMICS

Development economics was the first systematic effort to deal with the problems of the less developed countries.[5] Flourishing in the

---

[4] Neoliberalism refers to the application of the principles of neoclassical economics to economic development and other aspects of economic affairs. Neoliberalism and structural adjustment will be discussed in more detail below.

[5] A useful overview of theories and writings on economic development is James M. Cypher and James L. Dietz, *The Process of Economic Development* (London: Routledge, 1997).

1940s and 1950s, this theory became the predominant theoretical position in the United States and elsewhere to explain why some nations remained impoverished and what should be done to overcome the problems of the LDCs. In a strict sense, of course, the term "development theory" was a misnomer. Actually, a number of specific development theories competed with one another; these theories differed in their analysis of the precise causes of economic underdevelopment and appropriate solutions to economic problems. Moreover, development theory as a whole was a collection of general ideas rather than a single coherent theory. Among the more prominent members of the development school were Albert Hirschman, Arthur Lewis, Gunnar Myrdal, Raul Prebisch, Paul Rosenstein-Rodan, and Max Singer. These economists attempted to provide an overall explanation of economic underdevelopment and a strategy to lift the less developed nations out of poverty.

Development theory assumed that the less developed countries were fundamentally different in kind from the more advanced industrialized countries and functioned according to different economic principles. Development theorists believed that, although the precepts of neoclassical economics were applicable to the advanced industrialized economies, these theories were inapplicable to the LDCs because of their special conditions. For example, as Arthur Lewis argued, less developed economies were burdened by excess labor and low productivity in the agricultural sector; surplus workers were paid subsistence wages and constituted an immense reservoir that could be tapped to accelerate economic development.[6] These theorists also noted that the LDCs, which were mainly exporters of commodities and tropical products, suffered from unfavorable terms of trade. "Trade pessimism" led these economists to believe that trade could not serve as an "engine of growth" as it had for developing countries in the north during the nineteenth century. Furthermore, a number of market failures, including inflexible economic structures, very low savings rates, and poor educational systems, were believed to have locked the less developed economies into a vicious circle from which they could not escape without a strong interventionist state and significant international assistance.

Development theorists also believed the less developed countries were victims of "late-late" development. These economists argued that in the nineteenth century the then-developing countries such as

[6] W. Arthur Lewis, "Economic Development with Unlimited Supplies of Labour," *Manchester School* 22 (May 1954).

307

Japan and Germany enjoyed what Alexander Gerschenkron called "the advantages of backwardness," when they were able to draw upon the capital, technology, and experience of the early developers.[7] The late, late developing countries of the second half of the twentieth century, on the other hand, were considered to be so extremely far behind that they would face overwhelming problems competing with more developed economies, and would be unable to catch up with the more advanced economies unless extraordinary measures were taken. Development theorists therefore believed that the state and the international community had to play major roles.

The industrialized economies were judged so strong that LDC firms could not possibly compete against them and acquire market shares in the international economy. This view discouraged private entrepreneurship and undermined the belief in free trade and open markets. Some proponents of development theory thus believed that the path to economic development was trade protectionism and the strategy of "import substitution," and that every LDC should build an industrial structure behind high tariff walls. These ideas were set forth by Raul Prebisch, the Economic Commission for Latin America (ECLA), and the United Nations Commission for Trade and Development (UNCTAD) and became important in the import-substitution strategies of Latin America.

For Swedish economist Gunnar Myrdal, the essence of the underdevelopment problem was that the less developed economies were caught in a vicious circle of poverty or, according to his formulation, were locked into a process of "circular and cumulative causation" from which they could not escape without a massive state-led effort and generous international assistance.[8] Myrdal's argument proceeded like this: The less developed countries by definition were impoverished. As these countries were poor, they had very low rates of national savings. Because they had low savings rates, they also had low investment rates. Because they had low investment rates, their industries were inefficient and uncompetitive in world markets. Because their industries had low rates of productivity growth and were uncompetitive, these countries continued to be impoverished. And because they were poor. . . . and so on. The task of economic development, therefore, was to break this vicious circle of poverty in which the less developed countries were trapped.

[7] Alexander Gerschenkron, *Economic Backwardness in Historical Perspective* (Cambridge: Harvard University Press, 1962).

[8] Gunnar Myrdal, *Economic Theory and Underdeveloped Regions* (New York: Harper Torchbooks, 1957).

Following the implications of such ideas, development economists formulated the strategy of the "Big Push," which would enable LDCs to break through both domestic and international barriers to successful economic development. Set forth originally in an influential 1943 article by development economist Paul Rosenstein-Rodan, the idea of the Big Push may be said to have launched the field of development economics.[9] He argued that the state had to play a much more activist interventionist role in the economy than was needed in more advanced economies. In LDCs, it had to overcome such market failures as the lack of entrepreneurship, low national savings, and various economic uncertainties that weighed down these backward economies. In addition, due to low national savings rates and the absence of a strongly entrepreneurial private sector, the state itself had to become an entrepreneur and promote public investment. Development economists, however, differed among themselves about a number of issues, such as the importance of balanced growth strategies.

In addition, development economists prescribed that industrialized nations should provide massive foreign aid and other forms of financial and technical assistance. Moreover, they argued that the developed countries ought to extend trade preferences to the less developed countries and should not require the latter to reciprocate by opening their less competitive economies. If such policies were followed and a development regime were established, development economists believed that both the more developed and the less developed economies would benefit. Their optimistic belief that every economy had an interest in the development of all, set development economists apart from dependency theorists, economic nationalists, and Marxists, all of whom regarded the interests of undeveloped and those of developed economies as antithetical.

Triumph of Neoliberalism

The late 1970s and early 1980s witnessed the defeat of both development economics and the LDC strategy of import-substitution that had been intellectually supported by development theory. The foundations for the overthrow of development economics within the economics fraternity were laid in the 1960s with a profound change in the character of economic thought and methodology. The writings of

[9] Paul N. Rosenstein-Rodan, "Problems of Industrialisation of Eastern and South-Eastern Europe," *Economic Journal* (Quarterly Journal of the Royal Economic Society) 53, nos. 210–211 (June-September 1943): 202–211.

development economists had been mainly literary and descriptive; one can read Arthur Lewis and Albert Hirschman, for example, and only rarely encounter a graph or an equation. Then in the 1960s, influenced by Paul Samuelson's *Foundations of Economic Analysis* (1949) and the methodological writings of other neoclassical economists, formalization and abstract modeling began to displace the more literary style of most economists.[10] This shift meant that if an idea, however intellectually interesting it might be, could not be expressed in an abstract model, it was of little or no interest to the rising generation of mathematically inclined and model-oriented economists coming out of the Massachusetts Institute of Technology and elsewhere. One unfortunate consequence of this development was that problems of economic development suffered neglect because they were impossible to model.[11]

In addition to this methodological shift from literary to formal analysis, there was an intellectual revolution against development economics in the 1970s. As Hirschman pointed out in an intriguing essay entitled "The Rise and Fall of Development Economics," the emergence of development economics had been facilitated by the Keynesian revolution that posited two different types of economics and, therefore, also posited differing policy prescriptions.[12] On the one hand was what Keynes called "classical economics," with its emphasis on a full-employment equilibrium; this classical economic universe was composed of flexible prices and wages that could easily adjust to changes in demand and thereby restore a full-employment equilibrium. In this economic universe, the market did all the work and there was little that the state could or should do.

On the other hand, Keynes pointed out that there were situations characterized by market failure (as in the Great Depression) where equilibrium could not be restored by the free play of market forces and the government therefore had to intervene with demand management policies (macroeconomic policies) that would reestablish a full-employment equilibrium. Such departures from full-employment

---

[10] Paul A. Samuelson, *Foundations of Economic Analysis* (Cambridge: Harvard University Press, 1983).

[11] The interesting story of this methodological shift has been told by Paul R. Krugman in his *Development, Geography, and Economic Theory*. (Cambridge: MIT Press, 1995).

[12] Discussed in Albert O. Hirschman, "The Rise and Fall of Development Economies," in Hirschman, *Essays in Trespassing: Economics to Politics and Beyond* (New York; Cambridge University Press, 1981), Chapter 1. See also Lloyd G. Reynolds, *The Three Worlds of Economics* (New Haven: Yale University Press, 1971).

equilibrium were produced by economic behavior fundamentally different from that predicted by classical economics and that thus necessitated state intervention in the economy in order to overcome market failures. In effect, Keynesianism not only created a rationale for government intervention, but implied that classical economics was not a unified, universal science applicable to every economy and economic situation. In this way, Keynesianism supported the fundamental assumption of development economics that less developed economies were different from developed economies, and therefore the state should play a central role.

The attack on Keynesian economics in the 1960s and 1970s by monetarists and by the theory of rational expectations undermined the intellectual foundations of development economics. The essence of this criticism was that there is only *one* economics, and that economics is a universal science equally applicable to all societies. These arguments challenged the basic idea of development economics that the LDCs were fundamentally different from developed economies and functioned according to a different economic logic. The critics of development economics argued that such behavioral assumptions of neoclassical economics as individual rationality, the principle of marginal utility, and the importance of relative prices were as applicable to less developed as they were to developed countries. For example, in an important study for which he received the Nobel Prize, Theodore Schultz demonstrated that LDC farmers were rational maximizers who responded to market incentives and were not the hapless people depicted by development economists.[13]

Neoclassical economists argued that the principal source of underdevelopment is government policies that distort economic incentives, inhibit market forces, and actually work against economic development.[14] Neoclassical economists argued that the LDCs' problems were due to government failures rather than, as development economists contended, to market failures requiring government intervention. The

[13] Theodore W. Schultz, *Transforming Traditional Agriculture* (New Haven: Yale University Press, 1964). Schultz's research showed that peasants were rational and responded to price incentives. In one of the more bizarre episodes in the history of the Nobel Prize for economics, the award was made jointly to Arthur Lewis and Theodore Schultz for contributions to economics that contradicted one another. It is hardly conceivable that two physicists would get the physics prize for research that came to opposed conclusions about the nature of the universe. This curious episode is discussed by Hirschman, *Essays in Trespassing: Economics to Politics and Beyond,* Chapter 1.

[14] An important critique of development economics and statement of the neoclassical position is Ian M. D. Little, *Economic Development: Theory, Policy, and International Relations* (New York: Basic Books, 1982).

LDC state, neoclassical economists concluded, was the problem and not the solution in the failure of these economies to develop. They pointed out that, for example, reckless government policies were responsible for the excessively high rates of inflation and the huge government debts that distorted economic incentives and discouraged entrepreneurship. Their message to LDC governments was to "get the prices right," rely on the fundamentals of the market, and get their hands off the economy. If these simple neoclassical policy prescriptions were pursued, they contended, the less developed economies would permit a proper environment to emerge in which private initiatives would lead to economic development.

This neoclassical attack on development economics considered the world of economics to be unitary and the theories and principles of neoclassical economics to be just as applicable to the less developed countries as they were to the developed countries. State intervention, however, had distorted these economies and bore primary responsibility for their failure to develop. Fiscal irresponsibility, hyperinflation, and markets closed to international competition were among the major problems afflicting them. Neoclassical economists totally rejected the argument that the less developed economies were caught in a vicious circle of poverty and cumulative causation that could be broken only by state intervention and massive international assistance. Instead, they argued that if the governments of less developed countries stepped aside, pursued sound or "market-conforming" economic policies, and opened their markets to the world, their growth rates and national wealth would eventually converge with those of the more developed countries. That is, market openness, fiscal discipline, and noninterventionism constituted the route to economic development.

By the late 1970s, neoclassical orthodoxy had triumphed in the economics profession. Development economics literally disappeared, and development economists despaired and took up other intellectual interests. Albert Hirschman, for example, began to write about social theory, and the writings of the pioneers of development economics rarely appeared on the syllabi of American departments of economics. The ideas and policy proposals of development economics survived only in those less developed countries that continued to pursue import-substitution strategies and in certain specialized agencies of the United Nations that advocated the strategy of import-substitution. However, even in these remaining outposts, development economics and the policies it advocated suffered a severe defeat in the 1980s.

312

THE DEBT CRISIS AND STRUCTURAL ADJUSTMENT

The international debt problem that surfaced in the Mexican financial crisis of 1982 spread rapidly throughout the developing world, especially in Latin America and a number of African and East European countries. When Arab oil-producing countries had suddenly and sharply raised oil prices in 1973, severe balance of payments deficits were incurred by LDCs. Recycling of the resultant OPEC surplus to deficit LDCs through loans by large international banks increased the likelihood of an eventual crisis. The decision of the Federal Reserve in the fall of 1979 did precipitate a crisis when it shifted from a loose to a tight monetary policy in order to defeat hyperinflation. LDC debtors then suddenly found themselves saddled with huge interest payments on their debt and were unable to service their debt because of the global recession and loss of income from their exports.

The consequent LDC debt crisis during the 1980s had a devastating impact on a large number of developing countries and, subsequently, also had profound consequences for the economic policies of the LDCs, the role of the International Monetary Fund in economic development, and the relations between industrial and developing economies. In effect, the debt crisis signaled the failure of the development strategy based on import-substitution and of the idea that the state should play a substantial role in the less developed economy. Throughout the 1970s, LDCs had financed their economic development through "sovereign borrowing," that is, government borrowing, in Western capital markets, a strategy that permitted escape from dependence on both northern MNCs and the "conditionality" policies of the IMF and the World Bank.[15] By the mid-1980s reliance on bank loans had become impossible. Later in the decade, the collapse of the Soviet Union and the failure of its command economy further strengthened belief in the superiority of the market system. However, it was the LDC debt crisis, more than any other development, that led to the triumph of the doctrine of neoliberalism and the policy of structural adjustment.

When Mexico informed the United States in 1982 that it could no longer service its huge debt, the Federal Reserve launched a concerted effort to contain the crisis so as to prevent damage to the American banking system and extension of the crisis to other debtor countries in Latin America. While the Fed arranged for short-term loans to

---

[15] "Conditionality" refers to the imposition by the IMF of certain requirements that must be met before assistance is forthcoming.

prevent a Mexican default, the IMF assumed responsibility for working out a long-term solution. The arrangement for dealing with the Mexican debt crisis became the model followed with other LDC debtors. Although the debtors attempted to present a united front against imposition of the strict terms dictated by the lender countries, the latter were in firm control. However, it soon became apparent that the initial assessment of the debt crisis had been deeply flawed. The debt problem in many countries was really one of *insolvency*—they could not service their debts without major economic and structural reforms—rather than a *liquidity* problem that could be solved by short-term lending and policy adjustments. Many debtors could not possibly repay or even service (pay the interest on) their debts under the best of circumstances. It became obvious that a long-term, more fundamental solution to the debt problem was required.

In 1985, responding to this reassessment of the nature of the debt crisis, U.S. Secretary of the Treasury James Baker initiated the policy of structural adjustment.[16] This doctrine, resulting from the neoorthodoxy of the 1970s, assumed that the debtor countries' persistent trade and fiscal imbalances had deep structural causes. Therefore, along with changed macroeconomic policies, such structural reforms as a shift toward export-led growth, reductions of the role of the state in the economy, and public sector reforms were required. This approach was also based on the lessons drawn from the East Asian successes in the 1960s and 1970s. This new conventional wisdom coincided with rising opposition to big government in the United States, the United Kingdom, and elsewhere.

The doctrine of structural adjustment meant that a debtor country applying for financial assistance from the IMF and/or World Bank had to commit itself to a number of stringent economic and structural reforms. Over the short term, these reforms were intended to achieve balance of payments adjustment; over the long term, restructuring of these economies would be necessary if they were to return to successful economic development. Underlying this significant policy reorientation of lender governments and the IMF was the realization that only more rapid rates of economic growth would enable the debtors to overcome the problem of national insolvency.

The doctrine of structural adjustment was based on what John Williamson called the "Washington Consensus."[17] This term refers to

---

[16] Joan M. Nelson, ed., *Economic Crisis and Policy Choice: The Politics of Adjustment in the Third World* (Princeton: Princeton University Press, 1990).

[17] John Williamson, "Democracy and the 'Washington Consensus,'" *World Development* 21, no. 8 (1993): 1329–36.

Williamson's perception of broad agreement among public officials in both the industrial economies and international institutions on the importance of the neoliberal program for economic development and its emphasis on free markets, trade liberalization, and a greatly reduced role for the state in the economy. Although some LDCs charged that the demand for structural adjustment was a new form of capitalist imperialism, the LDCs had little choice other than compliance if they wanted financial assistance. While later developments complemented or supplemented the policy of structural adjustment, this basic approach soon defined the position of the industrial countries and the IMF toward the LDCs and economic development.

Belief that the role of the state in the economy should be drastically reduced and the economy should be opened to the outside world was a vital component of this neoliberal consensus; governments should deregulate and privatize the economy as well as shift from an import-substitution to an export-led growth strategy. Another component of structural adjustment was that governments should pursue prudent fiscal and monetary policies and should definitely maintain balanced budgets in order to eliminate runaway inflation. It was particularly important that the economy should "get prices right" and not permit government policies to distort them. After such reforms, it was argued, private initiatives and desirable social outcomes would be likely to emerge. Nations were encouraged to recognize that economic development requires an "effective" state, meaning a government run by incorruptible economic technocrats. Although a number of important disagreements (primarily of a political nature) persisted within this broad neoliberal agenda, the Washington Consensus became the principal approach of the developed countries to the less developed countries.[18]

The debt crisis transformed the international role of the IMF and the World Bank. The IMF had originally been established as a monetary institution to manage the Bretton Woods system of fixed exchange rates; for example, it provided short-term loans to deal with balance-of-payments problems. To receive such a loan, the recipient country had to fulfill certain macroeconomic policy conditions (conditionality). These conditions were imposed to force the country to bring its international payments back into equilibrium. In response to the debt crisis, the role of the IMF changed dramatically as it began

[18] These political disagreements have been over such matters as economic priorities, the speed and sequencing of economic liberalization, and how to reform the civil service. These highly controversial issues are at the core of the political problems that must be resolved if economic development is to succeed.

to make medium-term loans. In addition, implementation of the doctrine of structural adjustment meant that conditionality was expanded from requirements of changes in *macro*economic policy to fundamental changes in *micro*economic policies and in the overall economy. This made the IMF become an economic development agency with considerable influence over the economic affairs of less developed countries.

With its response to the debt crisis, the Fund joined the World Bank to play a major role in the affairs of both developing economies and the transitional economies in Eastern Europe and the former Soviet Union. Warranted or not, the Fund became known as the "bad guy," and was subjected to severe criticism by many economists, less developed countries, and politicians on both the political left and right. The Left turned against the IMF because of its inflexible demands that governments seeking assistance had to carry out major reforms and austerity programs, whose impact proved heaviest on the poor. The Right believed that IMF policies had actually harmed less developed countries and thus preferred a market solution to the financial troubles of developing and transitional economies. Opposition to the Fund reached its zenith during the 1997 East Asian financial crisis and led to proposals for fundamental reforms.

THEORY OF THE "DEVELOPMENTAL STATE"

In the late 1980s and early 1990s, the theory of the developmental state arose to challenge neoliberal orthodoxy explaining the rapid and successful industrialization of the Newly Industrializing Economies (NIEs) in East Asia. According to this position, the outstanding economic success of Japan and other East Asian countries was due to their adoption of the developmental state model in which the state had to play the central role in guiding economic development and had to lead rather than follow the market. The acrimonious debate between proponents of the developmental state and proponents of the neoliberal, market-centered approach has become central to determination of the best route to successful economic development.[19]

---

[19] Two useful analyses of this debate are Stephan Haggard, *Pathways from the Periphery: The Politics of Growth in the Newly Industrializing Countries* (Ithaca: Cornell University Press, 1990); and Richard F. Doner and Gary Hawes, "The Political Economy of Growth in Southeast and Northeast Asia," in Manochehr Dorraj, ed., *The Changing Political Economy of the Third World* (Boulder, Colo.: Lynne Rienner, 1995), Chapter 6.

The neoliberal interpretation of the extraordinary economic success of the NIEs (South Korea, Taiwan, Hong Kong, and Singapore) was that these economies had pursued "market conforming" economic development strategies; markets rather than government policies had determined the path of development. The extraordinary performance of these "miracle" economies, neoliberal thinkers believed, provided strong support for the Washington Consensus, the doctrine of structural adjustment, and neoclassical reliance on the market. According to this interpretation, East Asian governments had followed neoliberal policy prescriptions; they had opened their economies to the world, reduced the role of the state in the economy to permit markets to function properly, and pursued export-led growth strategies. This interpretation of Japanese and East Asian economic success, however, was challenged by theorists of the developmental state, who argued that success was due to the crucial role played by the state and its industrial policies in the process of economic development.

The theory of the developmental state is really a collection of several theories sharing important ideas. These several theories assert that East Asian governments have played a central role in the development of their economies. Two outstanding interpretations of East Asian economies as developmental states are found in Alice Amsden's *Asia's Next Giant* (1989), which analyzes the industrialization of South Korea, and Robert Wade's *Governing the Market* (1990), which deals with the industrialization of Taiwan.[20] Although Amsden's and Wade's ideas differ on a number of issues, I shall emphasize those points on which they and most other proponents of the developmental state are in agreement.

Theories of the developmental state argue that the governments of Taiwan, South Korea, and the other NIEs devised an array of incentives that encouraged private investment in strategic industries. Also, through a variety of techniques, these governments played a key role in creating an entrepreneurial class, identified critical economic areas for development, and exposed priority sectors to international competition that forced them to become efficient. These state policies encouraged development of an industrial and economic structure that would not have arisen merely in response to market signals. According to the theory of the developmental state, the policies of these governments deliberately got prices "wrong" in order to change the

[20] Alice H. Amsden, *Asia's Next Giant: South Korea and Late Industrialization* (New York: Oxford University Press, 1989); and Robert Wade, *Governing the Market: Economic Theory and the Role of Government in East Asian Industrialization* (Princeton: Princeton University Press, 1990).

behavior of firms; they also used nonprice means to alter firm behavior. Scholars argue that this state-led industrialization strategy worked by using the price mechanism to encourage private entrepreneurs to take actions that the government considered to be in the interest of rapid industrialization.

The industrial, protectionist, and other policies employed by the developmental state were based on the assumption (which had been shared by members of the first generation of development theorists) that these economies suffered from the consequences of "late, late industrialization." Market failure was assumed to be prevalent among these less developed economies, and market failure necessitated an active role for the state. Governing elites believed that their societies faced "collective action problems"; that is, they had to find a way to motivate members of their societies to work together. State policies were needed to bring private returns in line with public returns. States had to create an incentive structure to ensure that private entrepreneurs invested in those economic activities that would be the most socially beneficial. In addition to trade protection and government subsidies, their industrial policies included such "financial repression" policies as selective credit allocation and deliberate distortion of interest rates in order to channel cheap credit to favored economic sectors. Elites also believed that government policies should anticipate the future comparative advantage of the economy and that industrial policy should lead rather than follow the market.[21]

Although proponents of the developmental state agree with neoclassical economists that the strategy of export-led growth was a key factor in the economic success of the East Asian economies, they argue that neoclassical analysis is not sufficiently comprehensive. For example, they ask why business firms selected particular products for export.[22] As Amsden points out in her study of South Korean industrialization, that government used a number of mechanisms to promote particular industrial sectors and encourage export drives, including export contests to promote rapid industrialization of those sectors considered of strategic importance to the overall economy. Those industries that performed best in export markets were especially favored by government industrial policies and programs of financial assistance.

---

[21] Richard Auty makes the interesting point that industrial policy was a consequence of the uncertain political situation after the defeat of the United States in Vietnam. Richard M. Auty, *Economic Development and Industrial Policy: Mexico, Indonesia, and China* (New York: Mansell, 1994).

[22] Another area of disagreement has been the relationship of exports and growth. Did exports cause growth, as neoclassical economists assume, or did growth cause exports, as proponents of the development state believe?

Proponents of the developmental state maintained that the theory of the "governed market," to use Wade's appropriately descriptive term, rather than the neoclassical theory of the free market, accounted for the outstanding economic success of the East Asian NIEs.

The theory of the developmental state maintains that the East Asian state was able to play a guiding role in economic development because of a number of unique domestic and international factors. In all these societies, the state has been relatively autonomous and therefore able to pursue policies free from public pressure. Yet, this state autonomy was deeply embedded in a society where the state worked very closely with business interests to promote rapid industrialization.[23] Some observers believe that such Asian social values as hierarchical deference, a tradition of hard work, and subordination of the individual to the community played a crucial role; celebration of Asian values also provided ideological support to the authoritarian regimes of the region. The national political economy was based on trust and subordination rather than Western-style compliance and accountability. Although these states were authoritarian, they also carried out important reforms and implemented policies favorable to economic growth and social harmony; for example, they promoted land reform, education, and income equality.

At the core of the developmental state and the reason for its outstanding success were close ties among government, local banks, and industry. These intimate relationships, which Wade calls "alliance capitalism," facilitated channeling bank capital into promising industries and thus promoted rapid industrialization. At the same time, domestic governments frequently restricted both foreign direct and portfolio investments by international firms and thus insulated their economies from disruptive external influences. Although this system produced liabilities disproportionate to their assets in the larger enterprises such as the South Korean *chaebol*, the system worked very effectively and was stable as long as local governments controlled domestic financial markets and the capital account, a situation that changed dramatically in the 1990s and was a significant factor in the post-1997 East Asian financial crisis. Development of these economies was also supported by a number of sociological and political factors, such as a hard-working labor force and only moderate levels of inequality.

In addition to these domestic features, a number of international factors were of benefit to the Newly Industrializing Economies (NIEs). As Cold War allies of the United States, they received special

[23] Peter Evans, *Embedded Autonomy: States and Industrial Transformation* (Princeton: Princeton University Press, 1995).

treatment in American economic and other policies. National security concerns motivated Taiwan and South Korea, in particular, to place a high priority on rapid economic development. Moreover, as some writers have pointed out, Japanese imperialism had left a legacy of physical infrastructure, an educated population, and effective institutions that favored economic development. Another very important factor was that these economies were able to pursue an export-led growth strategy because of the global free-trade environment.

Despite the importance of East Asia's unique domestic and international circumstances, governments in other parts of the world have looked to this Asian experience for guidance and have sought to incorporate key components of that developmental model into their own strategies. Although many developing economies have been strongly influenced by the neoliberal agenda of export-led growth and structural reforms and have made important market-conforming reforms, many also have tended to be very pragmatic and have not been prepared to adopt completely the neoliberal emphasis on open markets and noninterference in the economy by the state. Also, they continue to be wary of what Stephan Haggard calls "deep integration" in the global economy.[24] As a consequence, industrializing economies and even most developed countries tend to pursue strategies of selective opening to the world economy, in which the state mediates between domestic and international markets and thereby attempts to guide the economy so as to promote the nation's economic and political interests. For example, although Brazil has given up its futile effort to create its own computer industry, it has continued to use protectionist devices to promote the development of a Brazilian automobile industry.

For Latin America and other industrializing countries, the ultimate attractiveness of the theory of the developmental state is that it appears to be the appropriate means for combining economic development with political independence.[25] Economic development and industrialization have never been considered ends in themselves. The ultimate goal of developing economies has always been to achieve economic autonomy and political independence. In a world of highly concentrated market power, states desire to control their national economies as much as possible and do not want their position in the

---

[24] Stephan Haggard, *Developing Nations and the Politics of Global Integration* (Washington, D.C.: Brookings Institution, 1995).

[25] I am indebted to Peter Kingstone of the University of Vermont for his assistance in my understanding of these matters. A relevant interpretation is Luiz Carlos Bresser Pereira, *Economic Crisis and State Reform in Brazil: Toward a New Interpretation of Latin America* (Boulder, Colo.: Lynne Rienner, 1996).

international division of labor to be determined solely by the free play of market forces.

Despite the strong support in many LDCs for the theory of the developmental state, most neoclassical economists reject it. Paul Krugman, writing in the *Foreign Affairs* journal (1994), attacked the idea that East Asian governments had succeeded because government policies had substantially raised the productivity levels of their economies.[26] Krugman argued that these societies were successful primarily because of their rapid accumulation of capital and labor, the basic factors of production. He further argued that the development experience of these countries supported the neoclassical growth model; there was no "miracle." While there had been a one-time leap forward, future growth would require increased emphasis on innovation and productivity growth, except in China. Whether or not Krugman's critique is correct, these societies should at least be credited for effective mobilization of their human and material resources.

THE EAST ASIAN MIRACLE PROJECT

The developmental state interpretation of East Asia's economic success could have remained an academic dissent from the Washington Consensus; however, the Japanese government's agreement with the theory's basic assumption about the important role of the state in economic development gave prominence to the theory.[27] In the 1980s,

[26] Paul R. Krugman, "The Myth of Asia's Miracle," *Foreign Affairs* 73, no. 6 (November/December 1994): 62–78. The emphasis on factor accumulation rather than technological progress was first set forth by Alwyn Young in the *1992 NBER Macroeconomic Annual*. Krugman, drawing upon Young's finding, downplayed the East Asian "miracle." The success of East Asia, he argued, was attributable mainly to capital investment and high population growth rather than to technological innovation and productivity growth. This argument is extended in Alwyn Young, "The Tyranny of Numbers: Confronting the Statistical Realities of the East Asian Growth Experience," *Quarterly Journal of Economics* 110 (August 1995): 641–80. Other economists have given support to the important role of technological progress in the "miracle." This work is discussed in Robert J. Barro, "The East Asian Tigers Have Plenty to Roar About," *Business Week*, 27 April 1998, 24. A report by the Paris-based Organization for Economic Development supports the Krugman-Young position that these economies suffered from serious weaknesses in technological development, skilled workers, and other technology-related matters. Organization for Economic Development, *Asia and the Global Crisis: The Industrial Dimension* (Paris: Organization for Economic Development, 1999). And thus the argument continues.

[27] The Japanese criticism of the Washington Consensus is set forth in The Overseas Economic Cooperation Fund, *Issues Related to the World Bank's Approach to Structural Adjustment: Proposal from a Major Partner* (October 1991), OECF Occasional Paper No. 1 (unpublished).

321

the World Bank (WB), having subscribed to the Washington Consensus, rejected what the Japanese believed to be their own superior model of economic development based on the central role of the state in the economy. The Japanese had been especially irked by the WB's *World Development Report 1991*, which praised the neoliberal position and had little good to say about the Japanese model.[28] As John Page, a high World Bank official, had told a Princeton University audience, the Japanese continued to sign the checks, but they felt that the World Bank did not appreciate the reasons for Japan's own outstanding economic success. Japan wanted the bank to pay greater attention to the distinctive features of the East Asian economies. It also wanted greater emphasis in World Bank policy on the important and necessary role of the state in economic development rather than a nearly exclusive emphasis on macroeconomic issues and structural adjustment. Therefore, the Japanese insisted that the World Bank carry out an empirical study to determine the specific reasons for the economic success of the East Asian economies before deciding on policy advice for other developing countries. This Japanese demand generated what became known as the East Asian Miracle Project.

The East Asian Miracle Project was intended not only to meet Japanese concerns but also to review the World Bank's policies toward less developed countries and to evaluate alternative approaches to economic development. John Page, director of the Project, labeled one possible approach "fundamentalism"; that is, the Solow or neoclassical theory of economic growth, which attributes economic growth primarily to "getting the prices right" and to accumulation of the basic factors of production.[29] The alternative approach, pejoratively labeled "mystical" by Page, was based on the theory of endogenous growth set forth by Paul Romer and other economists. This "new growth theory" implied that state interventionism could accelerate the process of economic growth and that, through industrial and other policies, the state could expedite technological innovation and productivity growth. The Project was intended to determine once and for all whether economic growth is better explained by factor accumulation, and thus accords with neoclassical theory and World Bank orthodoxy, or by technological advance and productivity growth, which would be in accord with endogenous growth theory and the idea of the "developmental state."

[28] World Bank, *The Challenge of Development: World Development Report 1991* (Washington, D.C.: World Bank, 1991).

[29] As the reader will recall, according to this theory technological change and productivity growth are exogenous and the role of the state in economic growth is negligible.

The Project concentrated on the East Asian NIEs and their unique development experience. Economic growth in these economies had been rapid and persistent; moreover, the benefits of economic development had been broadly distributed throughout the societies. The study looked for answers to particular questions: What did the process of economic development actually look like in these economies? What, if anything, did the industrial and other economic policies of various governments contribute to the process of economic growth? And, was the experience of the NIEs in any way transferrable to the great majority of less developed countries that were falling farther behind rather than converging as economic theory predicted? Answers to these questions would greatly facilitate World Bank decision-making regarding the economic policies it should pursue in promoting development. Unfortunately, the study and its report did not resolve the issue, at least not to the satisfaction of proponents of alternative explanations of East Asian economic development.

Report on the Project

The *World Development Report*'s main finding was that there had been no East Asian miracle. It concluded, instead, that the outstanding success of the East Asian NIEs was due to the fact that these economies had pursued market-conforming economic policies and had fostered such economic fundamentals as high rates of savings/investment, education, and prudent macroeconomic policy.[30] These economies were successful because they conformed to the Solow model of economic growth based on factor accumulation. Neither state intervention, technological progress, nor the theory of endogenous growth, the Report concluded, had much to do with the rapid industrialization of these economies. The Report included the following specific conclusions:

(1) The East Asian economies followed prudent macroeconomic policies that kept government deficits down or even reduced accumulated deficits, kept inflation low, and held foreign debt to modest levels. Pursuing market-conforming economic policies and minimizing price distortions, they got prices right by allowing domestic prices to fall into line with international prices, thereby encouraging industries with a natural comparative advantage to flourish.

[30] World Bank, *The East Asian Miracle: Economic Growth and Public Policy* (New York: Oxford University Press, 1993).

(2) They maintained higher levels of savings and investment and had harder working and more skilled workers than did other LDCs. For example, 7 to 10 percent of Gross Domestic Product (GDP) went into investment; this high rate of investment greatly facilitated rapid capital accumulation.

(3) The export push or export-led growth strategy of these economies was another reason for their success. Focus on foreign markets promoted economic efficiency by keeping domestic prices closely in line with international prices and also accelerated introduction of foreign technologies; this then facilitated increased productivity.

The Report was very critical of the "mystics," the theory of endogenous growth, and the idea of the developmental state. Although it acknowledged that industrial policy and other forms of state intervention might indeed have assisted the process of economic development, its message was quite negative about the efficacy of state intervention. The Report reached the following conclusions about the developmental state:

(1) Industrial policies to promote particular sectors, to determine the structure of the economy, and thereby to accelerate development and productivity growth failed to explain the region's rapid growth. State intervention was ineffective at best and counter-productive at worst. The major source of economic growth was capital accumulation, which accounted for 60 to 70 percent of the growth, whereas productivity growth—technological input—accounted for only about 30 percent of economic growth.

(2) Even without public-sector intervention, market forces by themselves would have brought about the changes in industrial structure that were encouraged by governments.

(3) Government controls of financial markets, the Report did point out, had lowered the cost of capital and directed credit to favored sectors. In light of the crisis of 1997, it is ironic that the Report had praised governments' interventions in financial markets.

The *World Development Report*, based on such findings, described the theory or model of economic growth it used to explain East Asian economic success as functionalist and concluded that a developing country would be successful if it carried out specific mutually reinforcing functions. The country had to find a way to rapidly accumulate such assets as human capital and capital investments. It had to allocate resources efficiently. And the country also had to achieve rapid productivity growth by catching up technologically with advanced countries. Although the Report gave some credit to effective state intervention in the economy, this was played down due to concern that LDCs with less competent and/or more corrupt governments might attempt to use the Report to defend undesirable interventionist policies. Ironically, this project that began as an attempt by the Japanese to support their heterodox concept of an Asian model of economic development had been transformed into a defense of neoliberal orthodoxy and was hailed as a decisive vindication of neoliberal emphasis on the central role of the market in economic development.

Criticisms of the Report

Release of the *World Development Report 1991* precipitated debate between its supporters and its critics.[31] Although some neoclassical economists believed that the Report had erred in giving even minimal credit to East Asian governments for promoting rapid economic development, the most severe critics were proponents of the developmental state who fiercely denounced it as blatantly ideological, representative of the laissez-faire position of the United States and the interests of private capital, and as an effort to assuage growing Western fears of competition from the rapidly industrializing countries of East Asia. The following criticisms of the Report are especially noteworthy.

The Report's emphasis on fundamentals suggests that economic growth is a fairly straightforward process of factor accumulation through private domestic investment, education, and exports. Such a view is contradicted by the emphasis in the new-growth models on the importance in the developmental process of imperfect information, increasing returns, multiple equilibria, path dependence, self-reinforcing mechanisms, historical lock-ins, and other dynamic properties. Critics argue strongly that growth processes are so complex that there can be no single explanation and that therefore the Report's considerable emphasis on factor accumulation was inappropriate.

Furthermore, the Report's assumption that one can disentangle macro basics or fundamentals—investment, education, exports—

---

[31] Excellent evaluations of the Report are Albert Fishlow, Catherine Gwin, Stephan Haggard, Dani Rodrik, and Robert Wade, *Miracle or Design? Lessons from the East Asian Experience*, Policy Essay no. 11 (Washington, D.C.: Overseas Development Council, 1994); and Robert Wade, "Japan, the World Bank, and the Art of Paradigm Maintenance: The East Asian Miracle in Political Perspective," *New Left Review* 217 (May/June 1996): 3–36.

from their micro foundations, or supporting sociopolitical institutions, is deeply flawed. Critics charge that fundamentals and institutions cannot be separated from one another; a high savings rate does not just happen but is the result of government policies and financial institutions. When one factors in domestic policies and institutions, the growth process becomes as complex as the new growth models suggest.

The authors of the Report deliberately played down their own findings regarding the important role of the state and of industrial policies in expediting rapid industrialization, and they also neglected the crucial importance of public financial institutions in mobilizing savings, evaluating projects, managing risk, monitoring managers, and facilitating transactions. For example, although the Report acknowledged that the most successful interventions by the state were the generous subsidies provided for manufactured exports, critics of the Report charge that this important point was not accorded appropriate weight in the overall assessment of industrial policy. In fact, many of the "market-friendly" policies praised by the Report, such as export contests, are actually examples of successful industrial policy.[32] According to Report critics, these contests proved a very effective method for the state to "pick winners" and thus to accelerate economic development.

Moral of the Tale

A close reading of the *World Development Report 1991* brings to mind the sage advice to literary critics set forth by D. H. Lawrence in his *Studies in Classic American Literature* (1964).[33] The critic, Lawrence admonished, should always contrast the author's proclaimed moral with the moral of the tale itself, as derived from a close reading of what the author had actually written. The proclaimed moral of the Report is that state interventionism did not work; however, this moral is contradicted over and over again as the Report describes the successful policies actually followed by East Asian gov-

---

[32] Under the terms of these contests, the government set forth certain conditions under which private firms competed for a valuable asset controlled by the government, such as access to easy credit or foreign exchange. The contest was organized so that the companies most likely to make successful use of the resource would win. Thus, an important criterion of success was export penetration of foreign markets. The state, it should be added, also protected these sectors from imports and foreign direct investment.

[33] D. H. Lawrence, *Studies in Classic American Literature* (New York: Viking, 1964).

ernments. The Report's own assessment of the results strongly suggests that state intervention and industrial policy were indeed vital factors in the economic success of the East Asian economies. And there was a particularly excellent example of this in South Korea's export contests.

However, the most basic weakness of the Report is its assumption that one can disentangle economic fundamentals—investment, education, exports—from government development strategies and the overall society in which an economy is embedded. The Report assumes that markets already exist and that economic development takes place in an economic and social vacuum. This approach totally neglects the national system of political economy—ideology, public institutions, and private business practices—that nurtures, facilitates, or frustrates the efficacy of markets. Although there is no single East Asian model, the countries' economic and political institutions have set the East Asian economies apart and produced their economic fundamentals. Would or could the economic fundamentals in East Asia have been put into place if there had been no developmental state or certain sociopolitical institutions? That is unlikely! The economic fundamentals and the developmental state are closely interrelated. Recognizing that the state and the fundamentals are integrated with one another and that economic fundamentals are anchored in their institutional context really supports the new growth theory. It is clear that understanding economic development requires greater knowledge of a society's economic and political system than the Report indicates. Although the fundamentals provide the sufficient causes of successful economic development, a well-functioning state is the necessary cause; without an effective state, the fundamentals would not even exist.

The Report erred by separating national economic policies from the fundamentals of these economies. In these societies, the state played a crucial role in accumulation of the factors emphasized by neoclassical economists. The high savings rate, the skilled and disciplined workforce, and large investments in education were all promoted by the state and did not just happen in response to the invisible hand of the market. Moreover, the Report relies excessively on Solow-type capital accumulation and ignores the importance of technological innovation and productivity growth. Despite the argument put forth by some prominent economists, the rapid and successful industrialization of these economies was due to both factor accumulation and technological progress. And both capital accumulation and productivity gains, at least indirectly, resulted from effective government policies.

This interpretation of the important part played by the developmental state in the East Asian Miracle Project is supported in part by Paul Krugman's qualified vindication of the insights of early postwar development economics. "High development theory," Krugman points out in *Development, Geography, and Economic Theory* (1995), was essentially correct in its emphasis on "strategic complementarity" with respect to investment and the problem of coordination.[34] Early development economists recognized the need for coordinated investment to assure individual firms that other firms would make complementary or supportive investments. The less developed countries, economic development theorists believed, are at a decided disadvantage in their attempts to develop in the world of the strong. How could these impoverished nations possibly develop industries capable of competing in world markets against such strongly established firms as Mitsubishi and General Motors!

Krugman argues that economies of scale and imperfect competition were missing from development theory and that without these two central ideas, the theory and policies for economic development could not be sustained. Development theorists did recognize the need for economies of scale at the plant level to give the less developed economy the comparative advantage it needed for economic development and international competitiveness. However, these theorists ignored the importance of scale economies and of imperfect competition at the national level.[35] Development requires promoting strategic complementarity through investment decisions, supporting domestic firms until they achieve scale economies in their production, and breaking the vicious cycle of poverty in which the LDCs have been trapped. These tasks in turn require the guiding hand of a strong state. Economic development cannot be left to the market alone. The state must play the key role in starting and managing the process of economic development. Solow himself has written that neoclassical growth theory tells us what determines the rate of economic growth, but Solow does not tell us what gets growth started in the first place.[36]

---

[34] Paul R. Krugman, *Development, Geography, and Economic Theory* (Cambridge: MIT Press, 1995).

[35] Economists identify two types of economies of scale: internal and external. The former refers to the expansion of production by an individual firm and the resulting reduction of production costs. The latter refers to expansion of an industry that makes possible greater specialization and other benefits that reduce the costs of the whole industry. David W. Pearce, ed., *The MIT Dictionary of Modern Economics*, 4th ed. (Cambridge: MIT Press, 1992), 12.

[36] Quoted in *IMF Survey*, 16, December 1991, 378.

A few comments are in order about a highly controversial issue in economic development. The initial success of the East Asian economies raised the important but unresolved issue of the relationship between development and democracy. Successive American administrations, following Milton Friedman although not necessarily knowingly, have believed that development and democracy proceed hand in hand.[37] During East Asia's miracle period, conservatives such as Nobel Laureate Gary Becker attributed the outstanding success of the East Asian economies to their "democratic" regimes; subsequently, conservatives blamed the problems following the 1997 financial crisis on the "authoritarian" nature of these political regimes. From the other side of the intellectual/political spectrum, Laureate Amartya Sen also argued that democracy and development complement, or at least should complement, one another.[38] Other scholars are not convinced that there actually is a close connection between democracy and development. Robert Barro believes that the relationship of democracy and development is ambiguous, and political scientist Atul Kohli, after a careful review of the literature, finds the connection equally elusive.[39] A United Nations report released in April 2000 concludes that successful economic development requires "good" government, a quality scarce in too many LDCs.[40]

THE EAST ASIAN FINANCIAL/ECONOMIC CRISIS

In the summer of 1997, the East Asian economies suffered a severe blow when a serious financial crisis and subsequently a much more general economic crisis brought the East Asian miracle to an abrupt halt. By the summer of 2000, the stricken nations had rapidly recovered from the crisis and its consequences. Nevertheless, it will take many years for the full social and political effects of this economic

[37] Alberto Alesina and Roberto Peroti, "The Political Economy of Growth: A Critical Survey of the Recent Literature," *World Bank Economic Review* 8, no. 3 (1994): 351—71.

[38] Amartya Sen, *Development as Freedom* (New York: Alfred A. Knopf, 1999).

[39] Robert J. Barro, *Getting It Right: Markets and Choices in a Free Society* (Cambridge: MIT Press,1997), 3; and Atul Kohli, "Democracy Amid Economic Orthodoxy: Trends in Developing Countries," *Third World Quarterly* 14, no. 4 (1993): 671–89.

[40] United Nations Development Program, *Overcoming Human Poverty: UNDP Poverty Report 2000.* Included in the Report's definition of good government were free elections, accountable and noncorrupt officials, and ambitious national programs to alleviate poverty. For LDC governments that tend to blame the rich countries for their economic difficulties, the Report was not well received. *New York Times,* 5 April 2000, A11.

329

disaster to be fully understood. Despite the inconclusive nature of this situation, there has been an acrimonious debate over the explanation and meaning of the crisis. The devastating setback of these miracle economies was immediately seized by many Western economists, public officials, and commentators as a convincing indictment of the developmental state; it is clear, they proclaimed, that the East Asian economies should adopt the neoclassical development model based on free markets and minimal state intervention in the economy. Many defenders of the East Asian developmental state model charged, in turn, that these economies were hapless victims of international financial interests and the reckless policies of the Clinton Administration. They contended that the developmental state model remains the most appropriate model for successful economic development.

According to the prominent Western "crony capitalism" interpretation, the East Asian developmental state contained the seeds of its own destruction. Those characteristics of the Asian model of economic development that have been credited with the extraordinary success of these economies and their rapid industrialization were alleged to be the very ones that led to the financial crisis and to subsequent economic disaster. Critics, who have included high officials in the IMF and the American Treasury, blamed the following "flawed" components of crony capitalism: (1) the intimate ties among local politicians, banks, and industry; (2) bank rather than stock market financing of economic development; and (3) nontransparent (or secret) financial arrangements involving government-favored businesses and banks. This government-manipulated system encouraged questionable overinvestment, especially in particular economic sectors, by appearing to guarantee investors, at least implicitly, that their investments were not at risk. In this way, the developmental state created moral hazard that ultimately led to the crisis.

Proponents of the developmental state reject the above analysis and instead blame the crisis on the pernicious behavior of international financial markets. As had happened many times before, investors became caught up in a frenzy of investment in these "miracle economies." The excitement surrounding the possibility of "easy money" caused investors to throw caution to the winds and ignore such obvious signs of impending trouble as the large number of short-term liabilities that had been assumed by East Asian borrowers. The huge investments in the region, well above rational profit expectations, were driven by the irrational euphoria of international investors. In addition, the premature liberalization of financial markets and capital accounts (freedom of capital movements) in these countries (for which the United States bears a large responsibility) must be assigned much of the blame. Thus, the crisis was due to the irrational functioning of international financial markets along with certain irresponsible policies of the U.S. Treasury.

And, thus, the controversy over the developmental state continues.

The Future of the Developmental State

It is obviously too early to reach final conclusions regarding the future of the East Asian developmental state and the proper role for the state in the process of economic development.[41] Yet there is strong evidence to support the idea that states must be very involved in economic development. It is worth noting that several months prior to the crisis, the World Bank had devoted its annual *World Development Report 1997* to the crucially important issue of the political prerequisites of successful economic development.[42] In this report, titled *The State in a Changing World,* the World Bank declared that economic development is dependent on a society's getting its *political* as well as its *economic* fundamentals "right." Without the former, such characteristics of the latter as openness to trade and sound macroeconomic policies cannot work because social norms, institutions, and customs determine how economic inputs will be used and whether success will in fact be forthcoming.[43]

The Report rejected the implicit logic of the "retreat-of-the-state" doctrine that the minimal state is the optimal state; a minimal state, the Report pointed out, can do no harm, but a weak state can do no good either. Neither state-dominated nor stateless development constitute the means to successful economic development. Although the Report refused to set forth "a single recipe for state reforms worldwide," it did provide a two-part strategy to forge an effective state capable of supporting rather than distorting economic development: (1) the state must match its activities with its capabilities and not attempt to do too much; and (2) improvement of the state's effec-

---

[41] Economists tried to assess these matters in the symposium, "The State and Economic Development," *Journal of Economic Perspectives* 4, no. 3 (summer 1990).

[42] World Bank, *World Development Report 1997: The State in a Changing World* (Washington, D.C.: World Bank, 1997).

[43] As Dani Rodrik has argued, contrary to the impression given by some economists, trade by itself will not lead to economic development. Dani Rodrik, *The New Global Economy and Developing Countries: Making Openness Work* (Washington, D.C.: Overseas Development Council, 1999).

331

tiveness requires vigorous public institutions and includes "restraints to check corrupt behavior" by public officials.[44]

In the same report, the World Bank recognized that economic development entails much more than solution of technical economic problems and is, at its core, a social and political problem. In its early years, the World Bank had followed the prescriptions of economists that economic development results when crucial economic and technical obstacles have been overcome. During the 1980s, under the reign of neoliberalism and the Washington Consensus, the doctrine of structural adjustment assumed that economic reforms and elimination of state interventionism would release economic forces that would speed development. The Bank and its economists have since learned to appreciate that more than "economic fundamentals" are necessary to achieve economic development.

The World Development Report 1997 returned to a truth first set forth in 1952 by Moses Abramowitz, a pioneer in the study of economic growth.[45] The fundamental requirement for economic development, Abramowitz wrote, was "social capacity." Economic development is not a technical economic problem involving factor accumulation and getting the "fundamentals right"; it is a social process that cannot be completed unless the state creates economic institutions, fosters social behavior, and pursues policies favorable to economic development. The then-new formal modeling of economic growth, Abramowitz pointed out, deals with the immediate source of economic growth and not with the social and other factors behind the immediate factors. His emphasis on the social and political aspects of economic development suggested that there was no single best way for a society to foster economic development.

At the turn of the century, efforts to understand the task of economic development again emphasized the need for a national development strategy.[46] Official thinking about economic development has,

---

[44] World Bank, World Development Report 1997: The State in a Changing World. A valuable history of the central role of states in economic development is Linda Weiss and John M. Hobson, States and Economic Development: A Comparative Historical Analysis (London: Polity Press, 1995).

[45] Abramovitz first set forth his notion of social capacity in Thinking About Growth and Other Essays on Economic Growth (Cambridge: Cambridge University Press, 1989); a restatement of his position is "Following and Leading," in Horst Hanusch, ed., Evolutionary Economics: Applications of Schumpeter's Ideas (New York: Cambridge University Press, 1988), 339.

[46] Dani Rodrik in his book, The New Global Economy and Developing Countries, argues that a country needs a strategy for domestic investment and a sound framework for resolving political conflict. Also, see Rodrik, "Getting Interventions Right: How South Korea and Taiwan Grew Rich," Economic Policy (April 1995): 55–107.

in fact, passed through several distinct stages. In the 1960s, the World Bank regarded economic development as a matter of solving a number of discrete technical problems regarding efficient use of resources and capital transfers. In the 1970s and early 1980s, emphasis was on trade liberalization and elimination of market dislocations caused by government intervention (structural adjustment). Later in the 1980s, the focus shifted to macroeconomic adjustment intended to eliminate inflation and macroeconomic instability (the Washington Consensus). In the 1990s, the World Bank and many experts began to appreciate that development requires transformation of the society. Joseph Stiglitz, an economist's economist, is purported to have conceded at a meeting that economists are beginning to understand that development is complex and that there is more to development than trade liberalization and macroeconomic adjustment. Similar lessons are applicable to the problems facing transitional economies.

Transitional Economies

The transition of the former command or communist economies of China, the Soviet bloc, and elsewhere to democratic, market-based societies is one of the most important issues of the post–Cold War era. I use the term "transition" advisedly. As Stephen Holmes has pointed out, transition suggests that these economies are on a known and predictable trajectory from communism to democratic capitalism.[47] The truth is that no one really knows what economic, political, and other factors led to the overthrow of communism, and even less is known about the forces at work in these "postcommunist societies" or about the direction in which economic and political forces are propelling them. Theories and speculations of various kinds abound as scholars, intellectuals, and public officials attempt to provide an overall explanation of this extraordinary and historically unprecedented situation. Yet, as Holmes suggests, no guidelines can help us to determine where these unfortunate postcommunist societies are heading: democracy, fascism, or even a return to communism. Nevertheless, despite its misleading implications, I shall follow convention and use the term "transitional societies."

The mere size of the transition problem is overwhelming. The magnitude and diversity of the swath of countries from the Baltic to the Balkans and from Eastern Europe across the steppes of central Asia to the Pacific Ocean defy comprehension. The twenty-seven or more

[47] Stephen Holmes, "Cultural Legacies or State Collapse? Probing the Postcommunist Dilemma," in Michael Mandelbaum, ed., *Postcommunism: Four Perspectives* (New York: Council on Foreign Relations, 1996), 22–76.

countries involved (excluding China) contain more than 400 million people. Many of these countries are mired in economic and political chaos with declining economies and corrupt governments. The end of communism has taken many different forms, and each different form strongly influences the path of the transition. Also, consideration of the transition issue is greatly compounded by the fact that individual countries are in very different economic and political situations. At one end of the spectrum is Russia, which has sought to create simultaneously both a democratic and a market economy. At the other end is China, where an effort is being made to combine a highly authoritarian political regime with a market-type economy. In between these extremes are numerous unfortunate countries with a host of social, economic, and political problems.

There is no historical experience on which one can draw for insights, nor are there economic, political, or other social theories on which one may rely for guidance, and economics has failed miserably as a guide. The transition problem is novel in the sense that the world has never before experienced the transition from one type of highly industrialized economy to a different type of highly industrialized economy. Although the rise of capitalism in the modern period provides some lessons, such as the need for an entrepreneurial class and a nonoppressive state, the implications of these lessons for a developed economy in transition are not clear. The former communist countries must first tear down corrupt and inefficient structures before they can begin to build new, effective, and publicly responsible economic and political institutions. Therefore, this discussion of the transitional economies must be sketchy as well as tentative.

Transition Theories

Following the collapse of communism, every formerly communist country in East Europe, including Russia, suffered severe recession, deindustrialization, and economic chaos; by one estimate, recession reduced by one-quarter the national product of Eastern Europe.[48] These economic troubles set back reform and, in some cases, resulted in a retrenchment of the reform effort. More generally, recession and its aftermath had a profound negative impact. Reform has been recognized as much more complicated and difficult than most econo-

---

[48] Kazimierz Z. Poznanski, "The Post-Communist Transition as an Institutional Disintegration: Explaining the Regional Economic Recession" (unpublished and undated); Janos Kornai, "Transformational Recession: Main Causes," *Journal of Comparative Economics* 19, no. 1 (August 1994), 39–63.

mists, public officials, and others had anticipated.[49] Scholars and others have set forth different explanations of what went wrong. One explanation is based on the doctrine of neoliberalism, another is the theory of cultural legacy, and yet another emphasizes the crisis of governance. Although each of these theories provides insights into the nature of postcommunist societies, the third is the most compelling explanation.

The neoliberal convergence explanation is strongly influenced by the neoliberal ideas and perspective on structural adjustment and includes a minimal role for the state in the economy and heavy reliance on the market.[50] According to this position, the postcommunist recession was an inevitable consequence of the transition from a command to a free market economy. In a communist-type economy, a number of serious hidden problems exist that only become known following the collapse of communism. For example, a major aspect of the transition problem is "unwanted production." Under a planned economy, firms produce a large number of goods that consumers are not interested in buying. The shift from a seller-oriented economy to a buyer-oriented, or market, economy takes time, and not enough time has yet elapsed to solve the resultant problems. For example, it takes time to create the type of middle class essential to the functioning of a market-type economy. It is the nature of reforms, this position argues, that matters get worse before they get better.

According to the cultural legacy explanation, the bad habits and mentalities of the past change slowly. Communism created passive and dependent peoples. Communist culture molded societies characterized by duplicity, disinformation, extreme self-interest, reliance on personal connections, and avoidance of any responsibility for one's actions. In addition, the triumph of communism suppressed issues, traditions, and problems that resurfaced when communism disappeared and that have made the transition process more difficult. Among these vestiges from the past, the revival of nationalism and ethnic conflict has proved particularly important. The collapse of Yugoslavia into internecine war exemplifies dramatically just how extreme the possible problems can be.

The most valuable explanation for the severe problems of the post-

---

[49] Joseph Stiglitz, "Quis Custodiet Ipsos Custodes?" *Challenge* 42, no. 6 (November/December 1999): 26–67.

[50] A powerful critique of this position is in Alice H. Amsden, Jacek Kochanowicz, and Lance Taylor, *The Market Meets Its Match: Restructuring the Economies of Eastern Europe* (Cambridge: Harvard University Press, 1994).

communist countries is the crisis-of-governance explanation.[51] For a number of reasons, the political elites of Eastern Europe engineered the collapse of the state as rapidly as possible and before society was ready for such drastic change. There had been uncritical acceptance of the neoliberal doctrine of the minimal state, and the important functions of the state in democratic market-oriented societies were not really understood. Another reason for abandoning the state as quickly as possible was the intense fear of a communist resurgence; elimination of the state bureaucratic apparatus would make a return to power by the communists much more difficult. Another cause of the collapse of the state was the extraordinarily rapacious and corrupt behavior of public officials. These officials had an interest in elimination of the state, and through one means or another they and their allies, including criminal elements in Russia, grabbed state assets for self-enrichment. Political elites in most postcommunist societies forsook the commonweal for short-term private advantage.

The Transition Record

Application of the three transition explanations to the experience of postcommunist society supports the crisis of governability or collapse-of-the-state explanation. In general terms, the transition problem involves implementation of several complex and difficult tasks. New public institutions must be established and old institutional structures, reformed or eliminated, while rules and regulations required for a market-type economy must be established. Privatization of state-owned economic sectors and change of ownership of the means of production from public to private owners must be accomplished. The inefficient state-managed economic structure must be liquidated, and privately owned firms that can adapt to a market-type economy must be installed. Marketization must also be implemented; the command or plan system of communism must be replaced by the price mechanism, in which economic decisions and the direction of the economy are determined by the response of individuals and firms to changes in relative prices. Beyond these economic reforms is the far more demanding challenge of creating a new civic culture of public virtue as well as a national sense of social responsibility. Without such a moral or psychological change in the sentiments of the people,

---

[51] See Holmes, "Cultural Legacies or State Collapse?", p. 50. Holmes's position is supported by Andrei Shleifer and Daniel Treisman, *Without a Map: Political Reform in Russia* (Cambridge: MIT Press, 2000).

the goal of a successful transition to a democratic capitalist system will never be achieved.

Institutional Reform. The experience of institutional reform has differed greatly across Eastern Europe. At one extreme is Poland, which has moved slowly but has implemented a number of important reforms; at the other is Bulgaria, which has made few efforts to transform its economy. However, the task of institutional reform everywhere has been strongly influenced by neoliberalism and its emphasis on the market. It is not excessive to state that the guiding idea of transition was that private enterprises were considered to be key agents of economic and political change in Eastern Europe and other former communist countries. Institutional transformation was believed to entail the simple substitution of the market for the state. The market in turn would lead to creation of impersonal public institutions and a civic culture required for the proper functioning of a market economy.

The collapse-of-the-state position, however, argues that the reformers eliminated a state apparatus that was necessary for managing the economy and did not replace it with public and private institutions required for an effective market-managed economy. The greater the reform or "state withdrawal" (e.g., in Russia and East Germany), the greater the depth of the postcommunist crisis. According to this position, it was essential that the state manage the transition from communism and make a market economy work. An effective and accountable state must elicit voluntary cooperation from its citizenry if it is to solve collective problems. It must also rebuild the infrastructure of the society laid waste by communism: education, the judicial system, and institutions concerned with energy, banking, health, and other necessities. State policy must establish the rules governing the market economy and guaranteeing private property rights; policies should be fair and consistent. The neoliberal-inspired transition process produced many corrupt and ineffective states. Without an effective and responsible state, successful transition could not take place.

Privatization. The purpose of privatization in Eastern Europe was to transfer state-owned property to the private sector. For reasons that I have already discussed, selling-off of state assets was carried out as rapidly as possible and with many disastrous consequences. In a number of countries there was a rush to create an indigenous middle class that would ensure political stability and strongly resist the return of communism. However, the various types of privatization schemes, such as property vouchers and sales to workers, were abject failures or at least resulted in very serious problems.[52] In many countries, state property was "sold" to former communists, corrupt public officials, and political favorites at very low prices; privatization in Russia even spawned a powerful criminal class. Although it is too soon to make a definitive judgment on privatization, at least one can say that it failed to create the strong middle class desired by many reformers. It also constituted one of the most significant redistributions of wealth in world history.

In addition to the speed of privatization and prevalence of corruption as obstacles to successful privatization were a low level of savings and serious troubles within the banking systems. Reforms had weakened the financial position of local firms and of the banking systems; many countries suffered from a liquidity crisis, and potential investors in these countries lacked sufficient capital to purchase those businesses and factories put up for quick sale. As a consequence, foreign firms, especially German, purchased a substantial portion of the assets sold. The resulting level of foreign ownership is quite high, particularly in Poland, the Czech Republic, and Hungary; few countries have so many business enterprises and important industries in foreign hands. Kazimierz Poznanski has estimated, for example, that 70 percent of Hungarian industry and banking are foreign-owned.[53] This situation has both benefits and possible costs for the host societies. On the one hand, foreign ownership has meant a rapid inflow of needed capital, technology, and know-how. On the other, it has fostered a highly oligopolistic economic structure that could result in exploitation, and it raises the fear of being drawn into a German sphere of economic domination.

Marketization. The principal goal of transition is to change from a command to a market system based on the price mechanism. This important structural change entails "a move from a sellers' to a buyers' market" and "enforcing a hard budget constraint" through privatization and elimination of such government support mechanisms as subsidies to favored enterprises.[54] Such reforms constituted, according to the neoliberal agenda, incentives to encourage profit-maximizing market behavior by all economic actors. Incentives would lead to a

---

[52] The various methods to privatize the economy are briefly discussed in Oleh Harvylyshyn and Donal McGettigan, *Privatization in Transition Countries: Lessons of the First Decade* (Washington, D.C.: International Monetary Fund, 1999), 7–9.

[53] Poznanski, "The Post-Communist Transition."

[54] Harvylyshyn and McGettigan, *Privatization in Transition Countries*, 2.

338

shift from old to new and more efficient economic activities and to restructuring (labor rationalization, new product lines, etc.) of those firms not eliminated by the shift to a market-based system based on private enterprise. Released economic forces would then transform postcommunist economies to market-type economies.

The necessary conditions for marketization have not been fully achieved. The rules, laws, and regulations necessary to a well-func-tioning market economy have been put in place only partially. Privati-zation has been very uneven throughout the region and has been dis-torted by corrupt behavior in many instances. Many government support mechanisms are still in place, and backtracking on privatiza-tion has appeared in response to public protests. A large part of eco-nomic activity is, in fact, still in state hands. In addition, withdrawal of financial support and protection through elimination of state sub-sidies and drastic lowering of trade barriers ruined many enterprises and set back the process of marketization. The overall impact of these developments has been extraordinarily harmful. In effect, partial and uneven reform has created what Joel Hellman has called a "winner take all" politics.[55] The beneficiaries of partial reform who were able to take advantage of the absence of a competent, honest state and to profit from the spoils of privatization have become powerful oppo-nents of further economic reform. This situation in some countries has resulted in a new class structure of winners and losers that could make further reform much more difficult.

The postcommunist experience has taught that creation of an effec-tive market economy requires a state with the power to establish and enforce the rules of the market. In some countries, especially Poland and Hungary, considerable progress toward a market economy based on private enterprise and impersonal rules has been made. Too many postcommunist countries, however, have failed to create a civic cul-ture based on mutual trust and public responsibility, a culture that can support a market-type economy. It is illusory to speak of a transi-tion because it is anyone's guess where these postcommunist countries are really heading.

Conclusion

As this is written in the year 2000, the international community has not yet come to terms with the immense problems of economic devel-

[55] Joel S. Hellman,"Winner Take All:The Politics of Partial Reform in Postcommu-nist Transitions," *World Politics* 50, no. 2 (January 1998).

opment. Whether or not a development regime is a possible or appropriate solution may be moot. In an era of neoliberalism with stress on the free market, a development regime is out of the question. On the other hand, free trade and economic openness do not by themselves constitute an adequate solution to the problem of underdevelopment or to the problems of the transition economies. A compromise must be found somewhere between the two extremes of abandonment of neoliberalism and total reliance on the market. Jeffrey Sachs has made an important start in this direction with his argument that the long-term solution to LDC problems will require that the fundamental problems that they face be solved by the international community: tropical and arid agriculture must be improved (a similar point was made long ago by Arthur Lewis), science and technology must be mobilized for development purposes, and major problems of environmental degradation and public health (HIV, malaria, and other tropical diseases) must be reduced or, better, eliminated.[56] Solving such problems would benefit rich and poor alike.

[56] "Sachs on Development," *The Economist,* 14 August 1999, 17–20.

CHAPTER THIRTEEN

The Political Economy of Regional Integration

T HE MOVEMENT toward economic regionalism or regional trade
agreements (RTAs), which accelerated in the mid-1980s, produced a significant impact on the shape of the world economy.[1] This
new regionalism differed in fundamental respects from an earlier regional movement in the 1950s and 1960s; it had much greater significance for the world economy. The earlier movement, whose only
survivor is the European Union, was limited largely to trade and just
a few other areas. The new regionalism is more global in scope and
involves integration not only of trade but also of finance and foreign
direct investment. Also, the goal of the movement toward regional
integration in Western Europe became political unification as well as
creation of a single unified market. In Western Europe and elsewhere,
trade has become increasingly regionalized, and this development has
caused concern that the international economy may be moving in the
direction of regional economic blocs.

The European Single Market Act (1986) triggered the "new regionalism" and stimulated development of other similar efforts. In the
early 1980s, European reticence to join the American-initiated Uruguay Round of trade negotiations, fear in the United States that Europe was turning inward, and impatience with the slowness of the
General Agreement on Tariffs and Trade (GATT) negotiations led to
the American decision to support North American economic regional-

---

[1] The writings on economic regionalism and preferential trading arrangements have
greatly expanded in recent years. Among the numerous writings on this subject, the
following are especially noteworthy: Jagdish N. Bhagwati and Arvind Panagariya, eds.,
The Economics of Preferential Trade Agreements (Washington, D.C.: AEI Press, 1996);
Richard Gibb and Wieslaw Michalak, eds., *Continental Trading Blocs: The Growth
of Regionalism in the World Economy* (New York: John Wiley, 1994); Vincent Cable
and David Henderson, eds., *Trade Blocs? The Future of Regional Integration* (London:
Royal Institute of International Affairs, 1994); Paul De Grauwe, *The Economics of
Monetary Integration*, 2d rev. ed. (New York: Oxford University Press, 1994); Jaime
De Melo and Arvind Panagariya, eds., *New Dimensions in Regional Integration* (New
York: Cambridge University Press, 1995); Miles Kahler, *Regional Futures and Transat-
lantic Economic Relations* (New York: Council on Foreign Relations, 1995); and Jef-
frey A. Frankel, *Regional Trading Blocs in the World Economic System* (Washington,
D.C.: Institute for International Economics, 1997).

341

ization. Once launched, the slow and drawn-out Uruguay Round as well as the regional movements in Western Europe and North America undoubtedly also contributed to the spread of regional trade agreements elsewhere in the world. Many nations, fearing that the Round would never succeed or that they would be shut out of other regional arrangements, initiated regional efforts, and regional trade agreements proliferated. By the late 1990s, there were approximately 180 regional agreements, and almost all members of the World Trade Organization (with the notable exception of Japan, Hong Kong, and Korea) were included in one or more formal regional arrangements.

Previously, initiatives toward development of regional free trade areas had been followed by new rounds of multilateral trade negotiations. The United States had responded to the Treaty of Rome (1957) and the subsequent creation of the European Community by initiating multilateral trade liberalization within the GATT; the Kennedy Round (1963–1967) of trade negotiations was a response by the United States to the creation of the European Community (Common Market) and the Tokyo Round (1973–1979), a response to the first enlargement of that Community. However, the multilateral American approach to the movement toward European integration changed in the 1980s. When it became clear that the Single Market Act in the mid-1980s could create a united and possibly closed West European market, the United States followed Canada's lead and shifted its policy toward development of a regional arrangement of its own: the North American Free Trade Agreement (NAFTA).

In Pacific Asia, largely in response to European and North American regional developments, Japan intensified its own efforts to create and lead a regional economy. As more and more developing countries liberalized their economies unilaterally to achieve greater efficiency and abandoned import-substitution strategies in favor of a greater emphasis on export-led growth, they too began to perceive the advantages of regional initiatives that would promote economies of scale for their industries and provide some counterbalance to regionalization in Europe and in North America. This expanding movement toward regional integration can be characterized as a response to what political scientists call a "security dilemma" in which each regional movement attempts to enhance its own bargaining position vis-à-vis other regions.

Albert Fishlow and Stephan Haggard have made a useful distinction between market-driven and policy-driven regional integration; certainly both political and economic considerations are involved in

342

every regional movement.[2] However, the relative importance of economic and political factors differs in each. Whereas the movement toward integration of Western Europe has been motivated primarily by political considerations, the motivation for North American regionalism has been more mixed, and Pacific Asian regionalism has been principally but not entirely market-driven. Attainment of such political objectives as ending French-German rivalry and creating a political entity to increase Europe's international standing and strengthen its international bargaining position has been of vital importance in European integration. North American regionalization, on the other hand, has been primarily market-driven; establishment of the free trade area reflected the natural integration of the three North American economies (Canada, Mexico, and the United States) by market forces. However, some political motives, such as strengthening North America's position vis-à-vis Western Europe and reducing illegal Mexican migration into the United States, have also been factors. And in Pacific Asia, although market forces have been the most important factors in integration of the economies, political considerations and Japanese policies have also played significant roles.[3]

Moreover, even though economic regionalism has become a universal phenomenon, regionalism has also assumed quite diverse forms.[4] In addition to the differing mix of political and economic goals, regional arrangements vary in their institutional form. For example,

[2] Albert Fishlow and Stephan Haggard, *The United States and the Regionalization of the World Economy*, Development Centre Documents (Paris: OECD, 1992).

[3] Although the Asia Pacific Economic Cooperation (APEC) organization could be considered an example of regional integration, its achievements have been quite modest.

[4] Ali M. El-Agraa, ed., with contributions, *The Economics of the European Community* (London: Harvester Wheatsheaf, 1994), provides a useful discussion of the various types of regional integration. These arrangements include the following in order of the stage of integration: (1) *Free trade area*: Members eliminate all trade restrictions against each other's goods; an example is the North American Free Trade Agreement (NAFTA). (2) *Customs union*: Although similar to a free trade area, participating countries adopt uniform tariffs and other trade restrictions vis-à-vis countries outside the union; the most prominent example was the European Economic Community or Common Market created by the Rome Treaty (1957). (3) *Common market*: Extends a customs union to include the free movement of the factors of production (goods, services, people, capital). (4) *Economic union*: The highest form of economic integration incorporates the previous stages of integration and adds monetary and fiscal policy harmonization; the only example is the movement toward European economic integration. (5) *Political Union*: Moves beyond economic union to supranational decision-making beyond the purely economic; a political union is the ultimate goal of the movement toward European unity.

343

whereas Western Europe is attempting to create an integrated political/economic entity, has erected an external tariff, and has become highly institutionalized, Pacific Asian regionalization has no external tariff, a very low level of institutional development, and every economy in the region has retained high tariffs. North American regionalism stands somewhere between the other two. The North American Free Trade Agreement created a free trade area without an external tariff, does not have a common market, and has only a few formal institutions. The movement toward greater unity as Europe seeks to achieve both economic and political integration is the only example of what scholars call *deep* regional integration.

The diversity of regional arrangements makes broad generalizations and overarching theories or explanations of regionalism impossible. One cannot confidently assess these regional efforts or predict their effects upon the world economy. It is nonetheless desirable to present a summary and critique of the principal attempts by economists and political scientists to develop theories or explanations regarding economic and, to a lesser extent, political regionalism. In general, economists have been interested in the welfare consequences of regional arrangements for members and nonmembers, and political scientists have been more concerned with ways to explain economic and political integration. While writings thus far have provided important insights into many aspects of economic regionalism, they leave many questions unanswered.[5]

ECONOMIC THEORIES

Integration of formerly self-contained economic areas into larger economic entities has been important in modern history. The modern era has been characterized by integration of small and relatively distinct territories into larger nation-states and into national economies surrounded by trade barriers. Despite this process of economic integration, when Fritz Machlup conducted an extensive review of the economic literature in 1976, he learned that prior to 1947 economists

---

[5] It is worth noting that the subject of political fragmentation has received very little attention from scholars of political economy. One exception is Patrick Bolton and Gérard Roland, "The Breakup of Nations: A Political Economic Analysis," April 1995 (unpublished).

had written little about economic integration.[6] Such neglect is startling because of the obvious importance of the integration of national
markets to the nature and evolution of the world economy. Beginning
with the European movement toward economic integration in the
early post–World War II period, the economics profession began to
pay more attention to international integration. Yet theoretical results
have been sparse and have not significantly advanced our understanding of the actual process of economic integration or of its consequences. In fact, the subject of economic integration remains largely
empirical rather than theoretical.[7]

The principal approaches that economists have taken in their efforts to explain regional integration or free trade areas arise from
neoinstitutionalism and the new political economy. The *new institutionalism* approach assumes that international, including regional, institutions, such as those of Western Europe, are established to overcome market failures, solve coordination problems, and/or eliminate
other obstacles to economic cooperation. These institutions create incentives for states to cooperate and, through a variety of mechanisms,
to facilitate such cooperation. Although the new institutionalism provides valuable insights, it does not consider the political reasons for
regional arrangements. The *new political economy* explanation emphasizes interest group politics and the distributive consequences of
economic regionalism; it assumes that such regional trade arrangements as customs unions and free trade agreements have significant
redistributive consequences that are usually harmful to nonmembers
and create both winners and losers among the members themselves.
Indeed, economists frequently explain economic integration as resulting from efforts of domestic interests to redistribute national income
in their own favor. This approach provides important insights into
the domestic politics of economic integration but fails to explain the
costly efforts by Europeans to achieve regional integration.

[6] Fritz Machlup, ed., *Economic Integration: Worldwide, Regional, Sectoral* (London:
Macmillan, 1976), 63. Studies by economists on economic integration include Bela
Balassa, *The Theory of Economic Integration* (Homewood, Ill.: Richard D. Irwin,
1961); and Peter Robson, *The Economics of International Integration* (London: Allen
and Unwin, 1987). Two pioneering studies of economic integration are W. M. Corden,
Monetary Integration, Essays in International Finance no. 93, Princeton University,
Department of Economics, International Finance Section, April 1992 and J. E. Meade,
H. H. Liesner, and S. J. Wells, *Case Studies in European Economic Union: The Mechanics of Integration* (London: Oxford University Press, 1962).

[7] A discussion of economic theories of integration is found in Bhagwati and Panagariya, eds., *The Economics of Preferential Trade Agreements.*

345

The Marxist theory of economic and political integration is another economic approach to an explanation of integration. According to Belgian economist Ernest Mandel, economic integration in general, and the movement toward European economic and political integration in particular, are explained by the efforts of transnational capitalist classes to increase the scale of capital accumulation.[8] Over the course of modern history, the requirements of capital accumulation have driven the world toward ever larger economic and political entities. According to this point of view, technological developments and international competition are forcing the dominant European capitalist class to overthrow the narrow confines of national capitalism and forge a regional economy that will strengthen the international competitiveness of European capitalism. However, as I shall point out later, economic determinism omits certain important political and strategic motives responsible for economic integration.

Economic theories do not provide a satisfactory explanation of economic integration. This is because economic analysts generally assume that a political decision has been made to create a larger economic entity, and that economists need only analyze the welfare consequences of that decision and concern themselves with just a few aspects of the process of economic integration. Another theoretical subject of interest to economists has been the theory of an "optimum currency area" (OCA); this theory specifies the conditions necessary for establishment of a common currency within an economic region. This theory is of special relevance to the effort to achieve the European Economic and Monetary Union (EMU). There is also a small literature on the "optimum regionalization" of the world economy; and attention is given to comparison of the political and economic consequences of a world containing two regionalized economies with the consequences of a world of three or more integrated regions.

An important body of economic literature deals with the welfare consequences for nonmembers of such regional arrangements as customs unions (the European Common Market) and of free trade areas (NAFTA). The classic work on the welfare consequences of regional trade agreements is Jacob Viner's The Customs Union Issue (1950), a study stimulated by growing concerns in the United States and elsewhere about the accelerating movement toward a Western European common market.[9] Prior to Viner's analysis, the conventional wisdom

[8] Ernest Mandel, Europe versus America?: Contradictions of Imperialism (London: N.L.B., 1970).

[9] Jacob Viner, The Customs Union Issue (New York: Carnegie Endowment for International Peace, 1950).

346

of the economics profession—based on the theory of comparative advantage—had been that regional agreements were beneficial to members and nonmembers alike, and that they produced much the same consequences as did global trade liberalization. In other words, the pre-Viner position was that the economic gains to both members and nonmembers were similar to those produced by free trade and included the benefits of specialization, improved terms of trade, greater efficiency due to increased competition, and increased factor flows among members. In his study, Viner not only challenged this optimistic assumption but also analyzed customs unions' implications for nonmembers.

Viner's analysis pointed out that a common external tariff would have trade-diverting as well as trade-creating effects. The initial or static consequences of an external tariff, say, around the European Common Market, would divert trade from foreign suppliers to suppliers located within the Common Market. However, as Viner also pointed out, the long-term or dynamic effects of a common market would lead to creation of a larger and more wealthy European market that would benefit not only local firms but also the market's external trading partners. Whether the trade-diverting or the trade-creating effects of a customs union would ultimately predominate, Viner concluded, was an empirical question that could be answered only from actual experience. Likewise, the welfare consequences for nonmembers could not be determined theoretically but only by observing the specific actions and policies of the European Economic Community or other regional arrangements.

Viner's pioneering analysis has been extended and modified by subsequent research; yet his insight into the basic indeterminacy of the welfare effects of economic regionalism remains valid.[10] Indeed, Viner's conclusions have been supported by a report in 1997 from a group of international experts.[11] Although these experts could draw upon theoretical developments and actual experience accumulated subsequent to Viner's study, they, too, concluded that neither economic theory nor empirical evidence can inform us whether or not

[10] See Alfred Tovias, "A Survey of the Theory of Economic Integration," in Hans J. Michelmann and Payayotis Soldatos, eds., *European Integration: Theories and Approaches* (Lanham, Md.: University Press of America, 1994).

[11] Jaime Serra et al., *Reflections on Regionalism: Report of the Study Group on International Trade* (Washington, D.C.: Carnegie Endowment for International Peace, 1997). See also Paul J. J. Welfens, "Economic Integration Theory," in Desmond Dinan, ed., *Encyclopedia of the European Union* (Boulder, Colo.: Lynne Rienner, 1998), 153–58.

a specific regional arrangement will harm nonmembers. No general conclusions can be drawn because of the very different and specific aspects of each regional arrangement. Indeed, economists answer the question of whether regional arrangements will lead to trade diversion or trade creation with the classic answer of economists and other scholars to difficult issues: "more research is needed."

Since Viner's early work, the new trade and growth theories have strongly influenced economists' thinking about regional integration. Whereas Viner's analysis was based on the neoclassical theories of trade and economic growth that assumed perfect competition, constant returns to scale, and diminishing returns, new thinking about economic integration is based on economies of scale and other favorable consequences of integration, such as R & D spillovers within the region. This means that firms within a regional arrangement can gain competitive advantages from which firms outside the arrangement are excluded. This theory implies that countries could and probably would support regional trade barriers and trade diversion so that firms within the region would have exclusive access to technological advances, economies of scale, and other advantages. External barriers could also protect such firms from external competition and enable them to achieve economies of scale and international competitiveness as well. Regional trade barriers could enhance the bargaining position of local firms and governments in their dealings with outside firms and governments. Evidence suggests that such strategic advantages of economic regionalism have played a role—but not a determining role—in the movement toward European integration.

POLITICAL THEORIES

Political scientists have had an interest in political and economic integration for a relatively long time, but before the movement toward European unity no one attempted to formulate general theories or explanations of regional integration.[12] Political scientists have emphasized institutional solutions to the problems of war and international political instability and have focused on the idea of federalism and political integration of the world. From the early postwar period on, the thinking of those interested in integration has been influenced

---

[12] An important volume on the ideas of political scientists regarding economic and political integration is Edward D. Mansfield and Helen V. Milner, eds., *The Political Economy of Regionalism* (New York: Columbia University Press, 1997). See also Andrew Moravcsik, "Integration Theory," in Desmond Dinan, ed., *Encyclopedia of the European Union* (Boulder, Colo.: Lynne Rienner, 1998), 278–91.

by federalism, neofunctionalism, neoinstitutionalism, intergovernmentalism, and realism.

Federalism

Throughout modern history, idealists have set forth schemes to solve
the problem of war by building federalist institutions to which parties
will consciously and voluntarily surrender their political autonomy
and sovereign rights. In the twentieth century, Woodrow Wilson's
proposal for a League of Nations, and the later establishment of the
United Nations, inspired additional federalist solutions to prevent another great war. Following World War II, the World Federalist movement, whose appeal arose from its emphasis on persuasion, convert-
ing public opinion, and building of institutions, expanded. Although
the federalist idea had some influence on the movement toward European integration, it appealed most of all to those interested in the
global level.

Despite its intellectual appeal, federalism has never proved to be a
successful route to political integration, and its successes have been
achieved only under unusual political circumstances. The few examples of successful federal experiments have been motivated primarily
by national security concerns. Indeed, the two most successful federal
republics—Switzerland and the United States—were created in response to powerful external security threats. And in the United States,
full political and economic integration were attained only after the
victory of the North over the South in the Civil War. The German
federalist state resulted from conquest by one nation (Prussia) of
other German political entities. Historically, political integration of
independent political entities has resulted from military conquest or
dynastic union, and neither of these methods will necessarily lead to
creation of an integrated economy.

Functionalism and Neofunctionalism

The theory of neofunctionalism was very influential in the 1950s and
1960s. Closely associated with the writings of Ernst Haas, neofunctionalism is the most important effort by political scientists to explain
political integration in general and European political integration in
particular.[13] Drawing upon the social sciences, Haas's theory of neofunctionalism, elaborated and extended by his students and other
scholars, argued that economic, technological, and other develop-

[13] Ernst Haas, "The Challenge of Regionalism," *International Organization* 12, no.
3 (1958): 444–58.

ments during the twentieth century have driven peoples and nation-states toward peaceful economic and political integration at both the regional and global levels.

The theory of neofunctionalism had its roots in pre–World War II functionalist theory that had appeared in response to the failure of the League of Nations to maintain the peace after World War I. Collapse of the League made people aware that something more than voluntary federalism was needed to ensure world peace. The British social democrat David Mitrany took up this challenge and systematically set forth his functionalist theory as a solution to the problem of war in his highly influential monograph *A Working Peace System* and other writings.[14] According to Mitrany, modern economic, technological, and other developments made political integration of the world possible and necessary. Technocratic management of an increasingly complex and integrated global economy and social system had become imperative.

The problem of war could be solved and the war-prone system of nation-states could be escaped, Mitrany argued, through international agreements in such specific functional or technical areas as health, postal services, and communications. Even though the political system remained fragmented into jealous and feuding nation-states, such functional and technical international institutions were feasible because the world in the twentieth century had become highly integrated both economically and physically by advances in communications and transportation. As functional international institutions succeeded and promoted social and economic welfare, they would gain legitimacy and political support and would over time triumph over the nation-state.

Mitrany assumed that an economically and technologically integrated world had given rise to many complex technical problems that individual competing states could not deal with effectively. If functional problems in the areas of health and postal services were to be solved, nation-states should, in their own self-interest, establish international organizations to carry out the required activities. Then, as the new organizations proved their effectiveness in dealing with various technical problems, states would delegate more and more tasks to international institutions. As new functional arrangements were put into place, the realm of independent political action, and hence also of international conflict, would become more and more circumscribed. In time, states would learn the advantages of peaceful

---

[14] David Mitrany, *A Working Peace System* (Chicago: Quadrangle, 1966).

cooperation, and the importance of political boundaries would diminish. Political integration of the world would thus result from economic and other forms of international cooperation.

Inspired by Mitrany's insights, Ernst Haas developed what he called "neofunctionalism" and applied this theory to both international institutions and the process of European integration.[15] Drawing on literature in social science, Haas produced *The Uniting of Europe* (1957) and *Beyond the Nation-State* (1964). Like Mitrany, Haas believed that modern democratic and, especially, welfare states required rational management of the economy and centralized technocratic control. However, for Haas, Mitrany's functionalism was too unsophisticated politically and lacked a theory of how integration actually took place. Whereas Mitrany had emphasized the deliberate actions of national leaders to create international institutions, Haas's focus was on domestic interest groups and political parties promoting their own economic self-interest. He also stressed the unintended consequences of previous integration efforts, which he called "spillover"; as groups realized that integration could serve their self-interest, there would automatically be spillover from one area of integration to another. In time, the process of spillover would lead to political cooperation and a transnational political community favoring more extensive and centralized regional or international governing mechanisms.

Haas was not especially interested in the reasons for initiating integration efforts; however, once an integration effort had been launched, Haas foresaw pressures for further integration. He expected that social and economic groups would demand additional economic integration, and that that would create new political actors interested in and ready to promote further integration. Political integration would be carried out by the actions of both domestic interest groups and international civil servants or entrepreneurs. Domestic interest groups, especially in business, would pressure their home governments to create regional institutions to perform particular tasks that would promote their economic interests. International civil servants, like the staff of the European Commission, would, as they fulfilled their assigned tasks,

---

[15] Haas was also influenced by the writings of Karl Deutsch. According to Deutsch, modernization leads to increasing levels of social interaction and communication among politically separated peoples, which in turn leads to a convergence of individual and group values in the direction of more cosmopolitan norms. This development results (at least among democratic societies) in the formation of a security community in which no state poses a threat to any other. Karl W. Deutsch, "Communications Theory and Political Integration," in Philip E. Jacob and James V. Toscano, eds., *The Integration of Political Communities* (Philadelphia: Lippincott, 1964).

develop a loyalty to the international institution rather than to their home governments. As powerful domestic interests and individual states learned the utilitarian value of international organizations, and as international civil servants transferred loyalty from their own states to international organizations, the role of international institutions in managing regional and global affairs would grow. Over time, the regional or global organization would be transformed from a means into an end itself. Thus, neofunctionalist theory, like functionalist theory, believed that economic cooperation would lead to political integration at either the regional or global level.

The idea that economic and technological forces are driving the world toward greater political integration is at the core of neofunctionalism. Forces leading to economic and political integration are embedded in the modern economic system and tend to be self-reinforcing, as each stage of economic integration encourages further integration. Neofunctionalism assumes that economic and other welfare concerns have become, or at least are becoming, more important than such traditional concerns as national security and interstate rivalry. Underlying this assumption is a belief that industrialization, modernization, democracy, and similar forces have transformed behavior. The theory assumes as well that the experience of integration leads to redefinition of the national interest and eventual transfer of loyalty from the nation-state to emerging regional or global entities.

It is worth noting several ways in which neofunctionalism modified functionalism. Whereas functionalism assumed that conscious political decisions would accelerate political integration, neofunctionalist theory assumes that, once the process of economic and technical integration has been launched, unanticipated consequences, spillovers from one functional area to another, and the effects of learning will propel the process toward eventual political and economic unification. One of neofunctionalism's core propositions is that the logic of functional spillovers would push political elites inevitably from economic cooperation toward political unification. Neofunctionalism concentrates on the process of regional integration itself and, unlike economic theory, does not attempt to evaluate explicitly the economic welfare consequences of regional integration. Yet, there is an unstated assumption that economic and political integration are beneficial to members and nonmembers alike.

Neofunctionalist ideas have strongly influenced the thinking of scholars and public officials about European regional integration. For example, Western Europeans, in their concerted effort to create both a single market and a single European currency (the euro), have assumed that economic and monetary unity would eventually force further steps toward economic and political unification. However, especially following the French veto in 1967 of Britain's effort to join the European Community, it became obvious that the neofunctionalist logic of spillovers and feedbacks was not working. And in 1975 Haas repudiated his own neofunctionalist theory.[16] Few scholars have been equally honest and courageous in rejecting their own theories when faced with contrary evidence.

Neoinstitutionalism, Domestic Politics, and Intergovernmentalism

Since scholars have recognized that functionalist and neofunctionalist thinking about regional integration has proved inadequate, new approaches—neoinstitutionalism, domestic politics, and intergovernmentalism—have influenced the writings of political scientists interested in economic and political integration.[17] Neoinstitutionalism emphasizes the role of institutions in solving economic and other problems; it maintains that institutions could help ameliorate market failures and solve collective action problems in economic and political integration. The most prominent scholar in this school of thought is Robert Keohane who, along with others, has emphasized the need for international institutions to deal with market failures, reduce transaction costs, and counter other problems. Scholars argue that international institutions (or regimes) assist states to solve collective action problems, promote cooperation through facilitation of reciprocity (tit-for-tat strategies), and link various issue areas. In such ways, regional international institutions increase the incentives for states to solve their disputes and cooperate with one another. Although this position has been very influential in the development of thinking about regional institutions, it has not led to a specific theory of economic and political integration.

Political scientists have also studied the effects on economic and political integration of such factors as the pressures of domestic economic interests and the interests of political elites. Their literature,

---

[16] Ernst Haas, "The Obsolescence of Regional Integration Theory," Institute of International Studies, University of California, Berkeley, Research Series no. 25, 1975.

[17] Intergovernmentalism is discussed in Robert O. Keohane and Stanley Hoffmann, eds., *The New European Community: Decision Making and Institutional Change* (Boulder, Colo.: Westview Press, 1991). Also, Hans J. Michelmann and Panayotis J. Soldatos, eds., *European Integration: Theories and Approaches* (Lanham, Md.: University Press of America, 1994). A critique of intergovernmentalism is Geoffrey Garrett and George Tsebelis, "An Institutional Critique of Intergovernmentalism," *International Organization* 50, no. 2 (spring 1996): 269–99.

emphasizing the importance for domestic groups of the distributive consequences of integration, has noted that winners support integration and losers oppose it. It has also recognized that political leaders will be guided by the consequences of integration for their own political survival and that domestic interests and institutions may facilitate or discourage integration. Many writings produced by political scientists in this area are very similar to those of economists. Although this literature supplements explanations that focus on the international level, by the year 2000 the literature had not been developed into a coherent theory or approach to economic and political integration.

The most significant approach by political scientists to economic and political integration since neofunctionalism is intergovernmentalism or, more specifically, liberal intergovernmentalism. This approach, derived from neofunctionalism, neoinstitutionalism, and other earlier theories of political integration, shares with neofunctionalism an emphasis on economic interests as the principal driving forces of regional integration. Like neoinstitutionalism, it stresses the importance of international, that is regional, institutions as a necessary means of facilitating and securing the integration process. However, intergovernmentalism differs from earlier approaches in its concentration on the central role of national governments, on the importance of powerful domestic economic interests, and on bargaining among national governments over distributive and institutional issues.

The most ambitious effort to develop a theory of economic and political integration based on intergovernmentalism is found in Andrew Moravcsik's *The Choice for Europe* (1998)[18] which concentrates on the pivotal responses of national governments to the increasing interdependence of national economies and emphasizes the importance of international institutions in solving problems generated by increasing economic interdependence. In Moravcsik's words:

My central claim is that the broad lines of European integration since 1955 reflect three factors: patterns of commercial advantage, the relative bargaining power of important governments, and the incentives to enhance the credibility of interstate commitments. Most fundamental of these was commercial interest. European integration resulted from a series of rational choices made by national leaders who consistently pursued economic interests—primarily the commercial interests of powerful economic producers and secondarily the

[18] Andrew Moravcsik, *The Choice for Europe: Social Purpose and State Power from Messina and Maastricht* (Ithaca: Cornell University Press, 1998).

macroeconomic preferences of ruling governmental coalitions—that evolved slowly in response to structural incentives in the global economy. When such interests converged, integration advanced.[19]

Thus, private economic interests and short-term macroeconomic policy preferences are considered responsible for European integration and, as Moravcsik is proposing a general theory of regional integration, for other integration efforts as well.

Moravcsik's belief that political motives, such as French-German reconciliation and the integration of West Germany into a denationalized European political structure, have played only a minor or secondary role in European political integration constitutes a serious weakness in his argument. The statements of European leaders about the political imperative of economic and political integration make Moravcsik's disregard of the political motives quite astounding. If Moravcsik is correct that regional integration efforts around the world are due to national responses to increasing international economic interdependence, then one would expect similar movements toward political integration elsewhere. As he argues, European integration differs only in that Europe has been "touched more intensely" by global economic developments.[20]

If one accepts Moravcsik's reasoning, one would expect that North America would also be moving toward political integration. After all, the three North American economies—the United States, Canada, and Mexico—are far more closely integrated in trade, financial flows, and foreign direct investment than are the economies of Western Europe. Although intra-European trade has certainly increased greatly since World War II, trade flows among the three North American economies, especially between the United States and Canada, are still considerably larger. North American corporate linkages across national borders dwarf those among European firms; and services, finance, and manufacturing in North America are more closely integrated than are those in Western Europe. Transnational European corporate integration, in fact, is just beginning, and progress toward economic integration has led to corporate integration, rather than vice versa. European national financial markets also remain highly fragmented and separated from one another. Yet, despite the higher level of North American economic integration, there is no pressure whatsoever for political unity. Political integration is not occurring, because the North American nations have no political motive to inte-

[19] Ibid., 3.
[20] Ibid., 5.

grate with one another as the nations of Western Europe have. Surely, the geopolitical concerns of the major West European powers should be given greater attention.

Realism

Although a number of realists have written on political integration, there is no generally accepted realist theory. However, the realist approach does emphasize the importance of power, national political interests, and interstate rivalries in the integrative process. Realism regards regional integration, especially political integration like that taking place in Western Europe, as a political phenomenon pursued by states for national political and economic motives. Realism, which I have labeled state-centric realism, assumes that a successful process of economic and political integration must be championed by one or more core political entities that are willing to use their power and influence to promote the integration process. In West European integration, regional leadership has been exercised by France and Germany.

Perhaps there is no better example of the realist approach to political integration than the following passage from Viner's *The Customs Union Issue* on the unification of Germany in the mid-nineteenth century:

It is generally agreed that Prussia engineered the customs union [*Zollverein*] primarily for political reasons, in order to gain hegemony or at least influence over the lesser German states. It was largely in order to make certain that the hegemony should be Prussian and not Austrian that Prussia continually opposed Austrian entry into the Union, either openly or by pressing for a customs union tariff lower than highly protectionist Austria could stomach.[21]

The realist approach to economic regionalism also calls attention to several factors that limit peaceful economic and political integration. Joseph Grieco, for example, stresses the importance of relative gains and of distributive issues in state calculations; these inevitably make the type of long-term cooperation necessary to integration efforts very difficult to achieve.[22] States, for example, are unlikely to willingly compromise their national security for economic gains in a regional arrangement; thus far, the European Union has experienced little

[21] Jacob Viner, *The Customs Union Issue*, 98–99.
[22] For a realist discussion of regional integration, consult Joseph Grieco, "Systemic Sources of Variations in Regional Institutionalization in Western Europe, East Asia, and the Americas," in Edward D. Mansfield and Helen V. Milner, *The Political Economy of Regionalism* (New York: Columbia University Press, 1997).

progress in reaching agreement on common security or foreign policies. In addition, the economic concessions required to achieve regional integration may be granted to allies but certainly not to potential adversaries. Therefore, economic and political integration may require a powerful leader that has an interest in and a capacity to promote a regional arrangement. Ready examples are Germany in Western Europe (EU), the United States in North America (NAFTA), Japan in Pacific Asia, and Brazil in South America (Mercosur).

The historical experience in national development reveals that despite neofunctionalist assertions, economic unification has followed rather than preceded political unification. Once a political decision has been made to achieve economic and monetary union, neofunctionalist logic and the solution of technical issues may propel deeper integration. However, at least to my knowledge, there is no example of spillover from economic and monetary unification that has led automatically to political unification. Indeed, in some ways, even the movement toward economic and political unification of Europe thus far has been historically unique. Integration by peaceful means of such a large region has never before been attempted, and there simply are no precedents to provide guidance regarding the future of European regionalization. Whether or not Europe will ultimately succeed depends more on political than on economic developments.

Every regional arrangement represents cooperative efforts of individual states to promote both national and collective objectives. Some believe that economic regionalism, and especially the effort to achieve European political unity, signals a movement away from a state-centric world and the beginning of a postnational international order. To the contrary, this effort and economic regionalism in general have been a response by nation-states to shared political and economic problems. As the world economy has become more closely integrated, regional groupings of states have increased their cooperation in order to strengthen their autonomy, increase their bargaining position in disputes about distributive issues, and promote other political or economic objectives. Regionalization is a means to extend national concerns and ambitions rather than an alternative to a state-centered international system.

Economic regionalism has spread because nation-states want the absolute benefits of a global economy at the same time that they seek to increase their own relative gains and protect themselves against external threats to their economic welfare and national security. Concerns over distributive issues and worries over national autonomy reflect the belief of national political and economic leaders that eco-

357

nomic competition must necessarily be a central concern in world politics. Furthermore, international economic competition necessitates large domestic markets that enable domestic firms to achieve economies of scale. In order to survive and prosper in an uncertain and rapidly changing world, individual states and groups of states are adapting to the evolving economic, technological, and political environment, as they have done many times in the past. In the 1990s, states have responded to intensely competitive and threatening globalization by forming or extending regional economic alliances or arrangements under the leadership of one or more major economic powers.

Economic regionalism has become an important component in the national strategies of the major economic powers to strengthen their respective domestic economies and their international competitiveness. They attempt to achieve at the regional level what they are no longer able to achieve at the national level.[23] The Maastricht Treaty was intended to create a politically and economically unified European Union (EU) that would be the economic equal of Japan and the United States. In North America, ratification by Canada, Mexico, and the United States of the North American Free Trade Agreement (NAFTA) established a free trade area intended to create a strong North American, and perhaps eventually a Western Hemisphere, integrated economy. The third important regional movement, in Pacific Asia, has been led by a Japan determined to strengthen its regional and global position. Although this Asian Pacific movement has been made manifest primarily through bilateral trade and investment linkages between Japan and other economies in the area, an effort to increase political integration of the Asian Pacific region began with the founding of the Asian Pacific Economic Cooperation (APEC) community. These three movements toward regional integration and the interrelationships among them will have a profound impact on the nature and structure of the world economy for some time to come.

AN ECLECTIC APPROACH

Efforts to develop a general theory of regional integration are unlikely to succeed. The realist approach also has serious limitations. There are too many different factors involved in regional movements around

---

[23] Gibb and Michalak, eds, *Continental Trading Blocs: The Growth of Regionalism in the World Economy*, 1.

the world, the differences among various regional efforts are too great, and too many assumptions that cannot be tested are necessarily involved in analysis of regional efforts. My realist bias is to stress the political and strategic sources of regional efforts; yet I acknowledge that this approach cannot fully account for every example of regional integration and/or for the important differences among these efforts. For example, although political considerations have certainly been important in NAFTA and in Japan's efforts to create an Asian Pacific economic bloc, the principal motive in those cases has been fulfillment of private and national economic interests. The dozens of efforts to create regional economies do possess one or more common elements: an economic motive, establishment of an external tariff of some kind, and/or a leader or leaders interested in promoting integration of the region. Yet, further generalization is difficult, if not impossible. Motives, external tariffs, and the role of leadership differ from one regional arrangement to another, and for this reason one must take an eclectic approach to understanding regional integration.

A universal theory or explanation of such a diverse and wide-ranging phenomenon is undoubtedly impossible to formulate. An eclectic approach is reasonable and should stress a number of factors. First of all, every regional effort involves some political motive, sometimes one that is very ambitious, as in European regional integration, and sometimes quite modest, as in North American regionalism. Although the interests and pressures of powerful domestic groups may shape regional arrangements, those arrangements are produced primarily by national interests as defined by the ruling elites of the states involved.

An eclectic approach should also incorporate recognition that regionalism is stimulated when there is no strong international leadership.[24] As the United States became less willing to continue the leadership role that it once performed, groups of states framed their own solutions to international economic problems. Weakening of the Bretton Woods System of rule-based trade and monetary regimes encouraged the search for regional solutions. Growing numbers of participants and the increasing complexity of the problems in international negotiations also encourage the movement toward regional arrangements. For example, the large number of participants in GATT/WTO trade negotiations has led groups of states to seek other solutions frequently easier to find at the regional than at the global level.

---

[24] Paul R. Krugman, "The Move Toward Free Trade Zones," in *Policy Implications of Trade and Currency Zones: A Symposium Sponsored by the Federal Bank of Kansas City* (Jackson Hole, Wyoming, 22–24 August 1992), 28.

Additional important factors in the spread of economic regionalism include the emergence of new economic powers, intensification of international economic competition, and rapid technological developments. The increased pace of economic change makes the choice between adjusting to new developments or resorting to protectionism even more vital. In the 1970s, nation-states usually responded to such challenges with New Protectionism; that is, the use of nontariff barriers. As that approach became less effective, states in Western Europe, North America, and elsewhere formed customs unions and free trade areas to slow the adjustment process and protect themselves from the rapidly industrializing and highly competitive economies of Pacific Asia. In the late 1990s, protectionist efforts increased once again.

There are other factors that should be recognized in a new approach. Economic regionalism is also driven by the dynamics of an economic security dilemma. For example, the movement toward European unity became a factor in the U.S. decision to support the North American Free Trade Agreement. Japan, fearing exclusion from both of those regional blocs, stimulated Asian Pacific regionalism. Other regional efforts around the world were also responses to earlier regional movements. In effect, nations have been trapped in a rather traditional Prisoner's Dilemma of mutual distrust from which escape has become very difficult.

Finally, additional factors influencing the movement toward economic regionalism have included the increasing importance for world trade of oligopolistic competition, the theory of strategic trade, and economies of scale. Earlier postwar economic thinking about regionalism emphasized the trade creation and diversion consequences of regional trading arrangements, but more recently the focus has been on the importance of internal and external economies of scale that could be achieved through economic integration.[25] In principle, of course, the best route to promote economies of scale would be through free trade and completely open markets. However, many business and political leaders believe that protected regional arrangements enable local firms to achieve such economies and thereby to increase their competitiveness vis-à-vis foreign firms. Then when the firms are sufficiently strong, they will be able to compete more successfully against established oligopolistic firms in global markets.

[25] As noted earlier, the term "internal economies of scale" refers to the decreased average costs enjoyed by a single, large firm over a smaller firm. The term "external economies of scale" refers to the fact that firms near one another can benefit from technological and other spillovers from neighboring firms. Desmond Dinan, ed., *Encyclopedia of the European Union* (Boulder, Colo.: Lynne Rienner, 1998), 153–58.

Such reasoning and efforts to increase international competitiveness have certainly been factors underlying the movement toward regional integration.

CONCLUSION

In Western Europe, North America, and Pacific Asia as well as elsewhere, dominant powers and their allies within a region have joined forces to solve regional problems and increase their bargaining leverage in global economic negotiations. The countries of the European Union already participate in international trade negotiations as a regional bloc. Economic regionalism has also become a means to increase the international competitiveness of regional firms. Various forms of economic regionalism (customs unions, free trade areas, and single markets) provide, to some extent, such advantages of free trade as increased competition and economies of scale while simultaneously denying these advantages to outsiders unless they invest in the internal market and meet member-country demands for local content, technological transfers, and job creation. Regionalism also facilitates pooling of economic resources and formation of regional corporate alliances. For all these reasons, regionalism has become a central strategy used by groups of states to increase their economic and political strength and therefore has become an extremely important feature of the global economy.

The Nation-State in the Global Economy

THE IDEA that the nation-state has been undermined by the transnational forces of economic globalization has appeared in writings on the international system and on the international economy. Many writings have argued that international organizations (IOs) and nongovernmental actors are replacing nation-states as the dominant actors in the international system. Books that have made this claim include those with such dramatic titles as *The Retreat of the State*, *The End of Geography*, and the *End of Sovereignty?*[1] Daniel Yergin and Joseph Stanislaw maintain that the market has wrested control from the state over the commanding heights of the economy and that the economic role of the nation-state is just about at an end.[2] Other writers believe a global economy has emerged or is emerging in which distinct national economies no longer exist and national economic policies are no longer possible.[3] This chapter disagrees with such views and argues that the nation-state continues to be the major actor in both domestic and international affairs.

At the beginning of the twenty-first century, the nation-state is clearly under serious attack from both above and below, and there is no doubt that there have been very important changes. Within many nations, the politics of identity and ethnic conflict is challenging the integrity of states, as ethnic and regional groups seek independence or at least greater autonomy.[4] Yet it is important to understand that the Kurds, Palestinians, and many other groups all want nation-states

---

[1] Richard O'Brien, *Global Financial Integration: The End of Geography*; Walter B. Wriston, *The Twilight of Sovereignty: How the Information Revolution Is Transforming Our World* (New York: Scribner's, 1992); Joseph A. Camilleri and Jim Falk, *End of Sovereignty? The Politics of a Shrinking and Fragmenting World* (Brookfield, Vt.: Elgar, 1992); Susan Strange, *The Retreat of the State: The Diffusion of Power in the World Economy* (New York: Cambridge University Press, 1996).

[2] Daniel Yergin and Joseph Stanislaw, *The Commanding Heights: The Battle Between Government and the Marketplace That Is Remaking the Modern World* (New York: Simon and Schuster, 1998).

[3] Paul Hirst and Grahame Thompson, *Globalization in Question: The International Economy and the Possibility of Governance* (London: Polity Press, 1996), 1.

[4] Vincent Cable, "The Diminished Nation-State: A Study in the Loss of Economic Power," in *What Future for the State? Daedalus* 124, no. 2 (spring 1995): 44–46.

of their own; they do not wish to eliminate nation-states but to divide present nation-states into units that they themselves can control. It is also accurate to say that economic globalization and transnational economic forces are eroding economic sovereignty in important ways. Nevertheless, both the extent of globalization and the consequences of economic globalization for the nation-state have been considerably exaggerated. For better or for worse, this is still a state-dominated world.

As Vincent Cable of the Royal Institute of International Affairs (London) has noted, it is not easy to assess globalization's implications for the nation-state.[5] Although the economic role of the state has declined in certain significant ways, it has expanded in others and, therefore, it is inaccurate to conclude that the nation-state has become redundant or anachronistic. As Cable says, the situation is "much messier" than that. The impact of the global economy on individual nations is highly uneven, and its impact varies from issue to issue; finance is much more globalized than are services and industrial production. While globalization has reduced some policy options, the degree of reduction is highly dependent on national size and economic power; the United States and Western Europe, for example, are much less vulnerable to destabilizing financial flows than are small economies. Indeed, the importance of the state has even actually increased in some areas, certainly with respect to promoting international competitiveness through support for R & D, for technology policy, and for other assistance to domestic firms.

Economic globalization is much more limited than many realize, and consequently, its overall impact on the economic role of the state is similarly limited. Moreover, although economic globalization has been a factor in whatever diminishment of the state may have occurred, ideological, technological, and international political changes have had an even more powerful influence. Furthermore, many and perhaps most of the social, economic, and other problems ascribed to globalization are actually due to technological and other developments that have little or nothing to do with globalization. Even though its role may have diminished somewhat, the nation-state remains preeminent in both domestic and international economic affairs. To borrow a phrase from the American humorist Mark Twain, I would like to report that the rumors of the death of the state "have been greatly exaggerated."[6]

[5] Ibid., 38.
[6] Mark Twain was a nineteenth-century American author whose obituary was mistakenly published before his death, leading Twain to comment that rumors of his death were greatly exaggerated.

THE LIMITED NATURE OF ECONOMIC GLOBALIZATION

In one sense, globalization has been taking place for centuries whenever improvements in transportation and communications have brought formerly separated peoples into contact with one another. The domestication of the horse and camel, the invention of the sailing ship, and the development of the telegraph all proved powerful instruments for uniting people, although not always to their liking. For thousands of years, ideas, artistic styles, and other artifacts have diffused from one society to another and have given rise to fears similar to those associated with economic globalization today. Nevertheless, it is important to discuss the economic globalization that has resulted from the rapid economic and technological integration of national societies that took place in the final decades of the twentieth century, especially after the end of the Cold War. This recent global economic integration has been the result of major changes in trade flows, of the activities of multinational corporations, and of developments in international finance.

Despite the increasing significance of economic globalization, the integration of the world economy has been highly uneven, restricted to particular economic sectors, and not nearly as extensive as many believe. As a number of commentators have pointed out, there are many ways in which the world is less integrated today than it was in the late nineteenth century. This should remind us that although the technology leading to increased globalization may be irreversible, national policies that have been responsible for the process of economic globalization have been reversed in the past and could be reversed again in the future.

As the twenty-first century opens, the world is not as well integrated as it was in a number of respects prior to World War I. Under the gold standard and the influential doctrine of laissez-faire, for example, the decades prior to World War I were an era when markets were truly supreme and governments had little power over economic affairs. Trade, investment, and financial flows were actually greater in the late 1800s, at least relative to the size of national economies and the international economy, than they are today. Twentieth-century changes appear primarily in the form of the greatly increased speed and absolute magnitude of economic flows across national borders and in the inclusion of more and more countries in the global economy. Yet, economic globalization is largely confined to North America, Western Europe, and Pacific Asia. And even though these industrial economies have become much more open, imports and investments from abroad are still small compared to the size of the domestic economies. For example, American imports rose from 5 percent of the total U.S. production in 1970 to just 13 percent in 1995, even though the United States was the most globalized economy.

Although trade has grown enormously during the past half century, trade still accounts for a relatively small portion of most economies; moreover, even though the number of "tradables" has been increasing, trade is still confined to a limited number of economic sectors. The principal competitors for most firms (with important exceptions in such areas as motor vehicles and electronics) are other national firms. The largest portions of foreign direct investment flows are invested in the United States, Western Europe, and China; a very small portion of the investment in sectors other than raw materials and resources has been invested in most less developed countries. International finance alone can be accurately described as a global phenomenon. Yet, even the globalization of finance must be qualified, as much of international finance is confined to short-term and speculative investment.

The most important measure of the economic integration and interdependence of distinct economies is what economists call the "law of one price." If identical goods and services in different economies have the same or nearly equal prices, then economists consider these economies to be closely integrated with one another. However, evidence indicates that the prices of identical goods around the world differ considerably whether measured by *The Economist* magazine's Big Mac index or by more formal economic measures.[7] When the law of one price is applied to the United States, it is clear that American prices differ greatly from those of other countries, especially Japan's. Price differentials in the cost of labor around the world are particularly notable, and there are large disparities in wages. All of this clearly suggests that the world is not as integrated as many proclaim.

The significant and sizable decline in migration is one of the major differences between late-nineteenth-century globalization and globalization of the early twenty-first century. During the past half century, the United States has been the only country to welcome large numbers of new citizens. Although Western Europe has accepted a flood of refugees and "guest workers," the situation in those countries has been and remains tenuous; few have been or will be offered citizen-

---

[7] Charles Engel and John H. Rogers, "Regional Patterns in the Law of One Price: The Roles of Geography versus Currencies," in Jeffrey A. Frankel, ed., *The Regionalization of the World Economy* (Chicago: University of Chicago Press, 1998), 153.

ship. The globalization of labor was considerably more advanced prior to World War I than afterward. In the late nineteenth century, millions of Europeans crossed the Atlantic to settle as permanent residents in North America; West Europeans also migrated in significant numbers to such "lands of recent settlement" as Australia, Argentina, and other temperate-zone regions. There were large migrations of Indians and Chinese to Southeast Asia, Africa, and other tropical regions. All these streams of migration became powerful determinants of the structure of the world economy.[8] In the early twenty-first century, labor migration is no longer a major feature of the world economy, and even within the European Union, migration from one member nation to another is relatively low.

Barriers to labor migration are built by policies intended to protect the real wages and social welfare of the nation's citizens, and the modern welfare state is based on the assumption that its benefits will be available only to its own citizens.[9] Some reformers in industrialized countries have constructed an ethical case that national wealth should be shared with the destitute around the world, but to my knowledge, even they have not advocated elimination of the barriers to international migration in order to enable the poor to move to more wealthy countries and thus decrease international income disparities. I find it remarkable that in the debate over globalization, little attention has been given to the most important factor of production; namely, labor and labor migration. For the billions of people in poor countries, national borders certainly remain an important feature of the global economy.

ALLEGED CONSEQUENCES OF ECONOMIC GLOBALIZATION

The conjuncture of globalization with a number of other political, economic, and technological developments transforming the world makes it very difficult to understand economic globalization and its consequences. Among far-reaching economic changes at the end of the twentieth century have been a shift in industrialized countries from manufacturing to services and several revolutionary technological developments associated with the computer, including emergence of the Internet and information economy. The skills and education

[8] W. Arthur Lewis, *The Evolution of the International Economic Order* (Princeton: Princeton University Press, 1978).

[9] James Mayall, *Nationalism and International Society* (Cambridge: Cambridge University Press, 1990), Chapter 5.

required by jobs in the computer age place unskilled labor in the industrialized countries at a severe disadvantage in their wages and job security.

Although some economic and technological developments associated with the computer, including the rapid advances in telecommunications, have certainly contributed to the process of globalization, and globalization in some cases has accentuated these economic and technological changes, the two developments are not synonymous. In fact, the contemporary technological "revolution" has been a far more pervasive and, in many ways, a much more profound development than is globalization, at least thus far. For example, the most important development currently altering individual lives is the incredible revolution in the biological sciences, such as biological engineering. Yet this important development in human affairs has nothing whatsoever to do with globalization as it is commonly conceived.

Many of the problems alleged to be the result of economic globalization are really the consequence of unfortunate national policies and government decisions. Environmentalists rage against globalization and its evils; yet, most environmental damage is the result of the policies and behaviors of national governments. Air, water, and soil pollution result primarily from the lax policies of individual nations and/or from their poor enforcement procedures. The destruction of the Amazon forest has been caused principally by the Brazilian government's national development policies; in the United States, forest clear-cutting is actually promoted by generous government subsidies to logging companies. Land-hungry peasants in Southeast Asia are permitted to destroy forests to acquire cultivable land. Small farmers in France, the United States, and elsewhere blame globalization for their economic plight, but small farms are victims of economic/technological changes that have increased the importance of economies of scale in agriculture. Unfortunately, large farms and agribusinesses are now best suited to take full advantage of such economic/technological changes. The American agricultural sector, especially the large farms, even benefit from generous government subsidies. It would be easy to expand the list of problems generally attributed to globalization that have really been caused by technological changes, by national government policies, or by other wholly domestic factors.

In Western Europe, globalization is frequently blamed for many of the problems that have emerged from the economic and political integration of the region. Both globalization and regionalism are characterized by lowered economic barriers, restructuring of business, and other economic/social changes; it is easy, therefore, to see why some have conflated the two developments into one. Yet, globalization and regionalism are different, especially in the goals that each is seeking to achieve.

The tendency to blame globalization for many vexing problems of modern life is due in part to nationalistic and xenophobic attitudes on the political right and an anticapitalist mentality on the political left. Nationalistic attitudes have been expressed by Ross Perot, Patrick Buchanan, and American organized labor; the latter long ago gave up the slogan "workers of the world unite" in favor of their own parochial interests. The leftist criticism of capitalism runs deep in some peoples and countries and within advanced capitalist economies, most notably France. The antagonism toward capitalism is directed at the principal representatives of the capitalist system in the modern world: the United States, large multinational firms, and such international economic institutions as the International Monetary Fund and World Trade Organization. When I note these criticisms, I myself do not intend to endorse such excesses of capitalism as rampant commercialism, enormous disparities in wealth and privilege, advertising's creation of "wants," or the worship of wealth as the measure of all things. Capitalism is a system based on self-interest that is too frequently made manifest in outright greed. Despite capitalism's serious flaws, the evils of today's world will not be solved by attacks on globalization. One may say about capitalism what Winston Churchill is reputed to have said about democracy, that it is the worst of all social systems except for all the others.

Elsewhere in this book and in another of my books, *The Challenge of Global Capitalism*, I have addressed many of the negative consequences alleged to have been caused by globalization and have argued that most of the charges against globalization are wrong, misleading, or exaggerated.[10] Domestic and international income disparities, the problems of unskilled workers, and the alleged "race to the bottom" in modern welfare states in general should not be attributed to economic globalization. In almost all cases, such other factors as technological changes, national policies, or the triumph of conservative economic ideologies carry primary responsibility for these developments. Those particularly concerned about income inequalities among national societies should recognize that globalization in the form of exports from industrializing to industrialized countries has actually

---

[10] A very effective critique of the antiglobalist position is found in Geoffrey Garrett, "Global Markets and National Politics," *International Organization* 52, no. 4 (autumn 1998): 787–824.

greatly benefited the industrializing countries; furthermore, very few countries have developed in this century without active participation in the global economy.

EFFECTIVENESS OF MACROECONOMIC POLICY

Since the end of World War II, and especially since governments accepted Keynesian economics in the early postwar era, national governments in the advanced industrialized economies have been held responsible for national economic performance. States were assigned the tasks of promoting national economic stability and steering their economies between the undesirable conditions of recession and inflation. Through macroeconomic policies, the state has been able to control, at least to some extent, the troubling vicissitudes of the market. However, the argument that the power of the state over economic affairs has significantly declined implies that national governments can no longer manage their economies. While it is true that macroeconomic policy has become more complicated in the highly integrated world economy of the twenty-first century, these policies do still work and can achieve their goals at least as well as in the past. What better example than the Federal Reserve's very successful management of the American economy in the mid-to-late 1990s! Moreover, today as in the past, the principal constraints on macroeconomic policy are to be found at the domestic rather than at the international level.

Macroeconomic policy consists of two basic tools for managing a national economy: fiscal policies and monetary policies. The principal instruments of fiscal policy are taxation and government expenditures. Through lowering or raising taxes and/or increasing or decreasing national expenditures, the federal government (Congress and the Executive) can affect the national level of economic activities. Whereas a federal budget deficit (spending more than tax receipts) will stimulate the economy, a budget surplus (spending less than tax receipts) will decrease economic activities. Monetary policy works through its determination of the size and velocity of a nation's money supply. The Federal Reserve can stimulate or depress the level of economic activities by increasing or restricting the supply of dollars available to consumers and producers. The principal method employed by the Federal Reserve to achieve this goal is to determine the national level of interest rates; whereas a low interest rate stimulates economic growth, a high rate depresses it.

Many commentators argue that the effectiveness of monetary policy has been significantly reduced by increased international financial

369

flows. If, for example, a central bank lowers interest rates to stimulate the economy, investors will transfer their capital to other economies with higher interest rates and thus counter the intended stimulus of lower rates. Similarly, if a central bank increases interest rates in order to slow the economy, investment capital will flow into the economy, counter the intended deflationary effects of higher rates, and stimulate economic activities. In all these ways, economic globalization is believed to have undermined the efficacy of fiscal and monetary policy. Therefore, some consider national governments no longer able to manage their economies.

To examine this contention, it is helpful to apply the logic of the "trilemma" or "irreconcilable trinity" discussed in Chapter 9. Every nation is confronted by an inevitable trade-off among the following three desirable goals of economic policy: fixed exchange rates, national autonomy in macroeconomic policy, and international capital mobility. A nation might want a stable exchange rate in order to reduce economic uncertainty and stabilize the economy. Or it might desire discretionary monetary policy to avoid high unemployment and steer the economy between recession and inflation. Or a government might want freedom of capital movements to facilitate the conduct of trade, foreign investment, and other international business activities. Unfortunately, a government cannot achieve all three of these goals simultaneously. It can obtain at most two. For example, choosing a fixed and stable exchange rate along with some latitude for independent monetary policies would mean forgoing freedom of capital movements, because international capital flows could undermine both exchange rate stability and independent monetary policies. On the other hand, a country might choose to pursue macroeconomic policies to promote full employment, but it then would have to sacrifice either a fixed exchange rate or freedom of capital movement.

Such an analysis tells us that although economic globalization does constrain government policy options, it does not impose a financial straitjacket on national macroeconomic policies. Whether an individual nation does or does not have the capacity for an independent macroeconomic policy is itself a policy choice. If a nation wants the capability to pursue an independent macroeconomic policy, it can achieve that goal by abandoning either fixed exchange rates or capital mobility. Different countries do, in fact, make different choices. The United States, for example, prefers independent monetary policy and freedom of capital movements and therefore sacrifices exchange rate stability; members of the European Economic Monetary Union (EMU), on the other hand, prefer fixed exchange rates and have created a common currency to achieve this goal. Some other countries that place a high value on macroeconomic independence—China, for example—have imposed controls on capital movements.

Different domestic economic interests also have differing preferences. Whereas export businesses have a strong interest in the exchange rate, domestic-oriented businesses place a higher priority on national policy autonomy. Investors prefer freedom of capital movement, whereas labor tends to be opposed to such movement, unless the movement should mean increased investment in their own nation. Economic globalization in itself does not prevent a nation from using macroeconomic policies for managing its economy.

The mechanisms employed to conduct monetary policy have not been seriously affected by globalization. Although various central banks operate differently from one another, an examination of the ways in which the American Federal Reserve (the Fed) steers the American economy is instructive and reveals that, at least in the American case, globalization has had only minimal effects.

Through its power to increase or decrease the number of dollars available to consumers and producers (liquidity), the Fed is able to steer the overall economy. The level of national economic activity is strongly influenced by the size of the nation's money supply; an increase in the money supply stimulates economic activities and a decrease slows down economic activity. The Fed has three basic instruments to influence the nation's supply of money. The first directly affects the money supply; the other tools work indirectly through the banking system.

The Fed's primary means for management of the economy is "open market operations," conducted through the Open Market Desk of the Federal Reserve Bank of New York. Through sale or purchase of U.S. government bonds directly to the public, the Fed can influence the overall level of national economic activity. If, for example, the Fed wants to slow the economy, it sells U.S. Government bonds. This takes money or liquidity out of the economy. If, on the other hand, the Fed wants to stimulate the economy, it uses dollars to purchase U.S. Government bonds and thus increases the money or liquidity in the economy.

The Fed can also change the discount rate, which is the interest rate on loans that the Fed makes directly to the nation's commercial banks. The Fed, for example, loans money to banks whose reserves fall below the Fed's reserve requirements (see below); this may happen if a bank has made too many loans or is experiencing too many withdrawals. By lending to private banks and increasing the reserves

371

of those banks, the Fed enables banks to make more loans and thus to increase the nation's money supply. Whereas raising the discount rate decreases loans and money creation, lowering of the discount rate increases loans and money creation. These changes in turn have a powerful influence on the overall level of economic activity.

Another tool that the Fed has available is its authority to determine the reserve requirements of the nation's banks. Reserve requirements specify the minimal size of the monetary reserves that a bank must hold against deposits subject to withdrawal. Reserve requirements thus determine the amount of money that a bank is permitted to lend and, thereby, how much money the bank can place in circulation. Through raising or lowering reserve requirements, the Fed sets a limit on how much money the nation's banks can inject into the economy. However, this method of changing the money supply is used infrequently because changed reserve requirements can be very disruptive to the banking system.

Globalization and a more open world economy have had only minimal impact on the Fed's ability to manage the economy. Yet the effectiveness of open market operations has probably been somewhat reduced by growth of the international financial market, and the purchase or sale of U.S. securities by foreigners certainly affects the national money supply. In the late 1990s, it was estimated that approximately $150 billion was held overseas. However, the effect of that large amount is minimized by the size of the more than $8 trillion domestic economy. Also, the American financial system (like that of other industrialized countries) exhibits a "home bias"; that is to say, most individuals keep their financial assets in their own currency. It is possible, however, that central banks in smaller and weaker economies find that their ability to manage their own money supply has been decreased, as was exemplified by the 1997 Asian financial crisis.

One should note that the continuing power of the Fed over the banks and the money supply through control of the interest rate has been challenged by the development of the credit card and other new forms of money. These credit instruments have decreased, at least somewhat, the effectiveness of the Fed's use of this instrument to control the economy. Still more problematic for the Fed is the increasing use of e-money in Internet commerce. In effect, these developments mean that the monopoly of money creation once held by the Fed and the banking system is being diluted. Through use of a credit card and/or participation in e-commerce, an individual or business can create money. Yet, at some point e-money and other novel forms of money must be converted into "real" or legal tender, and, at that point the

Fed retains control of the creation of real money. Thus, although the monetary system has become much more complex, the Fed still has ultimate control over that system and through it, the overall economy.

Although the power of central banks over interest rates and the money supply has been somewhat diminished, as long as cash and bank reserves remain the ultimate means of exchange and of settlement of accounts, central banks can still retain control over the money supply and hence of the economy. In fact, even if everyone switched to electronic means of payment but credit issuers still settled their balances with merchants through the banking system (as happens with credit cards now), central banks would still retain overall control. However, one day, e-money could displace other forms of money. If and when this develops, financial settlements could be carried out without going through commercial banks, and central banks would lose their ability to control the economy through interest rates. Such a development could lead to the "denationalization" of money. However, it seems reasonable to believe that some public authority would still be needed to control inflation and monitor the integrity of the computer system used for payments settlements.

With respect to *reserve requirements*, intense competition among international banks has induced some central banks to reduce reserve requirements in order to make the domestic banking industry more competitive internationally. Japanese banks, for example, have long been permitted by the government to keep much smaller reserves than American banks. One of the major purposes of the Basle Agreement (1988), was to make reserve requirements more uniform throughout the world. Rumor has it that this agreement was engineered by the Fed to decrease the international competitiveness of Japanese and other foreign banks vis-à-vis American international banks. Whatever the underlying motive, the agreement has been described as a response to financial globalization, and the establishment of uniform international reserve requirements has largely reestablished their effectiveness as instruments of policy.

The most important constraints on macroeconomic policy are found at the domestic level. If an economy were isolated from the international economy, fiscal policy would be constrained by the cost of borrowing. If a national government were to use deficit spending to stimulate its economy, the resulting budget deficit would have to be financed by domestic lenders. In that situation, an upper limit would be placed on government borrowing, because as the budget deficit and the costs of servicing that deficit rose, bond purchasers would become more and more fearful that the government might default on its debt and/or use monetary policy to inflate the money supply and thus reduce the real value of the debt. Increased risk as debt rises causes lenders to stop lending and/or to charge higher and higher interest rates; this then discourages further borrowing by the government. Also, another important constraint on monetary policy in a domestic economy is the threat of inflation; this threat places an upper limit on the ability of a central bank to stimulate the economy by increasing the money supply and/or lowering the interest rate. At some point, the threat of inflation will discourage economic activity. In short, there are limits on macroeconomic policy that have nothing whatsoever to do with the international economy—and these domestic constraints existed long before anyone had heard the term "globalization."

Economic globalization has made the task of managing an economy easier in some ways and more difficult in others. On the one hand, globalization has enabled governments to borrow more freely; the United States in the 1980s and 1990s borrowed heavily from Japanese and other foreign investors in order to finance a federal budget deficit and a high rate of economic growth. However, this debt-financed growth strategy, as Susan Strange pointed out first in *Casino Capitalism* (1986) and again in *Mad Money* (1998), is extraordinarily risky and can not continue forever. Fearing collapse of the dollar, investors could one day flee dollar-denominated assets for safer assets denominated in other currencies.[11] The consequences of such flight could be devastating for the United States and for the rest of the world economy. Thus, although economic globalization has increased the latitude of governments to pursue expansionary economic policies through borrowing excessively abroad, such serious financial crises of the postwar era as the Mexican crisis in 1994–1995, the 1997 East Asian financial crisis, and the disturbing collapse of the Russian ruble in August 1998 demonstrate the huge and widespread risks associated with such a practice.

Economic globalization and the greater openness of domestic economies have also modified the rules of economic policy. Certainly, the increasing openness of national economies has made the exercise of macroeconomic policy more complex and difficult. This does not mean that a national government can no longer guide the economy around the dangerous shoals of inflation and recession, but it does mean that the risk of shipwreck has grown.

[11] Susan Strange, *Casino Capitalism* (Oxford: Blackwell,1986); and *Mad Money: From the Author of Casino Capitalism* (Manchester, U.K.: Manchester University Press, 1998).

The Need for a Historical Perspective

The globalization thesis lacks a historical perspective. Those individuals who argue that globalization has severely limited economic sovereignty appear to believe that governments once possessed unlimited national autonomy and freedom in economic matters. Their argument assumes that nation-states have enjoyed unrestricted ability to determine economic policy and manage their economies and that governments were free because they were not subordinate to or encumbered by transnational market forces. As proponents of the globalization thesis contrast economic policy in the twenty-first century to this imagined past, they conclude that nation-states, for the first time ever, have become constrained by the increased integration of national economies through trade, financial flows, and the activities of multinational firms. In effect, having assumed that states once had complete economic freedom, these individuals misperceive the reality of the fundamental relationship between the state and the economy. When viewed from a more accurate historical perspective, the relationship of state and market in the contemporary era is neither particularly startling nor revolutionary.

In the decades prior to World War I, national governments had little effective control over their economies. Under the classical gold standard of fixed exchange rates, governments were more tightly bound by what Barry Eichengreen has called "golden fetters" than they are in the early-twenty-first century world of flexible rates. Moreover, as Nobel Laureate Arthur Lewis has noted, prior to World War I the economic agenda of governments everywhere was limited to the efforts of central banks to maintain the value of their currencies.[12] As Keynes pointed out in *The Economic Consequences of the Peace* (1919), national economic policy did not concern itself with the welfare of the "lower orders" of society.[13] This minor and highly constrained role of the state in the economy changed dramatically with World War I and subsequent economic and political developments.

Throughout the twentieth century, the relationship of state and market indeed changed significantly as governments harnessed their economies for total war and to meet their citizens' rising economic

---

[12] Barry Eichengreen, *Golden Fetters: The Gold Standard and the Great Depression* (New York: Oxford University Press, 1992); and W. Arthur Lewis, *Growth and Fluctuations, 1870–1913* (London: Allen and Unwin, 1978).

[13] John Maynard Keynes, *The Economic Consequences of the Peace* (London: Macmillan, 1919).

expectations. The world wars of the twentieth century, the Great Depression of the 1930s, and the immense economic demands of the Cold War elevated the state's role in the economy. During periods of intense concern about security, national governments used new tools to manage their economies and began to exercise unprecedented control over their economies. The Great Depression, the rise of organized labor, and the sacrifices imposed on societies by World War II led Western governments to expand their activities to guarantee the welfare of their citizens. For some years, the perceived success of the communist experiment also encouraged governments to help Keynes's "lower orders," and after World War II, governments in every advanced economy assumed responsibility for promotion of full employment and provision of a generous and high level of economic welfare.

Conclusion

The argument that the nation-state is in retreat is most applicable to the United States, Western Europe, and perhaps Japan. The end of the Cold War represented the end of a century and a half of rapid economic development and political/military conflict. Since the American Civil War (1861–1865), the Franco-Prussian War (1870–1871), and the Russo-Japanese War (1904–1905), the forces of nationalism, industrialization, and state-creation had driven the industrialized powers of Europe, the United States, and Japan. World War I, World War II, and the Cold War forged the modern nation-state as an economic and war-making machine. During these decades of interstate rivalry, the economy was often harnessed to the needs of the national war machine. This bellicose epoch appears to have ended, and the industrialized countries may be retreating to their more modest late-nineteenth-century status. Yet, one must ask whether the forces of nationalism, industrialization, and state-creation might not be causing a repeat of the tragic Western experience in the developing economies of Asia, Africa, and elsewhere! Thus far, there is little evidence to suggest that these countries will avoid repeating the mistakes made by the industrialized world.

CHAPTER FIFTEEN

Governing the Global Economy

I N HIS PIONEERING *Economics of Interdependence* (1968), Richard Cooper argued that the most serious problem of the postwar international economy was the intensifying clash between the economic and technological forces unifying the globe and the world's continuing political fragmentation.[1] Trade, investment, and financial flows, Cooper pointed out, were creating an increasingly integrated and highly interdependent global economy. Yet nation-states through such means as trade protection, subsidies, and industrial policies were resisting these integrating forces and, in doing so, were undermining the world economy. Tension between the evolving global economy and political fragmentation, Cooper argued, was causing economic instability and threatening to undermine the openness and efficiency of the world economy.

Cooper went on to evaluate various solutions that had been proposed to the clash between the "irresistible force" of economics and the "immovable object" of politics. He concluded that the ideal solution was some type of international governance of the global economy.[2] However, he doubted that nations would be willing to sacrifice national sovereignty and political/economic autonomy for the sake of a well-functioning international economy.

Since Cooper's 1968 advocacy of improved international governance of the world economy, a number of significant developments have increased the relevance of his diagnosis but made his solution even more difficult to attain. When Cooper published his book, the relevant world economy (reflected in the book's subtitle, *Economic Policy in the Atlantic Community*) was composed primarily of Western Europe, North America, and a weak periphery. Since that time, industry and economic power have diffused from the North Atlantic to Japan, the industrializing countries of Pacific Asia, and other industrializing powers in Latin America and elsewhere. In 1968, despite

---

[1] Richard N. Cooper, *The Economics of Interdependence: Economic Policy in the Atlantic Community* (New York: McGraw-Hill, 1968). Although Cooper's book is obviously dated, its analytical and theoretical framework continues to be important for anyone interested in international political economy.

[2] Ibid., 262.

important differences between the continental European tradition of stakeholder/corporatist capitalism and Anglo-Saxon shareholder/free market capitalism, the North Atlantic economies have shared a market-oriented concept of capitalism with modest state intervention. Today, Japan and most industrializing economies have very different cultural traditions and national systems of political economy; these differences include extensive state interventionism and close government-business ties. In 1968, the level of economic interdependence among national economies was still rather modest. Now, more than thirty years later, the forces of economic globalization have created a more integrated global economy.

Cooper's analysis strongly emphasized the necessary political foundations of international economic cooperation. Cooper argued that international cooperation in economic matters was unlikely unless there was political support from the major economic powers. At that time, he believed that the political foundation for improved cooperative management of the international economy could be found within the Atlantic Community. He suggested, however, that if the American/West European political alliance should prove unable to provide the political glue for economic policy cooperation, then it would be preferable to break up the North Atlantic countries into smaller units that could cooperate closely and more easily.[3] Cooper's words have proved prescient. Economic regionalism has made governance of the global economy both more necessary and more difficult to attain. Today, the North Atlantic region is divided into the European Union and the North American Free Trade Agreement areas, and their future relationships cannot be predicted. Throughout the global economy other regional blocs have been emerging.

Three decades after publication of Cooper's book setting forth the great need for international governance, the rapid globalization of the world economy has elevated the governance issue to the top of the international economic agenda.[4] Neither domestic economies nor the increasingly integrated world economy can rely on markets alone to police themselves. An international governance mechanism is needed to assume several functions in the new global economy; in particular, it must provide certain public goods and resolve market failures. Pro-

---

[3] Ibid., 77–78.

[4] A useful and wide-ranging exploration of the governance issue is James N. Rosenau and Ernst-Otto Czempiel, eds., *Governance without Government: Order and Change in World Politics* (New York: Cambridge University Press, 1992). Another valuable writing on the subject is Raimo V. Vayrynen, ed., *Globalization and Global Governance* (London: Rowman and Littlefield, 1999).

vision of international public goods must include maintaining the rule of law (and especially provide for the settlement of disputes in trade, FDI, and other areas), ensuring monetary and financial stability, setting common standards and regulations for business, managing global communication and transportation, and solving environmental problems.

Although many neoclassical economists and some liberal thinkers believe that only minimal rules are necessary, many scholars of international political economy argue that extensive rules or formal regimes are needed. There are three predominant positions regarding governance: neoliberal institutionalism, new medievalism, and trans-governmentalism.[5] Neoliberal institutionalism, based on the continued importance of the state, believes that formal international regimes and institutions are necessary. Whereas state-realism emphasizes the ever-present problem of interstate conflict and rivalry, neoliberal institutionalism stresses interstate cooperation. The new medievalism is based on the assumption that the state and the state-system have been undermined by economic, technological, and other developments and are being eclipsed by nongovernmental actors and the emergence of an international civil society. New medievalists believe that the end of national sovereignty and the resulting diffusion of power will enable selfless nongovernmental organizations (NGOs) to solve the world's pressing environmental and other problems. Transgovernmentalism argues that international cooperation by domestic government agencies in specific functional areas is rapidly replacing the decision-making functions of centralized national governments in the management of the global economy.

NEOLIBERAL INSTITUTIONALISM

Like realism, neoliberal institutionalism accepts the continued existence and importance of the nation-state in international affairs; however, it generally assumes that the state is a liberal, market-oriented state in the American sense, more interested in cooperation and absolute gains than in conflicts over relative gains. Neoliberal institutionalists believe that international institutions have become sufficiently strong to meet the challenges of a globalized international economy. Moreover, if existing regimes are found deficient, new ones can be created or easily modified, as they have been in the past. An impor-

[5] These useful categories are based on Anne-Marie Slaughter, "The Real New World Order," *Foreign Affairs* 76, no. 5 (September/October 1997): 183–97.

tant example of a substantial reform of an international institution is found in the 1995 replacement of the General Agreement on Tariffs and Trade (GATT) by the World Trade Organization (WTO); the latter has greater authority over trade matters, more resources, and more power to enforce its decisions. The World Bank and the International Monetary Fund are being reformed as the twenty-first century opens. New international conventions on environmental and other important matters have been implemented.

The types of international regimes and institutions advocated by neoliberal institutionalism have achieved considerable success. Despite some failings, the IMF, WB, and GATT/WTO have improved significantly the ways in which the international economy functions. However, this approach to international governance has a number of limitations. As the world has become more integrated and complex new issues have arisen, a number of existing regimes have proven to be quite inadequate to fulfill the tasks assigned to them. For example, the regimes governing the areas of finance and money have proved seriously deficient. The increased integration and instability of financial markets and exchange rate fluctuations pose a serious threat to the stability of the global economy. Efforts to create an international regime for multinational corporations, such as the Multilateral Investment Agreement, have reached stalemate because of strong opposition from many countries and powerful interest groups. There is no regime for economic development, one of the most pressing issues in the world. Although Article XXIV of the GATT/WTO was intended to regulate formation of regional economic arrangements, it is almost totally ineffective. In short, the task of reforming existing regimes and creating new ones is exceptionally difficult.

There are formidable obstacles to achievement of the neoliberal institutionalist ideal of a regime-based international economy, and the issue of compliance is particularly challenging. This problem continues to limit the effectiveness of international organizations; the many books and articles on compliance have not helped very much. There are few generally accepted principles and policy prescriptions upon which regimes can be constructed. The Bretton Woods regimes dealing with trade and monetary affairs, were based on such Western legal and economic ideas as the transparency of commercial dealings and limited state intervention in the economy, and the triumph of neoliberalism in the 1980s reinforced such liberal principles. However, as economic integration spread among many and more diverse economies and also deepened, fundamental differences among national systems of political economy regarding economic principles

380

and legitimate policy have challenged Western ideals. American and Japanese notions of what is fair in international economic competition are particularly divergent. Increasing regionalization of the global economy has proved to be a popular way of dealing with the problems created by such national differences.

The clash between different national systems of political economy has intensified, but most American economists and public officials expect that the process of convergence will eventually lead to worldwide acceptance of the policy prescriptions of neoclassical economics and a free market following the American model. Some aspects of the Asian model were certainly discredited by the 1997 financial crisis, and some states have retreated from prior aggressive government intervention in the economy. Yet, in many countries there is strong resistance to permitting the whims of the market to determine a society's welfare and/or the nation's position in the global system. Many national leaders bitterly resent the constraints that the emphasis on the "market" imposes on economic policy; notable examples of such resentment have appeared in Malaysia and South Korea. In defiance of free market ideology, Malaysia in the 1990s imposed capital controls and South Korea strongly resisted American demands to liquidate the *chaebol*. There have also been serious revolts against trade liberalization in the West, including the U.S. congressional defeat in 1997 of "fast track" legislation. Furthermore, the American and British model of shareholder capitalism (Anglo-Saxon capitalism) is rejected by Japan, continental Europe, and many other nations. Although important changes are taking place in these countries, they still consider a corporation to be a community with social responsibilities and resist thinking of corporations as bundles of contracts and commodities to be bought and sold. It is noteworthy that in Japan, East Asia, and other countries, corporations are important providers of social insurance and other forms of social welfare. As this role becomes threatened by global competition, resentment against the Anglo-Saxon model is likely to increase.

At the opening of the twenty-first century, international institutions are faced with a number of immediate issues whose outcome will determine their future. A pressing issue, given public prominence in 1999 by the Seattle protestors against the World Trade Organization, is what scholars call the "democratic deficit"; international economic institutions are criticized because they are not accountable to any democratic electorate. Closely tied to this issue is the gap between the authority of existing institutions and the changing distribution of power in the international system. Despite the significant shift in eco-

381

nomic power that occurred in the last half of the twentieth century, decision-making authority and responsibility in the IMF, WTO, and World Bank continue to be disproportionately accorded to the United States and, to a lesser extent, Western Europe. Still another issue is the question of institutional reform; this is especially relevant for the IMF because of intense criticism of the organization by both the political left and right in the United States.

Democratic Deficit

In the interest of efficient decision-making and in deference to member governments' desires to keep their national affairs confidential, every important international organization—including the WTO, IMF, and World Bank—operates largely in secrecy. The predilection toward secrecy is reinforced by the fear that negotiations on trade, monetary, and other important economic matters could roil and seriously destabilize global markets; a proposed change in exchange rates, for example, could wreak havoc in markets. Nevertheless, more and more people are coming to believe that their daily lives, cultures, and social well-being are subject to secret decisions by faceless international bureaucrats. These growing concerns contribute to a backlash against globalization and threaten the foundations of the global economy managed by international institutions.

The 1999 Seattle meeting of the World Trade Organization illustrated the difficulties encountered in the search for a solution to the democratic deficit. In addition to launching the Millennium Round of trade negotiations, the Seattle conclave of trade ministers was expected to begin a concerted effort to reform the organization and strengthen the WTO's authority over trade-dispute settlement and other matters. The WTO has more authority over national policies than any other international economic organization. Although the IMF and the World Bank do have significant influence over less developed countries needing financial and other forms of assistance, the WTO's authority over trade matters extends to every one of its members, including the United States, the European Union, and Japan. Unlike every other international organization, the WTO has the authority to penalize and impose a monetary fine on any country that defies the decisions of its dispute settlement panels. The WTO's judicial and regulatory powers are unprecedented for an international organization. It approaches the neoliberal institutionalist ideal of an effective supranational institution.

Moreover, despite the beliefs of many Seattle protesters, the World Trade Organization is the most democratic of the important international institutions, with the possible exception of the United Nations

General Assembly. In the World Trade Organization, each of the 130 or so members has only one vote; the major economic powers have no formal privileged position. Both the World Bank and the International Monetary Fund, on the other hand, have a system of weighted voting that greatly favors the United States, Western Europe, and, to a lesser extent, Japan. Despite its more democratic nature, the WTO's legitimacy is still questioned.

One of the most important demands of the Seattle protestors was that decisions of the World Trade Organization and, by implication, other international institutions as well, be made transparent to the public. In addition to openness, they demanded that nongovernmental organizations (NGOs), including those dealing with the subjects of human rights, labor, and environmental problems, should be permitted to participate in the decision-making process of the WTO and other international organizations; they should be permitted, for example, to submit briefs and provide testimony, regarding matters under consideration. Superficially, these demands for greater democratic accountability appear reasonable. If the international institutions and their decisions are to be accepted by the larger public as legitimate, then greater openness and accountability may be necessary. Yet, there are formidable obstacles to achievement of increased openness. Some international organizations are notoriously inefficient and inclusion of more participants would significantly complicate decision-making. In addition, the decisions of international organizations involve sovereign nations. Making the WTO's dispute-settlement mechanism more transparent, for example, would mean that the states who are the parties to these disputes would have to reveal sensitive information that they and powerful domestic constituents would prefer to keep secret. In such a situation, member governments could lose confidence in the WTO and be tempted to move outside the organization to resolve their differences.

Although a serious effort must be made to solve the democratic deficit, achieving a solution will not be easy. How does one achieve both increased efficiency and greater transparency, two seemingly contradictory goals set forth by EU Trade Commissioner Pascal Lamy following the Seattle debacle? The WTO is indeed undemocratic in the sense that it is not *directly* accountable to any electorate. However, it is difficult to envisage an electorate to which it and other international institutions could be made accountable. Although the NGOs at Seattle asserted that international institutions be made accountable to them, they themselves are not accountable to any general electorate. Who elected Ralph Nader to speak on behalf of all consumers? After all, nearly every international, regional, and even national organization responsible for managing our highly complex and integrated world is also characterized by a democratic deficit and is not directly accountable to a citizenry; this group includes the Security Council of the United Nations, the International Court of Justice, the World Health Organization, the European Commission, the U.S. Supreme Court, the Federal Reserve, and such American independent regulatory agencies as the Pure Food and Drug Administration and the Security and Exchange Commission. However, these organizations, as well as the WTO and other international organizations, are ultimately accountable to national governments that, at least in democratic systems, are themselves accountable to an electorate. The ultimate responsibility for governing the world has to rest with national governments, at least until the peoples of the world come together in one global society.

Authority and Power

Another important problem confronting neoliberal institutionalism—and other proposals for governing the global economy—is the growing gap between the distribution of authority within existing international institutions and the international distribution of economic power. When the original Bretton Woods institutions—the IMF, World Bank, and GATT/WTO—were established and subsequently modified, authority over these organizations was, in essence, vested in the United States and Western Europe. By custom, the selection of the directorship of the World Bank has been the prerogative of the United States, while selection of the head of the IMF has been the prerogative of Western Europe; moreover, these major powers can block any action that they disapprove. Japan and the LDCs, especially the larger ones such as Brazil and India, as they have developed and gained greater economic strength, have increasingly resented this arrangement and have demanded more authority and more leadership roles. This issue precipitated a crisis in early 2000 regarding appointment of a new director-general of the IMF after the resignation of Michel Camdessus as managing director. Following tradition, the West Europeans proposed their nominee, German finance official Caio Koch-Weser, whom they fully expected would be chosen. Unexpectedly, both Japan and an unusual coalition of LDCs nominated alternative candidates.[6] Although the United States did not contest

[6] The candidate of the coalition of African and Arab states was Stanley Fischer, a distinguished American economist and highly experienced IMF official. The Japanese, supported by some East Asian countries, nominated Eisuke Sakakibara, a former high official in the Ministry of Finance, colloquially known as "Mr. Yen," in part because of his strong and outspoken criticisms of American policy.

the "right" of the Europeans to choose the head of the IMF, it raised serious questions about Koch-Weser's qualifications. Eventually, the dispute was settled by the selection of an "acceptable" German nominee, Horst Kohler.

Underlying this seemingly minor dispute was the more fundamental question of which nation or nations will control or predominate in those institutions responsible for managing the global economy.[7] This issue has long divided the United States and Western Europe. In this instance, even though many Europeans had reservations about Mr. Koch-Weser, they, especially the French, regarded his candidacy as a means to prevent growing American domination of the IMF and other international institutions. West Europeans have become very concerned about their diminishing position in the international economic and political system. German insistence that it was their turn to select the IMF head reflected their desire to be recognized again as a great power. National pride is still very much with us.

In practice, the United States has been the dominant power in the International Monetary Fund as well as the World Bank and the General Agreement on Tariffs and Trade/World Trade Organization. In the several financial crises that have afflicted the international economy, including the 1994–1995 Mexican crisis and the post-1997 East Asian crisis, the United States in effect dictated IMF responses. In the realm of trade, the United States has initiated every round of trade negotiations and has largely set their agendas. The United States has frequently performed this leadership role against the opposition of Western Europe, Japan, and other powers; the United States had to put considerable pressure on Europeans even to participate in the Uruguay Round. West Europeans have also exercised inordinate influence in both the GATT and the WTO. It is not excessive to say that the United States and Western Europe, because of historical precedents and their sheer economic strength, have been and continue to be the dominant players in the international trading economy.

Continuing American and West European dominance in the WTO, IMF, and World Bank has become increasingly noxious to the Japanese, and Japan is very unhappy about its subordinate role in these institutions. Although Japan is the second-largest donor to international institutions like the OECD and the IMF, no Japanese has ever been chosen head of, or even been seriously considered for, any important international economic institution other than the Asian De-

---

[7] Votes in the IMF are based on a country's financial contribution. On this basis, the United States has 17 percent of the votes; the combined vote of the fifteen EU members is 37 percent. Thus, the United States and the European Union together control just over a majority of the votes.

velopment Bank. In addition, Japan is very resentful over the IMF's handling of the 1997 Asian financial crisis and the way in which the IMF has operated in the region. The Japanese, as well as other East Asians, believe that the IMF is too much under American influence. In response to these concerns, in 1999 Japan for the first time proposed its own candidate to be the next director-general of the IMF and sought support for that candidate from other Asian nations. Japan's new assertiveness highlights the fact that leadership of the international institutions responsible for managing the global economy continues to reside with the West, despite the shift in the global balance of economic power toward non-Western powers. This discontinuity between authority and power must one day be rectified if these institutions are to survive.

The longer-term significance of the Seattle meeting is that Western dominance of this international institution was successfully challenged by the less developed countries for the first time when they blocked major items on the agenda developed by the Americans and Europeans. The Seattle conclave witnessed a new and potentially important development in WTO governance. Led by Brazil, Egypt, and India, the less developed countries, who possess an overwhelming majority of the votes in the WTO, were successfully mobilized. Although they were not able to achieve their own agenda, they did thwart the efforts of the United States to incorporate labor standards and environmental protection into the trade regime. The less developed countries discovered at Seattle that they could influence the rules governing the international economy and at least prevent adoption of new rules contrary to their interests. How the LDCs will choose to exercise this new-found power in the future remains unclear. The significance of the change that has taken place in the role of the LDCs in governance of the world economy may be illuminated by a brief history.

Throughout much of the postwar era, the less developed countries have sought to achieve greater influence in international economic institutions and to make these institutions serve their interests. Their first attempt to achieve such goals was a proposal at the Bretton Woods Conference to create an international development regime that would benefit the less developed countries directly. This effort was spurned by the United States and the other major powers. Believing that the world economy worked to their disadvantage, many LDCs chose protectionism and began to pursue import-substitution policies. They generally left management of the international economy to the Bretton Woods institutions and the major economic powers. This attitude of resignation changed dramatically following the first oil crisis (1973) and the resultant recognition that the less developed countries could translate their commodity exports into political power. Less developed countries then began a concerted effort to increase their influence over the international economy.

The LDC revolt in the mid-1970s against the major economic powers and their dominant position in the Bretton Woods institutions was led by the Group of 77, which demanded a New International Economic Order (NIEO).[8] In addition to a long list of specific economic demands, such as debt relief and greater access to ADC markets, the Group of 77 wanted the Bretton Woods institutions to be placed under the authority of the UN General Assembly where the LDCs have a voting majority and could force the World Bank and other international organizations to implement their own economic agenda. This assault on international liberalism, to use Stephen Krasner's formulation, was eventually defeated by the United States and other major economic powers. Subsequently, in the late 1970s and early 1980s, the huge debt crisis of many LDCs led to another revolt, but the LDCs were eventually forced to accept the dictates of the major powers.

The third—and this time more successful—attempt of the LDCs to increase their authority in governance of international economic affairs took place at Seattle in late 1999. Whereas earlier efforts to achieve the New International Economic Order and/or massive debt relief had failed, the less developed countries were now inside the system and had the votes needed to successfully oppose any decisions contrary to their interests, including President Clinton's proposal regarding labor standards. One can look at this development as a victory for the underdog, and of course it was. However, this "victory" could make management of the trading regime much more difficult. One lesson of Seattle was that the WTO with its more than 130 members has become a very cumbersome institution indeed. The great economic powers will at least have to pay much greater attention to the concerns of the less developed countries.

Developments at the 1999 Seattle meeting could cause the major economic powers to forsake the WTO's multilateral approach to lowering trade barriers and to conduct trade negotiations on a unilateral or bilateral basis on terms highly favorable to the major economic powers. Abandonment of multilateral trade negotiations would be

---

[8] The Group of 77 and its demands are discussed in Stephen D. Krasner, *Structural Conflict: The Third World Against Global Liberalism* (Berkeley: University of California Press, 1985).

highly detrimental to the world trading system, and especially to the LDCs. The protesters in Seattle believed that the WTO is a prisoner of corporate interests, yet they forget that the weak, and not the strong, benefit most from the rule of law. If unilateralism and bilateralism replace the WTO's multilateralism, regional trading arrangements would undoubtedly increase and eclipse the postwar effort to achieve a multilateral trading system based on accepted rules.

A liberal international order requires strong leadership and cooperation among the major economic powers, and the United States is still the only nation capable of providing such leadership, even though American leadership of the world economy in the last decades of the twentieth century was anything but inspiring. Moreover, the United States cannot lead alone. Cooperation among the major economic powers is necessary, and the rising economic powers of South and East Asia will need to be included. Unfortunately, the United States and its Cold War allies are drifting in different directions, and clashes among them have increased since the end of the Cold War. Many observers dismiss such concerns and argue that mutual economic interests will ensure continuing international cooperation. It is certain that the United States, Western Europe, and Japan do have a strong political and economic interest in cooperating with one another. It is also certain that obstacles to cooperation, such as attacks on globalization and intensifying economic competition, are increasing. This situation could become very serious in the event of economic adversity. Meanwhile, American leadership and interstate cooperation constitute the only possible foundation for an open and stable global economy.

In effect, a four-way contest has arisen concerning "who governs" those international institutions responsible for managing the global economy. With the waning of Cold War alliances and the increasing assertion by the United States of its superpower status, both the Japanese and the West Europeans have become more and more determined to counter American power in the IMF and other international economic agencies.[9] Demands have also increased from a coalition of LDCs and industrializing countries who believe their interests must be better served by the IMF, World Bank, and WTO. These countries have been energized because, in recent years, the IMF and other institutions have increased their power over these nations, and this was

---

[9] In addition to lacking influence comparable to their economic might and financial contribution to the IMF and World Bank, the Japanese were particularly incensed over the American-dominated IMF approach to the 1997 East Asian financial crisis.

dramatically witnessed in the role of the IMF in the East Asian and other financial crises.

As the authority of international institutions has grown, so have the demands of more and more nations for a greater say in these institutions. In addition, groups and individuals with widely divergent and conflicting opinions at both ends of the political spectrum have increasingly demanded that wide-ranging reforms be instituted.

Institutional Reform

Many believe that the IMF, WTO, and other international institutions must be reformed in response to the changed nature of the global cconomy. An important demand for reform has come from the United States, where the IMF has been strongly attacked by both political left and right. The most serious demand came in the late 1990s from the conservative-dominated House of Representatives, where the IMF was singled out for attack for, among other charges, being wasteful and antimarket. In response to these concerns and as a precondition for agreement to a 1998 replenishment of IMF funds, the House established the International Financial Institutions Advisory Commission to propose changes in the IMF. Under the chairmanship of Alan Meltzer, a respected conservative economist, the Commission's report recommended to the Congress that the IMF and World Bank should be radically reformed and restructured, because, in its opinion, these agencies frequently do more harm than good in the developing world and waste billions by making loans to middle-income countries that could rely on the market instead.[10]

The principal recommendation of the Commission was that the IMF should curtail its lending programs to developed countries and cease intervening in the politics and economics of these countries. In an era of huge international financial flows, the private sector should have the responsibility to supply capital to the industrializing countries. The majority members of the Commission argued that IMF interventionism in developing countries to relieve poverty, and especially IMF's implicit guarantee to assist in the event of financial trouble, encouraged "moral hazard" and overborrowing. They urged that the IMF should restrict itself to helping the very poor and those less developed countries with temporary liquidity problems; moreover, the IMF should make only short-term loans at market or above interest rates in order to discourage irresponsible financial behavior; that is, the IMF's activities should be limited to those of a lender of

[10] *New York Times*, 8 March 2000, C4.

last resort. The International Financial Advisory Commission's report also recommended that the World Bank, which makes $50 billion of development loans a year, should be renamed the World Development Agency, and that it too should refrain from competing against the private sector.

The report's critics maintain that its unstated purpose was to destroy the effectiveness of the IMF and, to a lesser extent, the World Bank, rather than to reform them.[11] The report assumed that, most of the time, in a market-oriented global economy, only minimal intervention by any form of government would be required except in unusual restricted circumstances and that any intervention would be likely to be counterproductive. Thus, the report questions whether or not international institutions that began in the early Cold War period are appropriate to the globalized economy of the twenty-first century. In the world of huge private international financial flows, what role can these international institutions usefully play? Is governance really necessary, or can matters be left up to the self-regulating market of neoclassical economic theory? These are issues that proponents of neoliberal institutionalism, as well as all other scholars of international political economy, must address.

THE NEW MEDIEVALISM

The "new medievalism," based on the belief that the world is experiencing the end of national sovereignty,[12] implicitly rejects the idea of a liberal international economic order based on cooperation among sovereign states. Set forth originally in the Treaty of Westphalia (1648), the doctrine of sovereignty asserts that governments enjoy complete control over the territory and persons within their legal jurisdiction. New medievalists believe that the concept of national sovereignty, which has guided international statecraft for three hundred and fifty years, is breaking down because of both internal and exter-

---

[11] There is a stinging critique of the Report in Barry Eichengreen and Richard Portes, "A Shortsighted Vision for IMF Reform," *Financial Times*, 9 March 2000, 13; also, *The Economist*, 18 March 2000, 80. Treasury Secretary Lawrence Summers, who has set forth his own plans for IMF reform, has also criticized the Report in *The Financial Times*, 23 March 2000, 17.

[12] The term "new medievalism" is attributed to Hedley Bull, *The Anarchical Society: A Study of Order in World Politics* (London: Macmillan, 1977). Expressions of this position are David Held, "Democracy, the Nation-state, and the Global System," *Economy and Society* 20, no. 2 (May 1991); and Jessica T. Mathews, "Power Shift," *Foreign Affairs* 76, no. 1 (January/February 1997): 50–66.

nal developments; states are fragmenting into substates as a result of ethnic and regional conflicts and, at the same time, are being eclipsed by rising nonstate and superstate actors such as multinational firms, international organizations, and especially, nongovernmental organizations (NGOs).[13]

New medievalists explain that this historic watershed has been reached because of transnational economic forces (trade, finance, etc.) and because of such contemporary technological developments as the computer, information technologies, and advances in transportation. In the era of the Internet, they allege that governments have lost their monopoly over information and can therefore be successfully challenged by nongovernmental actors. Concluding that these changes erode hierarchical organizations and undermine centralized power structures, they see the once-dominant hierarchic order of nation-states being supplanted by horizontal networks of states, voluntary organizations, and international institutions. This development in turn leads to cooperative problem solving by concerned individuals and groups from around the world. In place of the undivided loyalty formerly owed by the citizen to the sovereign, a world of multiple allegiances and responsibilities is envisioned, a world in which subnational, national, and supranational institutions will share authority over individuals.

The implications of this position for governance of the global economy are not clear.[14] Proponents of the new medievalism assert that something new is on its way to replace the state, but they do not precisely define what that something may be. However, one possibility has been set forth by Wolfgang H. Reinicke in his *Global Public Policy: Governing Without Government?* (1998).[15] The central proposition of Reinicke's interesting book is that government and the functions of governance can be disentangled from one another. In the modern world, "government" has referred to formal institutions that enjoy national sovereignty, possess a monopoly of power over a particular territory, and are not answerable to an external authority. Governments have been able to make domestic public policy and have

---

[13] A critique of the "end of sovereignty" position is Stephen D. Krasner, *Sovereignty: Organized Hypocrisy* (Princeton: Princeton University Press, 1999).

[14] A useful review of several ideas for global governance is Marie-Josée Massicotte, "Global Governance and the Global Political Economy: Three Texts in Search of a Synthesis," *Global Governance: A Review of Multilateralism and International Organizations 5*, no. 1 (January/March 1999): 127–48.

[15] Wolfgang H. Reinicke, *Global Public Policy: Governing Without Government?* (Washington: Brookings Institution, 1989).

remained politically independent actors in international affairs. Governance, on the other hand, is a social function that is essential to a market economy at the national or international level, and is not necessarily the same as government.[16] Governance, according to Reinicke, need not be equated with government, but can be achieved through networks of public and private groups or institutions at national, regional, and international levels. In this fashion, a global economy can gain the benefits of government without a formal government.[17]

Assessing the feasibility of international governance, Reinicke's analysis concentrates on three case studies in the areas of finance, crime, and dual-use technology that he believes establish the feasibility of international governance as he defines it. One of his case studies directly relevant here is concerned with the negotiation and establishment of the Basle Accord (1988) to develop international regulatory standards for international banks. The principal component of the Accord was specification of minimum capital adequacy requirements; that is, it specified the size of the funds that international banks had to maintain to prevent bank failures and decrease the risk of destabilizing crises. In this case study, Reinicke argues that the Accord resulted from complex and successful negotiations among national governments, private interests, and the Bank for International Settlements. He concludes that the Basle Accord resulted from successful cooperation among governments, NGOs, and international institutions that were able to create an international governance mechanism in this particular area of international finance.

Although Reinicke's example does illustrate that national, private, and international organizations can cooperate and find a solution to an economic problem, his argument does not provide convincing support for the idea that governance (as opposed to government) by itself can deal with the many pressing problems created by increasing integration of the world economy. As Reinicke himself shows, the Basle Accord was achieved largely through strong American pressure. American money-center banks in New York and California had complained to the Federal Reserve that foreign international banks were permitted to maintain bank reserves lower than those required for American banks and that, as a result, the international competitive

---

[16] Ibid., 87.

[17] Reinicke's idea of Global Public Policy Networks is set forth in greater detail at www.globalpublicpolicy.net.

position of American international banks had declined. Responding to these concerns, the Federal Reserve put pressures on foreign governments to raise reserve requirements; this resulted in the Basle Accord, which required European and Japanese banks to increase their reserves. Although it was undoubtedly desirable that a universal standard on reserves be established, the United States clearly pressured others to accept its own banking regulations and did so in the interests of U.S. domestic banks.[18] This episode indicates that the problem of governing without government exists, because international governance will not work without power and, unfortunately, Reinicke's governance mechanism lacks the power needed to achieve compliance with its decisions.

A major theme of the new medievalism is that nongovernmental organizations (NGOs) have, or at least should have, a central role in the governance of international, or perhaps I should say "postnational," affairs. Organized primarily around such specific issues as safeguarding the environment, protecting human rights, and promoting a safer world, NGOs are believed to have become a significant force in particular issue areas. The number of nongovernmental organizations has greatly increased in recent decades to approximately 30,000 at the beginning of the twenty-first century.[19] Among the most important of these grass-roots organizations are the Worldwide Fund for Nature with about 5 million members and the Sierra Club with approximately 600,000 members. Most NGOs are located in the United States and, to a lesser extent, in Western Europe, but have become increasingly active in some less developed countries. Japan appears to have few important NGOs. Although NGOs were initially involved primarily with domestic issues, they have become increasingly concerned over the alleged negative consequences of globalization upon various international issues. Moreover, through the Internet, NGOs around the world have greatly improved their ability to communicate with one another. As was demonstrated by the street protests in Seattle against the WTO, these developments have also encouraged and facilitated formation of international NGO alliances that can bring considerable pressure on governmental agencies to change their policies.

[18] For a very different interpretation of the Basle Accord, consult Ethan Kapstein, *Governing the Global Economy: International Finance and the State* (Cambridge: Harvard University Press, 1994).

[19] *The Economist*, 11 December 1999, 21; and 29 January 2000, 25–27. The discussion in this section on NGOs draws heavily from these articles.

According to Anne-Marie Slaughter, the increasing importance of nonstate actors is due to several developments.[20] The end of the Cold War has lessened security concerns and opened the way for the rise of what she calls "transnational civil society." In addition, the information economy and the Internet have made possible emergence of an international civil society, because they have broken the information monopoly of corporations and governments; the Internet also greatly facilitates communications among nonstate actors. Finally, and perhaps most importantly, the globalization of the economy through integration of financial markets enhances the power of multinational corporations, and they are further integrating national economies.

Although there is some truth in Slaughter's characterization of the present era, several important caveats should be noted. The security environment in Europe has improved since 1989, except for the Balkans. On the other hand, the situation in South Asia has significantly deteriorated, while the increasing threat of war in East Asia, the Middle East, and parts of Africa is worrisome. It is far, far too early to know what impact the Internet and information economy will have on either domestic or international society: Will they have benign or negative consequences? Some experts worry about threats to privacy, improved methods of monitoring and controlling people, and, in light of huge corporate mergers, a massive concentration of economic power. In a provocative article, Joseph Nye and William Owens argue that control over information will be the ultimate source of power in the international politics of the Internet age.[21] Recognizing this possibility, major military establishments around the world are preparing for cyber warfare; the Nye/Owens prediction and these military activities do not accord with more benign views of the information revolution such as Anne-Marie Slaughter's. Whether these two experienced foreign affairs experts, Nye and Owens, or the advocates of global civil society are correct remains to be seen. Possible future consequences of increasing globalization are unknown. It is a mistake to consider only the benefits of economic and technological change.

NGOs have succeeded impressively in influencing the policies of national governments and international institutions, at least in some areas. One of the most important accomplishments was the Earth Summit (1992) in Rio de Janeiro, where NGOs brought enough pub-

---

[20] Anne-Marie Slaughter, commentary in "The Challenge of Non-State Actors," Proceedings of the 92d Annual Meeting of the American Society of International Law (Washington, D.C., April 1–4, 1998), 20–21.

[21] Joseph S. Nye Jr. and William A. Owens, "America's Information Edge," *Foreign Affairs* 75, 2 (March/April 1996): 20–36.

lic pressure to bear to achieve a number of agreements to eliminate greenhouse gases. Two years later, NGO protestors besieged the World Bank and forced the latter to reconsider some of its policies. Other examples of successful NGO campaigns were the treaty to eliminate land mines, the agreement to reduce the huge indebtedness of many less developed countries, and the derailment of the American-sponsored Multilateral Agreement on Investment that would have harmonized rules on foreign direct investment. Whatever one may think about the wisdom of one or another of these successes, it is certain that NGOs have become a force in the contemporary world.[22]

However, it remains uncertain whether or not NGOs can become the most effective or at least one of the most effective means to govern the global economy. Although NGOs' record is impressive, is it correct to conclude that we are truly witnessing the beginnings of a movement that can transform the world? Certainly, evidence does suggest that in their confrontations with the American government and those of some other nations, NGOs do frequently triumph. NGOs can lobby and pressure national governments to heed their wishes. Undoubtedly responding to their demonstrated power, international institutions such as the World Bank have established close ties with NGOs, especially those possessing technical expertise. In the aftermath of the Seattle debacle, pressures mounted for the World Trade Organization to open its proceedings to interested NGOs. It would require a giant step, however, to move from efforts to increase cooperation between international organizations and non-governmental organizations toward establishment of a global governing mechanism incorporating the growing number of NGOs.[23]

Neomedievalists believe that the increasing importance of NGOs in international affairs is a positive factor in the emergence of a global "civil society."[24] The idea of a global civil society has been set forth by many proponents of the new medievalism, and a number of writings present it as an alternative to a capitalist, nation-state world or-

[22] An attempt to measure the effectiveness of NGOs is Margaret E. Keck and Kathryn Sikkink, *Activists Beyond Borders: Advocacy Networks in International Politics* (Ithaca: Cornell University Press, 1998).

[23] The journal *Global Governance: A Review of Multilateralism and International Organizations* is dedicated to the idea of a governing mechanism based on civil society and incorporating NGOs.

[24] A wide-ranging and sympathetic discussion of global civic society is contained in *International Affairs* 75, no. 3 (July 1999.) Also, Adam Watson, *The Evolution of International Society: A Comparative Historical Analysis* (London: Routledge, 1992).

der. Robert Cox has argued that civil society is composed of people and groups seeking alternatives to globalization of the capitalist system. He believes that global civil society and social protest movements can provide a basis for an alternative world order.[25] Many neomedievalists would agree with Cox's statement. Many of those who accept this concept of a global civil society believe that the nation-state has become a servant of global capitalism and should share with capitalism the responsibility for such economic and social ills as inequality, environmental degradation, and widespread abuses of human rights. Similarly, international regimes and institutions are viewed as following the dictates of powerful multinational firms and the international capitalist elite.

The emerging international civil society is said to be composed of domestic and transnational nongovernmental groups, organized primarily around strong policy concerns, focusing on such subjects as the environment and elimination of nuclear weapons. The nongovernmental organizations (NGOs) and global social movements that constitute global civil society are strongly motivated by opposition to the alleged evils of national governments, multinational firms, and globalization. However, they themselves are a product of globalization. Paradoxically, as was demonstrated at Seattle, they could not have organized, allied with one another, and been politically effective without the revolutionary advances in global media and communications. It is worth noting that these advances are a product of the global capitalist system that many neomedievalists so heartily condemn.

Consideration of the medieval model of governance suggests the magnitude of the problem faced by the neomedievalist agenda. The medieval world of Western Europe, from approximately the fifth to the fifteenth centuries, shared a heritage of Christianity and Roman law. The ruling aristocracy of each major European country shared many similar ideas, norms, and values. Across Western Europe, one found much the same social and political structures: feudalism, the Church, and kingship. Despite its continual political, religious, and social strife, one can reasonably speak of medieval Europe as having possessed a unified civic culture. This thousand-year era before the rise of the modern territorial state was also characterized by fragile and dispersed concentrations of economic and political power. The

---

[25] Robert Cox, "Civil Society at the Turn of the Millennium: Prospects for an Alternative World Order," *Review of International Studies* 25, no. 1 (January 1999): 10–11.

level of technology and the level of organizational skills limited mobilization and effective use of economic and military capabilities.

Although proponents of the new medievalism speak of the emergence of a global civic culture of shared values and understandings that could provide social and political foundations for an NGO-managed world, evidence supporting such a contention is hardly convincing. Insofar as a postnational, global civic culture does exist, it is mainly limited to Western civilization; yet, even in the West, powerful nationalistic, ethnic, and racial conflicts persist. Despite stirrings in the non-Western world regarding the importance of human rights, toleration of religious differences, and Western liberal ideals, these other civilizations do not share the civic culture and/or core values of the West.[26] Knowledge of the history of the twentieth century makes it difficult to accept the argument of many human rights advocates that abusers of human rights will be deterred from further abusive activities because they have become subject to international exposure. One need not accept Samuel Huntington's argument in *The Clash of Civilizations* (1996) to appreciate that hundreds of millions of individuals do not subscribe to the West's secular values, nor do they accept the idea of a global civic culture incorporating religious toleration, human rights, and respect for individualism.[27] In China, India, and other parts of the less developed world, the state is certainly alive and well. NGOs are very unlikely to become as influential in these cultures as they have in the United States and some other Western countries. One day perhaps, especially as a consequence of economic development and emergence of a strong middle class, these civilizations may gravitate toward Western values of democracy, individualism, and human rights. But this time has not yet arrived.

It is much too soon to know what the long-term impact of NGOs will be on the management of an integrated global economy. At present, the observer should keep in mind that the modern state has been around for over three centuries and that generally effective international institutions have existed for a half century, while the active era of NGO activity on an international level began only two decades ago. If history is any guide, one can anticipate that the highly favorable picture that we have today of NGOs will become quite different in the future. It is the nature of politics—and politics is what we are talking about—for power to beget countervailing power and for the

---

[26] *The Economist*, 5 December 1998, special section, "A Survey of Human-Rights Law."

[27] Samuel Huntington, *The Clash of Civilizations and the Remaking of World Order* (New York: Simon and Schuster, 1996).

tactics of the politically successful to be imitated by others. The "good" NGOs of our time, which in most cases are pursuing noteworthy objectives, may one day be joined by NGOs whose goals are much less praiseworthy. Such a possibility was foreshadowed by the unholy alliance in Seattle between the "good" NGOs seeking to achieve such selfless objectives as human rights and environmental protection with American organized-labor NGOs that cynically exploited the former's goals in its campaign to keep LDC exports out of the American economy. It is sobering to recognize that the National Rifle Association and the Russian Mafia, whose agendas do not coincide at all with the political agenda of the new medievalists, have been among the most successful of all NGOs!

TRANSGOVERNMENTALISM

Transgovernmentalism poses a third possibility for a rule-based international economic and political order. Like liberal internationalism, and unlike the new medievalism, this position accepts the continued existence of nation-states. However, the nature of the state envisioned by this intellectual position is fundamentally different from that in state-centric liberal internationalism and political realism. Like the new medievalism, this position assumes that the governance functions of the state can be divided and delegated to intergovernmental bodies or networks dealing with specific policy issues. As Anne-Marie Slaughter has pointed out, many transgovernmental organizations already exist to deal with such matters as banking regulations (the Basle Accord), antitrust regulation, and judicial matters.[28] These transnational networks composed of technical experts, business executives, and lawyers are needed to manage an increasingly complex and integrated world in which extensive technical input is required. Yet, it would be a large leap from transgovernmental mechanisms in specific policy areas to international governance of the globe.

Transgovernmentalism is a quite conscious throwback to what Robert Keohane and Joseph Nye identified in their earlier writings as "transnationalism" and also, although to a lesser extent, as neofunctionalism.[29] Like transnationalism and neofunctionalism, transgovernmentalism makes three crucial closely related assumptions regarding national governments. Transgovernmentalism assumes that

---

[28] Anne-Marie Slaughter, "The Real New World Order."

[29] Robert O. Keohane and Joseph S. Nye, *Transnational Relations and World Politics* (Cambridge: Harvard University Press, 1972). Thomas Risse-Kappen, ed., *Bringing Transnational Relations Back In* (New York: Cambridge University Press, 1995).

nation-states can be divided into their component parts, an idea set forth in 1971 by Graham Allison.[30] The divided parts can then deal directly with their counterparts in other governments. Another assumption is that technical and other functional problems can be solved in isolation from larger national concerns and parochial political matters. Thus, like transnationalism and neofunctionalism, transgovernmentalism assumes that technical issues can be separated from politics and solved independently. Regulatory matters, for example, can be isolated from national economic priorities and from the pressures of powerful interests. Finally, transgovernmentalism ignores matters of national security and foreign policy and assumes no hierarchy or priority among the issues of interest to governments. National concern over the proliferation of nuclear weapons or the future of the NATO alliance is treated no differently than regulation of ocean fisheries.

Transgovernmentalism foresees a world stripped of power, national interests, and interstate conflict, a world in which technocrats, bureaucrats, and the like solve issues outside the realm of politics. While stressing the absolute gains from transgovernmental cooperation, transgovernmentalism is silent on the matters of relative gains and distributive questions that arise in almost every serious international discussion of substantive issues. Thus, transgovernmentalism envisions a world nearly devoid of both domestic and international politics.

Transgovernmental networks can be very useful in the solution of the many issues that have arisen and will continue to arise. However, this approach to governance of the global economy is severely limited by the political rivalries and conflicting interests among nation-states and powerful domestic constituencies. As we have already seen, even such a technical matter as the Basle Accord on banking practices, frequently cited as an example of successful intergovernmentalism at work, was laced with intense political and economic conflicts. Bureaucrats in the Japanese Ministry of Finance were acutely aware of the crucial role of American coercive power and economic interest in the outcome of the negotiations over that Accord! Any effort to resolve the governance issue must take into account the fact that we still live in a world of states, power, and national interests.

Each approach to governance of the global economy discussed above offers useful contributions. As proponents of neoliberal institutionalism correctly argue, formal international institutions and agreed-

---

[30] Graham T. Allison, *Essence of Decision: Explaining the Cuban Missile Crisis* (New York: HarperCollins, 1971).

399

upon rules or regimes have greatly facilitated cooperation among sovereign nation-states and have been a significant factor in the management of the international economy over half a century. Yet, the continued resistance of states to restrictions on their sovereignty, the limited coverage of international regimes/institutions, and serious problems of compliance mean that neoliberal institutionalism alone cannot govern the global economy. The argument of the new medievalism that NGOs are becoming more important in solving the world's pressing problems is supported by the fact that the strong commitment and concentrated energy of these associations have been, on the whole, positive forces for dealing with many of the world's serious issues. Yet, these groups cannot function without the national governments and international institutions on which they must bring pressure to achieve their goals. It is much too early to know the true long-term significance of the NGOs.

Finally, the approach of transgovernmentalism is an important complement to the other two approaches. Cooperation and information-sharing across national borders and among the agencies and branches of national governments can be effective means of dealing with many complex technical issues at both the domestic and international levels. However, the legalistic and technocratic approach of transgovernmentalism not only suffers from a democratic deficit, but its usefulness declines steeply as issues become more entwined with matters of national security, domestic partisan politics, and issues of distributive economic importance. Although all three approaches can facilitate the governance of the global economy, none of these approaches can fulfill the many demands placed upon international governance. Resolution of the governance issue must confront an even more fundamental issue, however.

Governance for What?

Governance first and last is about the exercise of power to achieve political, social, and other objectives. Every scheme to govern the global economy, therefore, must confront the fundamental question: Governance for what? The primary purpose to be served by the proposed mechanisms for governance of the global economy is the first issue that must be resolved. During the Cold War, this issue had been resolved; the purpose then was to strengthen the economies of the anti-Soviet alliance and solidify the political unity of the United States with its allies. With the end of the Cold War and the triumph of neoliberalism, the purpose of governance seemed clear again; for most American officials, business leaders, and professional economists, the purpose of governance was to facilitate free trade, freedom of capital movements, and unrestricted access by multinational firms to markets around the globe. The global economy, according to this position, should be governed in accordance with the policy prescriptions of neoclassical economics, and its rules should be based on market principles.

On April 15–16, 2000, the neoliberal consensus was challenged on two fronts. In Washington, D.C., thousands of protestors gathered in the streets to denounce the alleged evils of economic globalization and to demand that the IMF, WTO, and World Bank be made more accountable to environmental, human, and worker's rights, and to other humanitarian concerns. However misguided some protestors may have been, they represented millions of Americans and others who have grown worried over the alleged negative consequences of economic globalization for wages, job security, the environment, and other concerns. At the time of the Washington protests, several hundred miles to the south, in Havana, the Group of 77, representing the world's less developed countries, was drafting demands for a larger share of the world's wealth and a strengthened voice in the governance of the global economy. Unlike the protesters in Washington, these countries were not opposed to globalization but rather demanded a more equitable distribution of its fruits. Moreover, although both the Washington protesters and the Group of 77 demanded increased control over the global economy, their social, economic, and political purposes were largely in opposition to one another, although on some issues, such as debt relief for poor countries, increased financial assistance to LDCs, and greater control over MNCs, their agendas did coincide. However, with respect to more fundamental issues such as delegating greater authority to the WTO over environmental matters, human rights, and labor standards, the protestors and the Group of 77 could not have been farther apart.

Both the Washington protestors and the Group of 77 demanded fundamental changes in the purposes to be pursued by the governing institutions of the global economy. Making their respective demands, they rejected an international economy based on the principles of neoclassical economics and market principles whose ultimate purpose was maximization of consumer choice and global wealth. In place of the exclusively economic objectives of neoliberalism, they sought to substitute such nonmarket objectives as protecting the environment, safeguarding the jobs of American workers, or redistributing global wealth to less wealthy countries. Thus, the battle was joined once again between those who desired a world governed by the market and those who wanted the market subordinated to some higher political authority that would pursue one or another social purpose. Throughout much of modern history, this battle over the ends of economic activity has been fought principally at the domestic level between the representatives of capital and labor. In the increasingly integrated global economy of the twenty-first century, the battleground has become the entire globe, and the types as well as the number of participants have greatly expanded to include states, international organizations, and nongovernmental organizations. This is the new global economic order that those interested in international political economy must confront.

Conclusion

Governance at any level, whether national or international, must rest on shared beliefs, cultural values, and, most of all, a common identity. Unfortunately, we do not yet live in a global civic culture, and few common values unite all the peoples of the world. Identity and loyalties are still national or even local, ethnic, and racial. As more and more nations are formed, national identities are becoming more numerous and, in some cases, more intense. The value of human rights appears to be shared by many people throughout the world; all governments—even those who violate human rights—believe that they must at least give it lipservice. Although some notable triumphs of human rights have occurred, nationalistic ideals still prevail. Modern states are highly self-centered and are seldom concerned with the welfare of other peoples. For example, there is little sharing by the rich with the poor. Under such circumstances, talk of substituting global governance for the primacy of nation-states is in vain. The best for which one can hope is that the major powers, in their own self-interest as well as that of the world in general, will cooperate to fashion a more stable and humane international political and economic order.

Select Bibliography

This select bibliography does not include many of the books, articles, and other references cited in the text; nor does it include many of the items in the bibliography of my book, *The Political Economy of International Relations* (Princeton: Princeton University Press, 1987).

Anderson, Kym, and Richard Blackhurst, eds. *Regional Integration and the Global Trading System.* New York: Harvester Wheatsheaf, 1993.

Arrighi, Giovanni. *The Long Twentieth Century: Money, Power, and the Origins of Our Times.* London and New York: Verso, 1994.

Barro, Robert J. *Economic Growth and Convergence.* Occasional Papers No. 46. San Francisco: International Center for Economic Growth, 1994.

Becker, Gary S. *The Economic Approach to Human Behavior.* Chicago and London: University of Chicago Press, 1976.

Berger, Suzanne, and Ronald Dore, eds. *National Diversity and Global Capitalism.* Ithaca and London: Cornell University Press, 1996.

Bergsten, C. Fred. *America in the World Economy: A Strategy for the 1990s.* Washington, D.C.: Institute for International Economics, 1988.

Bergsten, C. Fred, and C. Randall Henning. *Global Economic Leadership and the Group of Seven.* Washington, D.C.: Institute for International Economics, 1996.

Bhagwati, Jagdish N. *Protectionism.* Cambridge: MIT Press, 1988.

———. *The World Trading System at Risk.* Princeton: Princeton University Press, 1991.

———. "The Capital Myth: The Difference between Trade in Widgets and Dollars." *Foreign Affairs* 77, no. 3 (May/June 1998): 7–16.

Bliss, Christopher. *Economic Theory and Policy for Trading Blocks.* Manchester, U.K.: Manchester University Press, 1994.

Burtless, Gary, Robert Z. Lawrence, Robert E. Litan, and Robert J. Shapiro. *Globaphobia: Confronting Fears About Open Trade.* Washington, D.C.: Brookings Institution, 1998.

Cable, Vincent, and David Henderson. *Trade Blocs? The Future of Regional Integration.* London: Royal Institute of International Affairs, 1994.

Cohen, Benjamin J. *Organizing the World's Money: The Political Economy of International Monetary Relations.* New York: Basic Books, 1977.

———. *The Geography of Money.* Ithaca: Cornell University Press, 1998.

Cooper, Richard N. *The Economics of Interdependence: Economic Policy in the Atlantic Community.* New York: McGraw-Hill, 1968.

Cox, Robert W. *Production, Power, and World Order: Social Forces in the Making of History.* New York: Columbia University Press, 1987.

Crane, George T., and Abla Amawi, eds. *The Theoretical Evolution of International Political Economy—A Reader.* New York and Oxford: Oxford University Press, 1991.

Deane, Phyllis. *The State and the Economic System: An Introduction to the History of Political Economy.* New York: Oxford University Press, 1989.

De Grauwe, Paul. *The Economics of Monetary Integration.* 2d rev. ed. New York: Oxford University Press, 1994.

De Melo, Jaime, and Arvind Panagariya, eds. *New Dimensions in Regional Integration.* New York: Cambridge University Press, 1995.

Destler, I. M. *American Trade Politics.* 3d ed. Washington, D.C.: Institute for International Economics; and New York: Twentieth Century Fund, 1995.

Destler, I. M., and C. Randall Henning. *Dollar Politics: Exchange Rate Policymaking in the United States.* Washington, D.C.: Institute for International Economics, 1989.

Doremus, Paul N., William W. Keller, Louis W. Pauly, and Simon Reich. *The Myth of the Global Corporation.* Princeton: Princeton University Press, 1998.

Dorraj, Manochehr, ed. *The Changing Political Economy of the Third World.* Boulder, Colo.: Lynne Rienner, 1995.

Dosi, Giovanni, Christopher Freeman, Richard Nelson, Gerald Silverberg, and Luc Soete, eds. *Technical Change and Economic Theory.* London and New York: Pinter, 1988.

Downs, George W., and David M. Rocke. *Optimal Imperfection? Domestic Uncertainty and Institutions in International Relations.* Princeton: Princeton University Press, 1995.

Eichengreen, Barry. *International Monetary Arrangements for the 21st Century.* Washington: Brookings Institution, 1994.

————. "Dental Hygiene and Nuclear War: How International Relations Looks from Economics." *International Organization* 52, no. 4 (autumn 1998): 993–1012.

———— *Towards a New International Financial Architecture: A Practical Post-Asian Agenda.* Washington, D.C.: Institute for International Economics, 1999.

Eichengreen, Barry, and Jeffry Frieden, eds. *The Political Economy of European Monetary Integration.* Boulder, Colo.: Westview Press, 1994.

Encarnation, Dennis J. *Rivals Beyond Trade: America versus Japan in Global Competition.* Ithaca: Cornell University Press, 1992.

Esty, Daniel C. *Greening the GATT: Trade, Environment, and the Future.* Washington, D.C.: Institute for International Economics, 1994.

Evans, Peter. *Embedded Autonomy: States and Industrial Transformation.* Princeton: Princeton University Press, 1995.

Fishlow, Albert, and Stephan Haggard. *The United States and the Regionalization of the World Economy.* Paris: Organization for Economic Co-operation and Development, Development Centre, 1992.

Fishlow, Albert, Catherine Gwin, Stephan Haggard, Dani Rodrik, and Robert Wade. *Miracle or Design? Lessons from the East Asian Experience.* Washington, D.C.: Overseas Development Council, 1994.

Frankel, Jeffrey A., ed. *The Regionalization of the World Economy.* Chicago: University of Chicago Press, 1998.

Frankel, Jeffrey A., and Miles Kahler. *Regionalism and Rivalry: Japan and the United States in Pacific Asia.* Chicago and London: University of Chicago Press, 1993.

Frieden, Jeffry A., and David B. Lake. *The International Political Economy: Perspectives on Global Power and Wealth.* New York: St. Martin's Press, 1987.

Gibb, Richard, and Wieslaw Michalak, eds. *Continental Trading Blocs: The Growth of Regionalism in the World Economy.* New York: John Wiley, 1994.

Gilpin, Robert. *The Political Economy of International Relations.* Princeton: Princeton University Press, 1987.

———. *The Challenge of Global Capitalism: The World Economy in the 21st Century.* Princeton: Princeton University Press, 2000.

Goldstein, Judith. *Ideas, Interests, and American Trade Policy.* Ithaca: Cornell University Press, 1993.

Goldstein, Morris. *The Asian Financial Crisis: Causes, Cures, and Systemic Implications.* Washington, D.C.: Institute for International Economics, 1998.

Goodwin, Craufurd D. *Economics and National Security: A History of Their Interaction.* Durham: Duke University Press, 1991.

Gourevitch, Peter. *Politics in Hard Times: Comparative Responses to International Economic Crises.* Ithaca: Cornell University Press, 1986.

Gourevitch, Peter, and Paulo Guerrieri, eds. *New Challenges to International Cooperation: Adjustment of Firms, Policies, and Organizations to Global Competition.* San Diego: University of California Press, 1993.

Gowa, Joanne. "Rational Hegemons, Excludable Goods, and Small Groups: An Epitaph for Hegemonic Stability Theory?" *World Politics* 41, no. 3 (April 1989): 307–24.

———. *Adversaries and International Trade.* Princeton: Princeton University Press, 1994.

Graham, Edward M. *Global Corporations and National Governments.* Washington, D.C.: Institute for International Economics, 1996.

Grieco, Joseph M. *Cooperation among Nations: Europe, America, and Non-Tariff Barriers to Trade.* Ithaca: Cornell University Press, 1990.

Grossman, Gene M., and Elhanan Helpman. *Innovation and Growth in the Global Economy.* Cambridge: MIT Press, 1991.

Gruber, Lloyd. *Ruling the World: Power Politics and the Rise of Supranational Institutions.* Princeton: Princeton University Press, 2000.

Haas, Ernst B. *The Uniting of Europe: Political, Social and Economic Forces, 1950–57.* Stanford: Stanford University Press, 1957.

———. *Beyond the Nation-State: Functionalism and International Organization*. Stanford: Stanford University Press, 1964.

Haggard, Stephan. *Pathways from the Periphery: The Politics of Growth in the Newly Industrializing Countries*. Ithaca: Cornell University Press, 1990.

———. *Developing Nations and the Politics of Global Integration*. Washington, D.C.: Brookings Institution, 1995.

Haggard, Stephan, and Robert R. Kaufman, eds. *The Politics of Economic Adjustment*. Princeton: Princeton University Press, 1992.

Haggard, Stephan, and Simmons, Beth A. "Theories of International Regimes." *International Organization* 41, no. 3 (summer 1987): 491–517.

Heilbroner, Robert, and William Milberg. *The Crisis of Vision in Modern Economic Thought*. New York: Cambridge University Press, 1995.

Held, David, Anthony McGrew, David Goldblatt, and Jonathan Perraton. *Global Transformations: Politics, Economics, and Culture*. Stanford: Stanford University Press, 1999.

Helleiner, Eric. *States and the Reemergence of International Finance: From Bretton Woods to the 1990s*. Ithaca: Cornell University Press, 1994.

Helpman, Elhanan, and Paul R. Krugman. *Market Structure and Foreign Trade: Increasing Returns, Imperfect Competition, and the International Economy*. Cambridge: MIT Press, 1985.

———. *Trade Policy and Market Structure*. Cambridge: MIT Press, 1989.

Henning, C. Randall. *Currencies and Politics in the United States, Germany, and Japan*. Washington, D.C.: Institute for International Economics, 1994.

———. *Cooperating with Europe's Monetary Union*. Washington, D.C.: Institute for International Economics, 1997.

Hicks, John. *A Theory of Economic History*. London, Oxford, and New York: Oxford University Press, 1969.

Hirschman, Albert O. *National Power and the Structure of Foreign Trade*. Berkeley: University of California Press, 1945.

Hirst, Paul, and Grahame Thompson. *Globalization in Question: The International Economy and the Possibilities of Governance*. Cambridge: Polity Press, 1996.

Irwin, Douglas A. *Against the Tide: An Intellectual History of Free Trade*. Princeton: Princeton University Press, 1996.

James, Harold. *International Monetary Cooperation Since Bretton Woods*. Washington, D.C.: International Monetary Fund, and New York: Oxford University Press, 1996.

Johnson, Chalmers. *MITI and the Japanese Miracle: The Growth of Japanese Industrial Policy, 1925–1975*. Stanford: Stanford University Press, 1982.

Jones, R. J. Barry. *Globalization and Interdependence in the International Political Economy: Rhetoric and Reality*. London: Pinter, 1995.

Jones, R. J. Barry, ed. *Perspectives on Political Economy*. London: Frances Pinter, 1983.

Julius, DeAnne. *Global Companies and Public Policy: The Growing Challenge of Foreign Direct Investment*. London: Pinter, 1990.

Kahler, Miles. *International Institutions and the Political Economy of Integration.* Washington, D.C.: Brookings Institution, 1995.

_____. *Regional Futures and Transatlantic Economic Relations.* New York: Council on Foreign Relations, 1995.

_____, ed. *Capital Flows and Financial Crises.* New York: Council on Foreign Relations, 1999.

Kasper, Wolfgang. *Global Competition, Institutions, and the East Asian Ascendancy.* San Francisco: ICS Press, 1994.

Katzenstein, Peter J., ed. *Between Power and Plenty: Foreign Economic Policies of Advanced Industrial States.* Madison: University of Wisconsin Press, 1978.

_____. *Small States in World Markets: Industrial Policy in Europe.* Ithaca: Cornell University Press, 1985.

Katzenstein, Peter, Robert O. Keohane, and Stephen D. Krasner. "International Organization at Fifty: Exploration and Contestation in the Study of World Politics." *International Organization* 52, no. 4 (autumn 1998).

Keck, Margaret, and Kathryn Sikkink. *Activists beyond Borders: Advocacy Networks in International Politics.* Ithaca: Cornell University Press, 1998.

Kenen, Peter B., ed. *Managing the World Economy: Fifty Years After Bretton Woods.* Washington, D.C.: Institute for International Economics, 1994.

_____. *Understanding Interdependence: The Macroeconomics of the Open Economy.* Princeton: Princeton University Press, 1995.

Keohane, Robert O. *After Hegemony: Cooperation and Discord in the World Political Economy.* Princeton: Princeton University Press, 1984.

_____. *International Institutions and State Power: Essays in International Relations Theory.* Boulder, Colo.: Westview Press, 1989.

Keohane, Robert O., and Helen V. Milner, eds. *Internationalization and Domestic Politics.* Cambridge: Cambridge University Press, 1996.

Keohane, Robert O., and Joseph S. Nye. *Transnational Relations and World Politics.* Cambridge: Harvard University Press, 1972.

_____. *Power and Interdependence: World Politics in Transition.* Boston: Little, Brown and Company, 1977.

Kindleberger, Charles P. *Power and Money: The Economics of International Politics and the Politics of International Economics.* New York: Basic Books, 1970.

_____. *The World in Depression.* Berkeley: University of California Press, 1973.

_____. *Manias, Panics, and Crashes: A History of Financial Crises.* New York: Basic Books, 1988.

Kirshner, Jonathan. *Currency and Coercion: The Political Economy of International Monetary Power.* Princeton: Princeton University Press, 1995.

Krasner, Stephen D. *Defending the National Interest: Raw Materials, Investments, and U.S. Foreign Policy.* Princeton: Princeton University Press, 1978.

_____. *Structural Conflict: The Third World against Global Liberalism.* Berkeley: University of California Press, 1985.

_____. ed. *International Regimes*. Ithaca: Cornell University Press, 1983.

Krugman, Paul R. *Geography and Trade*. Cambridge: MIT Press, 1991.

_____. ed. *Strategic Trade Policy and the New International Economics*. Cambridge: MIT Press, 1996.

Krugman, Paul R., and Maurice Obstfeld. *International Economics: Theory and Policy*. 3d ed. New York: HarperCollins, 1994.

Lairson, Thomas D., and David Skidmore. *International Political Economy: The Struggle for Power and Wealth*. New York: Harcourt Brace Jovanovich, 1993.

Lawrence, Robert Z., Albert Bressand, and Takatoshi Ito. *A Vision for the World Economy: Openness, Diversity, and Cohesion*. Washington, D.C.: Brookings Institution, 1996.

Lindblom, Charles E. *Politics and Markets: The World's Political Economic Systems*. New York: Basic Books, 1977.

Little, Ian M. D. *Economic Development: Theory, Policy, and International Relations*. New York: Basic Books, 1982.

Loriaux, Michael, et al. *Capital Ungoverned: Liberalizing Finance in Interventionist States*. Ithaca: Cornell University Press, 1997.

Maddison, Angus. *The World Economy in the 20th Century*. Paris: Development Centre of the Organization for Economic Cooperation and Development, 1989.

Mankiw, N. Gregory, *Principles of Economics*. New York: Dryden Press, 1998.

Mansfield, Edward D. *Power, Trade, and War*. Princeton: Princeton University Press, 1984.

_____. "Effects of International Politics on Regionalism in World Trade." In Kym Anderson and Richard Blackhurst, eds. *Regional Integration and the Global Trading System*. New York: St. Martin's Press, 1993.

Mansfield, Edward D., and Helen V. Milner, eds. *The Political Economy of Regionalism*. New York: Columbia University Press, 1997.

Martin, Lisa. *Coercive Cooperation: Explaining Multinational Economic Sanctions*. Princeton: Princeton University Press, 1982.

Mayall, James. *Nationalism and International Society*. New York: Cambridge University Press, 1990.

McKenzie, Richard B., and Gordon Tullock. *Modern Political Economy: An Introduction to Economics*. New York: McGraw-Hill, 1978.

Milner, Helen V. *Resisting Protectionism: Global Industries and the Politics of International Trade*. Princeton: Princeton University Press, 1988.

_____. *Interests, Institutions, and Information: Domestic Politics and International Relations*. Princeton: Princeton University Press, 1997.

Moran, Theodore H. *Foreign Direct Investment and Development: The New Policy Agenda for Developing Countries and Economies in Transition*. Washington, D.C.: Institute for International Economics, 1998.

Murakami, Yasusuke. *An Anticlassical Political-Economic Analysis: A Vision for the Next Century*. Stanford: Stanford University Press, 1996.

North, Douglass C. *Institutions, Institutional Change, and Economic Performance*. Cambridge: Cambridge University Press, 1990.

Nye, Joseph S., Jr. *Bound to Lead: The Changing Nature of American Power*. New York: Basic Books, 1990.

Olson, Mancur. *The Logic of Collective Action: Public Goods and the Theory of Groups*. Cambridge: Harvard University Press, 1965.

Ostry, Sylvia. *Governments and Corporations in a Shrinking World: Trade and Innovation Policies in the United States, Europe, and Japan*. New York: Council on Foreign Relations, 1990.

——. *The Post–Cold War Trading System: Who's on First?* Chicago: University of Chicago Press, 1997.

Ostry, Sylvia, and Richard R. Nelson. *Techno-Nationalism and Techno-Globalism: Conflict and Cooperation*. Washington, D.C.: Brookings Institution, 1995.

Oye, Kenneth A., ed. *Cooperation under Anarchy*. Princeton: Princeton University Press, 1986.

Phelps, Edmund S. *Political Economy: An Introductory Text*. New York: W. W. Norton, 1985.

Preeg, Ernest H. *From Here to Free Trade: Essays in Post–Uruguay Round Trade Strategy*. Chicago: University of Chicago Press, 1998.

Risse-Kappen, Thomas, ed. *Bringing Transnational Relations Back In*. Cambridge: Cambridge University Press, 1995.

Rodrik, Dani. *Has Globalization Gone Too Far?* Washington, D.C.: Institute for International Economics, 1997.

Ruggie, John Gerard. *Winning the Peace: America and World Order in the New Era*. New York: Columbia University Press, 1996.

Ruigrok, Winfried, and Rob van Tulder. *The Logic of International Restructuring*. London and New York: Routledge, 1995.

Scherer, F. M. *International High-Technology Competition*. Cambridge: Harvard University Press, 1992.

Schott, Jeffrey J., ed. *The World Trading System: Challenges Ahead*. Washington, D.C.: Institute for International Economics, 1996.

Schumpeter, Joseph A. *Capitalism, Socialism, and Democracy*. New York: Harper and Brothers, 1942.

Shaw, Martin. *Global Society and International Relations*. Cambridge: Polity Press, 1994.

Smith, Adam. *An Inquiry into the Nature and Causes of the Wealth of Nations*. New York: Modern Library, 1937 [1776].

Snidal, Duncan. "The Limits of Hegemonic Stability Theory." *International Organization* 39 (1985): 579– 614.

Spiro, David E. *The Hidden Hand of American Hegemony: Petrodollar Recycling and International Markets*. Ithaca: Cornell University Press, 1999.

Stallings, Barbara, ed. *Global Change, Regional Response: The New International Context of Development*. New York: Cambridge University Press, 1995.

Stein, Arthur A. *Why Nations Cooperate: Circumstance and Choice in International Relations*. Ithaca: Cornell University Press, 1990.

409

Strange, Susan. *States and Markets*. New York: Basil Blackwell, 1988.

——. *The Retreat of the State: The Diffusion of Power in the World Economy*. Cambridge: Cambridge University Press, 1996.

——. *Mad Money: From the Author of Casino Capitalism*. Manchester, U.K.: Manchester University Press, 1998.

Volcker, Paul A., and Toyoo Gyohten. *Changing Fortunes: The World's Money and the Threat to American Leadership*. New York: Times Books, 1992.

Walters, Robert S., and David H. Blake. *The Politics of Global Economic Relations*. 4th ed. Englewood Cliffs, N.J.: Prentice-Hall, 1996.

Waltz, Kenneth N. *Theory of International Politics*. Reading, Mass.: Addison-Wesley, 1979.

——. "Reflections on Theory of International Politics: A Response to My Critics." In Robert O. Keohane, ed. *Neorealism and Its Critics*. New York: Columbia University Press, 1986.

Weiss, Linda. *The Myth of the Powerless State*. Ithaca: Cornell University Press, 1998.

Weiss, Linda, and John M. Hobson. *States and Economic Development: A Comparative Historical Analysis*. London: Polity Press, 1995.

Whalley, John, and Colleen Hamilton. *The Trading System after the Uruguay Round*. Washington, D.C.: Institute for International Economics, 1996.

Williamson, John, and Chris Milner. *The World Economy: A Textbook in International Economics*. New York: New York University Press, 1991.

Winham, Gilbert R. *The Evolution of International Trade Agreements*. Toronto: University of Toronto Press, 1992.

Young, Oran R. *International Cooperation: Building Regimes for Natural Resources and the Environment*. Ithaca: Cornell University Press, 1989.

Zysman, John. *Governments, Markets, and Growth: Financial Systems and the Politics of Industrial Change*. Ithaca: Cornell University Press, 1983.

Index

411